D1152848

A LION HANDBOOK

THE CASE FOR CHRISTIANITY

A LION HANDBOOK
The Case for Christianity

COLIN CHAPMAN

Copyright © 1981 Lion Publishing

Published by
Lion Publishing
Icknield Way, Tring, Herts, England
ISBN 0 85648 371 0
Albatross Books
PO Box 320, Sutherland, NSW 2232, Australia
ISBN 0 86760 339 9

First edition 1981

Copyright of Scripture quotations is as follows:
Revised Standard Version, copyright 1946 and 1952, second edition
1971, by the Division of Christian Education, National Council of
the Churches of Christ in the USA.
Good News Bible, copyright 1966, 1971 and 1976 American Bible Society,
published by the Bible Societies/Collins.

Phototypeset by
Tradespools Limited, Frome, Somerset, England
Printed in Italy
by New Interlitho SPA, Milan

INTRODUCTION

There are many ways of presenting the case for Christianity. This is just one. Inevitably it is a personal approach. The material was originally developed for a youth club and expanded in book form under the title *Christianity on Trial*. Since then it has been tested in discussion with international students, and completely re-cast to start with human rather than abstract questions.

In putting Christianity on trial, or making out a case for it, I have concentrated on Christian *beliefs*. We can hardly carry out a thorough investigation into Christianity as a historical phenomenon. What would we be trying to prove – that Christianity has done more good than harm, or more harm than good? What we can do is test the beliefs, understand the Christian world-view, appreciate what it feels like to see the world as the Christian sees it. We can ask: are these beliefs true? Do they fit the facts of history and experience? Do they make sense of the world as we know it?

We begin, therefore, not with Christian beliefs about God or even with Jesus Christ but with ourselves, with man. What are some of the most basic human questions which men have always been asking, and which we ourselves have asked at some stage in our lives?

We then look at Christian answers to these questions.

This leads us to try to understand the Christian world-view by studying basic Christian assumptions about man, God and the universe, and about truth and 'salvation'.

We then look for ways of testing these beliefs, to see if we can in any sense say that they are 'true'.

At this stage we turn to consider alternative claims to truth, and try to explore ways of deciding between these competing claims.

Then we begin to take a closer look at Jesus and see how the Christian world-view depends completely on who he was and what he claimed to be doing.

Finally, we consider different possible verdicts after such an enquiry, and what it means to 'see' and to 'believe'.

SECTION 1

STARTING WHERE WE ARE—BASIC HUMAN QUESTIONS

How can anyone discover what life means?
It is too deep for us, too hard to
understand.
But I devoted myself to knowledge and
study;
I was determined to find wisdom and the
answers to my questions ...
ECCLESIASTES

If death ends all, if I have neither to hope
for good to come nor to fear evil, I must ask
myself what I am here for, and how in these
circumstances I must conduct myself.
SOMERSET MAUGHAM

But why? Was it for all this? Who are we
that so much should converge on our little
deaths? ... To be told so little—to such an
end—and still, finally, to be denied an
explanation ...
TOM STOPPARD

What are we sure of? Not even of our
existence, dear comforting friend! And
whom can we ask the questions that
torment us? 'What is this place?' 'Where
are we?'—a fat old man who gives sly hints
that only bewilder us more, a fake of a
gipsy squinting at cards and tea leaves.
What else are we offered? The never-
broken procession of little events that
assure us that we and strangers about us
are still going on? Where? Why? And the
perch that we hold is unstable!
   We're threatened with eviction, for this
is a port of entry and departure, there are
no permanent guests! And where else have
we to go when we leave here? ... We're
lonely. We're frightened.
TENNESSEE WILLIAMS

In this section we look at some of the basic questions which most of us ask at some time in our lives, even if we cannot put them into words. At this stage we are not trying to find answers, but simply to feel the full force of these dilemmas . . .

Outline

THE INDIVIDUAL
Who or what am I?

THE MEANING OF LIFE
What's the point of it all?

VALUES
How are we to make moral choices?

TRUTH
Is it possible to know the truth about ourselves and the universe?

LOVE
What is love, and where can it be found?

SUFFERING
Why is there suffering, and how can we live with it?

DEATH
How am I to face death? Is there a life after death?

THE FUTURE OF MAN
What hope is there for the human race?

THE SUPERNATURAL
Is there anything more than the physical world?

EVIL
Is there any hope in fighting evil and injustice?

BASIC HUMAN QUESTIONS

THE INDIVIDUAL

Who or what am I?

JACOB BRONOWSKI, the American scientist and humanist (1908–74), expresses the feeling that we are individuals who are different from other people:

When I say that I want to be myself, I mean as the existentialist does that I want to be *free* to be myself. This implies that I too want to be rid of constraints (inner as well as outward constraints) in order to act in unexpected ways. Yet I do not mean that I want to act either at random or unpredictably. It is not in these senses that I want to be free but in the sense that I want to be allowed to be different from others. I want to follow my own way—but I want it to be a way, recognizably my own, and not a zig-zag. And I want people to recognize it: I want them to say, 'How characteristic!'

This feeling, however, is challenged and threatened by modern science which seems to say that man is basically a machine or a mechanism. BRONOWSKI continues:

This is where the fulcrum of our fears lies: that man as a species and we as thinking men, will be shown to be no more than a machinery of atoms. We pay lip service to the vital life of the amoeba and the cheese mite; but what we are defending is the human claim to have a complex of will and thoughts and emotions—to have a mind ...

The crisis of confidence ... springs from each man's wish to be a mind and a person, in the face of the nagging fear that he is a mechanism. The central question I ask is this: Can man be both a machine and a self?

THOMAS MANN, the German novelist (1875–1955) who lived through World War I and Hitler's rise to power in the 1930s, realized that the frightening political developments of the twentieth century force us to face questions about the individual in society. He believed that in this century the human problem is being put to us 'in political terms':

The whole question of the human being and what we think about him is put to us today with a life-and-death seriousness unknown in times that were not so stern as ours. For everybody, but most particularly for the artist, it is a matter of spiritual life or spiritual death; it is to use the religious terminology, a matter of salvation. I am convinced that that writer is a lost man who betrays the things of the spirit by refusing to face and decide for himself the human problem, put, as it is today, in political terms.

ALDOUS HUXLEY, the English writer (1894–1963), wrote a book in 1931 called *Brave New World*, in which he described an imaginary totalitarian state of the future. In 1958 he wrote a further book, called *Brave New World Revisited*, in which he pointed out that some of the developments he had foreseen had actually taken place in certain countries. He had realized what could happen when too much power is concentrated in the hands of a few individuals—in government, industry or the mass media: we as individuals are not as free as we think we are:

> **Meanwhile there is still some freedom left in the world. Many young people, it is true, do not seem to value freedom. But some of us still believe that, without freedom, human beings cannot become human and that freedom is therefore supremely valuable. Perhaps the forces that now menace freedom are too strong to be resisted for very long.**

He asked the question:

> **How can we control the vast impersonal forces that now menace our hard-won freedoms?**

COLIN WILSON, the English writer-philosopher (and one fascinated by the para-normal and psychic), describes the problem of the individual as it is felt by 'The Outsider' in a book of that name, published in 1956 and subsequently translated into many different languages.

> **Their problem is the unreality of their lives. They become acutely conscious of it when it begins to pain them, but they are not sure of the source of the pain. The ordinary world loses its values, as it does for a man who has been ill for a very long time. Life takes on the quality of a nightmare, or a cinema sheet when the screen goes blank. These men who had been projecting their hopes and desires into what was passing on the screen suddenly realise they are in a cinema. They ask: Who are we? What are we doing here? With the delusion of the screen identity gone, the causality of its events suddenly broken, they are confronted with a terrifying dream. In Sartre's phrase, they are 'condemned to be free'.**

> **Completely new bearings are demanded; a new analysis of this real world of the cinema has to be undertaken. In the shadow world on the screen, every problem had an answer; this may not be true of the world in the cinema. The fact that the screen world has proved to be a delusion arouses the disturbing possibility that the cinema world may be unreal too. 'When we dream that we dream, we are beginning to wake up!' Novalis says. Chuang Tzu had once said that he had dreamed he was a butterfly, and now wasn't sure if he was a man who dreamed he was a butterfly or a butterfly dreaming he was a man.**

Jacob Bronowski

BASIC HUMAN QUESTIONS
THE MEANING OF LIFE

What's the point of it all?

The personal question of identity is part of the wider issue of the meaning of life.

The writer of Ecclesiastes, in the Old Testament, describes his determination to find answers to his questions:

> I used my wisdom to test all of this. I was determined to be wise, but it was beyond me. How can anyone discover what life means? It is too deep for us, too hard to understand. But I devoted myself to knowledge and study; I was determined to find wisdom and the answers to my questions . . .

Leo Tolstoy, the famous Russian novelist (1828–1910), describes how he found it impossible to escape from the question of the meaning and purpose of life:

> What is life for? To die? To kill myself at once? No, I am afraid. To wait for death till it comes? I fear that even more. Then I must live.

> But what for? In order to die? And I could not escape from that circle. I took up the book, read, and forgot myself for a moment, but then again, the same question and the same horror. I lay down and closed my eyes. It was worse still.

Somerset Maugham, the English novelist (1874–1965), rejected any kind of religious beliefs, but was still faced with questions about the meaning of life:

> If . . . one puts aside the existence of God and the possibility of survival as too doubtful to have any effect on one's behaviour, one has to make up one's mind what is the meaning and use of life. If death ends all, if I have neither to hope for good to come nor to fear evil, I must ask myself what I am here for, and how in these circumstances I must conduct myself.

Adam Schaff, the Polish Marxist philosopher, admits that questions of this kind remain in people's minds, however much the Marxist tries to avoid them or pretend that they do not exist:

> 'What is the meaning of life?' 'What is man's place in the universe?' It seems difficult to express oneself scientifically on such hazy topics. And yet if one should assert ten times over that these are typical pseudo-problems, problems would remain.

Martin Esslin, a drama critic, sees 'The Theatre of the Absurd' as an attempt to find answers to questions about man, which are all the more pressing because of the influence of writers such as Nietzsche and the events of the twentieth century:

> Zarathustra was first published in 1883. The number of people for whom God is dead has greatly increased since Nietzsche's day, and mankind has learned the bitter lesson of the falseness and evil nature of some of the cheap substitutes that have been set up to take his place. And so, after two terrible wars, there are still many

who are trying to come to terms with the implications of Zarathustra's message, searching for a way in which they can, with dignity, confront a universe deprived of what was once its centre and its living purpose, a world deprived of a generally accepted integrating principle, which has become disjointed, purposeless—absurd.

The Theatre of the Absurd is one of the expressions of this search.

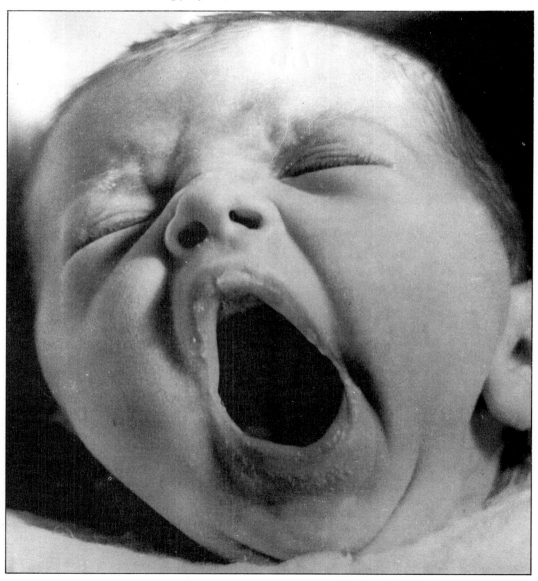

VALUES

How are we to make moral choices?

One possible source of meaning for man is in the realm of the moral choices he makes and the values he adopts.

MARCEL PROUST, the French novelist (1871–1922), describes in his novel *Remembrance of Things Past*, a situation in which Oriane has no moral values which can help her to decide between two courses of action:

Placed for the first time in her life in the presence of two duties as different as whether to leave by car and dine in town, or to show pity to a man who was going to die, she saw nothing in her code which told her which choice to make, and not knowing where her preference should be directed, she decided to pretend that the second option had not been presented to her, which would allow her to follow the first course of action and demanded less effort, thinking that the best way of resolving the conflict was to deny it.

ARTHUR KOESTLER, the novelist, political and scientific writer, raises the question of values in a vivid way by describing the moral dilemma which must have faced Scott during his return from the South Pole in 1912: either he must take the sick Oates along with him and accept the risks of delay, or he must leave him behind in the hope of saving his own life and the lives of the other three in the party.

This dilemma ... symbolises the eternal predicament of man, the tragic conflict inherent in his nature. It is the conflict between expediency and morality ... This conflict is at the root of our political and social crisis, ... it contains in a nutshell the challenge of our time ...

That both roads end as blind alleys is a dilemma which is inseparable from man's condition; it is not an invention of the philosophers, but a conflict which we face at each step in our daily affairs ... The more responsible the position you hold, the sharper you feel the horns of the dilemma. When a decision involves the fate of a great number of people, the conflict grows proportionately. The technical progress of our age has enormously increased the range and consequence of man's actions, and has thus amplified his inherent dilemma to gigantic proportions. This, therefore, is the reason for our acute awareness of a crisis. We are like the patient who for the first time hears in a loudspeaker the irregular ticking of his heart.

The problem is expressed in a variety of ways. EDMUND LEACH, in his 1967 Reith Lecture, raised the question in this form:

The question I am asking is: can scientists and politicians who have acquired god-like power to alter our way of life be restrained by the application of moral principles? If so, what moral principles?

ALBERT CAMUS, the French writer (1913–60) who spent much of his life in Algeria, took it for granted that God does not exist. He realized, however, that since he could not relate the idea of justice to God, he had to find some other basis for morality:

> **When man submits God to moral judgement, he kills Him in his own heart. And then what is the basis of morality? God is denied in the name of justice but can the idea of justice be understood without the idea of God?**

In his book *The Rebel* he asks the question in this way:

> **The controversial aspect of contemporary history compels us to say that rebellion is one of man's essential dimensions. It is our historical reality. Unless we ignore reality, we must find our values in it. Is it possible to find a rule of conduct outside the realm of religion and absolute values? That is the question raised by revolt . . .**

JEAN-PAUL SARTRE, the French existentialist philosopher (1905–80), found that what made the problem so acute for him was that we *have* to make some kind of judgements in order to live, and at the same time find it *impossible* to make them:

> **If I have excluded God the Father, there must be somebody to invent values.**
>
> **If God does not exist . . . man is in consequence forlorn, for he cannot find anything to depend upon, either within or outside himself.**
>
> **Any morality which does not present itself explicitly as *impossible today* contributes to the mystification and alienation of man. The moral 'problem' arises from the fact that morals are *for us* both unavoidable and impossible. Action must give itself its ethical norms in this climate of unsurmountable impossibility. It is in this light, for**

example, that one should consider the problem of violence or that of the relation between the means and the end.

> **I do not present these contradictions to condemn Christian morals: I am too deeply convinced that *any* morals are both impossible and necessary.**

ALVIN TOFFLER in his best-seller *Future Shock*, published in 1970, asks how we should think about the 'new stage of human development' before us. Instead of asking about values, he suggests that we need to define 'the goals of "progress"':

> **The moment is right for the formation in each of the high-technology nations of a movement for total self-review, a public self-examination aimed at broadening and defining in social, as well as merely economic, terms, the goals of 'progress'. On the edge of a new millennium, on the brink of a new stage of human development, we are racing blindly into the future. But where do we *want* to go?**
>
> **What would happen if we actually tried to answer this question?**

Increasing technological ability means increasing potential for disaster.

BASIC HUMAN QUESTIONS
TRUTH

Is it possible to know the truth about ourselves and the universe?

C.E.M. JOAD, an English philosopher (1891–1953), summed up the aims of traditional philosophy in this way:

> The object of philosophy, as I conceive it, is not to help people, but to discover truth. I want to know *qua* philosopher what the universe is like.
>
> It is the business of philosophy, as I conceive it, to seek to understand the nature of the universe as a whole, not, as do the sciences, some special department of it, but the whole bag of tricks to which the moral feelings of the Puritan, the herd instinct of the man in the street, the religious consciousness of the saint, the aesthetic enjoyment of the artist, the history of the human race and its contemporary follies, no less than the latest discoveries of science contribute. Reflecting upon this mass of data, the philosopher seeks to interpret it. He looks for a clue to guide him through the labyrinth, for a system wherewith to classify, or a purpose in terms of which to make meaningful.

BERTRAND RUSSELL, the English mathematician and philosopher (1872–1970), explained that one of the most basic questions of philosophy is the question of knowledge: how can we know anything?

> Is there any knowledge in the world which is so certain that no reasonable man could doubt it? This question, which at first sight might not seem difficult, is really one of the most difficult that can be asked. When we have realized the obstacles in the way of a straightforward and confident answer, we shall be well launched on the study of philosophy—for philosophy is merely the attempt to answer such ultimate questions, not carelessly and dogmatically, as we do in ordinary life and even in the sciences, but critically, after exploring all that makes such questions puzzling, and after realizing all the vagueness and confusion that underlie our ordinary ideas.

PAUL HAZARD, the French historian, (1878–1944), described how questions about truth became extremely important in seventeenth-century Europe, after centuries in which Christian beliefs had almost been taken for granted:

> What men craved to know was what they were to believe, and what they were not to believe. Was tradition still to command their allegiance, or was it to go by the board? Were they to continue plodding along the same old road, trusting to the same old guides, or were they to obey new leaders who bade them turn their back on all those outworn

things and follow them to other lands of promise? The champions of Reason and the champions of Religion were ... fighting desperately for the possession of men's souls, confronting each other in a contest at which the whole of thoughtful Europe was looking on.

Bertrand Russell

MICHAEL POLANYI, a scientist and philosopher, speaks about the tension created by the modern scientist's approach to truth and knowledge, in his book *Knowing and Being*:

Our task is not to suppress the specialisation of knowledge but to achieve harmony and truth over the whole range of knowledge. This is where I see the trouble, where a deep-seated disturbance between science and all other culture appears to lie. I believe that this disturbance was inherent originally in the liberating impact of modern science on medieval thought and has only later turned pathological.

Science rebelled against authority. It rejected deduction from first causes in favour of empirical generalisations. Its ultimate ideal was a mechanistic

theory of the universe, though in respect of man it aimed only at a naturalistic explanation of his moral and social responsibilities.

Our answers to these questions are not purely theoretical or philosophical; they have a profound effect on everyday life. This is how JOHN RUSSELL TAYLOR, a drama critic, describes the frightening atmosphere of the plays of Harold Pinter:

The technique of casting doubt upon everything by matching each apparently clear and unequivocal statement with an equally clear and unequivocal statement of its contrary ... is one which we shall find used constantly in Pinter's plays to create an air of mystery and uncertainty ... in these ordinary surroundings lurk mysterious terrors and uncertainties—and by extension, the whole external world of everyday realities is thrown into question. Can we ever know the truth about anybody or anything? Is there any absolute truth to be known?

BASIC HUMAN QUESTIONS
LOVE

What is love, and where can it be found?

BERTRAND RUSSELL asked if there is any way of overcoming some of the obstacles which stand in the way of human progress:

What stands in the way? Not physical or technical obstacles, but only the evil passions in human minds; suspicion, fear, lust for power, intolerance . . .

The root of the matter is a very simple and old-fashioned thing, a thing so simple that I am almost ashamed to mention it, for fear of the derisive smile with which wise cynics will greet my words. The thing I mean—please forgive me for mentioning it—is love, Christian love, or compassion . . .

THOMAS MANN's novel *The Magic Mountain* describes a frightening world in which no one can be certain of anything. The last sentence of the book, which raises a question about love, springs not from hope, but from despair:

Out of this universal feast of death, out of this extremity of fever, kindling the rain-washed evening sky to a fiery glow, may it be that Love one day shall mount?

MOTHER THERESA, a Roman Catholic nun who has devoted her life to serving the poor and dying in Calcutta, believes:

The biggest disease today is not leprosy or tuberculosis, but rather the feeling of being unwanted, uncared for and deserted by everybody. The greatest evil is the lack of love and charity, the terrible indifference towards one's neighbour who lives at the roadside assaulted by exploitation, corruption, poverty and disease.

WILLIAM GOLDMAN, in *Marathon Man*, describes the excitement of a young and naive man who finds his love responded to:

She loves me back. She really does. A beautiful girl, a beautiful, non-competitive, sweet, sensible girl, and she *cares* for me. After all these crummy years, my cup is running over.

It is one of the novel's supremely ironical twists that the girl betrays him and has faked love from the start.

In Bernardo Bertolucci's film *Last Tango in Paris*, the doomed sadness of sex without names is portrayed:

'I don't want a name. I'm better off with a grunt or a groan. Do you want to know my name?'

He raised himself on his hands and knees. He formed his mouth into the shape of a snout, lifted his head and growled loudly. Then he began to grunt, deep in his throat— a primal sound that excited them both . . .

'It's so masculine,' she said. 'Now listen to mine.'

She pulled him down next to her on the mattress, and held him tightly. She mewed, and asked, 'Do you like it?'

They laughed. He grunted again, and she answered. Together they filled the circular room with the strident courtship of beasts.

EDWARD ALBEE, the American playwright, shows the destructiveness of a marriage which has lost its meaning:

I'm numbed enough ... and I don't mean by liquor, though maybe that's part of the process—a gradual, over-the-years going to sleep of the brain cells—I'm numbed enough, now, to be able to take you when we're alone. I don't listen to you ... or when I *do* listen to you, I sift everything, I bring everything down to reflex response, so I don't really *hear* you, which is the only way to manage it. But you've taken a new tack, Martha, over the past couple of centuries— or however long it's been I've lived in this house with you—that makes it just too much ... too much.

... I've got to find some way to really get at you.

... You're a monster ... you *are*.

'The biggest disease today is . . . the feeling of being unwanted, uncared for, deserted by everybody.' Mother Theresa.

The entire country of Kampuchea has been devastated by war.

SUFFERING

Why is there suffering, and how can we live with it?

THE PSALMIST in the *Old Testament* pours out his complaint that God has abandoned him in his suffering:

> My God, my God, why have you
> abandoned me?
> I have cried desperately for help,
> but still it does not come.
> During the day I call to you, my God,
> but you do not answer;
> I call at night,
> but get no rest.

ALDOUS HUXLEY saw this as one of the most basic aspects of 'the Riddle of the Universe':

> In the form in which men have
> posed it, the Riddle of the Universe
> requires a theological answer.
> Suffering and enjoying, men want
> to know why they enjoy and to what
> end they suffer. They see good
> things and evil things, beautiful
> things and ugly, and they want to

find a reason—a final and absolute reason—why these things should be as they are.

EUGENE IONESCO, a French playwright of the school known as 'The Theatre of the Absurd', describes the profound impression made on him by the violence he witnessed early in his life:

> Shortly after my arrival in my
> second homeland, I saw a man, still
> young, big and strong, attack an old
> man with his fists and kick him with
> his boots . . . I have no other images
> of the world except those of
> evanescence and brutality, vanity
> and rage, nothingness or hideous,
> useless hatred. Everything I have
> since experienced has merely
> confirmed what I had seen and
> understood in my childhood: vain
> and sordid fury, cries suddenly
> stifled by silence, shadows
> engulfed forever in the night.

ADAM SCHAFF, as a Marxist, rejects all religious answers to these questions, but believes that Marxism must find convincing answers:

> The fact alone of some agnostics
> undergoing deathbed conversions
> gives much food for thought.
> Philosophy must take the place of
> religion here. It must tackle a
> number of diverse questions which
> have remained from the wreck of
> the religious view of life—the
> senselessness of suffering, of
> broken lives, of death, and many
> other questions relating to the fate
> of the living, struggling, suffering
> and dying individuals. Can this be
> done scientifically, that is in a way
> that is communicable and subject
> to some sort of verification?

Violent earthquakes in Algeria in 1980 left thousands upon thousands homeless.

BASIC HUMAN QUESTIONS
DEATH

How am I to face death?
Is there a life after death?

The writer of ECCLESIASTES, reflecting on all the injustice in the world, concludes that men are not too different from animals:

> I concluded that God is testing us, to show us that we are no better than animals. After all, the same fate awaits man and animal alike. One dies just like the other. They are both the same kind of creature. A human being is not better off than an animal, because life has no meaning for either. They are both going to the same place—the dust. They both came from it; they will both go back to it. How can anyone be sure that a man's spirit goes upwards while an animal's spirit goes down into the ground? ... There is no way for us to know what will happen after we die.

JAMES PACKER, a theologian, puts the question in very personal terms:

Death has been called 'the new obscenity', the nasty thing which no polite person nowadays will talk about in public. But death, even when unmentionable, remains inescapable. The one sure fact of life is that one day, with or without warning, quietly or painfully, it is going to stop. How am I, then, going to cope with death when my turn comes?

ALFRED TENNYSON, the English poet (1809–92), wrote these words in 1850 after the death of a close friend; he expressed the wishful hope that there is a life after death and that we have something better to look forward to:

Behold, we know not anything;
I can but trust that good shall fall
At last—far off—at last, to all
And every winter change to spring.

So runs my dream; but what am I?
An infant crying in the night;
An infant crying for the light;
And with no language but a cry.

ADAM SCHAFF takes it for granted that death is the end, but realizes that death makes us question many things about life:

'Vanity, vanity, all is vanity!' These words, repeated in various forms in all the philosophies of the East, seem to appeal to many who in old age begin to reflect on life and death. It is possible to shrug this off with a compassionate smile as nonsense, and yet the words echo a problem which simply cannot be ignored. Nor can the questions 'Why?', 'What for?', which force their way to the lips of people tired of the adversities and delusions of life. This applies still more to the compulsive questions which come from reflection upon death—why all this effort to stay alive if we are going to die anyway? It is difficult to avoid the feeling that death is senseless—avoidable, accidental death especially. Of course we can ask: senseless from what point of view? From the point of view of the progress of nature death is entirely sensible. But from the point of view of a given individual death is senseless and places in doubt everything that he does ... Attempts to ridicule this do not help ...

American novelist RAYMOND CHANDLER (1888–1959) chillingly presented the finality of death as seen by the non-Christian in his classic thriller, *The Big Sleep*:

What did it matter where you lay when you were dead? In a dirty sump or in a marble tower on top of a high hill? You were dead, you were sleeping the big sleep, you were not bothered by things like that. Oil and water were the same as wind and air to you. You just slept the big sleep, not caring about the nastiness of how you died or where you fell.

WOODY ALLEN, the American film-director and comedian, frequently illuminates the twentieth-century obsession with, and fear of, death. In *Death (a play)*, he presents the problem with characteristic wit:

It's not that I'm afraid to die, I just don't want to be there when it happens ...

Woody Allen

BASIC HUMAN QUESTIONS
THE FUTURE OF MAN

What hope is there for the human race?

P.T. FORSYTH, the English theologian (1848–1921), was concerned to ask questions about the meaning and goal of history:

> There are happily still people who ask what all the long and tragic train of history means, what great things does it intend, what destiny is it moving to, where its close shall be ... Do all its large lines converge on anything ... do they all curve in some vast trend and draw together to a due close? ... Do they all work together for good and love? What does man mean? Or are you so happy with the children, or so engrossed in your enterprises, that you can spare no attention to ask about the movement, the meaning, the fate of the race?

The majority of writers today tend to be pessimistic about the future. For W.E. HOCKING,

American educationalist and philosopher (1873–1966), death—not only of the individual but also of the human race—condemns us all to a feeling of frustration:

> What we see is the moment-to-moment boundary of our being, the nothingness that completes itself in death, our own and that of the race: in such a world, riddled the while with horror-filled actualities, how can a being aspiring and infinite be other than condemned to frustration? And in this world we are nevertheless condemned to engage and to act as men: is it possible?

ALDOUS HUXLEY, writing in 1936, was convinced that there would be more and more anarchy in the world, which would lead to a 'nihilist revolution':

> The time is not far off when the whole population and not merely a few exceptionally intelligent individuals will consciously realize the fundamental unlivableness of life under the present regime. And what then? ... The revolution that will then break out will not be communistic—there will be no need for such a revolution ... and besides, nobody will believe in the betterment of humanity or in anything else whatever. It will be a nihilist revolution. Destruction for destruction's sake. Hate, universal hate, and an aimless and therefore complete and thorough smashing up of everything.

BERTRAND RUSSELL was very concerned about the threat of nuclear war, and in an interview with a journalist once admitted:

> I have to read at least one detective book a day to drug myself against the nuclear threat.

ALVIN TOFFLER, in his book *Future Shock*, says that what makes men so worried about the future is 'the roaring current of change, a current so powerful today that it overturns institutions, shifts our values and shrivels our roots':

In 1965, in an article in *Horizon*, I coined the term 'future shock' to describe the shattering stress and disorientation that we induce in individuals by subjecting them to too much change in too short a time.

Can one live in a society that is out of control? That is the question posed for us by the concept of future shock. For that is the situation we find ourselves in. If it were technology alone that had broken loose, our problems would be serious enough. The deadly fact is, however, that many other social processes have also begun to run free, oscillating wildly, resisting our best efforts to guide them.

Urbanization, ethnic conflict, migration, population, crime—a thousand examples spring to mind of fields in which our efforts to shape change seem increasingly inept and futile.

With chilling clarity, Sir Geoffrey Vickers, the eminent British social scientist, has identified the issues: 'The rate of change increases at an accelerating speed, without a corresponding acceleration in the rate at which further responses can be made; and this brings us nearer the threshold beyond which control is lost'.

Alvin Toffler

MICHAEL HARRINGTON, writing in *The Accidental Century*, describes the fears which many have about the future. These fears arise not simply because of events happening around us; they spring from the basic uncertainty that we don't know what life is all about or where we're going:

Once destiny was an honest game of cards which followed certain conventions, with a limited number of cards and values. Now the player realizes in amazement that the hand of his future contains cards never seen before and that the rules of the game are modified by each player.

The whole world has become a dialectical nightmare; there are no more certainties.

FRANZ FANON, writing out of his experience of the Algerian Revolution in the 50s and 60s, optimistic that the Third World could show the way forward and start 'a new history of Man' urged:

Come, then, comrades ... Leave this Europe where they are never done talking of Man, yet murder men everywhere they find them ... Let us decide not to imitate Europe; let us combine our muscles and our brains in a new direction. Let us try to create the whole man, whom Europe has been incapable of bringing to triumphant birth ... The Third World today faces Europe like a colossal mass whose aim should be to try to resolve the problems to which Europe has not been able to find the answers ...

In 1976 the Italian town of Seveso was contaminated by noxious gases from a chemical factory, giving a grim foretaste of what chemical warfare could be like.

It is a question of the Third World starting a new history of Man, a history which will have regard to the sometimes prodigious theses which Europe has put forward, but which will also not forget Europe's crimes, of which the most horrible was committed in the heart of man, and consisted of the pathological tearing apart of his functions and the crumbling away of his unity. And in the framework of the collectivity there were the differentiations, the stratifications and the bloodthirsty tensions fed by classes; and finally, on the immense scale of humanity, there were racial hatreds, slavery, exploitation and above all the bloodless genocide which consisted in the setting aside of fifteen thousand millions of men ...

For Europe, for ourselves and for humanity, comrades, we must turn over a new leaf, we must work out new concepts, and try to set afoot a new man.

BASIC HUMAN QUESTIONS
THE SUPERNATURAL

Is there anything more than the physical world?

The philosophy of materialism, combined with modern scientific theory has tended to convince many people that the only things that are real are those that we can see, touch and feel. There is no 'heaven', no supernatural world.

In recent years, however, there has been an increasing interest in the occult, which suggests that many people still believe in the supernatural and want to find ways to control unseen forces.

ALVIN TOFFLER, traces some of these new interests back to the feeling that we can no longer control our environment:

> One response to the loss of control, for example, is a revulsion against intelligence. Science first gave man a sense of mastery over his environment, and hence over the future. By making the future seem malleable, instead of immutable, it shattered the opiate religions that preached passivity and mysticism.

Today, mounting evidence that society is out of control breeds disillusionment with science. In consequence, we witness a garish revival of mysticism. Suddenly astrology is the rage. Zen, yoga, seances, and witchcraft become popular pastimes.

PETER L. BERGER, the American sociologist, argued powerfully for a reaffirmation of the place of the supernatural in *A Rumour of Angels*:

> It may be conceded that there is in the modern world a certain type of consciousness that has difficulties with the supernatural ... We may say that contemporary consciousness is such and such; we are left with the question of whether we will assent to it. We may agree, say, that contemporary consciousness is incapable of conceiving either angels or demons. We are still left with the question of whether, possibly, both angels and demons go on existing despite this incapacity of our contemporaries to conceive of them ...
>
> What follows is not ... a total paralysis of thought. Rather, it is a new freedom and flexibility in asking questions of truth.

HAL LINDSEY, the American evangelist and writer, gives many examples of occult involvement in his best-selling book *Satan is Alive and Well on Planet Earth*:

> Cheryl may have answered an ad on how to be a witch. Who knows? She didn't tell me that, but as we sat on the floor of the coffee house rapping about her experiences, she told me she was sixteen—well, almost sixteen ...
>
> She became a witch. At first she pretended it was just a prank. Someone bought her a crystal ball, and she spent hours staring into it and interpreting the visions she

saw. One day she told one of her friends in school that her friend's father was going to die. When he met with an accidental death two days later, Cheryl felt little sadness; she was high with power!

'It shook me at first,' she said, 'but I was fascinated by it. I had something nothing else had! . . . I knew I had this power over people. I could burn a hole right through someone by just looking at them.'

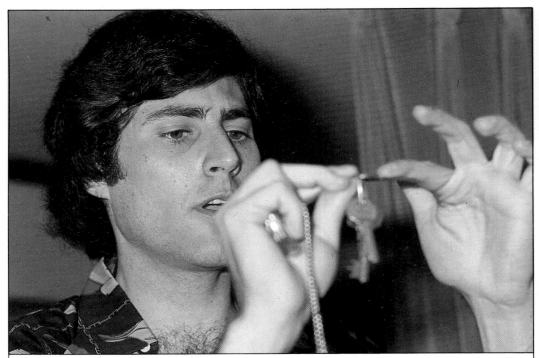

What is the source of Uri Geller's paranormal powers? One of his investigators believes that Geller is being made use of by evil spiritual beings.

EVIL

Is there any hope in fighting evil and injustice?

The *Old Testament* prophet HABAKKUK wrote in a situation where 'justice is never done':

> **O Lord, how long must I call for help before you listen, before you save us from violence? Why do you make me see such trouble? How can you endure to look on such wrongdoing? Destruction and violence are all round me, and there is fighting and quarrelling everywhere. The law is weak and useless, and justice is never done. Evil men get the better of the righteous, and so justice is perverted.**

The problem was specially acute for him because he believed that God is utterly holy: how could he allow evil to triumph?

> **Lord, from the very beginning you are God. You are my God, holy and eternal. Lord, my God and**

protector, you have chosen the Babylonians and made them strong so that they can punish us. But how can you stand these treacherous, evil men? Your eyes are too holy to look at evil, and you cannot stand the sight of people doing wrong. So why are you silent while they destroy people who are more righteous than they are?

The writer of ECCLESIASTES found that the problem of evil and injustice contributed to his feeling of the meaninglessness of life:

> **I looked again at all the injustice that goes on in this world. The oppressed were weeping, and no one would help them. No one would help them, because their oppressors had power on their side. I envy those who are dead and gone; they are better off than those who are still alive. But better off than either are those who have never been born, who have never seen the injustice that goes on in this world.**

MARTIN LUTHER KING JR, the American civil rights leader (1929–68), spoke of the urgent need to find ways of curbing violence throughout the world:

> **It is no longer merely the idealist or the doom-ridden who seeks for some controlling force capable of challenging the instrumentalities of destruction. Many are searching. Sooner or later all the peoples of the world, without regard to the political systems under which they live, will have to discover a way to live together in peace.**
> **Man was born into barbarism when killing his fellow man was a normal condition of existence. He became endowed with a conscience. And he has now reached the day when violence toward another human being must become as abhorrent as eating another's flesh.**

Can destruction be used to counter evil? In August 1945 the Pacific War was brought to an end by the bombing of Hiroshima and Nagasaki.

ALBERT CAMUS recognized that belief in a just God can give men the assurance that evil will ultimately be defeated. But since belief in God was no longer a real option for him, the problem he faced was much more acute, because there is no certainty that justice will ever be done:

The certainty of the existence of a God who would give meaning to life has a far greater attraction than the knowledge that without him one could do evil without being punished. The choice between these alternatives would not be difficult. But there is no choice, and that is where the bitterness begins.

Confronted with this evil, confronted with death, man from the very depths of his soul cries out for justice.

CHRISTIAN ANSWERS
TO HUMAN QUESTIONS

The Lord, who made the earth, who formed
it and set it in place, spoke to me. He whose
name is the Lord said, 'Call to me, and I will
answer you; I will tell you wonderful and
marvellous things that you know nothing
about . . .'

Who can understand the human heart?
There is nothing else so deceitful;
it is too sick to be healed.
I, the Lord, search the minds
and test the hearts of men.
I treat each one according to the way he
lives,
according to what he does.
JEREMIAH

The answers suggested in this section are not the kind of answers you find at the back of a book of mathematical problems or general knowledge!

These are simply some of the basic convictions which enable the Christian to start working out his answers.

In each case the quotations from the Bible and other writers give some indication of what it *feels like* to see the world in this way, and how these beliefs work out in practice.

Outline

THE INDIVIDUAL

THE MEANING OF LIFE

VALUES

TRUTH

LOVE

SUFFERING

DEATH

THE FUTURE OF MAN

THE SUPERNATURAL

EVIL

CHRISTIAN ANSWERS TO HUMAN QUESTIONS

THE INDIVIDUAL

Who or what am I?

If every human being is created in 'the image of God' he has real value to God the Creator. This, therefore, is how JESUS speaks about the value of the individual to God:

> Aren't five sparrows sold for two pennies? Yet not one sparrow is forgotten by God. Even the hairs of your head have all been counted. So do not be afraid; you are worth much more than many sparrows!

THE PSALMIST in the *Old Testament* has a deep sense of confidence and joy because he believes that God has made him and knows him intimately as an individual:

> You created every part of me;
> you put me together in my mother's womb.
> I praise you because you are to be feared;
> all you do is strange and wonderful.
> I know it with all my heart.
> When my bones were being formed,
> carefully put together in my mother's womb,
> when I was growing there in secret,
> you knew that I was there—
> you saw me before I was born.

JOB has a frightening sense of God's awareness of every individual. In his suffering he even wishes that God were *less* concerned about him:

> Why is man so important to you?
> Why pay attention to what he does?
> You inspect him every morning
> and test him every minute.
> Won't you look away long enough
> for me to swallow my spittle?
> Are you harmed by my sin, you jailer?
> Why use me for your target-practice?
> Am I so great a burden to you?
> Can't you ever forgive my sin?
> Can't you pardon the wrong I do?

LESSLIE NEWBIGIN shows how this belief in the value of the individual provides a compelling reason for fighting for the rights of the individual:

> During World War II, Hitler sent men to the famous Bethel Hospital to inform Pastor Bodelschwingh, its director, that the State could no longer afford to maintain hundreds of epileptics who were useless to society and only constituted a drain on scarce resources, and that orders were being issued to have them destroyed. Bodelschwingh confronted them in his room at the entrance to the Hospital and fought a spiritual battle which eventually sent them away without having done what they were sent to do. He had no other weapon for the battle than the simple affirmation that these were men and women made in the image of God and that to destroy them was to commit a sin against God which would surely be punished. What other argument could he have used?

The United States Declaration of Independence states that all men are created equal. They are endowed with certain inalienable rights . . . among these are life, liberty and the pursuit of happiness.

CHRISTIAN ANSWERS TO HUMAN QUESTIONS

THE MEANING OF LIFE

What's the point of it all?

The conviction that we live in a created universe is the starting point for understanding the meaning and purpose of life. The writer of ECCLESIASTES is able to get beyond the cynical and sceptical attitude that 'everything is useless', because he sees life as a gift from God, and can therefore enjoy everything that God has given us in this life:

> **I realized that all we can do is to be happy and do the best we can while we are still alive. All of us should eat and drink and enjoy what we have worked for. It is God's gift.**

> **This is what I have found out: the best thing anyone can do is to eat and drink and enjoy what he has worked for during the short life that God has given him; this is man's fate. If God gives a man wealth and property and lets him enjoy them, he should be grateful and enjoy what he has worked for. It is a gift from God. Since God has allowed**

him to be happy, he will not worry too much about how short life is.

His final conclusion is that God has created us to fear him and obey him. If there is a life after death, and if God is a righteous judge, we can be certain that we will one day understand the things in this life that appear meaningless and unjust:

> **After all this, there is only one thing to say: Fear God, and obey his commands, because this is all that man was created for. God is going to judge everything we do, whether good or bad, even things done in secret.**

In other parts of the Bible we find that what gives meaning and significance to man's life is the fact that God himself has a purpose for history, and wants men to know him and belong to his people:

> **I am the Lord . . . I will make you my own people, and I will be your God. You will know that I am the Lord your God . . .**

PAUL writes in this way about the plan of God which embraces the whole of the universe, and in which every individual who believes plays a significant part:

> **Let us give thanks to the God and Father of our Lord Jesus Christ! For in our union with Christ he has blessed us by giving us every spiritual blessing in the heavenly world. Even before the world was made, God had already chosen us to be his through our union with Christ, so that we would be holy and without fault before him.**
>
> **Because of his love God had already decided that through Jesus Christ he would make us his sons— this was his pleasure and purpose.**
>
> **Let us praise God for his glorious grace, for the free gift he gave us in his dear Son! For by the death of Christ we are set free, that is, our sins are forgiven. How great is the grace of God, which he gave to us in such large measure!**
>
> **In all his wisdom and insight God did what he had purposed, and**

The Bible teaches that God is supremely concerned for individual human beings.

With love and care, the handicapped, such as this blind boy, can be helped to live a normal life.

made known to us the secret plan he had already decided to complete by means of Christ. This plan, which God will complete when the time is right, is to bring all creation together, everything in heaven and on earth, with Christ as head.

JAMES PACKER writes about the summary of the purpose of life given in the *Westminster Shorter Catechism of Faith*:

'Man's chief end,' says the Shorter Catechism, magnificently, 'is to glorify God and to enjoy him forever.' End, note, not ends; for the two activities are one. God's chief end, purposed in all that he does, is his glory (and what higher end could he have?) and he has so made us that we find our own deepest fulfilment and highest joy in hallowing his name by praise, submission and service. God is no sadist and the principle of our creation is that, believe it or not (and of course many don't, just as Satan doesn't), our duty, interest and delight completely coincide.

Christians get so hung up with the pagan idea (very dishonouring to God, incidently) that God's will is always unpleasant, so that one is rather a martyr to be doing it, that they hardly at first notice how their experience verifies the truth that in Christian living duty and delight go together. But they do!—and if you think about your present life you will find it so!—and it will be even clearer in the life to come. To give oneself to hallowing God's name as one's life-task means that living, though never a joy-ride, will become increasingly a joy *road*. Can you believe that? Well, the proof of the pudding is in the eating! Try it, and you will see.

AUGUSTINE, bishop of Hippo in North Africa (354–430), wrote these well-known words in his *Confessions*:

Can any praise be worthy of the Lord's majesty? How magnificent is his strength! How inscrutable his wisdom! Man is one of your creatures, Lord, and his instinct is to praise you. He bears about him the mark of death, the sign of his own sin, to remind him that you thwart the proud. But still, since he is part of your creation, he wishes to praise you. The thought of you stirs him so deeply that he cannot be content unless he praises you, because you made us for yourself and our hearts find no peace until they rest in you.

CHRISTIAN ANSWERS TO HUMAN QUESTIONS
VALUES

How are we to make moral choices?

The ultimate standard of what is right for the Christian is the character of God himself. This is why PETER writes to fellow-Christians:

> Be holy in all that you do, just as God who called you is holy. The scripture says, 'Be holy because I am holy'.

The *Ten Commandments* revealed to MOSES give an outline of the standards which God sets for men; the first four speak of respect for God, and the last six speak of respect for our neighbours:

> Worship no god but me.
> Do not make for yourselves images of anything in heaven or on earth . . .
> Do not bow down to any idol or worship it . . .
> Do not use my name for evil purposes . . .
> Observe the Sabbath and keep it holy . . .

> Respect your father and your mother . . .
> Do not commit murder.
> Do not commit adultery.
> Do not steal.
> Do not accuse anyone falsely.
> Do not desire another man's house . . .

THE PROPHETS were constantly exposing injustice and corruption in personal and public life, applying the commandments in particular situations:

> The Lord says: 'I love justice and hate oppression and crime.'

> The Lord Almighty says, 'I will appear among you to judge, and I will testify at once against those who practise magic, against adulterers, against those who give false testimony, those who cheat employees out of their wages, and those who take advantage of widows, orphans, and foreigners— against all who do not respect me.'

JESUS extended some of the *Ten Commandments* to cover thoughts as well as outward actions. For example:

> You have heard that it was said, 'Do not commit adultery'. But now I tell you: anyone who looks at a woman and wants to possess her is guilty of committing adultery with her in his heart.

And he gave his own summary of the law of the *Old Testament* by bringing together two verses from different books:

> 'Love the Lord your God with all your heart, with all your soul, and with all your mind.' This is the greatest and the most important commandment. The second most important commandment is like it: 'Love your neighbour as you love yourself.' The whole Law of Moses and the teachings of the prophets depend on these two commandments.

While the Christian, therefore, does not have ready-made answers to all moral problems, he at least has a firm starting-point. Where there is doubt in particular situations, he can rely on the leading of the Holy Spirit who can make his conscience and the conscience of the Christian community sensitive to the mind of Christ. So PAUL writes:

> Be careful how you live. Don't live like ignorant people, but like wise people ... Don't be fools, then, but try to find out what the Lord wants you to do.

JUSTIN MARTYR was a well-known Christian apologist who lived in Palestine in the second century. His *First Apology* was addressed to the Emperor Antonius Pius to answer the popular charges that Christians were atheists and immoral. This is how he describes the change that Christianity had made to their way of life:

> We who used formerly to find our pleasures in fornication, now kiss Chastity alone. We who used magical arts, have devoted ourselves to the good and unbegotten God. We who loved more than anything being men of means, now bring what we have to a common fund and communicate to the needy. We were haters and murderers of one another; and when it came to foreigners, with different social customs, we could not make a common home. But now since the revelation of Christ we share the same manner of life, we pray for our enemies and seek to win over those who unjustly hate us.

JAMES PACKER emphasizes that Christian values are intended for society, and not just for the individual:

> What then should we say of the modern secular society? Should we see its emergence as a sign of progress? Is it not rather a sign of decadence, the start of a slide down a slippery slope with a pit at the bottom? When God's values are ignored, and the only community ideal is permissiveness, where will moral capital come from once the Christian legacy is spent? How can national policy ever rise above material self interest, pragmatic and unprincipled? How can internal collapse be avoided as sectional interests, unrestrained by any sense of national responsibility, cut each other down? How can an overall reduction, indeed destruction, of happiness be avoided, when the revealed way of happiness, the 'God first, others next, self last' of the Commandments, is rejected? The prospects are ominous. May God bring us back to himself and to the social wisdom of his Commandments before it is too late.

J.N.D. ANDERSON, formerly a professor of legal studies, explains how a Christian begins to grapple with difficult moral problems in the modern world. In a series of lectures entitled *Issues of Life and Death*, he concludes his first lecture on 'The Sanctity of Human Life' in this way:

> ... our basic concept, to which we shall continually have to return, is the unique significance and value of the human personality: man made in the image and after the likeness of God himself; man as he was created, as he now is, and as God would have him to be.
>
> It is in this light that we must approach the problems of artificial insemination, genetic engineering, birth control, sterilisation, abortion ... the prolongation of life, transplant surgery, euthanasia, suicide, capital punishment and the termination of life in the course of violence, revolution or war. Some of these subjects could justly be regarded by the humanist as man taking a conscious and active part in his own evolutionary development ... and they may certainly, I think, be considered by the Christian in the context of man attempting to obey the divine

In adopting two Vietnamese orphans, this family have obeyed the biblical command to care for the oppressed and the fatherless.

command to 'subdue the earth', to co-operate with God in his on-going creative purposes, and to 'replenish the earth' in an intelligent way. But whereas, in the animal kingdom, there would appear to be the widest scope for experimentation—provided always that this does not involve unnecessary pain, unacceptable exploitation or wrongful neglect of the principles of conservation—the situation is very different in the case of man. With an animal, for example, artificial insemination seems to involve no moral problems, but in the case of human beings a number of moral, aesthetic, psychological, social and even legal considerations must, of necessity, be taken into account; and this is also true of genetic engineering, sterilisation, euthanasia and much else. In other words, we must grapple with the problem of how far the command to subdue the earth includes man's own genetic and psychological make-up. And in this, and a number of other respects, the approach of the humanist may differ widely from that of the biblically minded Christian.

So we come back to where we began: the essential nature of man. On the one side of his nature man is indubitably part of the animal kingdom; but, in a unique degree, he is a rational creature, capable of conceptual thought. Partly for this very reason, he has the God-given ability to transform—or at least control—nature, and to participate in God's creative purposes. More important, from the spiritual standpoint, he is a moral creature, who can in part distinguish, even in his fallen condition, the difference between right and wrong. And, still more important, he is a creature with whom God himself can communicate . . .

So, as we approach the exceedingly complex and difficult questions to which we must turn . . . the Christian must insist that, while man is an integral part of the animal creation, he is also essentially distinct from it; that to speak of 'human nature' as in a category of its own is both meaningful and true; that, however much it may be right—and even mandatory—to attempt to improve the health, intelligence and enlightenment of our race, we cannot radically change human nature as such; and that any act or process designed to 'dehumanise' man stands, *ipso facto*, condemned.

CHRISTIAN ANSWERS TO HUMAN QUESTIONS
TRUTH

Is it possible to know the truth about ourselves and the universe?

The *Bible* makes the bold claim that the unseen God has revealed himself to men:

> **No one has ever seen God. The only Son, who is the same as God and is at the Father's side, he has made him known.**

To say that God has revealed the truth does not mean that he has revealed *everything* there is to be known. The revelation he has given is not exhaustive, but it is adequate. We can be sure that what has *not* been revealed is not inconsistent in any way with what *has* been revealed. What we still have to learn about God will not contradict what we already know about him.

MOSES, for example, makes a distinction between what has been revealed and what has not been revealed. What has been revealed provides an adequate basis for living both here and now, and in the future:

> **The secret things belong to the Lord our God, but the things revealed belong to us and to our children for ever, that we may follow all the words of this law.**

Similarly, PAUL contrasts his present knowledge of God with the knowledge he will have in heaven:

> **What we see now is like a dim image in a mirror; then we shall see face to face. What I know now is only partial; then it will be complete—as complete as God's knowledge of me.**

The incompleteness of his knowledge in this life, however, did not make him sceptical or agnostic. He believed that the truth which had already been revealed was utterly reliable and trustworthy:

> **We have not received this world's spirit; instead, we have received the Spirit sent by God, so that we may know all that God has given us. So then, we do not speak in words taught by human wisdom, but in words taught by the Spirit, as we explain spiritual truths to those who have the Spirit.**

The *Bible* also claims that God has revealed to us what he requires of us as men:

> **The Lord has told us what is good. What he requires of us is this: to do what is just, to show constant love, and to live in humble fellowship with our God.**

LACTANTIUS was a Christian apologist from North Africa who lived at the beginning of the fourth century. In this passage he speaks of three distinct stages by which he would try to help a person from a pagan background to understand the Christian faith. The experience of many in the twentieth century who have an atheistic or agnostic background often follows a similar pattern:

> **Since there are many steps by which one mounts to the home of truth, it is not easy for anyone to reach the top. For when lights are dazzling one with the brightness of the truth, if one does not keep a firm foothold, down one rolls to the**

In April 1981 the first American Space Shuttle was launched. The Bible teaches that it is right to explore our environment: but that we must acknowledge that there is a limit to what we can know.

bottom again. Now the first step is to understand religions which are false, and to cast aside the impious worship of gods made with hands. The second step is to perceive with the mind the fact that God is one most high, whose power and providence made the world from the beginning and direct it towards a future. The third step is to know His Servant and Messenger, whom He sent on embassy to Earth.

In another book he challenges pagans to present their beliefs in a reasonable and convincing way and emphasizes the Christians' willingness to discuss questions about truth:

Let them call us together to a meeting, exhort us to take part in worship of the gods, persuade us that the gods are many, by whose mysterious power and providence all is governed ... And let them confirm all this, not just by their own say-so—for the authority of mortal man can count for nought—but by some divine testimonies, as we do.

This is no case for violence or hurt, since religion cannot be forced. It must be conducted by words, more effective than blows in a matter affecting the will. Let them unsheath the keen blade of intellect. If their reasoning is true, let it be published. We are ready to hear if they should teach. Of course we do not believe those who keep mum, no more than we yield to outbursts of rage. Let them imitate us and set forth the reasoned statement of the whole matter. For we do not, as they complain, entice. We lead, we prove, we show. We keep no one against his will, for he is of no use to God who lacks devotion and faith. Yet no one deserts our side, since truth itself holds him. Let them teach in this manner ... But if they did, our 'old women', whom they despise, and 'local boys', would laugh their error and stupidity to scorn.

SIR ARTHUR S. EDDINGTON, a famous English scientist (1882–1944), was one of the observers of the 1919 eclipse, sent by the Royal Society to Africa to test Einstein's predictions regarding it, and so to test the truth of the relativity theory. This is how he wrote about the place of reason in man's search for the truth about God and the universe:

I am convinced that if in physics we pursued to the bitter end our attempt to reach purely objective reality, we should simply undo the work of creation and present the world as we might conceive it to have been before the Spirit moved upon the face of the waters. The spiritual element in our experience is the creative element, and if we remove it as we have tried to do in physics on the ground that it also creates illusion, we must ultimately reach the nothingness which was in the Beginning.

Reasoning is our great ally in the quest for truth. But reasoning can only start from premises; and at the beginning of the argument we must always come back to innate convictions... We are helpless unless we admit also (as perhaps the strongest conviction of all) that we have within us some power of self-criticism to test the validity of our own convictions ... I think that this power can be nothing less than a ray proceeding from the light of absolute Truth, a thought proceeding from the absolute Mind. With this guidance we may embark on the adventure of spiritual life uncharted though it be. It is enough that we carry a compass.

DONALD MACKAY describes how Christian convictions about the universe provide a firm basis for the scientific enterprise:

It is such a pathetic betrayal of truth to allow to grow in people's minds the idea that 'God had it all his own way until science came along and discovered mechanistic explanation'. To spread the idea deliberately, as some atheists do, seems sheer dishonesty when one thinks that from the biblical-theistic standpoint it is to God's own creative faithfulness, the faithfulness and regularity of his sustaining in being the universe that he has created, that we owe the success and worthwhileness of our mechanistic enterprise in science. It is *his* story that we are trying to tell in mechanistic terms. This conviction was one of the major motive factors in the rise of modern science; and it is not without significance that the great majority of the most famous developers of the mechanistic world-model— Newton, Boyle, Faraday, Maxwell, Compton, Eddington come to mind as examples—were believers in God. Their belief gave them all the greater confidence in the worthwhileness of studying nature. It is in the biblical doctrine of God as the Creator of our whole drama, its mechanistic level as well as its personal, that I see the one unifying perspective for the scientifically-structured world in which we live.

R. HOOKYAAS, a professor of the history of science, describes how Christian beliefs about the universe contributed to the development of modern science:

> Science is more a consequence than a cause of a certain religious view.
>
> The confrontation of Graeco-Roman culture with biblical religion engendered, after centuries of tension, a new science. This science preserved the indispensable parts of the ancient heritage (mathematics, logic, methods of observation and experimentation), but it was directed by different social and methodological conceptions, largely stemming from a biblical world view. Metaphorically speaking, whereas the bodily ingredients of science may have been Greek, its vitamins and hormones were biblical.

C.S. LEWIS, a professor of English literature (1893–1963), has become known as one of the greatest apologists of the twentieth century. In his autobiography *Surprised by Joy* he describes the first decisive stage in his conversion, when he came to believe in the truth of the existence of a personal God:

> Before God closed in on me, I was in fact offered what now appears a moment of wholly free choice. In a sense. I was going up Headington Hill on the top of a bus. Without words and (I think) almost without images, a fact about myself was somehow presented to me. I became aware that I was holding something at bay, or shutting something out. Or, if you like, that I was wearing some stiff clothing, like corsets, or even a suit of armour, as if I were a lobster. I felt myself being, there and then, given a free choice. I could open the door or keep it shut; I could unbuckle the armour or keep it on. Neither choice was presented as a duty; no threat or promise was attached to either, though I knew that to open the door or to take off the corset meant the incalculable. The choice appeared to be momentous but it was also strangely unemotional. I was moved by no desires or fears. In a sense I was not moved by anything. I chose to open, to unbuckle, to loosen the rein. I say, 'I chose', yet it did not really seem possible to do the opposite. On the other hand, I was aware of no motives. You could argue that I was not a free agent, but I am more inclined to think that this came nearer to being a perfectly free act than most that I have ever done.
>
> Amiable agnostics will talk cheerfully about 'man's search for God'. To me, as I then was, they might as well have talked about the mouse's search for the cat.
>
> I gave in, and admitted that God was God, and knelt and prayed: perhaps, that night, the most dejected and reluctant convert in all England. I did not then see what is now the most shining and obvious thing; the Divine humility which will accept a convert even on such terms.

LOVE

What is love and where can it be found?

The Christian has a very distinctive starting-point here because he believes that God is the source of all love. JOHN, for example, says that God *is* love, and that he has given us the supreme demonstration of love. He also draws conclusions about our relations with one another:

Dear friends, let us love one another, because love comes from God. Whoever loves is a child of God and knows God. Whoever does not know God, for God is love. And God showed his love for us by sending his only Son into the world, so that we might have life through him. This is what love is: it is not that we have loved God, but that he loved us and sent his Son to be the means by which our sins are forgiven.

Dear friends, if this is how God loved us, then we should love one another. No one has ever seen God, but if we love one another, God lives in union with us, and his love is made perfect in us.

The Bible gives space for a celebration of sexual love in *The Song of Solomon*, and in the framework of marriage, commitment and obedience is not a restriction but an enhancement of this love.

How beautiful you are, my darling! Oh, how beautiful! Your eyes behind your veil are doves. Your hair is like a flock of goats descending from Mount Gilead. Your teeth are like a flock of sheep just shorn, coming up from the washing. Each has its twin; not one of them is alone. Your lips are like a scarlet ribbon; your mouth is lovely. Your temples behind your veil are like the halves of a pomegranate. Your neck is like the tower of David, built with elegance; on it hang a thousand shields, all of them shields of warriors. Your two breasts are like two fawns, like twin fawns of a gazelle that browse among the lilies. Until the day breaks and the shadows flee, I will go to the mountain of myrrh and to the hill of incense. All beautiful you are, my darling; there is no flaw in you.

The Christian understanding of marriage is that God meant it to be a life-long union between husband and wife. After speaking about the creation of man and woman, the writer of GENESIS goes on to say:

That is why a man leaves his father and mother and is united with his wife, and they become one.

The demonstration of the love of God in Christ adds a further dimension. PAUL sees the way Christ gave himself for men as an example of how husband and wife need to give themselves to each other:

> Submit yourselves to one another because of your reverence for Christ.
>
> Wives, submit to your husbands as to the Lord. For a husband has authority over his wife just as Christ has authority over the church ...
>
> Husbands, love your wives just as Christ loved the church and gave his life for it. He did this to dedicate the church to God by his word, after making it clean by washing it in water, in order to present the church to himself in all its beauty— pure and faultless, without spot or wrinkle or any other imperfection. Men ought to love their wives just as they love their own bodies ...

WALTER TROBISCH comments in this way on the word used in the book of Genesis to describe sexual intercourse:

> The word 'know' is a great word. The Hebrew word for it used in the Bible means 'to know someone by name'. In other words, to know someone very well, to take care of that one, to love and respect him or her as a person. The Bible uses this word for the first time in Genesis 4:1, 'Adam knew Eve, *his* wife.' You can never know what *the* woman or *a* woman is like; you can only know *your* wife. That means you cannot know a woman except in marriage, in the atmosphere of faithfulness, where the sex act is one of the expressions of love.

The Christian understanding of love and marriage by no means excludes excitement, but its excitement comes from outside the individuals involved, in a way that non-Christians can find hard to understand. The English poet, JACK CLEMO, wrote:

> The man is in love in a sense which the materialist can never understand. He and the girl are 'one in Christ' in a sense which the spiritually-minded ascetic can never understand. They are united at a level which even the Marriage Service does not mention—chiefly because the Marriage Service was designed for all citizens of a 'Christian' State and therefore makes no special provision for couples who have been radically converted.
>
> ... This is the sexuality of the New Creation, a direct product of discipleship.

JAMES PACKER sums up the meaning of love and sex in marriage in this way:

> What then is the place and purpose of sex? God intends, as the story of Eve's creation from Adam shows, that the 'one flesh' experience should be an expression and a heightening of the partners' sense that, being given to each other, they now belong together, each needing the other for completion and wholeness (see Genesis 2:18–24). This is the 'love' that committed couples are to 'make' when they mate. Children are born from their relationship, but this is secondary; what is basic is the enriching of their relationship itself through their repeated 'knowing' of each other as persons who belong to each other exclusively and without reserve. So the place for sex is the place of life-long mutual fidelity, i.e. marriage, where sexual experience grows richer as the couple experience more and more of each other's loving faithfulness in the total relationship.

CHRISTIAN ANSWERS TO HUMAN QUESTIONS
SUFFERING

Why is there suffering and how can we live with it?

The *Bible* does not present a complete and systematic explanation of suffering; but it does at least give some important clues:

SUFFERING IS AN INTRUSION IN GOD'S UNIVERSE

The book of GENESIS insists that the universe as God originally made it was 'good':

> God saw all that he had made, and it was very good.

It then goes on to describe suffering (as we know it) as something which came in as a direct result of man's rebellion against God. Man disobeyed God at the suggestion of the serpent, who in other parts of the Bible is interpreted as the mouthpiece of Satan. As a result of this disobedience, God says to the woman:

> I will increase your trouble in pregnancy and your pain in giving birth...

And to the man:

> Because of what you have done, the ground will be under a curse. You will have to work hard all your life to make it produce enough food for you. It will produce weeds and thorns, and you will have to eat wild plants. You will have to work hard and sweat to make the soil produce anything, until you go back to the soil from which you were formed. You were made from soil, and you will become soil again.

This conviction is important because it excludes the idea that suffering was an integral part of the universe as God made it in the beginning, or that this is how he wanted it to be.

SOMETIMES THERE IS AN ELEMENT OF HUMAN RESPONSIBILITY, AND SOMETIMES THERE IS NONE

Some of our suffering is a result of our own ignorance or stupidity. If we abuse our bodies, for example, we usually have to suffer the consequences sooner or later.

Some of our suffering, however, is caused by other people—and we are sometimes responsible for the suffering of others. It is one of the frightening things about human freedom that since we are free to do *good* to other people, we are also free to do *harm*, either deliberately or unintentionally. This awareness that we are all 'bound up in the bundle of life', that our behaviour inevitably affects others, hardly needs to be illustrated from the Bible; this is simply the way life is, and we have to take 'the rough with the smooth'. All of creation has suffered because of what man has done, and it 'groans with pain' (Romans 8:22).

The *Bible*, however, does have some light to shed on the problem of innocent suffering—suffering where there is *no* element of human responsibility, where we cannot say that anyone has caused it.

The book of *Job* in the *Old Testament* deals with the problem of the suffering of the innocent. Job is portrayed as a God-fearing man (though not perfect or sinless), who suffers bereavement, the loss of his possessions and finally an intensely painful and unpleasant illness. The prologue of the book makes it clear that Job's suffering is not in any way connected with any sin or disobedience, but is brought about by the malicious activity of Satan. Job's friends do not know what has happened 'behind the scenes' in heaven, and they argue that Job's suffering is a direct result of his sin, or that it comes from God to teach him some lesson. But Job is naturally impatient with these half-truths which do not meet his need or explain his particular suffering.

At the end of the book, God breaks into the discussion and speaks to Job as the Sovereign Creator and Sustainer of the universe. What he says to Job in effect is this: 'I am the Creator of the universe and you are a creature. I am infinite, and know the answers to the questions about your suffering; but you are finite and cannot expect to know all the answers. If you did, you would be God. But look around you at the universe which I have created and which I still control. Can't you see enough evidence there to convince you that I am still in control? Can't you go on *trusting* me as Creator, even though you don't understand the reason for your suffering?'

After this Job reaches the point of surrendering himself to God in trust and humility:

> I know, Lord, that you are all-
> powerful;
> that you can do everything you
> want.
> You ask how I dare question your
> wisdom
> when I am so very ignorant.
> I talked about things I did not
> understand,
> about marvels too great for me to
> know.
> You told me to listen while you
> spoke
> and to try to answer your questions.
> Then I knew only what others had
> told me,
> but now I have seen you with my
> own eyes.
> So I am ashamed of all I have said
> and repent in dust and ashes.

The book of Job, therefore, teaches that suffering is sometimes totally undeserved. We cannot always say that we are suffering because of something which we or others have done. Part of the solution of the problem of undeserved suffering is to recognize that God, as a loving and all-powerful Creator, does know what he is doing in allowing us

to suffer, even when we don't know. (Although Job does not and cannot know it, there is a point in his suffering.)

JESUS DEDICATED HIMSELF TO RELIEVE SUFFERING

At the beginning of his public ministry, he applied some words of Isaiah to himself—words which have been described as 'the Nazareth Manifesto' because they outline the programme of action to which he was committed:

> The Spirit of the Lord is upon me,
> because he has chosen me to bring
> good news to the poor.
> He has sent me to proclaim liberty
> to the captives
> and recovery of sight to the blind;
> to set free the oppressed
> and announce that the time has
> come
> when the Lord will save his people.

He described himself as the one who is stronger than Satan, and pointed to his healing miracles as evidence that he had come to undo the ravages of Satan:

> It is ... by means of God's power
> that I drive out demons, and this
> proves that the kingdom of God has
> already come to you. When a strong
> man, with all his weapons ready,
> guards his own house, all his
> belongings are safe. But when a
> stronger man attacks him and
> defeats him, he carries away all the
> weapons the owner was depending
> on and divides up what he stole.

When he healed a woman who had been crippled for eighteen years, he was criticized by the religious authorities for having done this on a sabbath. This was his reply:

> You hypocrites! Any one of you
> would untie his ox or his donkey
> from the stall and take it out to give
> it water on the Sabbath. Now here is
> this descendant of Abraham whom
> Satan has kept bound up for
> eighteen years; should she not be
> released on the Sabbath?

Jesus gave his disciples special authority and power

to continue his healing ministry:

> Jesus called the twelve disciples together and gave them power and authority to drive out all demons and to cure diseases. Then he sent them out to preach the Kingdom of God and to heal the sick ...

JESUS TAUGHT THAT THERE IS SOMETHING WORSE THAN PHYSICAL SUFFERING

He taught his disciples that there is something very much worse than physical suffering in this life:

> I tell you, my friends, do not be afraid of those who kill the body but cannot afterwards do anything worse. I will show you whom to fear; fear God, who, after killing, has the authority to throw into hell. Believe me, he is the one you must fear!

JESUS EXPERIENCED SUFFERING WHICH WAS TOTALLY UNDESERVED

Many centuries before the time of Jesus, the prophet ISAIAH wrote about a mysterious figure whom he calls 'the Servant of the Lord'. Several writers in the New Testament see this as a picture of the undeserved suffering of Jesus:

> But he endured the suffering that should have been ours,
> the pain that we should have borne.
> All the while we thought that his suffering
> was punishment sent by God.
> But because of our sins he was wounded,
> beaten because of the evil we did.
> We are healed by the punishment he suffered,
> made whole by the blows he received.
> All of us were like sheep that were lost,
> each of us going his own way.
> But the Lord made the punishment fall on him
> the punishment all of us deserved.
> He was treated harshly, but endured it humbly;
> he never said a word.

> Like a lamb about to be slaughtered,
> like a sheep about to be sheared,
> he never said a word.
> He was arrested and sentenced and led off to die,
> and no one cared about his fate.
> He was put to death for the sins of our people.
> He was placed in a grave with evil men,
> He was buried with the rich,
> even though he had never committed a crime,
> or ever told a lie.

THERE WILL ONE DAY BE AN END TO SUFFERING

JOHN describes his vision of a new kind of universe in which there will be no suffering:

> Then I saw a new heaven and a new earth. The first heaven and the first earth disappeared, and the sea vanished. And I saw the Holy City, the new Jerusalem, coming down out of heaven from God, prepared and ready, like a bride dressed to meet her husband. I heard a loud voice speaking from the throne: 'Now God's home is with mankind! He will live with them, and they shall be his people. God himself will be with them, and he will be their God. He will wipe away all tears from their eyes. There will be no more death, no more grief or crying or pain. The old things have disappeared.'

These Christian beliefs about the problem of suffering have something to say to the person who is suffering. MICHEL QUOIST tries to sum up what God wants to say to the person who wonders why he is suffering:

> It is not I, your God, who has willed suffering, it is men ... Sin is disorder, and disorder hurts ... But I came, and I took all your sufferings upon me, as I took all yours since. I took them and suffered them before you.

Hope can come in the midst of disaster.

C.S. Lewis

C.S. Lewis writes of the way God can speak to men through pain and suffering:

> God whispers to us in our pleasures, speaks in our conscience, but shouts in our pains: it is his megaphone to rouse a deaf world.

These convictions also provide a strong motive for fighting suffering here and now. Jesus committed himself and his disciples to relieving suffering. Mother Theresa speaks about her work among the poor and the dying in Calcutta:

> I believe the people of today do not think that the poor are like them as human beings. They look down on them. But if they had that deep respect for the dignity of poor people, I am sure it would be—it would be easy for them to come closer to them, and to see that they, too, are the children of God, and that they have as much right to the things of life and of love and of service as anybody else. In these times of development everybody is in a hurry and everybody's in a rush, and on the way there are people falling down, who are not able to compete. There are the ones we want to love and serve and take care of.
>
> We ourselves feel that what we are doing is just a drop in the ocean. But if that drop was not in the ocean I think the ocean will be less because of that missing drop. For example, if we didn't have our schools in the slums—they are nothing, they are just little primary schools where we teach the children to love the school and to be clean and so on—if we didn't have these little schools, those children, those thousands of children, would be left in the streets. So we have to choose either to take them and give them just a little, or leave them in the street. It is the same thing for our Home for the Dying and our home for the children. If we didn't have that home, those people we have picked up, they would have died in the street. I think it was worth while having that home even for those few people to die beautifully, with God and in peace.

The example of the way in which Christ reacted to his suffering and violent death says something to those who suffer unjustly at the hands of others. This is a prayer written by BISHOP HASAN DEHQANI-TAFTI after the murder of his son in Iran in May 1980:

> O GOD
> We remember not only Bahram
> but also his murderers;
> Not because they killed him in the
> prime of his youth
> and made our hearts bleed and our
> tears flow,
> Not because with this savage act
> they have brought further disgrace
> on the name of our country among
> the civilised nations of the World;
> But because through their crime we
> now follow Thy footsteps
> more closely in the way of sacrifice.
> The terrible fire of this calamity
> burns up all selfishness and
> possessiveness in us;
> Its flame reveals the depth of
> depravity and meanness and
> suspicion,
> the dimension of hatred and the
> measure of sinfulness in human
> nature.
> It makes obvious as never before
> our need to trust in God's love
> as shown in the Cross of Jesus and
> His resurrection;
> Love which makes us free from hate
> towards our persecutors;
> Love which brings patience,
> forbearance, courage, loyalty,
> humility, generosity, greatness of
> heart;
> Love which more than ever deepens
> our trust in God's final victory and
> his eternal designs for the Church
> and for the World;
> Love which teaches us how to
> prepare ourselves to face our own
> day of death.
> O GOD
> Bahram's blood has multiplied the
> fruit of the Spirit in the soil of our
> souls;
> So when his murderers stand
> before THEE on the day of
> judgement
> Remember the fruit of the Spirit by
> which they have enriched our lives,
> And Forgive.

DIETRICH BONHOEFFER in his *Letters and Papers from Prison*, written while he was awaiting the death sentence in a Nazi prison in Germany in 1945, pointed out the link between the suffering of Jesus and the suffering of many of his disciples since then:

> It is infinitely easier to suffer in obedience to a human command than to accept suffering as free, responsible men. It is infinitely easier to suffer with others than to suffer alone. It is infinitely easier to suffer as public heroes than to suffer apart and in ignominy. It is infinitely easier to suffer physical death than to endure spiritual suffering. Christ suffered as a free man alone, apart and in ignominy, in body and in spirit, and since that day many Christians have suffered with him.

CHRISTIAN ANSWERS TO HUMAN QUESTIONS
DEATH

How am I to face death? Is there life after death?

The writer of ECCLESIASTES records his gloomy reflections on death:

> The same fate awaits man and animal alike. One dies just like the other. They are both the same kind of creature. A human being is no better off than an animal, because life has no meaning for either. They are both going to the same place— the dust. They both came from it; they will both go back to it. How can anyone be sure that a man's spirit goes upwards while an animal's spirit goes down into the ground? So I realized then that the best thing we can do is to enjoy what we have worked for. There is nothing else we can do. There is no way for us to know what will happen after we die.

This kind of realism enables him to give the following advice to young people:

> Young people, enjoy your youth. Be happy while you are still young. Do what you want to do, and follow your heart's desire. But remember that God is going to judge you for whatever you do.
>
> Don't let anything worry you or cause you pain. You aren't going to be young very long.
>
> So remember your Creator while you are still young, before those dismal days and years come when you will say, I don't enjoy life. That is when the light of the sun, the moon, and the stars will grow dim for you, and the rain clouds will never pass away. Then your arms, that have protected you, will tremble, and your legs, now strong, will grow weak. Your teeth will be too few to chew your food, and your eyes too dim to see clearly. Your ears will be deaf to the noise of the street. You will barely be able to hear the mill as it grinds or music as it plays, but even the song of a bird will wake you from sleep. You will be afraid of high places, and walking will be dangerous. Your hair will turn white; you will hardly be able to drag yourself along, and all desire will have gone.
>
> We are going to our final resting place, and then there will be mourning in the streets. The silver chain will snap, and the golden lamp will fall and break; the rope at the well will break, and the water jar will be shattered. Our bodies will return to the dust of the earth, and the breath of life will go back to God, who gave it to us.

People in the Old Testament period could believe that there is a life beyond death because they thought of man as a creature made in the image of the eternal God. But their ideas about life after death were very vague.

The resurrection of Jesus, however, changed the situation radically. For here was a man who died, but was raised from death by the power of God.

Is death really the end?

This is how different writers in the *New Testament* express their joyful confidence that Jesus has triumphed over death and robbed it of its power:

He (Jesus Christ) has ended the power of death and through the gospel has revealed immortal life.

Let us give thanks to the God and Father of our Lord Jesus Christ! Because of his great mercy he gave us new life by raising Jesus Christ from death. This fills us with a living hope, and so we look forward to possessing the rich blessings that

God keeps for his people. He keeps them for you in heaven, where they cannot decay or spoil or fade away. They are for you, who through faith are kept safe by God's power for the salvation which is ready to be revealed at the end of time.

Since the children, as he calls them, are people of flesh and blood, Jesus himself became like them and shared their human nature. He did this so that through his death he might destroy the Devil, who has the power over death, and in this way set free those who were slaves all their lives because of their fear of death.

Listen to this secret truth: we shall not all die, but when the last trumpet sounds, we shall all be changed in an instant, as quickly as the blinking of an eye. For when the trumpet sounds, the dead will be raised, never to die again, and we shall all be changed. For what is mortal must be changed into what is immortal; what will die must be changed into what cannot die. So when this takes place, and the mortal has been changed into the immortal, then the scripture will come true: 'Death is destroyed; victory is complete!' 'Where, Death, is your victory? Where, Death, is your power to hurt?'

JAMES PACKER sums up Christian beliefs about death:

Death is the fundamental human problem, for if death is really final nothing is worthwhile save self-indulgence. 'If the dead are not raised, let us eat and drink, for tomorrow we die' (1 Corinthians 15:32). And no philosophy or religion which cannot come to terms with death is any real use to us.

Here, however, Christianity stands out. Alone among the world's faiths and 'isms' it views death as conquered. For Christian faith is hope resting on fact—namely, the fact that Jesus rose bodily from the grave and now lives eternally in heaven. The hope is that when Jesus comes back—the day when history stops and this world ends— he will 'change our lowly body to be like his glorious body' (Philippians 3:21; see also 1 John 3:2). This hope embraces all who have died in Christ as well as Christians alive at his appearing: 'for the hour is coming when all who are in the tombs will hear his (Jesus') voice and come forth, those who have done good, to the resurrection of life' (John 5:28ff). And the raising of the *body* means the restoring of the *person*—not just part of me, but all of me—to active, creative and undying life, for God and with God.

BISHOP FESTO KIVENGERE describes how he was allowed to be present when three men from his diocese in Uganda were executed by firing squad in 1973:

February 10 began as a sad day for us in Kabale. People were commanded to come to the stadium and witness the execution by a firing squad of the three young men of our area. Death permeated the atmosphere in that stadium. A silent crowd of about three thousand was there to watch the spectacle.

I had permission from the authorities to speak to the men before they died, and two of my fellow ministers were with me.

They brought the men in a truck and unloaded them. They were handcuffed and their feet were chained. The firing squad stood at attention. As we walked away into the center of the stadium, I was wondering what to say to these men in the few minutes we had before their death. How do you give the Gospel to doomed men who are probably seething with rage?

We approached them from behind, and as they turned around to look at us, what a sight! Their faces were all alight with an unmistakable glow and radiance. Before we could say anything, one of them burst out:

'Bishop, thank you for coming! I wanted to tell you. The day I was arrested, in my prison cell, I asked the Lord Jesus to come into my heart. He came in and forgave me all my sins! Heaven is now open, and there is nothing between me and my God! Please tell my wife and children that I am going to be with Jesus. Ask them to accept Him into their lives as I did.'

The second man told us a similar story, excitedly raising his hands, which rattled his handcuffs. Then the youngest said:

'I once knew the Lord, but I went away from Him and got into political confusion. After I was arrested, I came back to the Lord. He has forgiven me and filled me with peace. Please tell my parents [they are evangelists in the diocese] and warn my younger brothers never to go away from the Lord Jesus.'

I felt that what I needed to do was to talk to the soldiers, not to the condemned. So I translated what the men had said into a language the soldiers understood. The military men were standing there with their guns cocked, and bewilderment on their faces. Those in the stadium who were near enough could hear it too, and the rest could see the radiance on the faces of the condemned which showed they were forgiven souls.

The soldiers were so dumbfounded at the faces and words of the men they were about to execute that they even forgot to put the hoods over their faces!

The three faced the firing squad standing close together. They looked toward the people and began to wave, handcuffs and all. The people waved back. Then shots were fired, and the three were with Jesus.

We stood in front of them, our own hearts throbbing with joy, mingled with tears. It was a day never to be forgotten. Though dead, the men spoke loudly to all of Kigezi District and beyond, so that there was an upsurge of life in Christ, which challenges death and defeats it.

The next Sunday, I was preaching to a huge crowd in the hometown of one of the executed men. Again, the feel of death was over the congregation. But when I gave them the testimony of their man, and how he died, there erupted a great song of praise to Jesus! Many turned to the Lord there, and in many other places.

We heard that the soldiers who were in the firing squad and the guards standing by could not shake off the reality of what they saw—the glory of God on the faces of dying men.

CHRISTIAN ANSWERS TO HUMAN QUESTIONS
THE FUTURE OF MAN

What hope is there for the human race?

Jesus did not predict a gradual improvement in man's condition until we reach a grand Utopia on this earth. Rather he spoke of men being deceived by false prophets, of war and natural disasters, persecution, cosmic disturbances, panic and fear about the future. The climax of history would be his own return to the world 'with great power and glory':

> Be on guard; don't be deceived. Many men, claiming to speak for me, will come and say, 'I am he!' and, 'The time has come!' But don't follow them. Don't be afraid when you hear of wars and revolutions; such things must happen first, but they do not mean that the end is near . . .
>
> Countries will fight each other; kingdoms will attack one another. There will be terrible earthquakes, famines, and plagues everywhere; there will be strange and terrifying things coming from the sky. Before all these things take place, however, you will be arrested and persecuted; you will be handed over to be tried in synagogues and be put in prison; you will be brought before kings and rulers for my sake . . .
>
> There will be strange things happening to the sun, the moon, and the stars. On earth whole countries will be in despair, afraid of the roar of the sea and the raging tides. People will faint from fear as they wait for what is coming over the whole earth, for the powers in space will be driven from their courses. Then the Son of Man will appear, coming in a cloud with great power and glory. When these things begin to happen, stand up and raise your heads, because your salvation is near.

DAVID BEBBINGTON, a historian, speaks about the Christian understanding of history:

> A Christian understanding supplies something that historicism lacks: confidence in the future. Its keynote of hope is grounded in the twin beliefs that God is guiding history forward in a straight line and that it will in due time reach his goal . . . Belief in the divine superintendence of history and expectations of the end of time provide ample grounds for the Christian hope. There will ultimately be victory for Jesus Christ at the goal of history. Indeed, the decisive engagement has already been fought. The battle against evil was won by Jesus on the cross. At that point God 'disarmed the principalities and powers and made a public example of them, triumphing over them in him' (Colossians 2:15). The outcome of world history is

The Bible teaches that God is in control; he will triumph over the evil in the cosmos.

therefore already assured. God will continue to direct the course of events up to their end when the outcome will be made plain.

HERMAN DOOYERWEERD, a Dutch professor of philosophy, makes a similar point:

Ultimately, the problem of the meaning of history revolves around the question: 'Who is man himself and what is his origin and final destination?' Outside the central biblical revelation of creation, the fall into sin and redemption through Jesus Christ, no real answer is to be found to this question ...

There would be no future hope for mankind and for the whole process of man's cultural development if Jesus Christ had not become the spiritual centre and his kingdom the ultimate end of world-history.

This centre and end of world-history is bound neither to the Western nor to any other civilization. But it will lead the new mankind as a whole to its true destination, since it has conquered the world by the divine love revealed in its self-sacrifice.

CHRISTIAN ANSWERS TO HUMAN QUESTIONS
THE SUPERNATURAL

Is there anything more than the physical world?

The Bible acknowledges the reality of the world of spirits and superhuman powers. It records, for example, how King Saul in his desperation asked a medium to call up the spirit of the prophet Samuel who had previously been his friend and advisor:

> Saul disguised himself; he put on different clothes, and after dark he went with two of his men to see the woman. 'Consult the spirits for me and tell me what is going to happen,' he said to her. 'Call up the spirit of the man I name ...'
> 'Whom shall I call up for you?' the woman asked.
> 'Samuel,' he answered.
> When the woman saw Samuel, she screamed and said to Saul, 'Why have you tricked me? You are King Saul!'
> 'Don't be afraid !' the king said to her. 'What do you see?'

> 'I see a spirit coming up from the earth,' she answered.
> 'What does it look like?' he asked.
> 'It's an old man coming up,' she answered. 'He is wearing a cloak.'
> Then Saul knew that it was Samuel, and he bowed to the ground in respect.
> Samuel said to Saul, 'Why have you disturbed me? Why did you make me come back?'...

The Old Testament law, however, contains strict warnings against dabbling in any kind of magic or contact with spirits:

> Don't sacrifice your children in the fires on your altars; and don't let your people practise divination or look for omens or use spells or charms, and don't let them consult the spirits of the dead. The Lord your God hates people who do these disgusting things ...

Several of the healing miracles of Jesus consisted of casting out evil spirits. But the greatest demonstration of Christ's victory over all the supernatural powers is to be seen in his death and resurrection. PAUL writes:

> On that cross Christ freed himself from the power of the spiritual rulers and authorities; he made a public spectacle of them by leading them as captives in his victory procession.

He therefore prays for believers:

> I ask that your minds may be opened to see his light, so that you will know what is the hope to which he has called you, how rich are the wonderful blessings he promises his people, and how very great is his power at work in us who believe. This power working in us is the same as the mighty strength which he used when he raised Christ from death and seated him at his right side in the heavenly world. Christ rules there above all heavenly rulers, authorities, powers, and lords; he has title superior to all

titles of authority in this world and in the next.

Os GUINNESS recounts the following experience to illustrate the reality of such spiritual powers, and the victory of Christ over them:

> Speaking once at Essex University, I saw sitting in the front row a strange-looking girl with an odd expression on her face. Remembering an incident the previous night when a radical had tried to disrupt the lecture, I spoke on but also prayed silently that she would create no trouble. She remained quiet the whole evening but came up as soon as it was finished with a very troubled look and asked me what spell I had cast to keep her quiet. She told me she was part of a spiritist circle in the South of England and that the spirits had ordered her to travel to Essex, where she had never been before, to disrupt a series of lectures beginning that week. The curious sequel to this was that when I arrived back in Switzerland someone else in the community, far from a fanciful visionary, asked me what had happened in the Essex lectures. Praying for them one morning, she had seen in a vision, as real as waking reality, the lecture hall and the strange girl about to disrupt the meeting. Having prayed for her, she was convinced that nothing had happened, but she wondered if it was just her imagination. The presence of a Christian praying in the power of the Holy Spirit is always enough to render the occult inoperable.

HAL LINDSEY recalls similar encounters:

> The comments at the breakfast table drifted to prophecy, and the Scottish kilt girl dropped a bomb in the conversation when she said, 'I've always been able to look into the future and foresee what is going to happen.'

> I gulped my coffee and snapped to attention. I began to question her.
> 'This isn't something new ... I've had a gift of psychic power all my life—inherited it from my mother and grandmother, I guess.'
> To this day I have a difficult time describing the change in the atmosphere ... It was a bright morning, yet I could feel an uncanny oppression around us ... What happened during the following hours was an amazing experience ... I witnessed a miracle! This woman was freed from an evil spirit. Not in Africa, not in the remote regions of the Amazon, but in the sunshine of an American college campus.

EVIL

Is there any hope in fighting evil and injustice?

The Christian world-view enables us to approach the difficult question of the problem of evil with certain basic convictions:

Evil (like suffering) is an intrusion into the universe God made. The universe as God made it was 'very good' (Genesis 1:31).

There is a personal Being behind all the powers of evil. The Bible calls him 'the Devil' or 'Satan', and thinks of him as a created heavenly being, who in his rebellion against God is working to ruin everything that God has made.

Man's original rebellion against the Creator came about through the influence and suggestion of Satan. Human nature is therefore corrupt and sinful, and it is this corruption in his nature rather than his situation or his circumstances which leads him to evil. This is where JESUS located the root of the problem of the evil in human nature:

It is what comes out of a person that makes him unclean. For from the inside, from a person's heart, come the evil ideas which lead him to do immoral things, to rob, kill, commit adultery, be greedy, and do all sorts of evil things; deceit, indecency, jealousy, slander, pride, and folly— all these evil things come from inside a person and make him unclean.

Jesus defeated the powers of evil on the cross by allowing them to do their worst to him.

The Christian hope is that since God is a righteous Judge, there will be a Day of Judgement when justice will be done, and will be seen to be done. We can therefore have the same confidence as THE PSALMIST that God is coming to judge the world:

**Be glad, earth and sky!
Roar, sea, and every creature in you;
be glad, fields, and everything in you!
The trees in the woods will shout for joy
when the Lord comes to rule the earth.
He will rule the peoples of the world with justice and fairness.**

This hope is not an excuse for doing nothing at the present time. ISAIAH, the prophet, spoke of 'the Servant of the Lord' or 'the Suffering Servant' bringing justice; while this hope will not be fulfilled completely before the second coming of Jesus, all his followers are committed to work for justice here and now in their own situation:

**The Lord says,
'Here is my servant, whom I strengthen—
the one I have chosen, with whom I am pleased.
I have filled him with my spirit,
and he will bring justice to every nation ...
He will bring lasting justice to all.
He will not lose hope or courage;
he will establish justice on the earth ...'**

And now the Lord God says to his servant,

J.I. Packer

'I, the Lord, have called you and given you power
to see that justice is done on earth . . .'

JAMES PACKER explains the essence of the problem for the Christian, and the starting point for an answer:

Does not the existence of evil—moral badness, useless pain and waste of good—suggest that God the Father is not almighty after all?—for surely he would remove these things if he could? Yes, he would, and he is doing so! Through Christ, bad folk like you and me are already being made good; new pain- and disease-free bodies are on the way and a reconstructed cosmos with them; and Paul assures us that 'the sufferings of this present time are not worth comparing with the glory that is to be revealed to us' (Romans 8:18; 19–23). If God moves more slowly than we wish in clearing evil out of his world and introducing the new order, that, we may be sure, is in order to widen his gracious purpose and include in it more victims of the world's evil than otherwise he could have done.

C.E.M. JOAD, the philosopher, came to accept Christian beliefs after many years of being an agnostic. He came to believe that they were true because he became convinced that they provided a far more convincing explanation of human nature than his previous beliefs. This is what he wrote in 1952 in his book *Recovery of Belief*:

What I have to record is a changed view of the nature of man, which in due course led to a changed view of the nature of the world . . .

This view of human evil (that evil is merely the product of heredity and environment and can be eradicated through progress) which I adopted unthinkingly as a young man I have come fundamentally to disbelieve. Plausible, perhaps, during the first fourteen years of this century when . . . the state of mankind seemed to be improving—though even then the most cursory reading of human history should have been sufficient to dispose of it—it has been rendered utterly unplausible by the events of the last forty years. To me, at any rate, the view of evil implied by Marxism, expressed by Shaw and maintained by modern psychotherapy, a view which regards evil as a by-product of circumstances, which circumstances can, therefore, alter and even eliminate, has come to seem intolerably shallow and the contrary view of it as endemic in man, more particularly in its Christian form, the doctrine of original sin, to express a deep and essential insight into human nature.

STEPHEN NEILL wrote these words while he was working as a bishop in India:

The best way to understand the doctrine of the wrath of God is to

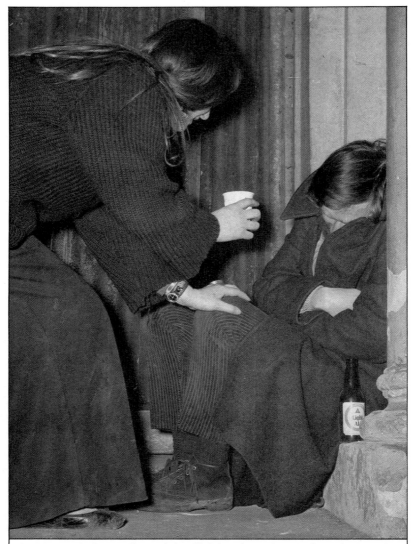

Confidence in God's over-all control gives Christians the starting point for combatting evil here and now.

consider the alternatives. The alternative is not love; since rightly considered, love and wrath are only the obverse and reverse of the same thing ... The alternative to wrath is neutrality—neutrality in the conflict of the world ... To live in such a world would be a nightmare. It is only the doctrine of the wrath of God, of his irreconcilable hostility to all evil, which makes human life tolerable in such a world as ours.

SECTION 3

UNDERSTANDING THE CHRISTIAN WORLD-VIEW

When I look at the sky, which you have
        made,
    at the moon and the stars, which you set
        in their places—
what is man, that you think of him;
    mere man, that you care for him?

Yet you made him inferior only to yourself;
    you crowned him with glory and
        honour.
You appointed him ruler over everything
        you made;
    you placed him over all creation:
    sheep and cattle, and the wild animals
        too;
    the birds and the fish
    and the creatures in the seas.

O Lord, our Lord,
    your greatness is seen in all the world!
PSALM 8

Christianity is a system which is
composed of a set of ideas which can be
discussed. By 'system' we do not mean a
scholastic abstraction, nevertheless we do
not shrink from using this word. The Bible
does not set out unrelated thoughts.
FRANCIS SCHAEFFER

In this section we are simply trying to *understand* the Christian world-view. We are not trying to find arguments for or against.

What are the basic Christian beliefs about man and the universe? What are the assumptions which make the Christian see the world as he does? What does it feel like to live in this kind of universe?

Outline

CHRISTIAN ASSUMPTIONS ABOUT GOD
Personal
Infinite
Creator
Sustainer
Loving
Holy
One
Three 'persons'
Christian responses

CHRISTIAN ASSUMPTIONS ABOUT MAN
A creature created in the image of God
A rebel against his Creator
Can become a 'son' of God

CHRISTIAN ASSUMPTIONS ABOUT THE UNIVERSE
Created
Sustained
God has a plan for the universe

CHRISTIAN ASSUMPTIONS ABOUT TRUTH
God has revealed the truth
The truth God revealed was open to verification

CHRISTIAN ASSUMPTIONS ABOUT SALVATION
God must judge—but wants to forgive
Death means more than physical death
Forgiveness is always something costly
Man cannot solve his problem by himself

CHRISTIAN ASSUMPTIONS ABOUT GOD

The following propositions do not exhaust the meaning of God for the Christian but simply lay down certain fundamental guidelines.

● God is personal and God is infinite.
● God is the Creator of the universe and God is the Sustainer of the universe.
● God is loving and God is holy.
● God is one and God is three 'persons'.

The two propositions in each pair must be taken closely together to balance each other. For example, it is not enough to say that God is the Creator of the universe, because this says nothing about his relationship to the universe now. So the statement that he is Creator must be paired with the statement that he is the Sustainer of the universe. Similarly, when we say that God is personal, we must immediately add that he is infinite. Although he has something in common with man who is conscious of being a person, he is not subject to the limitations of human personality.

All eight propositions must be held together. If we reject or seriously modify even one of them our whole belief about God will be seriously affected.

GOD IS PERSONAL

He is not an impersonal 'It', or a force like energy or electricity. Just as men have personal names, so God in the Old Testament gives himself a personal name, Yahweh (probably meaning something like 'the One who is', 'the One who is there').

God said to Moses, 'I am who I am ... the Lord (Yahweh) ... this is my name for ever, and thus I am to be remembered throughout all generations ...'

He has *mind* and can think: he is not in some realm beyond thought or reason:

**For my thoughts are not your thoughts,
neither are your ways my ways,
says the Lord.
For as the heavens are higher than the earth,**

> so are my ways higher than your
> ways
> and my thoughts than your
> thoughts.

He has *will* and can decide and make free choices: he is not controlled by any higher power like 'Fate':

> I know that the Lord is great,
> and that our Lord is above all gods.
> Whatever the Lord pleases he does,
> in heaven and on earth,
> in the seas and all deeps.

He has *emotions* and can feel. The prophet HOSEA describes God as speaking in this way about himself:

> How can I give you up, O Ephraim!
> ... My heart recoils within me, my
> compassion grows warm and
> tender.

Because he is 'personal', he can communicate truth and reveal himself to men; he can enter into personal relationships with us, and we can come to know him in a personal way.

> For thus says the high and lofty One
> who inhabits eternity, whose name
> is Holy:
> 'I dwell in the high and holy place,
> and also with him who is of a
> contrite and humble spirit,
> to revive the spirit of the humble,
> and to revive the heart of the
> contrite.'

> The friendship of the Lord is for
> those who fear him,
> and he makes known to them his
> covenant.

GOD IS INFINITE

Although he is personal, he does not have the limitations of human personality. He himself was not created by someone greater.

> 'You are my witnesses,' says the
> Lord,
> 'and my servant whom I have
> chosen,
> that you may know and believe me
> and understand that I am He.
> Before me no god was formed,
> nor shall there be any after me.'

He has always existed and will always exist. He is not limited by time, because he has created both space and time.

> Before the mountains were brought
> forth
> or ever thou hadst formed the earth
> and the world,
> from everlasting to everlasting thou
> art God.

He is not limited by the universe, because he is at work throughout it; he is omnipresent. Nothing in the universe works independently of him.

> Am I a God at hand, says the Lord,
> and not a God afar off? Can a man
> hide himself in secret places so that
> I cannot see him? says the Lord. Do
> I not fill heaven and earth? says the
> Lord.

He knows everything; he is omniscient. He knows everything about each individual person, and about the future.

> O Lord, thou hast searched me and
> known me!
> Thou knowest when I sit down and
> when I rise up;
> thou discernest my thoughts from
> afar.

> I am God, and there is none like me,
> declaring the end from the
> beginning.

He can do anything he wants (though he always acts 'in character'); he is omnipotent. There is no Chance or Fate or Luck behind God which works independently of him.

> But he is unchangeable and who
> can turn him?
> What he desires, that he does.
> For he will complete what he
> appoints for me;

and many such things are in his mind.

In this prayer HABAKKUK speaks of God as both personal and infinite:

Art thou not from everlasting, O Lord my God, my Holy One?

GOD IS THE CREATOR OF THE UNIVERSE

The universe of time and space has been brought into existence by him of his own free choice. He did not *have* to create the universe; he was perfectly complete without it.

In the beginning God created the heavens and the earth ...

Praise him, sun and moon, praise him, all you shining stars! Praise him, you highest heavens, and you waters above the heavens! Let them praise the name of the Lord! For he commanded and they were created.

The universe is completely distinct from God; he is transcendent. The universe is not a part of God or an emanation from God; neither is he a part of it.

By the word of the Lord the heavens were made, and all their host by the breath of his mouth. He gathered the waters of the sea as in a bottle; he put the deeps in storehouses. Let all the earth fear the Lord,

Cholesterol crystals, magnified 250 times. The Bible teaches that God sustains the most intricate workings of his universe.

> **let all the inhabitants of the world**
> **stand in awe of him!**
> **For he spoke, and it came to be;**
> **he commanded, and it stood forth.**

God created the universe 'out of nothing'; there was no 'raw material' for God simply to marshal into order.

> **By faith we understand that the**
> **world was created by the word of**
> **God, so that what is seen was made**
> **out of things which do not appear.**

God uses the same great power with which he created the world, to help man in his weakness:

> **Have you not known? Have you not**
> **heard?**
> **The Lord is the everlasting God,**
> **the Creator of the ends of the earth.**
> **He does not faint or grow weary,**
> **his understanding is unsearchable.**
> **He gives power to the faint,**
> **and to him who has no might he**
> **increases strength.**
> **Even youths shall faint and be**
> **weary,**
> **and young men shall fall**
> **exhausted;**
> **but they who wait for the Lord**
> **shall renew their strength,**
> **they shall mount up with wings like**
> **eagles,**
> **they shall run and not be weary,**
> **they shall walk and not faint.**

> **O Lord my God, thou art very great!**
> **Thou art clothed with honour and**
> **majesty,**
> **who coverest thyself with light as**
> **with a garment,**
> **who hast stretched out the heavens**
> **like a tent ...**
> **Thou dost cause grass to grow for**
> **the cattle,**
> **and plants for man to cultivate ...**
> **Thou makest darkness, and it is**
> **night ...**

> **He covers the heavens with clouds,**
> **he prepares rain for the earth,**
> **he makes grass grow upon the hills.**
> **He gives to the beasts their food,**
> **and to the young ravens which cry.**

NEHEMIAH links together the work of God in creating and sustaining the universe:

> **Thou art the Lord, thou alone; thou**
> **hast made heaven, the heaven of**
> **heavens, with all their host, the**
> **earth and all that is on it, the seas**
> **and all that is in them; and thou**
> **preservest all of them.**

GOD IS
THE SUSTAINER OF
THE UNIVERSE

The magnificent spiral nebula in Ursa Major.

Not only is the universe created by God, it is also 'maintained' by him. He is immanent within the universe, although he is not a part of it. He is not merely the First Cause. He is not like the watchmaker who leaves the watch to run by itself. The universe could not continue without God.

GOD IS LOVING

The Old Testament speaks in many different ways of the love of God towards man whom he has created in his image:

**I have loved you with an everlasting love;
therefore I have continued my faithfulness to you.**

As I live, says the Lord God, I have no pleasure in the death of the wicked, but that the wicked turn from his way and live ...

**Seek the Lord while he may be found,
call upon him while he is near;
let the wicked forsake his way,
and the unrighteous man his thoughts;
let him return to the Lord, that he may have mercy on him,
and to our God for he will abundantly pardon.**

**The steadfast love of the Lord never ceases,
his mercies never come to an end;
they are new every morning;
great is thy faithfulness.**

Hosea, the prophet, speaking on behalf of God:

**When Israel was a child, I loved him ...
The more I called them,
the more they went from me;
they kept sacrificing to the Baals,
and burning incense to idols.
Yet it was I who taught Ephraim to walk,
I took them up in my arms;
but they did not know that I healed them.
I led them with the cords of compassion,
with the bands of love,
and I became to them as one
who eases the yoke from their jaws,
and I bent down to them and fed them.**

In the New Testament the supreme revelation of the love of God is seen in the coming of the eternal Son:

For God so loved the world that he gave his only Son, that whoever believes in him should not perish but have eternal life.

God shows his love for us in that while we were yet sinners Christ died for us.

Some passages go further and speak of an eternal relationship of love between the Father, the Son and the Spirit. Love is thus part of the character of God: he did not become loving after he created man.

Jesus speaks in this way about the Father:

For the Father loves the Son, and shows him all that he himself is doing ...

He prays:

Father, I desire that they also, whom thou hast given me, may be with me where I am, to behold my glory which thou hast given me in thy love for me before the foundation of the world.

GOD IS HOLY

God is morally perfect; he is utterly good. He is not morally neutral; he is not beyond good and evil or above morality.

Thou who art of purer eyes than to behold evil and canst not look on wrong ...

**For thou art not a God who delights in wickedness,
evil may not sojourn with thee.**

> **Thus says the Lord: 'Let not the wise man glory in his wisdom, let not the mighty man glory in his might, let not the rich man glory in his riches; but let him who glories glory in this, that he understands and knows me, that I am the Lord who practice kindness, justice, and righteousness in the earth; for in these things I delight, says the Lord.'**

The moral laws he has revealed to men are an expression of his character. There is an absolute standard for right and wrong in the character of God himself.

> **The Lord appeared to Abram, and said to him, 'I am God Almighty; walk before me, and be blameless.'**

> **You shall be holy; for I the Lord your God am holy.**

> **For the Lord is righteous, he loves righteous deeds;**
> **the upright shall behold his face.**

> **You shall walk before the Lord your God and fear him, and keep his commandments and obey his voice, and you shall serve him and cleave to him ... You shall purge the evil from the midst of you.**

Man's revolt against God is a personal affront to him and a breach of his laws. God cannot simply overlook man's disobedience or behave as if it doesn't matter, or as if it doesn't really exist.

> **... thou who triest the minds and hearts,**
> **thou righteous God ...**
> **God is a righteous judge,**
> **and a God who has indignation every day.**

> **How can I pardon you?**
> **Your children have forsaken me,**
> **and have sworn by those who are no gods.**
> **When I fed them to the full,**
> **they committed adultery**
> **and trooped to the houses of harlots.**
> **They were well-fed lusty stallions,**

> **each neighing for his neighbour's wife.**
> **Shall I not punish them for these things? says the Lord;**
> **and shall I not avenge myself on a nation such as this?**

> **For wicked men are found among my people;**
> **they lurk like fowlers lying in wait.**
> **They set a trap;**
> **they catch men.**
> **Like a basket full of birds,**
> **their houses are full of treachery;**
> **therefore they have become great and rich,**
> **they have grown fat and sleek.**
> **They know no bounds in deeds of wickedness;**
> **they judge not with justice**
> **the cause of the fatherless, to make it prosper,**
> **and they do not defend the rights of the needy.**
> **Shall I not punish them for these things? says the Lord,**
> **and shall I not avenge myself on a nation such as this?**

In this revelation of the character of God given to MOSES we have the love of God and the holiness of God held closely together:

> **The Lord passed before him, and proclaimed, 'The Lord, the Lord, a God merciful and gracious, slow to anger, and abounding in steadfast love and faithfulness, keeping steadfast love for thousands, forgiving iniquity and transgression and sin, but who will by no means clear the guilty.**

ISAIAH similarly holds together love and holiness:

> **For a brief moment I forsook you,**
> **but with great compassion I will gather you.**
> **In overflowing wrath for a moment I hid my face from you,**
> **but with everlasting love I will have compassion on you,**
> **says the Lord, your Redeemer.**

PAUL saw no difficulty in holding together the wrath of God and the love of God and speaking of them in the same breath:

> God shows his love for us in that while we were yet sinners Christ died for us. Since, therefore, we are now justified by his blood, much more shall we be saved by him from the wrath of God.

JOHN, similarly, holds the love and the wrath of God together; the word 'propitiation' contains the idea of turning away wrath:

> In this is love, not that we loved God, but that he loved us and sent his Son to be the propitiation for our sins.

THERE IS ONLY ONE GOD

Other supernatural beings and powers do exist—Satan and the angels; but they are all created beings, and subordinate to God. There are not a number of gods, each controlling different parts of the universe.

> The Lord our God is one Lord; and you shall love the Lord your God with all your heart, and with all your soul, and with all your might.

Since there is only one God, all men are bound to acknowledge him:

> I am the Lord, and there is no other, besides me there is no God.
> I gird you, though you do not know me,
> that men may know, from the rising of the sun
> and from the west, that there is none besides me;
> I am the Lord, and there is no other.
>
> Turn to me and be saved, all the ends of the earth!
> For I am God, and there is no other.
> By myself I have sworn,

> from my mouth has gone forth in righteousness
> a word that shall not return:
> 'To me every knee shall bow, every tongue shall swear.'

THERE ARE THREE 'PERSONS' IN THE ONE GOD

The first Christians were orthodox Jews who had been brought up to believe that God is one. They never abandoned their belief that God is one; but they gradually came to understand the oneness of God in a new way, and to distinguish between the Father, the Son and the Spirit. This radical reinterpretation of the oneness of God came about because of three things:

● JESUS spoke of himself as 'the Son' who enjoyed an intimate relationship with 'the Father'. This relationship had existed before the creation of the world:

> All things have been delivered to me by my Father; and no one knows

the Son except the Father, and no one knows the Father except the Son and any one to whom the Son chooses to reveal him.

And now, Father, glorify thou me in thy own presence with the glory which I had with thee before the world was made.

● JESUS spoke about the Holy Spirit as distinct from himself and from the Father:

When the Counsellor comes, whom I shall send to you from the Father, even the Spirit of truth, who proceeds from the Father, he will bear witness to me.

You shall receive power when the Holy Spirit has come upon you; and you shall be my witnesses ...

● The early Christians experienced God working in their lives in a radically new way, and they understood this to be the work of the Holy Spirit.

When the day of Pentecost had come, they were all together in one place. And suddenly a sound came from heaven like the rush of a mighty wind, and it filled all the house where they were sitting. And there appeared to them tongues as of fire, distributed and resting on each one of them. And they were all filled with the Holy Spirit and began to speak in other tongues, as the Spirit gave them utterance.

The fruit of the Spirit is love, joy, peace, patience, kindness, goodness, faithfulness, gentleness, self-control ...

So PAUL writes of the three-in-one God:

I fall on my knees before the Father, from whom every family in heaven and on earth receives its true name. I ask God from the wealth of his glory to give you power through his Spirit to be strong in your inner selves and I pray that Christ will make his home in your hearts through faith.

CHRISTIAN RESPONSES

These convictions about God are not a set of cold, lifeless propositions. This is the kind of response they should arouse in the believer:

● Worship:
O come, let us worship and bow down,
let us kneel before the Lord, our Maker!

● Awe and reverence:
I through the abundance of thy steadfast love will enter thy house,
I will worship toward thy holy temple in the fear of thee.

● Thanksgiving and wonder:
I will give thanks to the Lord with my whole heart;
I will tell of all thy wonderful deeds.
I will be glad and exult in thee, I will sing praise to thy name, O Most High.

● Joy:
How lovely is thy dwelling place, O Lord of hosts!
My soul longs, yea, faints for the courts of the Lord;
my heart and flesh sing for joy to the living God.

● Love:
I love thee, O Lord, my strength.

● Trust:
The Lord is my strength and my shield;
in him my heart trusts;
so I am helped, and my heart exults, and with my song I give thanks to him.

CHRISTIAN ASSUMPTIONS ABOUT MAN

MAN IS A CREATURE CREATED IN THE IMAGE OF GOD

The Bible recognizes that man in his physical make-up has a great deal in common with the animals; the writer of Genesis speaks of man being made 'of dust from the ground' like the animals. But the basic difference between man and the animals is that man is in some ways like God:

> **Then God said, 'Let us make man in our image, in our likeness . . .' So God created man in his own image, in the image of God he created him; male and female he created them.**

The following passage later in the book of Genesis makes it clear that the 'image and likeness' is to be understood quite naturally as resemblance:

> **When God created man, he created him in the likeness of God. He created them male and female; at the time they were created, he blessed them and called them 'man'. When Adam had lived 130 years, he had a son in his own likeness, in his own image . . .**

To say that a man is like God means that:

● Just as God is personal, so man is personal.
● Just as God has mind and can think and communicate, so man has a mind and can think and communicate; he is rational.
● Just as God has a will and can decide and make free choices, so man has a will and can make certain free choices; he is responsible and accountable. He has not been 'programmed'; he has a real measure of freedom.
● Just as God has emotions and can feel, so man has emotions and can feel.
● Just as God is a moral being, so man is moral and can understand the difference between right and wrong.
● Just as God is creative, so man can be creative in many areas of life.

Man, however is clearly unlike God in certain respects:

● God is infinite, unlimited by space and time: man is not.

● God is Spirit and has no body: man has a physical body with all its limitations.

● God has absolute knowledge and absolute power: man does not.

As he was originally created man was perfect:

God saw all that he had made, and it was very good.

Although man is no longer perfect, he is still God's creation, bearing his image. The likeness has been spoiled, but not obliterated completely. Man still has something in common with God. So however much the writers of the Bible may stress man's fallen state, they never lose sight of the fact that he is the crown of God's creative work in the universe. To say that man is a created being, therefore, far from degrading him, is the very thing that gives him his greatness and dignity.

MAN IS NOW A REBEL AGAINST HIS CREATOR

The human race is now in a state of rebellion against its Creator. Men may recognize that God exists. They may even try to worship him in different ways. But they fail to love him as he deserves. They fail to live up to his standards.

Man was not *created* a rebel; he has *become* a rebel. When Adam was created, he was given a choice: either to depend on God and obey him, or to be independent.

God plainly warned what the consequences of disobedience would be:

> You may eat the fruit of any tree in the garden, except the tree that gives knowledge of what is good and what is bad. You must not eat the fruit of that tree: if you do, you will die the same day.

The effects of Adam's rebellion and sin were transmitted to the whole human race:

> Sin came into the world through one man, and his sin brought death with it. As a result, death has spread to the whole human race because everyone has sinned.

Man's rebellion against God at the present time thus consists in a refusal to live according to God's revealed laws. JOHN defines sin in terms of lawlessness:

> Whoever sins is guilty of breaking God's law, because sin is a breaking of the law.

PAUL defines sin as man's refusal to acknowledge the truth that he knows about God:

> God's anger is revealed from heaven against all the sin and evil of the people whose evil ways prevent the truth from being known. God punishes them, because what can be known about God is plain to them, for God himself made it plain. Ever since God created the world, his invisible qualities, both his eternal power and his divine nature, have been clearly seen; they are perceived in the things that God has made. So those people have no excuse at all! They know God, but they do not give him the honour that belongs to him, nor do they thank him. Instead, their thoughts have become complete nonsense, and their empty minds are filled with darkness.

Those who have not had the fuller revelation of God through the Bible and through Jesus Christ are in the same state of rebellion against God. PAUL writes that although they have not had the fuller revelation, they have set certain standards for themselves and others, and have failed to live up to them:

> Do you, my friend, pass judgement on others? You have no excuse at all, whoever you are. For when you judge others and then do the same things which they do, you condemn yourself. We know that God is right when he judges the people who do such things as these. But you, my friend, do those very things for which you pass judgement on others! Do you think you will escape God's judgement?

This means that men who have never heard the fuller revelation of God recorded in the Bible will be judged on the basis of whether or not they have lived up to the standards they have set for themselves and others—drawing on God's basic law which is written in the hearts of all men. And on this basis, there is no one who is innocent before God.

> ... all men, both Jews and Greeks, are under the power of sin.

> ... all have sinned and fall short of the glory of God.

God's reaction to this situation cannot be neutral. He cannot pretend that disobedience does not matter, or that it can be passed over or forgiven lightly. The prophets give many examples of situations in which God is compelled to act in judgement:

> I was ready to be sought by those
> who did not ask for me;
> I was ready to be found by those
> who did not seek me.
> I said, 'Here am I, here am I,' to a
> nation that did not call on my name.
> I spread out my hands all the day to
> a rebellious people,
> who walk in a way that is not good,
> following their own devices;
> a people who provoke me to my
> face continually . . .
> Behold, it is written before me:
> 'I will not keep silent, but I will
> repay,
> yea, I will repay into their bosom
> their iniquities and their fathers'
> iniquities together, says the Lord.'

The Bible uses the word 'wrath', or 'anger', to describe God's reaction to man's rebellion:

> . . . we all once lived in the passions
> of our flesh, following the desires of
> body and mind, and so we were by
> nature children of wrath . . .

PAUL speaks in this way about the final consequences of man's rebellion, if there is no repentance and turning to God:

> They shall suffer the punishment of
> eternal destruction and exclusion
> from the presence of the Lord and
> from the glory of his might.

But this punishment is not inevitable. God offers forgiveness, if only rebel man will seek it:

> Come now, let us reason together,
> says the Lord:
> Though your sins are like scarlet,
> they shall be as white as snow;
> though they are red like crimson,
> they shall become like wool.

MAN CAN BECOME A 'SON' OF GOD

Although man is a rebel by nature and under the judgement of God, God has taken the initiative and done something to restore the broken relationship:

> When we were still helpless, Christ
> died for the wicked at the time that
> God chose. It is a difficult thing for
> someone to die for a righteous
> person. It may even be that
> someone might dare to die for a
> good person. But God has shown
> how much he loves us—it was while
> we were still sinners that Christ
> died for us . . . We were God's
> enemies, but he made us his friends
> through the death of his Son . . . We
> rejoice because of what God has
> done through our Lord Jesus
> Christ, who has now made us God's
> friends.

Jesus is the 'Son of God' in a special and unique sense. But those who put their trust in him and accept the reconciliation which he offers are born into the family of God to become 'sons':

> Some . . . did receive him and
> believed in him; so he gave them
> the right to become God's children.
> They did not become God's
> children by natural means, that is,
> by being born as the children of a
> human father; God himself was
> their Father.

As God's children, we have an obligation to try to become more and more like him:

> Since you are God's dear children,
> you must try to be like him. Your life
> must be controlled by love, just as
> Christ loved us and gave his life for
> us as a sweet-smelling offering and
> sacrifice that pleases God.

Jesus brought his message to real human beings with real joys and real needs.

CHRISTIAN ASSUMPTIONS ABOUT THE UNIVERSE

THE UNIVERSE WAS CREATED BY GOD

The universe has been brought into existence by God. It is not eternal.

God created the universe of his own free choice. He was not under any compulsion to create the universe. He was not incomplete without it.

The universe is completely distinct from God; God is transcendent. The universe is not a part of God or an emanation from God, nor is God a part of the universe.

God created the universe 'out of nothing'; there was no raw material already there which he simply brought into order.

The material world is not in any sense 'evil' because everything that God made was 'good'.

All these convictions can be derived from the first chapter of the Bible:

> **In the beginning God created the heavens and the earth. The earth was without form and void, and darkness was upon the face of the deep; and the Spirit of God was moving over the face of the waters.**
> **And God said, 'Let there be light'; and there was light. And God saw that the light was good; and God separated the light from the darkness ...**

'God created' implies that he created 'out of nothing'.

'God said ...' implies that the creation of the universe was a free act, a free choice of God.

'God saw ...' implies that the universe is distinct from God.

THE UNIVERSE IS SUSTAINED BY GOD

The universe was not only created by God; it is also sustained by him all the time. The universe could not exist without God.

God sustains the universe according to certain 'laws'; but these laws do not work independently of

The planet Saturn, photographed by the Voyager 1 spacecraft.

him. Both the normal and the abnormal ordering of natural phenomena are the work of God. God is able to work miracles at any time in his own universe for a particular purpose.

God is responsible for what we *do* know about the universe as well as for what we *do not* know. He is not simply the 'God of the gaps', brought in to account for the areas of life we do not yet understand.

THE PSALMIST speaks of the activity of God in the regular and 'natural' processes of nature:

> **Thou makest springs gush forth in the valleys;**
> **they flow between the hills,**
> **they give drink to every beast of the field;**
> **the wild asses quench their thirst.**
> **By them the birds of the air have their habitation;**
> **they sing among the branches.**
> **From thy lofty abode thou waterest the mountains;**
> **the earth is satisfied with the fruit of thy work.**
> **Thou dost cause the grass to grow for the cattle,**
> **and plants for man to cultivate,**
> **that he may bring forth food from the earth,**
> **and wine to gladden the heart of man,**
> **oil to make his face shine,**
> **and bread to strengthen man's heart.**

The universe is not the product of chance, but of the purpose and design of God. It is God who is responsible for the 'natural' laws of the universe. After the flood, God says to Noah:

> **While the earth remains, seedtime and harvest, cold and heat, summer and winter, day and night, shall not cease.**

THE PSALMIST speaks of the stability and reliability of the universe as the work of God:

> **Thou didst set the earth on its foundations,**
> **so that it should never be shaken.**
> **Thou didst cover it with the deep as with a garment;**

> **the waters stood above the mountains.**
> **At thy rebuke they fled;**
> **at the sound of thy thunder they took to flight.**
> **The mountains rose, the valleys sank down to the place which thou didst appoint for them.**
> **Thou didst set a bound which they should not pass,**
> **so that they might not again cover the earth.**

Many writers do not draw any sharp line between God's work in creation and sustaining; they are aspects of the same activity.

> **It is he who made the earth by his power,**
> **who established the world by his wisdom,**
> **and by his understanding stretched out the heavens.**
> **When he utters his voice there is a tumult of waters in the heavens,**
> **and he makes the mist rise from the ends of the earth.**

GOD HAS A PLAN FOR THE UNIVERSE

The book of Genesis speaks of the physical world being affected by man's rebellion against God. After man's disobedience God says to him,

> **You listened to your wife and ate the fruit which I told you not to eat. Because of what you have done, the ground will be under a curse. You will have to work hard all your life to make it produce enough food for you. It will produce weeds and thorns, and you will have to eat wild plants. You will have to work hard and sweat to make the soil produce anything, until you go back to the soil from which you were formed. You were made from soil, and you will become soil again.**

PAUL speaks of the whole creation being caught up in frustration and decay, and 'groaning with pain'; but he looks forward to the time when it will be set free from its slavery to decay:

> **All of creation waits with eager longing for God to reveal his sons. For creation was condemned to lose its purpose, not of its own will, but because God willed it to be so. Yet there was the hope that creation itself would one day be set free from its slavery to decay and would share the glorious freedom of the children of God. For we know that up to the present time all of creation groans with pain, like the pain of childbirth. But it is not just creation alone which groans; we who have the Spirit as the first of God's gifts also groan within ourselves, as we wait for God to make us his sons and set our whole being free.**

PETER writes about the end of the universe and the creation of 'new heavens and a new earth'; this hope should affect the way we live:

> **The Day of the Lord will come like a thief. On that Day the heavens will disappear with a shrill noise, the heavenly bodies will burn up and be destroyed, and the earth with everything in it will vanish. Since all these things will be destroyed in this way, what kind of people should you be? Your lives should be holy and dedicated to God, as you wait for the Day of God and do your best to make it come soon— the Day when the heavens will burn and be destroyed, and the heavenly bodies will be melted by the heat.**

These beliefs about the universe lead the believer to worship God as Creator with amazement, wonder and joy:

> **Praise the Lord, my soul!
> O Lord, my God, how great you are!
> You are clothed with majesty and glory;
> you cover yourself with light.**

> **You spread out the heavens like a tent
> and built your home on the waters above ...**

They also make it possible to trust God to provide us with all that we need to live. JESUS teaches in the Sermon on the Mount:

> **I tell you not to be worried about the food and drink you need in order to stay alive, or about clothes for your body. After all, isn't life worth more than food? And isn't the body worth more than clothes? Look at the birds flying around: they do not sow seeds, gather a harvest and put it in barns; yet your Father in heaven takes care of them! Aren't you worth much more than birds? Can any of you live a bit longer by worrying about it?**
> **And why worry about clothes? Look how the wild flowers grow: they do not work or make clothes for themselves. But I tell you that not even King Solomon with all his wealth had clothes as beautiful as one of these flowers. It is God who clothes the wild grass—grass that is here today and gone tomorrow, burnt up in the oven. Won't he be all the more sure to clothe you? How little faith you have!**

At the same time we must recognize that God has made man responsible for the way he treats his environment. The creation story in Genesis emphasizes man's responsibility for looking after the earth and bringing it under control. Man has a divine mandate to be a responsible steward of his environment:

> **So God created human beings, making them to be like himself. He created them male and female, blessed them, and said, 'Have many children, so that your descendants will live all over the earth and bring it under control. I am putting you in charge of the fish, the birds, and all the wild animals. I have provided all kinds of grain and all kinds of fruit for you to eat ...'**

CHRISTIAN ASSUMPTIONS ABOUT TRUTH

GOD HAS REVEALED THE TRUTH

The Bible points to four different ways in which God has revealed truth to men: through the universe; through the nature of man; through Jesus Christ and through the written word: the Bible.

REVELATION THROUGH THE UNIVERSE
The universe tells us something about the God who made it. The character of the universe—its size, its complexity, its order and its beauty—tells us something about the Creator. It is not a revelation in words, but the universe does, as the psalmist says, 'say' something about God.

> **The heavens are telling the glory of God;
> and the firmament proclaims his handiwork.
> Day to day pours forth speech,
> and night to night declares knowledge.**

> **There is no speech, nor are there words;
> their voice is not heard;
> yet their voice goes out through all the earth,
> and their words to the end of the world.**

This kind of revelation, however, is limited. It tells us only certain things about God. Job, for example, is very conscious of the limitations of this kind of revelation:

> **He binds up the waters in his thick clouds,
> and the cloud is not rent under them.
> He covers the face of the moon,
> and spreads over it his cloud ...
> Lo, these are but the outskirts of his ways;
> and how small a whisper do we hear of him!**

But despite the incompleteness of this revelation, it leaves men with no excuse when they reject and suppress that amount of truth which is clearly revealed. PAUL writes:

For the wrath of God is revealed from heaven against all ungodliness and wickedness of men who by their wickedness suppress the truth. For what can be known about God is plain to them, because God has shown it to them. Ever since the creation of the world his invisible nature, namely, his eternal power and deity, has been clearly perceived in the things that have been made. So they are without excuse . . .

REVELATION THROUGH THE NATURE OF MAN

Everyone in certain situations has feelings that are described by the word 'ought':

'You ought to do this' or 'You ought not to do that'.

'I ought to do this' or 'I ought not to do that'.

None of us is so completely amoral that we feel that anything can be allowed and nothing discouraged.

Different societies have different social codes and different laws; but there is a large measure of agreement between them. The moral codes of the great religions have much in common with each other.

According to Christian beliefs, man is a fallen creature, and his conscience therefore does not invariably reflect the will of God. But at many points his own instincts correspond very closely with what God has revealed in a fuller way through the written word in the Bible and through Jesus Christ.

Christianity says that these basic instincts reveal something, however dimly, of the character of the God who has made man in his likeness. They are not simply the product of the society and the culture in which man lives. Furthermore, when we expect others to accept our standards, or judge others by our standards, we are assuming that these standards are right, and consistent with the way things are. This in itself points to the existence of a personal God who has made things this way. PAUL's letter to the Romans puts it like this:

Therefore you have no excuse, O man, whoever you are, when you judge another; for in passing judgment upon him you condemn yourself, because you, the judge, are doing the very same things . . .

When the Gentiles who have not the law do by nature what the law requires, they are a law to themselves, even though they do not have the law. They show that what the law requires is written on their hearts, while their conscience also bears witness and their conflicting thoughts accuse or perhaps excuse them . . .

These two kinds of revelation, however, are limited. The universe does not tell us anything about the moral character of God, of whether he is a loving God or a cruel God. And the sinfulness of

What is our reaction to obvious injustice?

man frequently blinds him to the limited amount of truth which he knows from his own nature.

REVELATION THROUGH JESUS CHRIST

JESUS spoke of himself as the one who reveals the Father:

> All things have been delivered to me by my Father; and no one knows the Son except the Father, and no one knows the Father except the Son and any one to whom the Son chooses to reveal him.

> Jesus said to him, 'I am the way, and the truth, and the life; no one comes to the Father, but by me. If you had known me, you would have known my Father also; henceforth you know him and have seen him.' Philip said to him, 'Lord, show us the Father, and we shall be satisfied.' Jesus said to him 'Have I been with you so long, and yet you do not know me, Philip? He who has seen me has seen the Father; how can you say, "Show us the Father"? Do you not believe that I am in the Father and the Father in me? ...'

This is the comment of one of the disciples who knew Jesus:

> Grace and truth came through Jesus Christ. No one has ever seen God, the only Son, who is in the bosom of the Father, he has made him known.

The writer of the letter to the Hebrews links together God's revelation of himself through the prophets in the Old Testament with his revelation of himself in Jesus Christ:

> In many and various ways God spoke of old to our fathers by the prophets; but in these last days he has spoken to us by a Son.

REVELATION THROUGH THE WRITTEN WORD OF GOD IN THE BIBLE

The authority of the Bible for the Christian is based on the authority of Jesus himself. If we see Jesus as a revelation of God, we should see the Bible as a revelation of God, because it bears the seal of Jesus' authority.

Jesus gave the apostles special authority to record and interpret the gospel. He promised his disciples that the Holy Spirit would enable them to give a reliable account of his teaching, and would show them more of the truth which would be revealed later.

> The Counsellor, the Holy Spirit, whom the Father will send in my name, he will teach you all things, and bring to your remembrance all that I have said to you.

> I have yet many things to say to you, but you cannot bear them now. When the Spirit of truth comes, he will guide you into all the truth; for he will not speak on his own authority, but whatever he hears he will speak, and he will declare to you the things that are to come.

PAUL claimed that he too had been commissioned as an apostle—in his case, through the exceptional circumstances of his conversion. He believed that the Holy Spirit had revealed the truth to him:

> Now we have received not the spirit of the world, but the Spirit which is from God, that we might understand the gifts bestowed on us by God. And we impart this in words not taught by human wisdom but taught by the Spirit, interpreting spiritual truths to those who possess the Spirit.

Jesus treated the Old Testament as the written word of God. While Jesus himself claimed to be a fuller revelation of God, he did not question the truth or the authority of what had already been revealed through the Old Testament. He assumed it had the highest possible authority and used it to explain his own authority.

> Think not that I have come to abolish the law and the prophets; I have come not to abolish them but to fulfil them. For truly, I say to you, till heaven and earth pass away, not an iota, not a dot, will pass from the law until all is accomplished.

Whoever then relaxes one of the least of these commandments and teaches men so, shall be called least in the kingdom of heaven; but he who does them and teaches them shall be called great in the kingdom of heaven.

Jesus answered them, 'Is it not written in your law, "I said, you are gods"? If he called them gods to whom the word of God came (and scripture cannot be broken), do you say of him whom the Father consecrated and sent into the world, "You are blaspheming," because I said, "I am the Son of God"?'

You search the scriptures, because you think that in them you have eternal life; and it is they that bear witness to me.

This is how JESUS speaks about the authority of certain specific parts of the Old Testament:

And as Jesus taught in the temple, he said, 'How can the scribes say that the Christ is the son of David? David himself, inspired by the Holy Spirit, declared,
"The Lord said to my Lord,
Sit at my right hand,
till I put thy enemies under thy feet."'

And Pharisees came up to him and tested him by asking, 'Is it lawful to divorce one's wife for any cause?' He answered, 'Have you not read that he who made them from the beginning made them male and female, and said, "For this reason a man shall leave his father and mother and be joined to his wife, and the two shall become one"?'

Then he said to them, 'These are my words which I spoke to you, while I was still with you, that everything written about me in the law of Moses and the prophets and the psalms must be fulfilled.'

In treating the Old Testament in this way he was simply recognizing the claims which certain writers made for themselves. Many of the Old Testament writers speak of God revealing himself both through his actions and through his words, i.e. by what he does in history, and by what he reveals in words communicated to the minds of the prophets.

The Lord used to speak to Moses face to face, as a man speaks to his friend.

Surely the Lord God does nothing, without revealing his secret to his servants the prophets.

Sometimes we are told that those who received this revelation wrote down what had been revealed:

Moses came and told the people all the words of the Lord and all the ordinances; and all the people answered with one voice, and said, 'All the words which the Lord has spoken we will do.' And Moses wrote all the words of the Lord.

Then the Lord put forth his hand and touched my mouth; and the Lord said to me, 'Behold, I have put my words in your mouth.
See, I have set you this day over nations and over kingdoms ...' And the word of the Lord came to me, saying, 'Jeremiah, ...'

Then Jeremiah called Baruch the son of Neriah, and Baruch wrote upon a scroll at the dictation of Jeremiah all the words of the Lord which he had spoken to him.

THE TRUTH GOD REVEALED WAS OPEN TO VERIFICATION

This does not mean that every single part of the revelation was subject to verification. It means simply that in the course of the revelation, there were certain vital points where the people involved were able to verify what came to them as a revelation from God. If the word 'verification' sounds a very modern word, this does not mean that the idea is modern. All through the Bible we find that men are concerned with the basic question: how can I *know* if this is true? They were not prepared to believe any and every miracle or revelation which purported to be from God.

● **Abraham** was promised by God that he would be the ancestor of a great nation, and that his descendants would inherit the land of Canaan. At first he simply believed the promise; he took it on trust. But then he asked for some more definite assurance that the promise would be fulfilled:

> He (God) brought him outside and said, 'Look toward heaven, and number the stars, if you are able to number them.' Then he said to him, 'So shall your descendants be.' And he *believed* the Lord; and he reckoned it to him as righteousness. And he said to him, 'I am the Lord who brought you from Ur of the Chaldeans to give you this land to possess.' But he said, 'O Lord God, *how am I to know* that I shall possess it?' ...

The account then goes on to describe something which God did before Abraham's eyes.

> Then the Lord said to Abram, '*Know of a surety* that your descendants will be sojourners in a land that is not theirs ... And they shall come back here in the fourth generation ...'

● When **Moses** met God in the wilderness, he was commissioned to lead his people out of slavery in Egypt. MOSES' reply has a very contemporary ring about it:

> Then Moses answered, 'But behold they *will not believe me* or listen to my voice, for they will say, "The Lord did not appear to you."' The Lord said to him, 'What is that in your hand?' He said, 'A rod.' ...

God then performed a miracle with the rod which Moses had in his hand; and the purpose of the miracle was:

> that they may *believe* that the Lord, the God of their fathers, the God of Abraham, the God of Isaac, and the God of Jacob, has appeared to you ... If they will not believe you ... or heed the first sign, they may believe the latter sign. If they will not believe even these two signs or heed your voice, you shall take some water from the Nile and pour it upon the dry ground; and the water which you shall take from the Nile will become blood upon the dry ground.

● When **Pharaoh** refused to let the people go, MOSES prophesied that there would be various plagues, and then pointed to these as evidence for his claims about God's revelation to him:

> Thus says the Lord, 'By this *you shall know* that I am the Lord ...'

Each of the subsequent plagues is prophesied with this intention:

> that you may *know* that there is no one like the Lord our God ...
> that you may *know* that I am the Lord in the midst of the earth.

● The record of the events at Mount Sinai includes several miracles which were witnessed by all the people. This is how MOSES reminds the people, at a later stage, of the events at Mount Sinai:

> Take heed ... lest you forget the things which your eyes have *seen* ... how on the day that you stood before the Lord your God at Horeb, the Lord said to me, 'Gather the people to me, that I may let them *hear* my words, so that they may learn to fear me all the days that they live upon the earth, and that they may teach their children so.' And you came near and stood at the foot of the mountain ... wrapped in darkness, cloud and gloom. Then the Lord spoke to you out of the midst of the fire; you *heard* the sound of words, but saw no form; there was only a voice. And he declared to you his covenant, which

he commanded you to perform, that is, the ten commandments; and he wrote them upon two tables of stone.

● **Elijah and the priests of Baal** witnessed one of the most striking examples of verification in the Old Testament. It came at a time of crisis in the history of the children of Israel, when false ideas of God associated with Baal had become very popular. ELIJAH, the prophet of God, issued a challenge to the prophets of Baal:

> And Elijah came near to all the people, and said, 'How long will you go limping with two different opinions? If the Lord is God, follow him; but if Baal, then follow him ... Let two bulls be given to us; and let them choose one bull for themselves, and cut it in pieces and lay it on the wood, but put no fire to it; and I will prepare the other bull and lay it on the wood, and put no

> fire to it. And you call on the name of your god and I will call on the name of the Lord; and the God who answers by fire, he is God.' And all the people answered, 'It is well spoken' ...

The prophets of Baal performed their rituals and called on Baal, but nothing happened. Then:

> Elijah the prophet came near and said, 'O Lord, God of Abraham, Isaac, and Israel, *let it be known this day that thou art God* in Israel, and that I am thy servant ... Answer me, O Lord, answer me, that *this people may know that thou, O Lord, art God* ...' Then the fire of the Lord fell, and consumed the burnt offering ... And when all the people saw it, they fell on their faces; and they said, 'The Lord, he is God; the Lord, he is God.'

Impurities in gold are removed by smelting. The Bible teaches that God is concerned to make the lives of his people pure and without fault.

● **The prophets** could never simply assume that everyone would automatically accept every word they said as a revelation from God. This is the test which MOSES said should be applied to messages claiming to come from God:

> If you say in your heart, '*How may we know* the word which the Lord has not spoken?'—when a prophet speaks in the name of the Lord, if the word does not come to pass or come true, that is a word which the Lord has not spoken; the prophet has spoken it presumptuously, you need not be afraid of him.

The prophet ISAIAH prophesied about what God is going to do in history. He said that God was telling them what would happen in advance, so that they could be quite certain that he has done it and that he has given the message to the prophet:

> ... that men may *see* and *know*,
> may consider and understand together,
> that the hand of the Lord has done this,
> the Holy One of Israel has created it.
>
> The former things I declared of old, they went forth from my mouth and I made them known;
> then suddenly I did them and they came to pass.
> Because I know that you are obstinate,
> and your neck is an iron sinew,
> and your forehead brass,
> I declared them to you from of old, before they came to pass I announced them to you,
> lest you should say, 'My idol did them ...'

EZEKIEL, similarly, predicted what was to happen at different periods of the future; and in each case the intention was that through the prediction and the event following, men might *know*:

> ... and you shall *know* that I am the Lord.

● **The first disciples** came to believe in Jesus gradually, through being with him and working with him over a period of three years. There was no sudden surrender or blind commitment; and they did not believe through the private illumination of any one individual. They were persuaded by the combined evidence of the character, teaching and miracles of Jesus.

They had ample opportunity to get to know almost every side of his *character*, and they could observe whether his life was consistent with what he taught.

They were able to test his *teaching* against what they already knew about God from the Old Testament. They came to see that Jesus' claims about himself were consistent with what God had already revealed.

> Lord, to whom shall we go? You have the words of eternal life; and we have *believed*, and have come to *know*, that you are the Holy One of God.

His *miracles* provided further evidence of his unique relationship with God and confirmed the claims he made for himself.

> This, the first of his signs, Jesus did at Cana in Galilee, and manifested his glory; and his disciples *believed* in him.

The climax of this evidence was the resurrection. When Thomas refused to accept the word of the other disciples that they had seen the risen Christ, and when he insisted on being able to verify the story before he believed, the risen Christ appeared to him and invited him to touch him, to assure himself that Christ really had been raised from death:

> Eight days later, his disciples were again in the house, and Thomas was with them. The doors were shut, but Jesus came and stood among them, and said, 'Peace be with you.' Then he said to Thomas, 'Put your finger here, and see my hands; and put out your hand, and place it in my side; do not be faithless, but believing.' Thomas answered him, 'My Lord and my God!'

● **The early preaching about Jesus.** PETER first preached about Jesus in Jerusalem, seven weeks after the resurrection. He could assume that his audience had heard the reports of what had happened and, if they wanted to, could check them for themselves by questioning those involved. All he need do therefore was to remind them of what had happened, and interpret its meaning:

> **Men of Israel, hear these words: Jesus of Nazareth, a man attested to you by God with mighty works and wonders and signs which God did through him in your midst, as you yourselves know—this Jesus, delivered up according to the definite plan and foreknowledge of God, you crucified and killed by the hands of lawless men ... This Jesus God raised up, and of that we all are witnesses ... Let all the house of Israel therefore know assuredly that God has made him both Lord and Christ, this Jesus whom you crucified.**

PAUL, in one of the earliest parts of the New Testament to be written, reminds the Corinthians in simple outline of the events of the resurrection:

> **I delivered to you as of first importance what I also received, that Christ died for our sins in accordance with the scriptures, that he was buried, that he was raised on the third day in accordance with the scriptures, and that he appeared to Cephas, then to the twelve. Then he appeared to more than five hundred brethren at one time, most of whom are still alive, though some have fallen asleep. Then he appeared to James, then to all the apostles. Last of all ... he appeared also to me.**

In this context Paul is saying in effect, 'If you want to check up on the facts, go and ask any of the eyewitnesses for yourselves. There are many still alive who claim to have seen what happened. Go and verify the story for yourself.'

LUKE explains his purpose in writing his Gospel in this way:

> **Inasmuch as many have undertaken to compile a narrative of the things which have been accomplished among us, just as they were delivered to us by those who from the beginning were eyewitnesses and ministers of the word, it seemed good to me also, having followed all things closely for some time past, to write an orderly account for you, most excellent Theophilus, that you may know the truth concerning the things of which you have been informed.**

From this carefully worded introduction we learn several significant things:

1. Many people before Luke had attempted to make some kind of record or narrative about the life of Jesus. They were not writing exhaustive records, but they were interested in recording what had happened.

2. Luke does not claim to have been an eyewitness himself, but he does claim to have been in close touch with those who were.

3. Luke wants his reader, Theophilus, to know the truth about the reports he has heard. In his companion volume, *the Acts of the Apostles*, Luke describes for Theophilus the beginnings of the Christian church after the resurrection. The last part of the book describes in detail the arrest of Paul and his various trials; and it ends with Paul in Rome on trial for his life.

If Theophilus was not actually involved in Paul's trial in some way, he must at least have been interested in it for some reason. And it seems that Luke is simply trying to explain the facts about the origin of Christianity and of how Paul came to be arrested and brought to Rome for trial. He is writing for a contemporary, and much of what he says would be open to verification. If Theophilus wanted to, he could check up on the details, for instance, the various Roman authorities Luke mentions.

At all these crucial stages, therefore, there were opportunities to *disprove* claims about God's revelation of himself. There were occasions in the Old Testament when people could apply certain tests to convince themselves that God's message revealed to a prophet was genuine. The gospel about Jesus was based on the combined testimony of several men about real historical events, and this testimony could be confirmed or discredited as long as the eyewitnesses were alive.

CHRISTIAN ASSUMPTIONS ABOUT SALVATION

Man's problem is not simply that he doesn't know the truth. It is rather that he *does* know some of the truth, and yet refuses to accept it and acknowledge God as his Creator.

We have already seen that the Bible describes man as a rebel against his Creator. We need here to spell out in greater detail the nature of man's need. If the word 'salvation' involves deliverance of some kind, what exactly is the condition from which man needs to be delivered? What is it that creates the need for salvation?

GOD MUST JUDGE SIN– BUT HE WANTS TO FORGIVE

God is both loving and holy. This means that he loves the sinner and longs for the very best for him; but at the same time he cannot accept man's rebellion lightly. He is not morally neutral, and he cannot simply forgive the sin of those who persist in their rebellion against him and refuse to accept their guilt before him. He cannot turn a blind eye or act as if nothing had happened. Man's sin is a personal affront to God; but it is also at the same time a violation of his laws. And when the laws are broken, the sanctions must be applied. Thus God's reaction to man in his sin can be summed up in two words: love and wrath.

This tension can be seen in some of the writings of the Old Testament prophets who speak on behalf of God. JEREMIAH, for example, asks: how can God *not* judge men for their wickedness? How can he fail to punish them?

The Lord asked, 'Why should I
forgive the sins of my people?
They have abandoned me
and have worshipped gods that are
not real.
I fed my people until they were full,
but they committed adultery
and spent their time with
prostitutes.
They were like well-fed stallions
wild with desire,
each lusting for his neighbour's
wife.

Christians believe that Jesus came to rescue us.

Shouldn't I punish them for these things ...?

On the other hand, speaking through the prophet HOSEA, God says:

**How can I give you up, Israel?
How can I abandon you?
Could I ever destroy you as I did Admah,
or treat you as I did Zeboiim?
My heart will not let me do it!
my love for you is too strong.
I will not punish you in my anger;
I will not destroy Israel again.
For I am God and not man.
I, the Holy One, am with you.
I will not come to you in anger.**

What can be done to resolve this tension? If God responds with judgement and condemnation, there is no hope for man. If, on the other hand, God simply extends a pardon to all who ask for it, how can he expect man to take his laws seriously?
● From God's side (if we may speak in these terms) the problem is: how to uphold the laws (which God must do if he is not to deny his nature) and at the same time acquit the sinner. How can God forgive *and* remain just? How can he forgive (as he longs to do) and at the same time register his hatred and condemnation of everything that spoils his universe?
● From man's side the problem is: how can I get right with God? If I have affronted him and broken his laws, how can I make my peace with him? How can the relationship be restored?

The message of the Bible is that God needs to do something which will demonstrate his love *and* his wrath at the same time. There has to be an 'atonement' which will deal with the problem of guilt and restore the broken relationship between God and man. B.B. WARFIELD, an American theologian (1851–1921) sums up the problem and the need for atonement in this way:

It is the distinguishing characteristic of Christianity ... not that it preaches a God of love, but that it preaches a God of conscience. A benevolent God, yes: men have framed a benevolent God for themselves. But a thoroughly honest God, perhaps never. That

has been left for the revelation of God himself to give us. And this is the really distinguishing characteristic of the God of revelation: he is a thoroughly honest, a thoroughly conscientious God—a God who deals honestly with himself and us, who deals conscientiously with himself and with us. And a thoroughly conscientious God, we may be sure, is not a God who can deal with sinners as if they were not sinners. In this fact lies the deepest ground of the necessity of the Atonement.

DEATH MEANS MORE THAN THE PHYSICAL DEATH OF THE BODY

The book of GENESIS speaks of death as something which is closely tied up with man's rebellion against God. It tells how God tested the obedience of Adam and Eve:

The Lord God commanded the man, saying, 'You may freely eat of every tree of the garden; but of the tree of the knowledge of good and evil you shall not eat, for in the day that you eat of it you shall die.'

Adam and Eve chose to disobey because they wanted to become gods themselves and to cease being dependent on their Creator. And these were some of the consequences of their disobedience:
● more acute physical suffering;
● physical death (although we are not told what human life would have been like if they had not been disobedient);
● they forfeited the possibility of living in constant fellowship and communion with God.

This Old Testament teaching about the connection between sin and death is summarized by PAUL and JAMES in these words:

Sin came into the world through one man and death through sin, and so death spread to all men because all men sinned.

The wages of sin is death ...

... desire when it has conceived gives birth to sin; and sin when it is full-grown brings forth death.

FORGIVENESS IS ALWAYS SOMETHING COSTLY

If the ruler of a country pardons someone who has been convicted as a criminal, his pardon doesn't *cost* him anything. He is not in any way involved personally with the criminal, but is acting in an official capacity as head of state. When God pardons, however, he *is* involved personally. It is *his* laws which have been broken, and he has been affronted personally.

When we think of forgiveness between people in ordinary life, we begin to see that forgiveness usually involves some kind of suffering. If someone hurts us in a small way and apologizes, it is easy to accept the apology. But the greater the wrong or injury, the harder it is to forgive. If a husband is unfaithful to his wife but comes back and asks forgiveness, she may be willing to forgive; but the forgiveness will not be an easy or casual thing. It will cost a great deal. It will hurt. For the essence of forgiveness is that we accept the wrong or the injury that has been done to us; we *bear the consequences* of it without retaliation, and without being bitter or resentful.

This element of suffering in forgiveness is illustrated in the parable JESUS told about the prodigal son. The son has insulted his father by demanding his share of his inheritance before his death; he has wasted it all in reckless living, and then decides to return to his father's home. While the father is overjoyed to see his son back, he has to bear all the shame and disgrace that his son has brought on him. It is not an easy or a light thing for him to welcome him home—it costs him some-

thing, and he personally *suffers the consequences* of his son's actions:

He was still a long way from home when his father saw him; his heart was filled with pity, and he ran, threw his arms round his son, and kissed him. 'Father,' the son said, 'I have sinned against God and against you. I am no longer fit to be called your son.' But the father called his servants. 'Hurry!' he said. 'Bring the best robe and put it on him. Put a ring on his finger and shoes on his feet. Then go and get the prize calf and kill it, and let us celebrate with a feast! For this son of mine was dead, but now he is alive; he was lost, but now he has been found.'

One of the ways in which God revealed some of these basic truths about the costliness of forgiveness was through the Old Testament law and its sacrificial system.

The laws often use the expression 'to bear sin (or sins)', which means 'to be responsible for sin' and 'to bear the consequences of sin'. For instance, when a person breaks any law governing social life and worship, it is said of him: 'he shall bear his iniquity' or 'he shall bear his sin'. In modern translations this is sometimes translated 'he must suffer the consequences' or 'he will be held responsible'. Bearing sin, therefore, means being held responsible for it and bearing the punishment for it. In one case we read that one person can bear the sins of another person: 'he shall bear her iniquity'.

In the sacrificial system certain animals are said to 'bear sin' or 'take away sin'.

The sin offering ... is very holy, and the Lord has given it to you in order to take away the sin of the community.

The Day of Atonement was a special day in the year on which Aaron as the chief priest had to confess the sins of the people as he laid his hands on the head of the goat. The goat was then sent off into the desert:

Then the goat is to be driven off into the desert by a man appointed to do it. The goat will carry all their sins

**away with him into some
uninhabited land.**

These sacrifices were intended to bring home in a
vivid and dramatic way certain basic truths:
● that sin and guilt have to be punished;
● that if men bear the consequences of their sin
and guilt, it means death;
● that forgiveness is available to men, not because
God turns a blind eye to sin and acts as if it does
not exist, but because the full responsibility and
consequences of it can be borne by another;
● that the sacrifices were not simply the expression
of homage of man the creature to his Creator, but
also of man the sinner to the God against whom he
had sinned;
● that there is a way by which the guilty party can
be acquitted and forgiven without setting aside or
annulling the law of God.

The Old Testament not only speaks of individuals in certain cases bearing the sins of another
person, or of animals bearing certain sins. The
prophet ISAIAH gives us a glimpse of one whom he
calls 'the Servant of the Lord'. The identity of this
mysterious person is left open, and one of the most
significant things about him is that in his suffering
and violent death he bears 'the sins of us all':

> He endured the suffering that
> should have been ours,
> the pain that we should have borne.
> All the while we thought that his
> suffering
> was punishment sent by God.
> But because of our sins he was
> wounded,
> beaten because of the evil we did.
> We are healed by the punishment he
> suffered,
> made whole by the blows he
> received.
> All of us were like sheep that were
> lost,
> each of us going his own way.
> But the Lord made the punishment
> fall on him,
> the punishment all of us deserved.

Jesus identified himself with the figure of 'the
Suffering Servant' in some of his sayings, and the
apostles made this identification very clearly in
their teaching about the meaning of the death of
Jesus.

MAN CANNOT SOLVE HIS PROBLEM BY HIMSELF

Man can do nothing to restore his broken relationship with God, and can do nothing to cancel the
sentence of death which stands over him. He also
finds himself defeated in the inner conflict between
his lower nature and his desire to do good. This is
how PAUL describes the intense conflict he experienced all through his life; it was only Christ who
was able to offer him hope of winning the victory:

**For even though the desire to do
good is in me, I am not able to do it. I
don't do the good I want to do;
instead, I do the evil that I do not
want to do. If I do what I don't want
to do, this means that I am no
longer the one who does it; instead,
it is the sin that lives in me.
So I find that this law is at work:
when I want to do what is good,
what is evil is the only choice I
have. My inner being delights in the
law of God. But I see a different law
at work in my body—a law that
fights against the law which my
mind approves of. It makes me a
prisoner to the law of sin which is at
work in my body. What an unhappy
man I am! Who will rescue me from
this body that is taking me to
death? Thanks be to God, who does
this through our Lord Jesus Christ!**

It is these four assumptions taken together that
explain what the Christian means by the word
'salvation'. Something needs to happen if men are
to escape the judgement of God on their sin. Death
is horrible enough in itself, but when it becomes a
final break in the relationship between man and his
Creator, it is even more of a curse. If forgiveness
among men usually costs something, forgiveness
will cost something to God and will not be merely a
matter of words. And finally, man needs someone
from outside to deliver him from his condition,
because he is completely helpless to save himself.

SECTION 4

TESTING THE CHRISTIAN WORLD-VIEW

Does this (concept) really work . . . ?
Do its consequences fit our
experience . . . ?
This is the simple but profound test of fact
by which we have come to judge the large
words of the makers of states and systems.
JACOB BRONOWSKI

The doors were locked, but Jesus came
and stood among them and said, 'Peace be
with you.' Then he said to Thomas, 'Put
your finger here, and look at my hands;
then stretch out your hand and put it in my
side. Stop your doubting, and believe!'
GOSPEL OF JOHN

A man can't always be defending the truth;
there must be a time to feed on it.
C.S. LEWIS

The Gospels describe how Jesus stood trial before Pontius Pilate, governor of Judea. In 1961, archaeologists at Caesarea discovered this stone slab bearing his name.

Testing the Christian world-view means that we set out to ask the difficult question: *is Christianity true?* We are not simply asking: does Christianity *contain truths?*

Does it contain individual truths which can be combined with truths from other religions and philosophies?

We are asking: Is Christianity *the truth?* Does the Christian world-view give us the right way to look at the world? Do Christian beliefs teach us 'the truth' about ourselves and the universe?

Many people today are convinced that such a question is so arrogant and presumptuous, or so totally unanswerable, that they are willing to settle for much more modest questions, such as: What is the value of Christian beliefs? Are they useful? Is Christianity true to me? Is it true to my experience? Is it true existentially?

We ought not, however, to settle for these questions unless we find good reasons for abandoning our original question.

If, therefore, we want to persevere with our original question, we need to apply two basic tests:

● Are Christian beliefs consistent with each other? Do they contradict each other at any point?

● Are Christian beliefs consistent with everything else that we know about ourselves and the universe? This is what Jacob Bronowski calls 'the simple but profound test of fact'. Does this concept really work? . . . Do its consequences fit our experience?

We have already seen that at several vital stages in biblical history the people involved were able to carry out certain tests to assure themselves of the truth of what they were seeing and hearing. But is there any way in which we today can test Christian beliefs? Are they in any way open to verification? Can they be tested in anything like the way other beliefs can be tested?

If we can find out what verification means in history, philosophy and science, we can see how the approach to testing truth in each of these areas can be applied to Christian beliefs.

Outline

VERIFICATION IN HISTORY

VERIFICATION IN PHILOSOPHY

VERIFICATION IN SCIENCE

**A Test-Case:
CREATION AND/OR EVOLUTION**

VERIFICATION IN HISTORY

When we think of verification in historical enquiry, we soon realize that there are many different levels or degrees of certainty. For instance, we cannot reach the same kind of certainty in history as in mathematics. We can illustrate some of these different levels of certainty in this way:

CERTAIN
that Winston Churchill is dead.
that there was a Second World War.

PROBABLE
that Hitler committed suicide in 1945.
that in 1700 the population of Scotland was just over one million.

POSSIBLE
that James IV was not killed at the battle of Flodden.
that Queen Elizabeth was really a man (a recent theory).
that Richard III did not murder the Princes in the Tower.
that Conan Doyle was Jack the Ripper (a recent suggestion).

IMPROBABLE
that Jesus visited the south of England (an old tradition).
that Bacon wrote Shakespeare's plays.

The modern historian is not as confident as his predecessors about his ability to reconstruct 'what really happened'. And even assuming that he has got the facts right, he is much more conscious of the difficulty of interpreting them objectively. PIETER GEYL, a Dutch historian:

To expect from history those final conclusions, which may perhaps be obtained in other disciplines, is, in my opinion, to misunderstand its nature ... The scientific method serves above all to establish facts; there is a great deal about which we can reach agreement by its use. But as soon as there is a question of explanation, of interpretation, of appreciation, though the special method of the historian remains valuable, the personal element can no longer be ruled out—that point of view which is determined by the circumstances of his time and by his own preconceptions. No human

The Bayeux Tapestry gives a contemporary picture of the eleventh-century occupation of England by the Normans.

intelligence can hope to bring together the overwhelming multiplicity of dates and of factors, of forces and movements, and from them establish the true, one might almost say the divine balance. This is literally a superhuman task. A man's judgement—for however solemnly some people may talk about the lessons of History, the historian is after all only a man sitting at his desk—a historian's judgement, then, may seem to him the only possible conclusion to draw from the facts, he may feel himself sustained and comforted by his sense of kinship with the past, and yet that judgement will have no finality. Its truth will be relative, it will be partial. Truth, though for God it may be One, assumes many shapes to men. Thus it is that the analysis of so many conflicting opinions concerning one historical phenomenon is not just a means of whiling away the time, nor need it lead to discouraging conclusions concerning the untrustworthiness of historical study. The study, even of contradictory conceptions can be fruitful . . . History is indeed an argument without end.

Some of the beliefs of Christianity are beliefs that certain events happened at particular places and at particular times. These beliefs, therefore, must be open to the ordinary methods of historical enquiry. Thus:

● *Just as* the historian asks questions about events; e.g. did the Battle of Hastings take place or did it not? And if it did happen, did it happen in the way in which the different accounts suggest? *So in the same way* we can and must ask questions about the events recorded in the Bible; e.g. Did Jesus rise from the dead or did he not? And if he did, did it happen in the way that the documents suggest?

● *Just as* the historian is concerned about the interpretation of events, and asks such questions as: what were the causes of World War II? . . . *So in the same way* we can ask such questions as: how are we to account for the origin and growth of Christianity?

● *Just as* in attempting to answer these questions, the historian can never be completely objective, but is inevitably influenced by his presuppositions; e.g. Marxist theory . . . *So in the same way* in considering the biblical documents we are bound to be influenced by our presuppositions; e.g. that miracles can, or cannot, happen.

● *Just as* the historian realizes that he cannot arrive at 100 per cent certainty about the past but is content to accept lesser degrees of certainty . . . *So in the same way* while we may not be 100 per cent certain about the events in the Bible, we need not therefore be completely sceptical, discounting the possibility of knowing anything about what happened. We are simply asking for the *same* standard for Christianity—not a less stringent one; not a harsher one, than is general.

● *Just as* historical events and theories are open to

falsification; i.e. they can be shown to be highly unlikely or improbable ... *So in the same way* the events recorded in the Bible are open to falsification; they are not immune from historical enquiry.

The Christian does not claim to be able to prove with 100 per cent certainty that Jesus rose from the dead. What he can say is that there are very good historical reasons for believing that he did. He can point out that the documentary evidence for the resurrection is at least as good as the evidence for other events of the period which are never questioned, and very much better than some.

Believing that the resurrection did happen can lead us on to enter into a relationship with the living Christ. It is the reality of this experience which brings complete conviction to the Christian about the resurrection.

The following quotations from three Christian writers show the place which historical verification has played or still plays in their faith.

C.S. LEWIS, speaking about one stage in his conversion:

> Early in 1926 the hardest boiled of all the atheists I ever knew sat in my room on the other side of the fire and remarked that the evidence for the historicity of the Gospels was really surprisingly good. 'Rum thing', he went on. 'All that stuff of Frazer's about the Dying God. Rum thing. It almost looks as if it had really happened once!'

FRANK MORISON, a lawyer, set out to prove that the resurrection did not happen, but through his study of the evidence was forced to change his mind:

> I wanted to take this Last Phase of the life of Jesus, with all its quick and pulsating drama, its sharp, clear-cut, background of antiquity, and its tremendous psychological and human interest—to strip it of its overgrowth of primitive beliefs and dogmatic suppositions, and to see this supremely great Person as He really was.
> ... Fully ten years later, the opportunity came to study the life of Christ as I had long wanted to

> study it, to investigate the origins of its literature, to sift some of the evidence at first hand, and to form my own judgement on the problem which it presents. I will only say that it effected a revolution in my thought. Things emerged from that old-world story which previously I should have thought impossible. Slowly but very definitely the conviction grew that the drama of those unforgettable weeks of human history was stranger and deeper than it seemed. It was the *strangeness* of many notable things in the story which first arrested and held my interest. It was only later that the irresistible logic of their meaning came into view.

A.R. VIDLER refers to N.P. Williams' extreme statement of the vulnerability of his faith:

> If an ostrakon were unearthed at Nazareth which showed conclusively that Joseph was the father of Jesus, he would abandon the Christian faith and look round for some other theory of the universe.

This attitude, however, is being increasingly challenged by writers who are influenced by different forms of existentialism in philosophy or theology. Rudolf Bultmann, for example, the German theologian (1884–1976), began to argue in the 1940s that the resurrection should not be regarded as a historical event, but that the Christian faith could survive without this foundation of 'myth'. This idea has come to be accepted by many.

RONALD GREGOR SMITH, writing in 1966, claimed that the historical evidence for the resurrection is altogether unconvincing; but he goes on to say that this does not destroy Christian faith:

> So far as historicity is concerned, ... it is necessary to explain: we may freely say that the bones of Jesus lie somewhere in Palestine.
> Christian faith is not destroyed by this admission. On the contrary, only now, when this has been said, are we in a position to ask about the meaning of the resurrection as an

integral part of the message concerning Jesus.

PAUL VAN BUREN, writing in 1963, argued that we should not think of the resurrection as a historical fact, because science makes it impossible to believe that a dead man could be raised to life:

If we speak of Easter as a fact, we shall have to be able to give a description of it. To take the latter tradition as a description of the appearances, however, raises far more problems than it solves. Because of the influence of the natural sciences, especially biology, on our thinking today, we can no more silence the questions concerning the changes in cells at death which spring to the mind when we read the Easter story of the Gospels, than we can deny that we live in the twentieth century.

Similarly, EDUARD SCHWEITZER believed that our faith in the resurrection should be based not on the supposed *event* of Jesus being raised from the dead, but on the *faith* of the first disciples:

Even if we had the best film of a Jerusalem newsreel of the year 30 AD (or whatever it was), it would not help us much since it could not show us what really happened on that day. Only Easter, the revelation of the Spirit, shows what really happened ... Historical facts never create faith, only faith creates faith.

Proof cannot be given of Jesus' resurrection ... God exposes himself to scepticism, doubt, and disbelief, renouncing anything that would compel men to believe.

The immediate effect of this conclusion is extremely liberating. The earliest Christians obviously cared astonishingly little about all the details of the Easter event—the where and how of it. But this means that the Easter faith does not depend on our success in believing in the possibility and historicity of all kinds of remarkable happenings,

like the ability of the risen Lord to eat. It means, furthermore, that our assurance of Jesus' resurrection does not wax or wane depending on how precisely we read these accounts and on what new sources are discovered. But if there are no guarantees for Easter faith, on what is our assurance based? ...

When ... assurance grows out of life with the word of the risen Lord and in obedience to him, the historical details of what happened at Easter become incidental. For faith no longer needs the guarantees of proof. To faith, the empty tomb will be a sign of what has taken place. It will not, however, fight for the empty tomb as for an article of faith, because the truth of Easter does not in fact depend on the empty tomb. What is important is whether the believer has such faith in the risen Lord that he will live under his dominion, will hold fast to the lordship of Jesus even when it leads him to his death. Only then will he find out whether he really relies on him 'who raises the dead' (2 Cor. 1. 8–9). And so the disciples, too, had to learn to understand what really took place at Easter through years of service under the living Christ, by living under his dominion and letting him show them what his resurrection really meant.

These attitudes are derived ultimately from the existentialist understanding of faith which was made popular by Søren Kierkegaard. Critics have every justification, however, for pointing out how impossible it is to maintain belief in the resurrection if we are not convinced that the resurrection happened in history.

T.W. FOWLE, who was not a convinced Christian, wrote these words in 1881 at a time when he could see theologians beginning to try to escape the challenge of the questioner who really wanted to know if Jesus rose from the dead or not:

The time is then, I think, rapidly drawing on when modern thought will demand of theology, and that with some excusable peremptoriness of tone, to state once for all upon which footing it elects to stand. At present the tone of many scientific minds seems to be somewhat as follows: 'We really cannot occupy ourselves in serious discussion, because we never quite know where we have you. You always seem to us to assume a supernatural standpoint, and then, when confronted with obvious difficulties involved in this, to fly elsewhere for refuge. Adopt the alternative that it is only a framework for moral ideas and spiritual truths, and that too we can make shift to estimate. But to halt uneasily between the two, and to say that so tremendous an event as the resurrection of a dead man may have happened or may not, but that on the whole it does not much matter, is to impose a fatal barrier to sincere discussion with minds that have been trained to estimate the nature and consequences of fact. If this story be true, then every conception that man can form of himself and his surroundings must be carefully modified; if it be false, then it should not be allowed to intrude itself upon a religion which, as more than half seem to assure us, having first succeeded in convincing themselves, was not founded upon it, does not need it, and would be better without it.

J.S. BEZZANT, an English theologian, has expressed his impatience with Bultmann and others who say that it is *because* Christian faith is immune from proof that we can continue to believe it:

It is even said (by Bultmann) that Christ crucified and risen meets us in the word of preaching and nowhere else. Faith in the word of preaching is sufficient and absolute ... Believe the message and it has

No one doubts that the Pilgrim Fathers set sail for America in 1620. Many historical events are attested beyond doubt.

saving efficacy. But what is the ground for believing? The answer given is Jesus' disciples' experience of the resurrection. But this is not, he holds, a historical confirmation of the crucifixion as the decisive saving event because the resurrection is also a matter of faith only, i.e. one act of faith has no other basis than another act of faith. And what is the resurrection? Another theologian who accepts the historical scepticism of Bultmann says 'the resurrection is to be understood neither as outward nor inward, neither mystically nor as a supernatural phenomenon nor as historical'. If this has any meaning it can only be that the resurrection is not to be understood in any sense. No intelligent person desires to substitute prudent acceptance of the demonstrable for faith; but

when I am told that it is precisely its immunity from proof which secures the Christian proclamation from the charge of being mythological, I reply that immunity from proof can 'secure' nothing whatever except immunity from proof, and call nonsense by its proper name. Nor do I think that anything like historical Christianity can be relieved of objections by making the validity of assertions depend upon the therapeutic function it plays in healing fractures in the souls of believers, or understand how it can ever have this healing function unless it can be believed to be true.

Attempts to detach the Christian faith from history have very serious consequences. But when we see how the Christian faith is so bound up with what has happened in history, the idea of verification in history points to one particular way in which we can test the truth of Christian beliefs.

Christian symbols carved in catacombs in Rome point clearly to the existence of a Christian community in the city in the third century AD.

VERIFICATION IN PHILOSOPHY

In traditional philosophy, there are two main lines of verification:

1. THE TEST OF COHERENCE OR CONSISTENCY

i.e. when we want to test the truth of a proposition, we first ask questions like these: Does it contradict itself in any way? Does it violate the basic rule of logic, the law of non-contradiction (that *a* cannot be *non-a*)?

2. THE TEST OF CORRESPONDENCE

i.e. correspondence with reality: Does it correspond with what we know of the real world?

ALASDAIR MACINTYRE explains that the idea of verification in philosophy includes the idea of falsification:

The original form of the Verification Principle put forward by the Vienna Circle of Linguistic Philosophers, stated that a proposition is meaningful *only* if it is open to verification: if it is not open to any kind of verification, then it does not make sense, and we cannot even begin to ask whether it is true or not. This principle can hardly be applied consistently, however, because the principle itself is not open to verification; and therefore on its own terms cannot make sense, let alone be true.

To these two basic tests can be added a third:

3. THE PRAGMATIC TEST

i.e. does this proposition fit the facts of our experience better than any other proposition? Does it really work in practice? Thus BERTRAND RUSSELL summarizes these different tests and the meaning of verification in philosophy in this way:

Philosophical knowledge ... does not differ essentially from scientific knowledge; there is no special source of wisdom which is open to philosophy but not to science ... Philosophy, like all other studies, aims primarily at knowledge.

It is customary to say that a general proposition is 'verified' when all of its consequences which it has been possible to test have been found to be true.

To say, therefore, that Christian beliefs are open to verification means that Christian beliefs can be discussed on the same level as philosophical beliefs. Therefore:

● *Just as* philosophers ask 'Does this theory make sense? Is it consistent with itself? Does it contradict itself?' ... *So in the same way* we can and must ask 'Does this Christian belief make sense? Is it consistent with itself? Does it contradict itself?'

● *Just as* the philosopher asks 'Is this theory consistent with everything else that I know?' ... *So in the same way* we ask 'Is this Christian belief consistent with everything else that I know?'

● *Just as* the philosopher has to use as his data all his own experience and knowledge, and the experience and knowledge of others ... *So in the same way* in putting Christian beliefs on trial we can use as evidence all our own experience and knowledge, and the experience and knowledge of others.

● *Just as* a philosophical belief is open to verification and is also open to falsification ... *So in the same way* Christian beliefs are open to falsification.

This does not mean that Christian beliefs can be reduced *permanently* to the level of an abstract hypothetical system. But it does mean that we can at least *begin* in this way. We have to ask ourselves whether this system fits the facts better than other beliefs claim to. If we consider them at all seriously, we will soon realize that we cannot remain in the position of the armchair philosopher or the disinterested spectator for ever. For if Christian beliefs *are* true, we have to come to terms with our Creator, and this will have a profound effect on the way we think and feel and behave.

It was through following this approach that C. E.M. JOAD eventually abandoned his agnosticism and became a Christian. In his book *The Recovery of Belief* he wrote:

Does Christian belief make sense? Does it contradict itself? Is it consistent with what we know of the world?

The following book is an account of some of the reasons which have converted me to the religious view of the universe in its Christian version. They are predominantly arguments designed to appeal to the intellect ...

While I admit that intellect cannot go all the way, there can, for me, be no believing which the intellect cannot, so far as its writ runs, defend and justify. I must, as a matter of psychological compulsion, adopt the most rational hypothesis, the most rational being that which seems to cover most of the facts and to offer the most plausible explanation of our experiences as a whole ...

It is because ... the religious view of the universe seems to me to cover more of the facts of experience than any other that I have been gradually led to embrace it ...

VERIFICATION IN SCIENCE

This is how JACOB BRONOWSKI describes the principle of verification in science:

We cannot shirk the historic question, What is truth? On the contrary: the civilization we take pride in took a new strength on the day the question was asked. It took its greatest strength later from Renaissance men like Leonardo, in whom truth to fact became a passion. The sanction of experienced fact as a face of truth is ... the mainspring which has moved our civilization since the Renaissance.

The first step is the collection of data ... Next comes the creative step ... which finds an order in the data by exploring likenesses ... and the third step is to create this concept (the central concept) ... This sequence is characteristic of science. It begins with a set of appearances. It organizes these into laws. And at the centre of the laws it finds a knot, a point at which several laws cross: a symbol which gives unity to the laws themselves. Mass, time, magnetic moment, the unconscious ... And we test the concept, as we test the thing, by its implications. That is, when the concept has been built up from some experiences, we reason what behaviour in other experiences should logically flow from it. If we find this behaviour, we go on holding the concept as it is. If we do not find the behaviour which the concept logically implies, then we must go back and correct it. In this way logic and experiment are locked together in the scientific method, in a constant to and fro in which each follows the other.

Science is the creation of concepts and their exploration in the facts. It has no other test of the concept than its empirical truth to fact. Truth is the drive at the centre of science: it must have the habit of truth, not as a dogma but as a process.

'*Science is the creation of concepts and their exploration in the facts.*' *Jacob Bronowski.*

The test of truth is the known factual evidence ...

We must be careful, however, not to make exaggerated claims about verification in science. Scientists in recent years have become much more modest in their claims for the experimental method. Karl Popper, for example, has suggested that we should think of the experimental method as a method of *disproof* rather than proof.

Historic Christianity has always believed that the universe was created by God and is sustained by God; and that man is different from the animals in that he bears 'the image of God'. These beliefs must inevitably have some point of contact with the theories of various sciences, and especially about the origin of the universe and man.

We must therefore be willing to accept the challenge of the scientist, and say that we believe the scientific method *is* relevant in considering the truth of Christian beliefs. We must be willing to approach Christian beliefs about the origin and nature of man and the universe as one possible theory among many. We must be willing to examine them alongside other beliefs and try to find out which of these theories accounts best for *all* that we know about man and the universe.

It can hardly be emphasized strongly enough that the question here is not simply: Did man evolve from the apes? This question is important (see *A Test-Case: Creation and/or Evolution*), but it is not the only question; and it must be considered in the context of the much larger question: which of these two ways of thinking about the universe fits the facts better:

● that the universe is a completely closed system of cause and effect; that there is no supernatural God; that all there is is what can be seen; and that the universe is the product of chance which has somehow produced purpose;

● or that the universe was created by God and depends for its existence on God; that man is what he is because he is stamped with God's likeness?

These two ways of thinking are completely incompatible, and we must make a decisive choice between them. This choice is far more fundamental than the choice we make about the specific question of the evolution of man.

The process of choosing between these two hypotheses can follow the scientific method closely, step by step. Just as the scientific method depends on presuppositions, observation, theory and experiment, so in the same way in testing Christian beliefs, presuppositions, observation, theory and experiment all play their part.

PRESUPPOSITIONS
Just as the scientist has presuppositions which he accepts but cannot prove with complete certainty ... *So in the same way* we are bound to approach Christian beliefs with our own presuppositions; e.g. that miracles can or cannot happen.

OBSERVATION
Just as the scientist must consider all the possible evidence (or as much of it as possible) ... *So in the same way* we must consider all the relevant evidence for Christian beliefs (or as much of it as possible)—and this will include the evidence about the origin of the universe and of man, and also the total experience of others and ourselves.

THEORY
Just as the scientist considers all the possible theories and tries to find the theory or hypothesis which accounts best for all that he observes; e.g. which theory makes the best sense of the data that we observe:—that the sun goes round the earth?—or that the earth goes round the sun? ... *So in the same way* we must try to find the theory which fits the facts best; i.e. which theory makes the best sense of what we observe in the universe and in man:—that the universe is a completely closed system of cause and effect, the product of impersonal energy which evolved by chance?—or that the universe was created by an infinite, personal God?

EXPERIMENT
Just as the scientist must conduct the necessary experiments to test all the possible theories, and to eliminate false theories ... *So in the same way* we can test these rival beliefs by the test of fact; i.e. by observing what happens when one lives consistently on the basis of one or other of these beliefs.

RICHARD WURMBRAND, in a book about Christians behind the Iron Curtain, tells how a Russian sculptress, who had been brought up to believe as a convinced atheist began questioning whether her atheistic world-view made sense of her own experience:

Once, we worked on a statue of Stalin. During the work, my wife asked me: 'Husband, how about the thumb? If we could not oppose the thumb to the other fingers—if the fingers of the hands were like toes—we could not hold a hammer, a mallet, any tool, a book, a piece of bread. Human life would be impossible without this little thumb. Now, who has made the thumb? We both learned Marxism in school and know that heaven and earth exist by themselves. They are not created by God. So I have learned and so I believe. But if God did not create heaven and earth, if he created only the thumb, he would be praiseworthy for this little thing.

'We praise Edison and Bell and Stephenson who have invented the electric bulb, the telephone and the railway and other things. But why should we not praise the one who has invented the thumb? If Edison had not had a thumb he would have invented nothing. It is only right to worship God who has made the thumb.'

The husband became very angry ... 'Don't speak stupidities! You have learned that there is no God. And you can never know if the house is not bugged and if we will not fall into trouble. Get into your mind *once and for all* that there is no God. In heaven there is *nobody*!'

She replied: 'This is an even greater wonder. If in heaven there were the Almighty God in whom in stupidity our forefathers believed, it would be only natural that we should have thumbs. An Almighty God can do everything, so he can make a thumb, too. But if in heaven there is nobody, I, from my side, am decided to worship from all my heart the "Nobody" who had made the thumb.'

JACOB BRONOWSKI accepted this method of discussing beliefs. The Christian will not agree with the *conclusion* at which he arrived; but his *method* sums up clearly what it means to test Christian beliefs:

... Does this (concept) really work ... without force, without corruption, and without another arbitrary superstructure of laws which do not derive from the central concept? Do its consequences fit our experience; do men in such a society live so or not so? This is the simple but profound test of fact by which we have come to judge the large words of the makers of states and systems.

There have always been two ways of looking for truth. One is to find concepts which are beyond challenge, because they are held by faith or by authority or the conviction that they are self-evident. This is the mystic submission to truth which the East has chosen, and which dominated the axiomatic thought of the scholars of the Middle Ages. So St Thomas Aquinas holds that faith is a higher guide to truth than knowledge is; the master of medieval science puts science firmly into second place.

Jacob Bronowski

But long before Aquinas wrote, Peter Abelard had already challenged the whole notion that there are concepts which can only be felt by faith or authority. All truth, even the highest, is accessible to test, said Abelard: 'By doubting we are led to inquire, and by inquiry we perceive the truth' . . .

The habit of testing and correcting the concept by its consequences in experience has been the spring within the movement of our civilization ever since. In science and in art and in self-knowledge we explore and move constantly by turning to the world of sense to ask, Is this so? This is the habit of truth . . .

Thomas Aquinas

Science is indeed a truthful activity. And whether we look at facts, at things, or at concepts, we cannot disentangle truth from meaning—that is, from an inner order. Truth therefore is not different in science and in the arts; the facts of the heart, the bases of personality, are merely more difficult to communicate. Truth to fact is the same habit in both, and has the same importance for both, because facts are the only raw material from which we can derive a change of mind. In science, the appeal to fact is the exploration of the concept in its logical consequences. In the arts, the emotional facts fix the limits of experience which can be shared in their language.

A TEST CASE: CREATION AND/OR EVOLUTION

There are three reasons why the subject of evolution is often extremely difficult to discuss:

1. Sometimes there is a breakdown in communication because words like 'creation' and 'evolution' mean different things to different people.

2. Not many people understand enough about sciences like biology and palaeontology to be able to understand technical books on these subjects. Most of us have to rely on the simplified version of the theory of evolution which we have picked up from school text-books or the popular press. While we don't need to be trained historians to study the documents concerning the life of Jesus, the vast majority of us find ourselves out of our depth when faced with amoeba and fossils!

3. It doesn't seem possible to settle the question simply by studying scientific evidence. There are eminent scientists who are experts in the different sciences concerned who are atheists; and there are many who are convinced Christians. If the purely scientific evidence is not decisive one way or the other, it would appear that philosophical and religious assumptions enter more fully than we realize into our thinking about creation and evolution. This is probably true for the non-Christian as much as for the Christian, since these other assumptions have nothing whatsoever to do with science.

How should we relate science and revelation?

The Christian should find no problem in relating science and revelation to each other, because he sees them *both* as ways in which God reveals himself. If God through his 'special revelation' (that is through Jesus and the Bible) shows himself as Creator of the universe, he also gives us through scientific study an opportunity to find out all that we can about the working of the universe. It is inconceivable that God should contradict himself and that what he reveals through the Bible should conflict with what he reveals through science.

To understand the Christian approach to science it is helpful to remember that modern science developed in a Christian context. The ancient Greeks had developed geometry, but their approach to science relied on deduction from first principles rather than observation and experiment.

The Arabs had developed arithmetic and algebra, and this was an important and necessary contribution. Christian Europe in the Middle Ages didn't make any significant progress because it was still under the influence of Greek ways of thinking.

The kind of world-view that was needed for modern science to emerge was one which insisted on the regularity of nature, the rationality of God the Creator and the certainty that the universe exists. There needed to be some way of relating the rational approach which relies purely on speculation and thinking and the experimental approach which relies on observation and experiment.

It was not an accident, therefore, that modern science developed from the sixteenth century onwards in a Christian context, because it was biblical beliefs about the universe which supplied these vital elements which had been missing before.

C.F. VON WEIZACKER, a German physicist, summarized these important concepts and described modern science as a 'legacy' or even 'a child of Christianity':

The concept of strict and generally valid laws of nature could hardly have arisen without the Christian concept of creation. Matter in the Platonic sense, which must be 'prevailed upon' by reason, will not obey mathematical laws exactly:

matter which God has created from nothing may well strictly follow the rules which its Creator had laid down for it. In this sense I called modern science a legacy, I might even have said a child, of Christianity.

DONALD MACKAY, a professor of communication and neuro-science, has written of the way in which the biblical assumptions about the universe provide a solid base for the activity of the scientist:

The biblical doctrine ... provides a more stable, rather than a less stable, foundation for our normal scientific expectations, in the stability of the will of a God who is always faithful.

We are emerging from a period of confused conflict during which the biblical doctrine of divine activity seems to have become largely distorted or forgotten. It is in this doctrine, untrimmed by any concessions to the spirit of our age, that I see the basis of the deepest harmony between Christian faith and the scientific attitude. There could be no higher guarantee of our scientific expectations than the rationality and faithfulness of the

This fossil of a pterodactyl is said to be 200 million years old.

**One who holds in being the stuff
and pattern of our world.**

If we then go on to ask how in principle we should relate science to the Bible, the most natural answer for the Christian is that we should try to find ways of reconciling what we learn from science with what we understand from the Bible. While we recognize that they approach the same subjects from different angles, we refuse to keep them totally separate in water-tight compartments.

How then does this approach work out in practice?

● We have to be aware of the tentative nature of most scientific theories. It is only too easy for the scientist to dogmatize about his theories, but then to find that they have to be revised radically in a few years time in the light of new knowledge. If we remember how confidently certain scientific theories were advanced, say 50 years ago, and how much they have had to be revised since then, we shall be less inclined to have an unjustifiable confidence in the theories which are propounded as certain today.

● We have to be willing to revise our interpretation of what the Bible means. We must acknowledge that we may not always have understood the meaning which the author intended to convey. Revising our *interpretation* of the Bible, however, does not demand a change in our estimate of its *authority*.

● We have to be prepared to suspend judgement when we find that we cannot make sense of all the different pieces of evidence. This means that we may have to say, 'Yes, there *is* a problem here, and we cannot *at present* see a solution to it. We are not running away from the evidence, and it *is* conceivable that compelling evidence would tell against Christian beliefs at this point and make us reject them. But the evidence is not so decisive as to make us abandon our understanding of the Bible's teaching. We must therefore simply suspend judgement now, and hope to be able to see a solution at some future date.' Far from being an escape or an excuse for lazy minds, this attitude can be a genuine expression of Christian and scientific humility.

DEREK KIDNER, in a commentary on Genesis, writes about the way he relates science to the story of Adam and Eve:

The exploratory suggestion is only tentative, as it must be, and it is a personal view. It invites correction and a better synthesis; meanwhile it may serve as a reminder that when the revealed and the observed seem hard to combine, it is because we know too little, not too much . . .

What do we mean by 'creation'?

The Christian believes that the creation of the universe and of man was not an accident, but the result of God's purposeful and deliberate action.

While some Christians still insist on a very literal interpretation of the early chapters of Genesis, others believe that we must be willing to revise our understanding in the light of new knowledge. This means that we are not bound to interpret these chapters as if they are an eye-witness report of the exact process by which the universe and man were created.

One of the opening scenes of de Laurentii's film *The Bible* shows Adam literally being formed out of dust—a heap of dust is transformed into a living man before our eyes in a few seconds. The text of Genesis, however, does *not* demand an interpretation of this kind. Nor does it demand the interpretation that man was created in an instant 'out of nothing'.

The writer of GENESIS reserves the word 'create' for three decisive stages in the creation of the universe:

In the beginning God created the heavens and the earth . . .
(the initial creation of the 'raw material' of the universe)

God created the great sea monsters and every living creature that moves, with which the waters swarm . . . and every winged bird . . .
(the creation of animal life)

God created man in his own image . . .
(the creation of man)

In the first of these stages the word 'create' must imply 'created out of nothing'. But in the other two stages, it is not a creation out of nothing, but rather a creation through working on matter that is already there:

> And God said, 'Let the waters bring forth swarms of living creatures . . .'

> The Lord God formed man of dust from tne ground, and breathed into his nostrils the breath of life; and man became a living being . . .

Thus, when the writer speaks of God creating man, he speaks of it as a decisively new stage in the unfolding process of creation. But he does not define precisely *how* God created man; and we must be careful not to read into the text ideas which are not there. If we are careful to distinguish between what the Bible *does say* and what it *does not say*, we can afford to have a more open mind over the process by which God created man.

JAMES PACKER gives this outline of how, as a theologian, he understands the first two chapters of Genesis which speak about the creation of the universe and man:

> Genesis 1 and 2, however, tell us *who* without giving many answers about *how*. Some today may think this a defect; but in the long perspective of history our present-day 'scientific' preoccupation with *how* rather than *who* looks very odd in itself. Rather than criticise these chapters for not feeding our secular interest, we should take from them a needed rebuke of our perverse passion for knowing Nature without regard for what matters most; namely, knowing Nature's Creator.
> 	The message of these two chapters is this: 'You have seen the sea? the sky? sun, moon and stars? You have watched the birds and the fish? You have observed the landscape, the vegetation, the animals, the insects, all the big things and little things together? You have marvelled at the wonderful complexity of human beings, with all their powers and skills and the deep feelings of fascination, attraction and affection that men and women arouse in each other? Fantastic, isn't it? Well now, meet the one who is behind it all!' As if to say: now that you have enjoyed these works of art, you must shake hands with the artist; since you were thrilled by the music, we will introduce you to the composer. It was to show us the Creator rather than the creation and to teach us knowledge of God rather than physical science, that Genesis 1 and 2, along with such celebrations of creation as Psalm 104 and Job 38–41, were written.

There are definite limits, however, to the ways in which Genesis can be reinterpreted. For example, many Christians hold that belief in a historic Adam is an essential part of Christian beliefs—for the following reasons.

● It is a basic principle in interpreting the Bible that we must always ask: 'what did the original writer intend?' When we ask this question about the early chapters of Genesis, we find an important clue in the phrase 'these are the generations of . . .' This phrase is repeated in different forms eleven times in the course of the book, and its meaning is: 'this is the genealogy, or genealogical history, of . . .' For example,

> These are the generations of the heavens and the earth

> This is the book of the generations of Adam

> These are the generations of Noah

> These are the generations of the sons of Noah, Shem, Ham and Japheth

It seems therefore that the original writer or editor of the book thought of Adam in the same way as all the other people who came after him—that is as real historical characters.

● The Jews always understood that the creation story referred to a single pair, and JESUS clearly accepted this view without question.

> Pharisees came up to him and tested him by asking, 'Is it lawful to

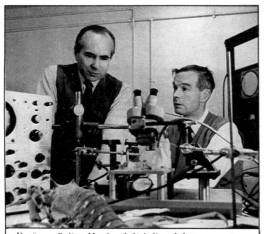

*Professor Julian Huxley (left) believed that every aspect
of the universe was enjoying a continual evolution.*

**divorce one's wife for any cause?'
He answered, 'Have you not read
that he who made them from the
beginning made them male and
female, and said, "For this reason a
man shall leave his father and
mother and be joined to his wife,
and the two shall become one"?'**

LUKE traces the genealogy of Jesus back to Adam,
the first man:

**Jesus, when he began his ministry,
was about thirty years of age, being
the son (as was supposed) of
Joseph, the son of Heli ... the son
of Enos, the son of Seth, the son of
Adam, the son of God.**

PAUL assumes that Adam was the first man, the
one through whom sin entered the world. His
whole argument in the following passage about the
effects of the death and resurrection of Jesus
depends on the assumption that the fall of Adam
was just as much a historical event as the death and
resurrection of Jesus:

**... sin came into the world through
one man and death through sin, and
so death spread to all men because
all men sinned ... If many died
through one man's trespass, much
more have the grace of God and the**

**free gift in the grace of that one man
Jesus Christ abounded for many.
And the free gift is not like the effect
of that one man's sin. For the
judgement following one trespass
brought condemnation, but the free
gift following many trespasses
brings justification. If, because of
one man's trespass, death reigned
through that one man, much more
will those who receive the
abundance of grace and the free gift
of righteousness reign in life
through the one man Jesus Christ.**

**Then as one man's trespass led
to condemnation for all men, so one
man's act of righteousness leads to
acquittal and life for all men. For as
by one man's disobedience many
were made sinners, so by one
man's obedience many will be made
righteous.**

● Rejection of the belief in a historic Adam creates
far more problems than it solves. If the early
chapters of Genesis have nothing to do with
origins—the origin of the universe, of man and sin
and suffering—then a host of very vital questions
are left completely unanswered: e.g. what does it
mean to say that man was 'created in the image of
God'? Did man grow into the image of God, and
did the divine likeness in man evolve gradually?
Was man created perfect, or was he created in the
same conditions as he is now? Was man always a
sinner and a rebel by nature?

What do we mean by 'evolution'?

It is harder to define 'evolution', because it is used
in at least three different senses:
   1. When we speak of evolution within limited
areas—for example, the evolution of the horse—we
are speaking about the way the horse has developed, and our theory is based on a considerable
amount of scientific evidence.
   2. When we speak of the theory of evolution in
a more general sense, however, we are thinking of

a biological theory which, it is claimed, accounts for the development of *all* living things from the amoeba to man. PROFESSOR W.R. THOMPSON, in the Introduction to the 1956 Everyman edition of *The Origin of Species*, summarizes Darwin's theory of evolution and the view of most representative modern Darwinians in this way:

> **Natural selection, leading to the survival of the fittest, in populations of individuals of varying characteristics and competing among themselves, has produced in the course of geological time gradual transformations leading from the simple primitive organism to the highest form of life, without the intervention of any directive agency or force . . . Purposeless and undirected evolution, says J. S. Huxley, eventually produced, in man, a being capable of purpose and of directing evolutionary change.**

3. In many cases 'evolution' is understood to be not only a biological theory, but also a philosophical theory which can be applied in many other fields. JULIAN HUXLEY writes of evolution as an all-embracing philosophy:

> **All reality is evolution . . . It is a one-way process in time; unitary, continuous; irreversible; self-transforming, and generating variety and novelty during its transformations.**
>
> **In the evolutionary pattern of thought there is no longer either need or room for the supernatural. The earth was not created: it evolved. So did all the animals and plants that inhabit it, including our human selves, mind and soul as well as brain and body. So did religion.**
>
> **All aspects of reality are subject to evolution, from atoms and stars to fish and flowers, from fish and flowers to human societies and values—indeed . . . all reality is a single process of evolution.**

Is it possible to reconcile creation and evolution?

The first thing we must say is: it all depends what we mean by 'evolution'.

If we use evolution in the first sense, as a theory which we use to explain the development of living things where there is convincing evidence, then there is no reason why evolution is incompatible with creation. There are many well-qualified scientists who are not convinced that the theory of evolution has provided a convincing explanation of the development of *homo sapiens*. There are still too many gaps in the data. PROFESSOR W.R. THOMPSON:

Charles Darwin

Darwin himself considered that the idea of evolution is unsatisfactory unless its mechanism can be explained. I agree, but since no one has explained to my satisfaction how evolution could happen I do not feel impelled to say that it has happened. I prefer to say that on this matter our information is inadequate.

There is a great divergence of opinion among biologists, not only about the causes of evolution but even about the actual process. This divergence exists because the evidence is unsatisfactory and

**does not permit any certain
conclusion. It is therefore right and
proper to draw the attention of the
non-scientific public to the
disagreement about evolution. But
some recent remarks of
evolutionists show that they think
this unreasonable. This situation,
where scientific men rally to the
defence of a doctrine they are
unable to define scientifically,
much less demonstrate with
scientific rigour, attempting to
maintain its credit with the public
by the suppression of criticism and
the elimination of difficulties, is
abnormal and undesirable in
science.**

PROFESSOR D.S.M. WATSON, a biologist, has
pointed out that many scientists have other
reasons, which have nothing to do with science, for
holding onto their belief in the theory of evolution:

**Evolution has been accepted by
scientists, not because it has been
observed to occur or proved by
logical coherent evidence to be
true, but because the only
alternative, special creation, is
clearly unacceptable.**

This is an example of how one theologian, JOHN
STOTT, believes that evolution in this sense can be
related to the creation story in Genesis:

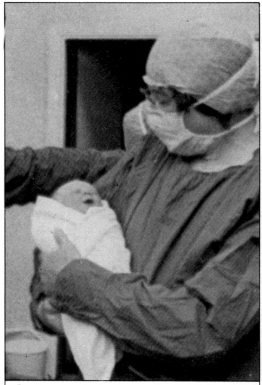

*Genetic engineering has become a live issue in the 1980s.
In 1980 Loise Brown, the first test-tube baby, was born.*

**It seems perfectly possible to
reconcile the historicity of Adam
with at least some (theistic)
evolutionary theory. Many biblical
Christians in fact do so, believing
them to be not entirely
incompatible. To assert the
historicity of an original pair who
sinned through disobedience is one
thing; it is quite another to deny all
evolution and to assert the separate
and special creation of everything,
including both subhuman creatures
and Adam's body. The suggestion
(for it is no more than this) does not
seem to me to be against Scripture
and therefore impossible that when**

**God made man in His own image,
what He did was to stamp His own
likeness on one of the many
'hominids' which appear to have
been living at the time.
 Speaking hesitatingly as a non-
scientist, the extraordinary
homogeneity of the human race
(physiological and psychological)
has always appealed to me as the
best available scientific evidence of
our common ancestry.
 The chief problem in the
reconciliation of Scripture and
science regarding the origins of
mankind concerns the antiquity of
Adam. If Adam and Eve were a
historical pair, when do you date**

them? There are two main alternatives.

The first is that they were very early indeed, many thousands of years BC, so that all the cave-drawing, tool-making hominids were descended from them. The difficulty here is that we would then have to postulate immense gaps in the Genesis story and genealogies.

The second alternative is that they were comparatively recent, even as late as 5 or 10,000 BC. This reconstruction begins with the biblical witness that the dawn of civilization, adumbrated in Genesis 4:17–22, almost immediately follows the Fall. If this is correct, then even the fairly advanced (although prehistoric) cave-drawing hominids were pre-Adamic. The difficulty here is the claimed scientific evidence that true humans were living in some parts of the world long before this period. But were they Adamic? Anatomically they may have been virtually indistinguishable from modern man; but by what criteria can we judge if they bore the image of God in a biblical sense?

It may be that we shall not be able to solve this problem until we know more precisely what 'the image of God' means, and how much cultural (and even primitive religious!) development may have been possible to pre-Adamic hominids who nevertheless did not possess the divine likeness.

If we use evolution in the second sense, as a biological theory which accounts for the evolution of everything from amoeba to man, we are faced with a basic choice:

● The first possibility is that we see the process of evolution as a purely chance process, which, by definition, rules out the activity of God as Creator. Thus PROFESSOR W.R. THOMPSON points out the 'anti-religious flavour' in many statements of the doctrine of evolution:

The doctrine of evolution by natural selection as Darwin formulated, and as his followers still explain it, has a strong anti-religious flavour. This is due to the fact that the intricate adaptations and co-ordinations we see in living things, naturally evoking the idea of finality and design and, therefore, of an intelligent providence, are explained, with what seems to be a rigorous argument, as the result of chance ... It is clear that in the *Origin* evolution is presented as an essentially undirected process. For the majority of its readers, therefore, the *Origin* effectively dissipated the evidence of providential control.

● The second possibility is that we believe that the process of evolution does not rule out the activity of God. We therefore say that it is not inconceivable that God should choose to use this chance process as *his way* of creating the universe. Those who believe that creation is compatible with evolution in this sense are forced to make a drastic reinterpretation of Genesis. For if the human race has evolved gradually from ape-like ancestors without any special 'break', there cannot have been a single 'Adam'. JOHN HABGOOD recognizes that such a reinterpretation of the Bible affects the whole structure of Christian beliefs:

Even if we believe, as most theologians now do, that the stories of Adam and Eve are profound myths and not literal history, some difficulties remain. The doctrines of the Fall and of the uniqueness of man are not just forced upon Christians because they happen to be there in Genesis 1:3. They are essential pieces of Christian theology, interlocking with the whole of the rest of theology, which cannot be removed without putting the whole structure in jeopardy.

If we think of evolution in the third sense, as a biological theory and a philosophy of evolution, it is hard, if not impossible to see how it can be reconciled with the idea of creation. JULIAN HUX-LEY insists that 'In the evolutionary pattern of thought there is no longer any need or room for the supernatural', and the Christian understanding of creation is therefore ruled out of court as 'unnecessary and illogical':

> **Supernatural creation runs counter to the whole of our scientific knowledge ... To postulate a divine interference with these exchanges of matter and energy at a particular moment in the earth's history is both unnecessary and illogical.**

There are some writers, however, who have accepted the philosophy of evolution and tried to use it to reinterpret their Christian understanding of the universe. TEILHARD DE CHARDIN, the Roman Catholic priest and scientist (1881–1955), accepted evolution not simply as a biological theory, but as an all-embracing philosophy which transforms everything, including Christian beliefs:

> **One might well become impatient or lose heart at the sight of so many minds (and not mediocre ones either) remaining today still closed to the idea of evolution, if the whole of history were not there to pledge to us that a truth once seen, even by a single mind, always ends up by imposing itself on the totality of human consciousness. For many, evolution is still only transformism, and transformism is only an old Darwinian hypothesis as local and dated as Laplace's conception of the solar system or Wegener's Theory of Continental Drift. Blind indeed are those who do not see the sweep of a movement whose orbit infinitely transcends the natural sciences and has successively invaded and conquered the surrounding territory—chemistry, physics, sociology and even mathematics and the history of religions. One after the other all the fields of human knowledge have been shaken and carried away by the same under-water current in the direction of the study of some**

> **development. Is evolution a theory, a system or a hypothesis? It is much more: it is a general condition to which all theories, all hypotheses, all systems must bow and which they must satisfy henceforward if they are to be thinkable and true. Evolution is a light illuminating all facts, a curve that all lines must follow.**
>
> **If as a result of some interior revolution, I were successively to lose my faith in Christ, my faith in a personal God, my faith in the Spirit, I think I would continue to believe in the World. The World (the value, the infallibility, the goodness of the World); that, in the final analysis, is the first and last thing in which I believe.**

THOMAS ALTIZER, a theologian of the 'Death of God' school which flourished in the 1960s pointed out what happened in de Chardin's reinterpretation of Christian language:

> **It is true that Teilhard occasionally and inconsistently introduces traditional Christian language into the pages of *The Phenomenon of Man*; but this fact scarcely obviates the truth that virtually the whole body of Christian belief either disappears or is transformed in Teilhard's evolutionary vision of the cosmos.**

One of our main conclusions at the end of this study of creation and evolution ought to be that whenever we find ourselves talking about evolution, we are not simply talking about whether or not man has evolved from the apes. In the end we are faced with a choice between two world-views which are totally incompatible:

1. that the universe is the product of a chance process; or
2. that there is a personal Creator who has been at work throughout the whole process of creation.

Which of these views best fits all the facts of our experience? We cannot resolve this question simply by looking at the fossils ...

SECTION 5

UNDERSTANDING AND TESTING THE ALTERNATIVES

It was the manifestly poisonous nature of the fruits that forced me to consider the philosophical tree on which they had grown.

An obviously untrue philosophy leads in practice to disastrous results.

. . .we realize the necessity of seeking an alternative philosophy that shall be true and therefore fruitful of good.
ALDOUS HUXLEY

What I have to record is a changed view of the nature of man, which in due course led to a changed view of the nature of the world.
C.E.M. JOAD

Atheism is a cruel, long-term business: I believe I have gone through it to the end.
JEAN-PAUL SARTRE

Sartre never felt any attraction to the Christian faith, and spent his life working out the implications of his atheism. His words about going 'through it to the end' give us a clue as to what it means to understand and test the alternatives to the Christian faith.

Following a belief to the end means that we try to be consistent and work it out to its logical conclusion. In many cases the question 'what would happen if. . .?' can become 'what has happened when. . .?' because there have always been people before us who have tried to be consistent in their search for truth, and have explored all the possible answers and their consequences. We may dislike or disagree with their conclusions; but if these are possible conclusions which follow logically from the initial assumptions, what is it that prevents us from following the same road? Can we show where they have gone wrong? Or are we holding back only because of habit or tradition, 'common sense' or pure sentiment?

FRANCIS SCHAEFFER gives two examples of people who have followed their beliefs to their logical conclusion and then found themselves caught in a dilemma. They are caught in a tension between the logical conclusions of their beliefs and the real world in which they live.

In the first example he describes a conversation with an atheist, who thought he had no reason for believing that anything was there outside of himself:

> He was an atheist, and when he found out I was a pastor he anticipated an evening's entertainment, so he started in. But it did not go quite that way. Our conversation showed me that he understood the implications of his position and tried to be consistent concerning them. After about an hour I saw that he wanted to draw the discussion to a close, so I made one last point which I hoped he would never forget, not because I hated him, but because I cared for him as a fellow human being. I noticed that he had his lovely little Jewish wife with him. She was very beautiful and full of life and it was easy to see, by the attention he paid to her, that he really loved her.
>
> Just as they were about to go to their cabin, in the romantic setting of the boat sailing across the Mediterranean and a beautiful full moon shining outside, I finally said to him, 'When you take your wife into your arms at night, can you be sure she is there?'
>
> I hated to do it to him, but I did it knowing that he was a man who would really understand the implications of the question and not forget. His eyes turned, like a fox caught in a trap, and he shouted at me, 'No, I am not always sure she is there', and walked into his cabin.

In the second place he speaks of lovers in the Left Bank of the River Seine in Paris, who fall in love and then cry because, according to their philosophy, there is no such thing as 'love':

> If I met any of these I would put my hand gently on their shoulders and say, '. . . at this moment you understand something real about the universe. Though your system may say love does not exist, your own experience shows that it does.' They have not touched the personal God who exists, but, for a fleeting moment, they have touched the existence of true personality in their love. This is indeed an objective reality . . .

If we can see that a particular belief leads to disastrous consequences, we must *either*

> live in a way that is consistent with what we believe and accept the full consequences;

> *or* we stay where we are, and admit the inconsistency between what we believe and how we live;

> *or* we turn round and look for a different belief which fits better with the world as it is.

ALDOUS HUXLEY, writing in 1937 about beliefs which he had held earlier in his life, gives an example of what this kind of change of mind can mean:

> **It was the manifestly poisonous nature of the fruits that forced me to consider the philosophical tree on which they had grown.**

> **An obviously untrue philosophy of life leads in practice to disastrous results.**

He speaks about

> **. . . the point where we realize the necessity of seeking an alternative philosophy that shall be true and therefore fruitful of good.**

The Christian is bound to feel that Huxley's earlier dissatisfaction with his position never led him to consider Christian faith as such an 'alternative philosophy' which would be true and therefore 'fruitful of good'. He will want to point to the 'poisonous nature' of Huxley's later position. C.E.M. JOAD, on the other hand, is an example of a philosopher who *was* willing to change his mind and came to be convinced of the Christian world-view:

> **What I have to record is a changed view of the nature of man, which in due course led to a changed view of the nature of the world . . .**

TEMPLE GAIRDNER, a missionary who worked in Egypt for many years and had a great deal of contact with Muslims, wrote these words in a booklet on *The Muslim Idea of God:*

> **When men get into a cul-de-sac and think their position hopeless, it means they have taken a wrong turn, and that they must go back to beyond the point where they took that turn, and start upon another path.**

Our choice of alternatives to the Christian faith must inevitably be selective. It would be impossible to discuss every individual religion, every kind of philosophy and modern cult.

We therefore confine ourselves to five different religions or kinds of religion—Primal religion, the Eastern religions—Hinduism and Buddhism, Judaism and Islam.

We then look at ten key thinkers who have had a profound influence on the way we think and helped to create what we sometimes call 'the modern mind'.

Finally we examine ten different 'isms'— different philosophies or religious outlooks.

In each case we need to try to *feel what it is like* to live with one of these different world-views. It isn't enough to outline different religions and philosophies and consider them as theories for abstract discussion. We need to put ourselves in the other person's shoes, and try to see the world as he sees it. The quotations should help us not only to understand the different world-views in a theoretical way, but to help us to enter into the experience of those who hold them and live by them.

We also try to test the different religions and 'isms' at points where they raise particular difficulties, and in particular over the answers they give to the basic human questions.

Outline

MAJOR RELIGIONS
Primal religion
Eastern religions—Hinduism and Buddhism
Judaism
Islam

TEN KEY THINKERS
Thomas Aquinas
René Descartes
John Locke
David Hume
Jean Jacques Rousseau
Immanuel Kant
George Frederick Hegel
Søren Kierkegaard
Karl Marx
Sigmund Freud
The legacy of these thinkers—'the modern mind'

TEN '-ISMS'
Catholic Scholasticism
Deism
Rationalism
Atheism
Agnosticism
Mysticism
Pantheism
Marxism
Existentialism
Humanism

MAJOR RELIGIONS

PRIMAL RELIGION

The religion of many tribal societies all over the world is sometimes called Primal religion, or Animism or Primitive religion. While there are significant differences in different continents, they have many basic features in common—for example, belief in good and evil spirits which control the world and need to be placated.

It was once thought that primal religion is the nearest thing one can find to the original religion of man. But the evidence is more easily explained by the assumption that this form of religion has developed (or degenerated) from an original worship of the one Creator-God.

Led by Fr. Wilhelm Schmidt of Vienna, anthropologists have shown that the religion of the hundreds of isolated tribes in the world today is not primitive in the sense of being original. The tribes have a memory of a 'High God', a benign Creator-Father-God, who is no longer worshipped because he is not feared. Instead of offering sacrifice to him, they concern themselves with the pressing problems of how to appease the vicious spirits of the jungle. The threats of the witch-doctor are more strident than the still, small voice of the Father-God.

We see, then, that the evolution of religion from a primitive Animatism can no longer be assumed as axiomatic and that some anthropologists now suggest that Monotheism may be more naturally primitive as a world-view than Animism. Their research suggests that tribes are not animistic because they have continued unchanged since the dawn of history. Rather, the evidence indicates degeneration from a true knowledge of God. Isolation from prophets and religious books has ensnared them into sacrificial bribery to placate the spirits instead of joyous sacrificial meals in the presence of the Creator.
ROBERT BROW

The following examples are all taken from African religions, and the quotations are from the book *African Religions and Philosophies* by JOHN MBITI:

● There is a strong awareness of the existence of a personal Creator God:

African knowledge of God is expressed in proverbs, short statements, songs, prayers, names, myths, stories and religious ceremonies. All these are easy to remember and pass on to other people, since there are no sacred writings in traditional societies. One should not, therefore, expect long dissertations about God. But God is no stranger to African peoples, and in traditional life there are no atheists. This is summarized in an Ashanti proverb that 'No one knows a child the Supreme Being'. That means that everybody knows of God's existence almost by instinct, and even children know Him.

This God, however, has withdrawn himself. He exists, but he is too distant for any man to enjoy communion with him:

It is particularly as Spirit that God is incomprehensible. So the Ashanti rightly refer to Him as 'the fathomless Spirit', since no human mind can measure Him, no intellect can comprehend or grasp Him ... Many people readily admit that they do not know what God is like, and that they do not possess the words of God— since words are vehicles of someone's thoughts and to a certain degree they give a portrait of the speaker. Some even say that God's proper name is unknown; or give Him a name like that of the Lunda, which means or signifies 'the God of the Unknown', or that of the Ngombe which means 'the Unexplainable', or of the Maasai which means 'the Unknown'. A person's name in African societies generally has a meaning descriptive of His personality and being. In the

case of God, people might know some of His activities and manifestations, but of His essential nature they know nothing. It is a paradox that they 'know' Him, and yet they do not 'know' Him: He is not a Stranger to them, and yet they are strangers to Him; He knows them, but they do not know Him. So God confronts men as the mysterious and incomprehensible, as indescribable and beyond human vocabulary. This is part of the essential nature of God.

The love of God is taken for granted, but is seldom made explicit:

As for the love of God, there are practically no direct sayings that God loves. This is something reflected also in the daily lives of African peoples, in which it is rare to hear people talking about love. A person shows his love for another more through action than through words. So, in the same way, people experience the love of God in concrete acts and blessings; and they assume that He loves them, otherwise He would not have created them.

The remoteness and unknowableness of God create the need for different kinds of mediators to put man in touch with the power which controls the universe. In this way the spirits of the ancestors and witchdoctors come to play an important role in man's quest for health, happiness and security.

● There is no question about the reality of the supernatural world:

It emerges clearly that for African peoples, this is a religious universe. Nature in the broadest sense of the word is not an empty impersonal object or phenomenon: it is filled with religious

significance. Man gives life even where natural objects and phenomena have no biological life. God is seen in and behind these objects and phenomena: they are His creation, they manifest Him, they symbolize His being and presence. The invisible world is symbolized or manifested by these visible and concrete phenomena and objects of nature. The invisible world presses hard upon the visible: one speaks of the other, and African peoples 'see' that invisible universe when they look at, hear or feel the visible and tangible world.

HOW DOES THIS WORLD-VIEW AFFECT MORAL VALUES?

God tends to have little to do with the standards or values adopted by any society:

Even if . . . God is thought to be the ultimate upholder of the moral order, people do not consider Him to be immediately involved in the keeping of it. Instead, it is the patriarchs, living-dead, elders, priests, or even divinities and spirits who are the daily guardians or police of human morality. Social regulations of a moral nature are directed towards the immediate contact between individuals, between man and the living-dead and the spirits. Therefore, these regulations are on the man-to-man level, rather than the God-to-man plane of morality.

HOW DOES THE INDIVIDUAL THINK OF DEATH?

African religions have their own mythology about the origins of the human race; but they can hold out little hope for the individual as he faces death:

Yet behind these fleeting glimpses of the original state and bliss of man, whether they

are rich or shadowy, there lie the tantalizing and unattained gift of the resurrection, the loss of human immortality and the monster death. Here African religions and philosophy must admit a defeat: they have supplied no solution. This remains the most serious cul-de-sac in the otherwise rich thought and sensitive feeling of our peoples.

According to African religions and philosophy, the grave is the seal of everything, even if a person survives and continues to exist in the next world. There is an accelerated rhythm from death through the state of personal immortality (as the living-dead) to the state of collective immortality (as ordinary spirits). This final 'beat' of the rhythm may or may not have an end. There is, however, nothing to hope for, since this is the destiny of everybody; though older people do not seem to fear, and may even long for, the 'departure' from this to the next world. There is no resurrection for either the individual or mankind at large ... The departed do not grow spiritually towards or like God, though some may act as intermediaries between men and God and may have more power and knowledge than human beings. Such is the anthropocentric view of the destiny of man, and as far as traditional African concepts are concerned, death is death and the beginning of a permanent ontological departure of the individual from mankind to spirithood. Beyond that point, African religions and philosophy are absolutely silent, or at most extremely vague. Nothing can reverse or halt that process, and death is the end of real and complete man.

All 'primal' groups have a great concern for the dead. The Torajo people of Indonesia entomb their dead along with life-sized wooden effigies.

HOW ARE WE TO EXPLAIN SUFFERING AND EVIL AND FIGHT AGAINST THEM?

Within this tightly knit corporate society where personal relationships are so intense and so wide, one finds perhaps the most paradoxical areas of African life. This corporate type of life makes every member of the community dangerously naked in the sight of other members. It is paradoxically the centre of love and hatred, of friendship and enmity, of trust and suspicion, of joy and sorrow, of generous tenderness and bitter jealousies. It is paradoxically the heart of security and insecurity, of building and destroying the individual and the community. Everybody knows everybody else: a person cannot be individualistic, but only corporate. Every form of pain, misfortune, sorrow or suffering; every illness and sickness; every death whether of an old man or of the infant child; every failure of the crop in the fields, of hunting in the wilderness or of fishing in the waters; every bad omen or dream: these and all the other manifestations of evil that man experiences are blamed on somebody in the corporate society.

By this ('natural evil') I mean those experiences in human life which involve suffering, misfortune, diseases, calamity, accidents and various forms of pain. In every African society these are well known. Most of them are explainable through 'natural' causes. But ... for African peoples nothing sorrowful happens by 'accident' or 'chance': it must all be 'caused' by some agent (either human or spiritual) ...

Ceremony and ritual are widely used to combat evil influences such as disease.

In some societies it is thought that a person suffers because he has contravened some regulation, and God or the spirits, therefore, punish the offender. In that case, the person concerned is actually the cause of his own suffering ... But in most cases, different forms of suffering are believed to be caused by human agents who are almost exclusively witches, sorcerers and workers of evil magic ... They are ... 'responsible' for 'causing' what would be 'natural evil', by using incantations, mystical power, medicines, by sending secondary agents like flies and animals, by using their 'evil eye', by wishing evil against their fellow man, by hating or feeling jealous, and by means of other 'secret' methods ... In the experience of evil, African peoples see certain individuals as being intricately involved, but wickedly, in the otherwise smooth running of the natural universe.

In African villages, disease and misfortune are religious experiences, and it requires a religious approach to deal with them. The medicine-men are aware of this, and make attempts to meet the need in a religious (or quasi-religious) manner—whether or not that turns out to be genuine or false or a mixture of both ...

Suffering, misfortune, disease and accident, are all 'caused' mystically, as far as African peoples are concerned. To combat the misfortune or ailment the cause must also be found, and either counteracted, uprooted or punished. This is where the value of the traditional medicine-man comes into the picture. So long as people see sickness and misfortune as 'religious' experiences, the traditional medicine-man will continue to exist and thrive.

EASTERN RELIGIONS— HINDUISM AND BUDDHISM

Hinduism sprang from a reaction against the debased polytheistic religion which developed in India before the eighth century BC. Buddhism was an offshoot which grew out of Hinduism under the influence of Siddhartha Gautama, the Buddha (563–483 BC).

ROBERT BROW describes the religion which the Aryan invaders brought with them to India in the second millennium BC, and which later developed into Hinduism:

If we could look down on the ancient world about 1500 BC we would see ordinary men and women still offering animal sacrifices as their normal way of approaching God or the gods. The earliest literature of India, the Sanskrit *Vedas*, picture the nomadic Aryan tribes who fought their way eastwards across the Indus and Ganges plains. The head of the family offered animal sacrifice with the same simplicity as Abraham. When they settled in India the Aryans developed a regular priesthood, and the *Vedas* are the hymns which the priests chanted as the sacrificial smoke ascended to God. The hymns address God under various names such as 'The Sun', 'The Heavenly One' and 'The Storm', but the interesting thing is that, whatever name they give to God, they worshipped him as the Supreme Ruler of the universe. This practice is called *Henotheism*. God has several names, just as Christians today have several names for God, but the names do not indicate different gods. They are different facets of the one God. Henotheism changes into Polytheism when the names of God are so personified that various gods are separated, and they begin to disagree and fight among themselves. The later Vedic literature has certainly become polytheistic by, say, 1000 BC, but the earliest Aryans must have been Monotheists.

The crucial step in the development of Hinduism was taken when someone began to identify 'God' more closely with the universe, and then said '*God is not different from or distinct from the universe*. God *is* everything there is, and everything there is *is* God.'

It is important to realize that this vital step has made the Eastern religions differ fundamentally from the Western religions (Judaism, Christianity and Islam). *Professor Zaehner*, who came from a Hindu background and was for many years a professor of Eastern religions at Oxford University, underlines the deep divisions between Eastern and Western religions:

To maintain that all religions are paths leading to the same goal, as is so frequently done today, is to maintain something that is not true.

Not only on the dogmatic, but also on the mystical plane, too, there is no agreement.

It is then only too true that the basic principles of Eastern and Western, which in practice means Indian and Semitic, thought are, I will not say irreconcilably opposed; they are simply not starting from the same premises. The only common ground is that the function of religion is to provide release; there is no agreement at all as to what it is that man must be released from. The great religions are talking at cross purposes.

'GOD' AND THE INDIVIDUAL 'SOUL'

The clue to all eastern thinking about man is contained in one of the most significant sayings of Hinduism: '*Thou art That*'—that is, the individual soul (*Atman*) is to be identified with the all-pervading 'God' (*Brahman*).

The following are different attempts (by a Hindu, a Buddhist and a Christian) to summarize the meaning and significance of this important saying:

The *Upanishads* point out that the *Brahman* and the *Atman* are the same. The Supreme has manifested Himself in every soul, and the student of religion is dramatically told in the *Upanishads*, 'Thou art That' (*tat tvam asi*). This idea provides the core of most Hindu religious thought and is developed later by Samkara into his doctrine of *advaita* (lit. non-duality). This is a monistic doctrine, which denies the existence of the world as separate from God.
K.M. SEN

The quintessence of Indian thought may be summed up by saying that the Atman of man and the Atman of the universe are one.

At the heart of the Universe is the One Reality of which the universe as we know it is but a periodic manifestation. This is the only Supreme Deity known

to Indian thought, for the Upanishadic philosophy, like Buddhism, 'revolts against the deistic conception of God' (Radhakrishnan) ...
CHRISTMAS HUMPHREYS

The phrase ... consists of three Sanskrit words, generally regarded in India as the most important sentence that that country has ever pronounced; the succinct formulation of a profound and ultimate truth about man and the universe. The phrase is: *tat tvam asi. Tat* means 'that'; *tvam* means 'thou'; and *asi* is the second person singular of the verb 'to be'. 'That thou art'; *tat tvam asi.* It means, thou art that reality, thou art God. The same truth is expressed in other ways; for instance, in the famous equation '*atman* equals *Brahman*'—or the soul of man is God, or the Ultimate Reality, with a very large capital U and capital R; the really real. The individual self is the world soul. The soul of man equals the ultimate of the universe. 'Thou', or to use our more colloquial term, 'you'—each one of you reading this book— are in some final, cosmic sense the total and transcendent truth that underlies all being, *Brahman* who precedes and transcends God himself, the Infinite and Absolute Reality beyond all phenomena, beyond all apprehension and beyond all form.
WILFRED CANTWELL-SMITH

GOD AND THE WORLD
PRESIDENT RADHAKRISHNAN, Indian philosopher and statesman and one-time professor of Eastern religions at Oxford (1888–1975), writing in *The Hindu View of Life* is content to remain agnostic about the origin of the universe and the relationship between God and the universe:

The hypothesis of creation is a weak one, and it assumes that God lived alone for some time and then suddenly it occurred to him to have company, when he put forth the world. The theory of manifestation is not more satisfying, for it is difficult to know how the finite can manifest the infinite. If we say that God is transformed into the world, the question arises whether it is the whole of God that is transformed or only a part. If it is the whole, then there is no God beyond the universe and we lapse into the lower pantheism. If it is only a part, then it means that God is capable of being partitioned. We cannot keep one part of God above and another part below. It would be like taking half the fowl for cooking, leaving the other half for laying eggs. Samkara believes that it is not possible to determine logically the relation between God and the world. He asks us to hold fast both ends. It does not matter if we are not able to find out where they meet.

The history of philosophy in India as well as Europe has been one long illustration of the inability of the human mind to solve the mystery of the relation of God to the world. The greatest thinkers are those who admit the mystery and comfort themselves by the idea that the human mind is not omniscient. Samkara in the East and Bradley in the West adopt this wise attitude of agnosticism. We have the universe with its distinctions. It is not self-sufficient. It rests on something else, and that is the Absolute. The relation between the two is a mystery.

He rejects an extreme form of pantheism; but there is still no possibility of the existence of a personal Creator God.

The Hindu view rebels against the cold and formal conception of God who is external to the world, and altogether remote and transcendent. The natural law of the world is but a working of God's sovereign purpose. The uniformity of nature, the orderliness of the cosmos, and the steady reaching forward and upward of the course of evolution proclaim not the unconscious throbbing of a soulless engine, but the directing mind of an all-knowing spirit. The indwelling of God in the universe does not mean the identity of God with the universe. According to the latter view God is so immanent in everything that we have only to open our eyes to see God in it, but also there is nothing of God left outside the whole of things. God lies spread out before us. The world is not only a revelation, but an exhaustive revelation of God. Hindu thought takes care to emphasise the transcendent character of the Supreme. 'He bears the world but is by no means lost in it.' The world is in God and not God in the world. In the universe we have the separate existence of the individuals. Whether the divine spark burns dimly or brightly in the individual, the sparks are distinct from the central fire from which they issue.

DOES THE INDIVIDUAL HAVE ANY SIGNIFICANCE?
RABINDRANATH TAGORE expresses the Hindu's hope that he will one day be merged with the universe:

Dark is the future to her, and the odour cries in despair,
'Ah me, through whose fault is my life so unmeaning?
Who can tell me, why I am at all?'
Do not lose heart, timid thing!
The perfect dawn is near when you will mingle your life with all

life and know at last your purpose.

Buddhism holds out the hope of Nirvana, a state in which the individual no longer exists as a separate individual:

Nirvana is the extinction of the not-Self in the completion of the Self. It is, therefore, to the limited extent that we can understand it, a concept of psychology, a state of consciousness. As such it is, as Professor Radhakrishnan points out, 'the goal of perfection and not the abyss of annihilation. Through the destruction of all that is individual in us, we enter into communion with the whole universe, and become an integral part of the great purpose. Perfection is then the sense of oneness with all that is, has ever been and can ever be. The horizon of being is extended to the limits of reality.' It is therefore not correct to say that the dewdrop slips into the Shining Sea; it is nearer to the truth to speak of the Shining Sea invading the dewdrop. There is here no sense of loss but of infinite expansion when, 'Foregoing self, the Universe grows I.'
CHRISTMAS HUMPHREYS

JACOB BRONOWSKI, as a scientist, points out the practical effects of these beliefs about the individual:

The cultures of the East still differ from ours as they did then. They still belittle man as individual man. Under this runs an indifference to the world of the senses, of which the indifference to experienced fact is one face. Anyone who has worked in the East knows how hard it is there to get an answer to a question of fact. When I had to study the casualties from the atomic bombs in Japan at the end of the war, I was dogged and perplexed by this difficulty. The man I asked, whatever man one asks, does not really understand what one wants to know: or rather, he does not understand that one wants to know. He wants to do what is fitting, he is not unwilling to be candid, but at bottom he does not know the facts because they are not his language. These cultures of the East have remained fixed because they lack the language and the very habit of fact.

Christmas Humphreys

C.E.M. JOAD spells out the logical conclusion of this way of thinking:

A condition in which I shall cease to think, to feel as an individual or, indeed to *be* an individual, is a condition in which *I* shall cease to be at all. Now why should I hope or seek to realise such a condition, unless I take my individual personality to be of no account?

HOW DO THE HINDU AND THE BUDDHIST DECIDE WHAT IS RIGHT AND WRONG?

RADHAKRISHNAN explains that in Hinduism morality is determined by the code of practice developed over the centuries in Hindu society. Values are based on the concept of *dharma*, a word which comes close to the word 'nature':

Hinduism is more a way of life than a form of thought. While it gives absolute liberty in the world of thought it enjoins a strict code of practice. The theist and the atheist, the sceptic and the agnostic may all be Hindu if they accept the Hindu system of culture and life . . . what counts is conduct, not belief.

Dharma is right action. In the *Rig Veda, rta* is the right order of the universe. It stands for both the *satya* or the truth of things as well as the dharma or the law of evolution. Dharma formed from the root *dhr*, to hold, means that which holds a thing or maintains it in being. Every form of life, every group of men has its dharma, which is the law of its being. Dharma or virtue is conformity with the truth of things; adharma or vice is opposition to it. Moral evil is disharmony with the truth which encompasses and controls the world.

The Buddhist code of morals is summed up in what is known as 'The Eight-fold Path': Right Belief, Right Thought, Right Speech, Action, Means of Livelihood, Exertion, Remembrance, and Meditation. This Path 'leads to the end of suffering by the elimination of personal and separative desire'. The essence of Buddhism is summed up in the words:

> 'To cease from all sin,
> To get virtue,
> To purify the heart.'

Values are based on the concept of *karuna*, love:

Karuna corresponds to love. It is like the sands of the Ganges: they are trampled by all kinds of beings: by elephants, by lions, by asses, by human

beings, but they do not make any complaints. They are again soiled by all kinds of filth scattered by all kinds of animals, but they just suffer them all and never utter a word of ill-will. Eckhart would declare the sands on the Ganges to be 'just', because 'the just have no will at all: whatever God wishes it is all one to them, however great the discomfort may be'.
D.T. SUZUKI

The basic problem with this approach to values is that there is ultimately no difference between good and evil, since they are merely different aspects of the one great reality:

The antitheses of cause and effect, substance and attribute, good and evil, truth and error, are due to the tendency of man to separate terms which are related. Fichte's puzzle of self and not-self, Kant's antinomies, Hume's opposition of facts and laws, can all be got over if we recognize that the opposing factors are mutually complementary elements based on one identity.
RADHAKRISHNAN

If good and evil are both aspects of the One Great Reality, ultimately there is no sure way of deciding between what is good and what is evil. FRANCIS SCHAEFFER relates the following incident to illustrate this dilemma:

One day I was talking to a group of people in the digs of a young South African in Cambridge. Among others, there was present a young Indian who was of Sikh background but a Hindu by religion. He started to speak strongly against Christianity, but did not really understand the problems of his own beliefs. So I said, 'Am I not correct in saying that on the

basis of your system, cruelty and non-cruelty are ultimately equal, that there is no intrinsic difference between them?' He agreed. The people who listened and knew him as a delightful person, an 'English gentleman' of the very best kind, looked up in amazement. But the student in whose room we met, who had clearly understood the implications of what the Sikh had admitted, picked up his kettle of boiling water with which he was about to make tea, and stood with it steaming over the Indian's head. The man looked up and asked him what he was doing and he said, with a cold yet gentle finality, 'There is no difference between cruelty and non-cruelty.' Thereupon the Hindu walked out into the night.

IS IT EVER POSSIBLE TO KNOW 'THE TRUTH'?
Hinduism starts from a profound agnosticism about the nature of God:

The Hindu never doubted the reality of the one supreme universal spirit, however much the descriptions of it may fall short of its nature. Whatever the doctrinaires may say, the saints of God are anxious to affirm that much is hidden from their sight. God hideth himself. It is a sound religious agnosticism which bids us hold our peace regarding the nature of the supreme spirit. Silence is more significant than speech regarding the depths of the divine. The altars erected to the unknown gods in the Graeco-Roman world were but an expression of man's ignorance of the divine nature. The sense of failure in man's quest for the unseen is symbolized by them. When asked to define the nature of God, the seer of the Upanishad sat silent, and when pressed to

answer exclaimed that the Absolute is silence. The mystery of the divine reality eludes the machinery of speech and symbol. The 'Divine Darkness', 'That of which nothing can be said', and such other expressions are used by the devout when they attempt to describe their consciousness of direct communion with God.
RADHAKRISHNAN

This means that according to the Hindu way of thinking it is impossible to say that any belief is either 'true' or 'false'; every possible kind of belief is permitted with an almost infinite tolerance:

Hinduism developed an attitude of comprehensive charity instead of fanatic faith in an inflexible creed. It accepted the multiplicity of aboriginal gods and others which originated, most of them, outside the Aryan tradition, and justified them all. It brought together into one whole all believers in God. Many sects professing many different beliefs live within the Hindu fold.
RADHAKRISHNAN

The religious beliefs of different schools of Hindu thought vary and their religious practices also differ; there is in it monism, dualism, monotheism, polytheism, pantheism, and indeed Hinduism is a great storehouse of all kinds of religious experiments.
K.M. SEN

Hindus are so cheerfully diverse, so insistent that religious ways are many, that only vast and distorting oversimplification could predicate that their diversity and their ways is (I say 'ways is' to enforce my point) true or false. No Hindu has said

Many Buddhists spend a number of years as monks, living in austerity.

**anything that some other
Hindu has not contradicted.**
WILFRED CANTWELL-SMITH

Buddhism similarly believes that
man is incapable of
understanding Reality with his
intellect, because it is
unknowable:

**As between the theist and
atheist positions, Buddhism is
atheistic, but it would be more
correct to say that it analyses
the complex of conflicting
ideas comprised in the term
God with the same
dispassionate care as it
analyses the so-called soul.
Such analysis, which all are
pressed to make for
themselves, proves, say
Buddhists, that the Western
ideas are inaccurate and
inadequate. The Buddhist
teaching on God, in the sense
of an ultimate Reality, is
neither agnostic, as is
sometimes claimed, nor vague,
but clear and logical. Whatever
Reality may be, it is beyond the
conception of the finite
intellect; it follows that
attempts at description are
misleading, unprofitable, and
waste of time. For these good
reasons the Buddha
maintained about Reality 'a
noble silence'. If there is a
Causeless Cause of all Causes,
an Ultimate Reality, a
Boundless Light, an Eternal
Noumenon behind phenomena,
it must clearly be infinite,
unlimited, unconditioned and
without attributes. We, on the
other hand, are clearly finite,
and limited and conditioned by,
and in a sense composed of,
innumerable attributes. It
follows that we can neither
define, describe, nor usefully
discuss the nature of THAT
which is beyond the
comprehension of our finite
consciousness. It may be
indicated by negatives and
described indirectly by
analogy and symbols, but**

*Buddhist doctrine is likened to a raft which can carry us across the ocean of the
world of suffering to salvation beyond.*

**otherwise it must ever remain
in its truest sense unknown
and unexpressed, as being to
us in our present state
unknowable.**
CHRISTMAS HUMPHREYS

ARNOLD TOYNBEE, the famous
historian (1889–1975), illustrates
how the understanding of truth
found in the Eastern religions has
become more popular in the
West:

**Since I do not believe in a
personal god, I don't have a
vested interest in any one
religion ... Although, of
course, I can't get away from
my Judaeo-Christian
background, temperamentally I
am a Hindu. As a Hindu, I don't
have any difficulty in believing
in many gods simultaneously,
or thinking that a syncretist
faith may be the answer for our
age. To Hindus, it's of no
consequence which road, Siva
or Vishnu, one travels—all
roads lead to heaven.**

WILFRED CANTWELL-SMITH is
under the same kind of influence

when he suggests that we must
give up asking the question 'Is
Christianity true or false?'
because it cannot be answered.
Instead we should ask the
question 'Is *my* Christianity true?
Can this belief *become true* to
me?' What we must search for is:

**... a new type of answer;
neither a simple 'yes' nor a
simple 'no' but some *tertium
quid*, more subtle, more
complex, tentative, yet to be
hammered out.**
    **There is so much diversity
and clash, so much chaos, in
the Christian Church today that
the old ideal of a unified or
systematic Christian truth has
gone. For this, the ecumenical
movement is too late. What has
happened ... is that the
Christian world has moved into
that situation where the Hindu
has long been: of open variety,
of optional alternatives. It
would seem no longer possible
for anyone to be told, or even
to imagine that he can be told,
what it means or should mean,
formally and generically, to be**

This determines his status in the next life which may be that of a god, a Brahman, an outcaste, a woman, a dog, a plant, and so on. Once again he is caught up in the round of desire, action and consequences, as the water in the water-wheel is passed from one plate to the next, and finds no release.

This doctrine gives an easy explanation for all the differences in human life. Bad and good fortune, health or sickness, poverty or riches, are all ascribed to *karma*. Not only every calamity of the world, but the caste system itself is explained by this doctrine. It also accounts to a great extent for the pessimism found in Hindus today, and largely explains the apparent callousness towards suffering. A man's moral and spiritual state are not really under his control since it is the result of a former life.

LESSLIE NEWBIGIN points out that these attitudes have very practical and far-reaching consequences:

It cannot be denied that the main thrust of the teaching of the ancient Asian religions has been away from a concern to change the world. Their dominant teaching has been that the wise man is he who seeks to be content with the world, to be released from attachment to it, but not to seek to change it. The idea of total welfare for all men as a goal to be pursued within history is foreign to the Asian religions, and modern Indian writers such as Sarma and Pannikar have no hesitation in acknowledging that, so far as India is concerned, it is part of the western invasion of the last few centuries.

a Christian. He must decide for himself—and only for himself.

He even makes the breath-taking assertion that Christians in the past never really claimed that Christianity was *true*.

I have urged the personalist quality of religious life as of ultimate significance, over against the abstract system ... It is a surprisingly modern aberration for anyone to think that Christianity is true or that Islam is—since the Enlightenment, basically, when Europe began to postulate religions as intellectualist systems, patterns of doctrine, so that they could for the first time be labelled 'Christianity' and 'Buddhism', and could be called true or false. Earlier this was not so. No classical Christian theologian, I have discovered, ever said that Christianity is true.

ARTHUR KOESTLER spells out some of the implications of this view of truth:

Behind the curtain there is the magic world of double-think. 'Ugly is beautiful, false is true, and also conversely.' This is not Orwell; it was written in all seriousness by the late Professor Suzuki, the foremost propounder of modern Zen, to illustrate the principle of the identity of opposites ... Facts and arguments which succeed in penetrating the outer defences are processed by the dialectical method until 'false' becomes 'true', tyranny the true democracy, and a herring a racehorse.

WHAT SHOULD BE OUR ATTITUDE TO SUFFERING?

G.T. MANLEY shows how the Hindu doctrine of *karma* (merit) explains common attitudes to suffering:

A man's life consists of actions, good and bad, each bearing fruit, and when he dies there is an accumulation of *karma*, merit and demerit, remaining to be worked off.

In Hinduism, the family is the most important religious group. Most ceremonies and rituals take place in the family.

IS THERE ANY DIFFERENCE ULTIMATELY BETWEEN GOOD AND EVIL?

In the Eastern way of thinking there is ultimately no difference between good and evil; they are purely relative.

RADHAKRISHNAN, writing about Hinduism:

Evil, error and ugliness are not ultimate. Evil has reference to the distance which good has to traverse. Ugliness is half-way to beauty. Error is a stage on the road to truth. They have all to be outgrown. No view is so utterly erroneous, no man is so absolutely evil as to deserve complete castigation ... In a continuously evolving universe evil and error are inevitable, though they are gradually diminishing.

CHRISTMAS HUMPHREYS, writing about Buddhism:

Nothing can be manifested in a finite world without its opposite. Light implies darkness, else it would not be known as light, and breathing could not be sustained unless we breathed both in and out. Like the double action of the human heart, the heartbeat of the universe implies duality, a cosmic pulse, an alternation of in-breathing and out-breathing, of manifestation and rest. To the Buddhist good and evil are relative and not absolute terms. The cause of evil is man's inordinate desires for self. All action directed to selfish separative ends is evil; all which tends to union is good.

JUDAISM

Judaism is based on the teaching of the Old Testament as it has been interpreted within the Jewish community over the centuries.

● The Jewish understanding of *God*, therefore, has a great deal in common with Christian beliefs.

Jew and Christian agree on certain essential characteristics of God ... A working basis of the doctrine of God, acceptable at least in outline to either faith, may be posited as follows. *God is One and unique, eternally existing, endowed with limitless power and knowledge, present throughout His creation, throned in unimaginable transcendent splendour, yet close to every creature, supreme in His decrees, righteous, just, holy and merciful.*
ROY A. STEWART

● Its understanding of *man* tends to be more optimistic about man's condition than Christianity. It denies that the individual inherits a sinful nature:

The divine relationship with man is indestructible. It can be strained or marred but cannot be severed entirely and broken beyond repair, not even by transgression and sin ... If by erring from the right path man yields to temptation and lapses into sin, regret and penitence can repair the ravages of his sin and restore perfect harmony to this relationship.
Judaism rejects the idea of human proneness to sin. A

natural tendency to evil would be a contradiction to the fundamental command of holiness, a contradiction to the holiness of God which man is called upon to reproduce in himself ... Sin lieth at the door, not within man himself, and this is followed by 'and thou shalt rule over him'.
ISIDORE EPSTEIN

● It has its own doctrine of *salvation*:

The initiative in atonement is with the sinner. He cleanses himself on the Day of Atonement by fearless self-examination, open confession, and the resolve not to repeat the transgressions of the past year. When our Heavenly Father sees the abasement of the penitent sinner, He sprinkles, as it were, the clean waters of pardon and forgiveness upon him.
On the Day of Atonement the Israelites resemble the angels, without human wants, without sins, linked together in love and peace. It is the only day of the year on which the accuser Satan is silenced before the throne of Glory, and even becomes the defender of Israel ... The closing prayer begins: 'Thou givest a hand to transgressors, and Thy right hand is stretched out to receive the penitent. Thou hast taught us to make confession unto Thee of all our sins, in order that we may cease from the violence of our hands and may return unto Thee who delightest in the repentance of the wicked.' These words

contain what has been called 'the Jewish doctrine of salvation'.
J.H. HERTZ

WHAT IS THE BASIS FOR MORALITY IN JUDAISM?
The moral values of Judaism are derived, with varying strictness, from the Old Testament law. In many cases they differ from Christian values because they are affected by Judaism's more optimistic diagnosis of man's present condition.

The Christian view of sin and atonement is sterner, more realistic, and more inward than the Jewish one. Its outward rules are fewer, less related to specific circumstance, centred in greater measure in the intangible realm of the human heart—which makes its canons loftier and more difficult for the observer. Much of what the Christian regards as sin might be re-defined as insufficiency of love, God-ward or manward ... It follows from this that a Jew may sometimes feel a satisfaction with his life and conduct which is impossible for the Christian ... If ever a Jew looks for some divine reward for his virtues, a Christian can look only for divine pardon for his sins.
ROY A. STEWART

HERBERT DANBY, writing about an article by Ahad ha-Am (Asher Ginsberg), a Jewish writer, points out some of the differences between Jewish and Christian ethics:

The Christian 'golden rule' is 'Do unto others what you would that men should do unto you.' Judaism has the same, or what seems to be the same rule in the negative form: 'What is hateful to thyself, do not do unto thy neighbour.' And Ahad ha-Am believes that in these two forms lies the ethical difference in the two religions:

egotism is the mark of Jewish ethics; but Christian altruism, he insists, is merely inverted egotism, the substitution of *other* for *self*.

Ahad ha-Am is not content to leave the matter at that. To make an apparently abstruse point clear as daylight he quotes the following case from the Talmud:

Imagine two men travelling in the desert; only one of them has a bottle of water; if both drink they will both die before their journey's end; if only one drinks he will reach safety, but his companion will certainly die. What should the man with the bottle of water do? Rabbi Akiba decided,(and Ahad ha-Am fully agrees that the decision counts as a fundamental principle of Jewish morality)—R. Akiba decided that the man with the water should keep it and drink it all himself; because *both* of them could not survive, it is more *just*, more in accord with God's righteousness, that a man should save himself rather than that he should save his neighbour and so lose his own life. Other things being equal, says Jewish morality, you have no right to assume that your neighbour's affairs are of more worth in God's eyes than your own affairs. Certainly Judaism approves of the laying down of life to fulfil a religious ideal (sanctification of the name of God, martyrdom); but it condemns the man who will suppress himself for the sake of his fellow. Christianity, on the contrary, teaches: 'Greater love hath no man than this, that a man lay down his life for his friends.'

Ahad ha-Am maintains that this, the basic difference between Jewish and Christian ethics, shows the superiority of Jewish ethics, in that it replaces the illogical Christian doctrine of self-sacrifice, self-renunciation, by the *absolute rule of justice*.

CAN WE LOOK AGAIN AT JESUS OF NAZARETH?

One of the biggest problems affecting discussion between Christians and Jews is that the Christian church has such a bad record in its dealing with Jews in the past.

If, however, there is a willingness for the Christian to admit 'both we and our fathers have sinned' (Psalm 106:6) it may be possible to look again at the figure of Jesus, and see how he fulfils the hopes and longings of the Old Testament. (See section 6: Focussing on Jesus of Nazareth.)

At the festival of Passover, Jews recall how God delivered them from slavery in Egypt.

ISLAM

With a world-wide community of between 700 and 800 million Muslims, Islam is now the second largest world religion.

Islam regards Muhammad (AD 560–632) as the last and greatest of the prophets sent by God. After working for several years as a merchant in Arabia, Muhammad believed that God was calling him to be a prophet. The revelations that came to him between that time and his death were recorded and collected in the *Qur'an*. During his lifetime he united all the tribes of Arabia in the worship of the One God, and within a century of his death Islam had spread throughout the Middle East, across North Africa and into Spain, and as far as Persia.

THE MUSLIM UNDERSTANDING OF GOD

The *Qur'an* lays great emphasis on the oneness of God, his transcendence and power, and his lordship over the whole universe:

Allah: there is no god but Him, the Living, the Eternal One. Neither slumber nor sleep overtakes Him. His is what the heavens and the earth contain. Who can intercede with Him except by His permission? He knows what is before and behind men. They can grasp only that part of His knowledge which He wills. His throne is as vast as the heavens and the earth, and the preservation of both does not weary Him. He is the Exalted, the Immense One.

He is Allah, besides whom there is no other god. He is the Sovereign Lord, the Holy One, the Giver of Peace, the Keeper of Faith; the Guardian, the Mighty One, the All-powerful, the Most High! Exalted be He above their idols! He is Allah, the Creator, the Originator, the Modeller. His are the most gracious names. All that is in heaven and earth gives glory to Him. He is the Mighty, the Wise One.

THE *QUR'AN* HAS MUCH TO SAY ABOUT THE DIGNITY OF MAN AS GOD'S CREATURE

Your Lord said to the angels: 'I am creating man from clay. When I have fashioned him and breathed of My Spirit into him, kneel down and prostrate yourselves before him.

The angels all prostrated themselves except Satan, who was too proud, for he was an unbeliever.

'Satan,' said Allah, 'why do you not bow to him whom My own hands have made? Are you too proud, or do you think he is beneath you?'

Satan replied: 'I am nobler than he. You created me from fire, but him from clay.'

... your Lord said to the angels: 'I am placing on the earth one that shall rule as My deputy' ...

ISLAM HAS ITS OWN UNDERSTANDING OF SALVATION

According to Islam, every child is born innocent and free from any sin whatever. Man neither inherits sin nor is he responsible for the sins of evil done by others.

'And no burdened soul can bear another's burden' (Qur'an 35:18). This is not only a question of justice, but such a concept of man as a responsible being implies also *human freedom and dignity*.

'And that man hath only that for which he makes effort.

And that this effort will be seen.' (Qur'an 53:39–40)

For instance, it was solely Adam's responsibility to expiate for the error of his disobedience. Moreover, the Qur'an teaches that Adam did pray for pardon and was forgiven. This is consistent with the very concept of God and His predominant attributes: Mercy and Forgiveness. God the Almighty, who is the Creator and Sustainer of all the universe, is also *the final authority to grant forgiveness*, of which He is the Source.

Moreover, God who created man and is aware of his weakness, never rejects sincere repentance and prayers for forgiveness, such as Adam requested.

According to Islam, man should appreciate his dignity as a responsible being, stand on his own feet, and work out his own salvation through God's guidance, for no one can act on behalf of another or intercede between God and Man.

'And when My servants ask you (Muhammad) concerning Me, I am indeed close (to them): I answer the prayer of the suppliant when he calls to Me. So let them hear My call and let them trust in Me, in order that they may be led aright.' (Qur'an 2:186)
BASIC PRINCIPLES OF ISLAM

IS THERE ANY POINT OF CONTACT BETWEEN GOD AND MAN?

When there is so much emphasis on the 'otherness' of God and the complete difference between God and his creatures, it becomes difficult to see what man has in common with God:

In ... setting man as it were face to face with God, without any mediating spiritual or personal elements, Islam necessarily emphasised the contrast between them. In spite of the passages of mystical intuition in the Koran, the dogmatic derived from it could not but start from the postulate of the opposition between God and man, and (as a necessary corollary) the equality of all men in their creaturely relation to God. In this stark contrast lies the original tension of Islam.
H.A.R. GIBB

Even when we use human language about God and say that he is wise or good, we have to recognize that God is so totally different from man, that these words do not mean the same when they are applied to God. Muhammad Abduh was a famous Muslim apologist in Egypt in the nineteenth century, who reaffirmed traditional teaching of Muslim theology regarding the 'attributes' of God:

The orthodox position ... is reaffirmed: although they may be similar in name to attributes and qualities ascribed to human beings, they are in reality not the same in nature. 'God does not resemble any of His creatures, and there is no relation between them and Him, except that He is the one who brought them into existence, and they belong to Him and will return to Him.'
C.C. ADAMS

IS IT POSSIBLE TO KNOW GOD?

One result of this emphasis on the sovereignty of God is that it is very difficult to establish any point of contact between God and man, and God can hardly be known.

AL-JUNAYD, the ninth-century mystic:

No one knows God save God Himself Most High, and therefore even to the best of His creatures He has only revealed His names in which He hides himself.

This kind of agnosticism about the nature of God has led many Muslims to move towards the mystical faith of the Sufis. Much of the teaching of Sufism, instead of being rejected as heretical, has been accepted into the mainstream of Islamic thought.

REYNOLD NICHOLSON, writing about the *Qur'an*:

Are there any germs of mysticism to be found there (in the Koran)? The Koran ... starts with the notion of Allah, the One, Eternal, and Almighty God, far above human feelings and aspirations—the Lord of His slaves, not the Father of His children; a judge meting out stern justice to sinners, and extending His mercy only to those who avert His wrath by repentance, humility, and unceasing works of devotion; a God of fear rather than of love. This is one side, and certainly the most prominent side, of Mohammed's teaching; but while he set an impassable gulf between the world and Allah, his deeper instinct craved a direct revelation from God to the soul. There are no contradictions in the logic of feeling. Mohammed, who had in him something of the mystic, felt God both as far and near, both as transcendent and immanent. In the latter aspect, Allah is the light of the heavens and the earth, a Being who worked in the world and in the soul of man.

Writing about the development of Islamic theology, he says:

The champions of orthodoxy had set about constructing a system of scholastic philosophy that reduced God's nature to a purely formal, changeless, and absolute unity, a bare will devoid of all affections and emotions, a tremendous and incalculable power with which no human creature could have any communion or personal intercourse whatsoever. That is the God of Mohammedan theology. That was the alternative to Sufism. Therefore, 'all thinking, religious Moslems are mystics,' as Professor D. B. Macdonald, one of our best authorities on the subject, has remarked. And he adds: 'All, too, are pantheists, but some do not know it.'

WHAT IS THE SIGNIFICANCE OF THE INDIVIDUAL BEFORE GOD?

The *Qur'an* stresses that every individual stands alone before God on the Day of Judgement:

There is none in the heavens or the earth but shall return to Him in utter submission. He has kept strict count of all His creatures, and one by one they shall approach Him on the Day of Resurrection. Invoke no other god with Allah. There is no god but He. All things shall perish except Himself. His is the judgement, and to Him you shall return.

The emphasis on the sovereignty of God, however, is such that there is the danger of the individual being swallowed up in the presence of the all-powerful God. The individual may come to feel that he has no freedom, because all his actions have already been determined by God:

This is an admonition to all men: to those among you that have the will to be upright. Yet you cannot will except by the will of Allah, the Lord of the Creation.

In some forms of Sufism (Muslim mysticism) the sense of the individual is in danger of being lost completely:

Does personality survive in the ultimate union with God? If personality means a conscious existence distinct, though not separate, from God, the majority of advanced Moslem mystics say 'No!' As the rain-drop absorbed in the ocean is not annihilated but ceases to exist individually, so the disembodied soul becomes indistinguishable from the universal Deity.
R.A. NICHOLSON

HOW CAN WE KNOW IF THE *QUR'AN* IS THE WORD OF GOD?
Muslims in the past have assumed that the *Qur'an* is the word of God. The impact of modern ways of thinking, however, is likely to make more and more people ask the question, 'How can I know if the *Qur'an* is the word of God?'

Muslims do not read the Qur'an and conclude that it is divine; rather, they believe that it is divine, and then they read it.
   The Muslim world, also, is moving into what may possibly become a profound crisis, too; in that it also is just beginning to ask this question, instead of being content only with answering it. Young people in Lahore and Cairo, labour leaders in Jakarta and Istanbul, are beginning to ask their religious thinkers, and beginning to ask themselves,

'Is the Qur'an the word of God?' Answering this question has been the business of the Muslim world for over thirteen centuries. Asking it is a different matter altogether, haunting and ominous.
W. CANTWELL-SMITH

The Muslim believes that God has revealed something of himself in the universe and in the nature of man. But if one asks, 'How can I know if the *Qur'an* is the word of God, a true revelation from God?' these are the kind of answers which the *Qur'an* itself gives:

● Muhammad performed no miracles to prove the truth of his claim to be a prophet. When challenged to produce his credentials, he simply pointed to the unique character of the *Qur'an* itself. The very fact of the *Qur'an* itself is therefore sufficient evidence that it is a true revelation from God.

They ask: 'Why has no sign been given him by his Lord?' Say: 'Signs are in the hands of Allah. My mission is only to give plain warning.'
   Is it not enough for them that We have revealed to you the Book for their instruction? Surely in this there is a blessing and an admonition to true believers.

This book is not to be doubted. It is a guide to the righteous, who have faith in the unseen and are steadfast in prayer; who bestow in charity a part of what We give them; who trust what has been revealed to you and to others before you, and firmly believe in the life to come . . .
   If you doubt what We have revealed to Our Servant, produce one chapter comparable to this book. Call upon your idols to assist you, if what you say be true. But if you fail (as you are sure to fail) then

guard yourselves against that fire whose fuel is men and stones prepared for the unbelievers.

● Belief and unbelief depend so entirely upon the will of Allah that if he wills a person to believe, he will believe, without any signs. The *Qur'an* does not seem to admit the possibility that the unbeliever, or even the believer, may have honest doubts and want to ask, 'How can I be sure if it is true?'

The unbelievers ask: 'Why has no sign been given him by his Lord?'
   Say: 'Allah leaves in error whom He will, and guides those who repent and have faith; whose hearts find comfort in the remembrance of Allah. Surely in the remembrance of Allah all hearts are comforted.'

● The punishment for unbelief is hell. The threat of hell should bring us to our senses and persuade us to believe.

Those who dispute our revelations shall know that they have no escape.
   He has revealed to you the Book with the truth, confirming the scriptures which preceded it; for He has already revealed the Torah and the Gospel for the guidance of men, and the distinction between right and wrong.
   Those that deny Allah's revelations shall be sternly punished; Allah is mighty and capable of revenge.
   When Our clear revelations are recited to them, the unbelievers say: 'This is plain magic.' Such is their description of the truth when it is declared to them.
   Do they say: 'He has invented it himself'?
Say: 'If I have indeed invented it, then there is nothing that you can do to save me from Allah's wrath. He well knows

Communal prayer is led by a mullah. *In Islam the idea of community is of great importance.*

what you say about it. He is our all-sufficient witness. He is the Benignant One, the Merciful.'

Say: 'I am no prodigy among the apostles; nor do I know what will be done with me or you. I follow only what is revealed to me, and my only duty is to give plain warning.'

Say: 'Think if this Koran is indeed from Allah and you reject it; if an Israelite has vouched for its divinity and accepted Islam, while you yourselves deny it with scorn. Truly Allah does not guide the wrongdoers.'

The appropriate response, therefore, is simply to listen and obey.

When you do not recite to them a revelation they say: 'Have you not yet invented one?' Say: 'I follow only what is revealed to me by my Lord. This Book is a veritable proof from your Lord, a guide and a blessing to true believers.'

When the Koran is recited, listen to it in silence so that Allah may show you mercy.

It is He who has revealed to you the Koran. Some of its verses are precise in meaning—they are the foundation of the Book—and others ambiguous. Those whose hearts are infected with disbelief follow the ambiguous part, so as to create dissension by seeking to explain it. But no one knows its meaning except Allah. Those who are well-grounded in knowledge say: 'We believe in it: it is from our Lord. But none takes heed except the wise. Lord, do not cause our hearts to go astray after You have guided us.'

When we raise this question of the truth of the revelation in the *Qur'an*, the authoritarianism of Islam leads in practice to reactions of this kind: either

1. a blind and unquestioning acceptance of the *Qur'an*; or

2. an intellectual scepticism about God, combined with a limited practice of the Muslim way of life; or

3. a total rejection of Islamic beliefs about God and the supernatural; or

4. a mysticism which enables the Muslim to bypass or transcend certain intellectual problems.

WHAT IS THE BASIS OF THE MORAL LAW?

The moral law for man cannot be based on the character of God— what he *is* by nature. It has to be based on the commands or decrees of God. And the Five Pillars of Islam express the most important things in the life of the Muslim: Recital of the Creed, Prayer, Fasting, Almsgiving, Pilgrimage.

It is these Five Pillars, and particularly the profession of the Creed and the performance of prayer and fasting, which

chiefly make up the practice of Islam to the average Muslim. He who acknowledges the Unity and Transcendence of God, pays Him His due in prayer and fast, and accepts Muhammed as the last and greatest of the Prophets, may well, indeed, have to taste the Fire, but hopes that he will not, like the infidel, remain in it for ever—through the timely intercession of the Prophet. The most heinous sins are polytheism, apostasy, scepticism and impiety, besides which social sins and all subtler forms of evil pale into comparative insignificance.
J.N.D. ANDERSON

The word 'holy' is applied to God, but it occurs only once in the *Qur'an*:

He is Allah, besides whom there is no other god. He is the Sovereign Lord, the Holy One, the Giver of Peace, the Keeper of Faith, the Guardian, the Mighty One, the All-Powerful, the Most High! Exalted be He above their idols!

This holiness, however, is not defined in terms of moral purity or perfection, but in terms of transcendence:
    BEIDHAWI, the great Muslim commentator on the *Qur'an* of the thirteenth century wrote:

Holy means the complete absence of anything that would make Him less than He is.

AL-GHAZZALI wrote in this way in the twelfth century about the justice of God:

Allah's justice is not to be compared with the justice of men. For a man may be supposed to act unjustly by invading the possession of another, but no injustice can be conceived on the part of God. It is in His power to pour down upon men torments, and if He

were to do it, His justice could not be arraigned. Yet he rewards those that worship Him for their obedience on account of His promise and beneficence, not of their merit or of necessity, since there is nothing which He can be tied to perform; nor can any injustice be supposed in Him nor can He be under any obligation to any person whatsoever.

WHAT IS LOVE?
Another consequence of the Islamic belief about God is that God's attitude towards man tends to be defined in terms of compassion and mercy, rather than of love. These, for example, are some of the Ninety Nine Names of God: The Merciful; the Compassionate, the Forgiver, the Forgiving; the Clement, the Generous, the Affectionate, the Kind.
    If the Muslim ever speaks about the love of God, he thinks not so much of God's love for man, as man's love for God, as the response which is aroused by contemplating the attributes of God.
    AHMAD GALWASH, a contemporary apologist:

Rightly to understand the love of God is so difficult a matter that one sect of philosophers have altogether denied that man can love a being who is not of his own species, and they have defined the love of God as consisting merely in obedience to Him. But this is not true ... The following prayer was taught by the Arabian Prophet to his followers: '*O God, grant me to love Thee and to love those who love Thee, and whatsoever brings me nearer to Thy love, and make Thy love dearer to me than cold water to the thirsty traveller in the desert.*' ...
    We now come to treat love in its essential nature,

according to the spiritual Muslim conception. Love may be defined as an inclination to that which is pleasant.

The Muslim is probably forced to speak of the mercy and compassion of God rather than the love of God because love sounds too human a word to apply to God. One could also say that if God is one in the sense that the Muslim understands, it does not make sense, logically, to speak of love as being part of the character of God. Love by definition demands an object, unless it is to become self-love. And if there is no Trinity which allows a relationship of love between the three persons of the godhead, then the only possible object of the love of God can be the universe and man. But this makes it difficult to think of God as sufficient in himself and not dependent on the existence of the universe.

WHAT KIND OF LIFE AFTER DEATH CAN WE LOOK FORWARD TO?
The *Qur'an* emphatically agrees with Christianity that 'man's chief end is to glorify God ...':

I created mankind and the jinn [spirits] in order that they might worship Me.

Many passages speak of the hope of Paradise which is held out to believers:

For the unbelievers We have prepared fetters and chains, and a blazing fire. But the righteous shall drink of a cup tempered at the Camphor Fountain, a gushing spring at which the servants of Allah will refresh themselves: they who keep their vows and dread the far-spread terrors of Judgement-day; who for love of Allah give sustenance to the poor man, the orphan, and the captive, saying: 'We feed you for Allah's sake only; we seek

Prayer is an act of submission to Allah. The very word 'Islam' means 'submission'.

of you neither recompense nor thanks: for we fear from Him a day of anguish and of woe.'

Allah will deliver them from the evil of that day and make their countenance shine with joy. He will reward them for their steadfastness with robes of silk and the delights of Paradise. Reclining there upon soft couches, they shall feel neither the scorching heat nor the biting cold. Trees will spread their shade around them, and fruits will hang in clusters over them . . .

They shall be arrayed in garments of fine green silk and rich brocade, and adorned with bracelets of silver. Their Lord will give them a pure beverage to drink.

Thus you will be rewarded; your high endeavours are gratifying to Allah.

Many Muslims would not interpret passages such as these in a literal way. But when every allowance has been made for metaphor and symbol, the Muslim cannot hold out the hope of enjoying a personal relationship with God. He may point to the mystic's hope of union with God, but this has to be understood in terms of absorption into God. So that although he can speak of man's goal as being 'to glorify God', he cannot consistently add with the Christian, 'and to enjoy him for ever.'

WHAT IS THE MUSLIM ANSWER TO THE PROBLEM OF SUFFERING AND EVIL?

Islamic theology has tried to maintain a balance between its teaching about the predestination of God and its insistence on human responsibility. MUHAMMAD ABDUH, for example, outlined the orthodox teaching in this way:

Islam is the main religion of many countries in South-East Asia.

All . . . Muslim sects believe that they have a share of free choice in their actions which they call 'acquisition' (*kasb*), and this is the basis of reward and punishment in the opinion of all of them.

At the same time he admits that, in practice, this balance has not always been held:

We do not deny that in the thought of the common people in Muslim lands this article has been contaminated with traces of the belief in compulsion, and this perhaps has been the cause of some of the misfortunes that have befallen them in past generations.

The *Qur'an* presents the balance by saying that while everything, both good and evil, has been determined by the will of God, man is still held responsible before God:

Allah does not change a people's lot unless they change what is in their hearts. If he seeks to afflict them with a misfortune, none can ward it off. Besides Him, they have no protector.

Whatever good befalls you, man, it is from Allah: and whatever ill from yourself.

The crucial difference between Islam and Christianity over the question of suffering is that Islam has no place for a suffering Saviour. In the early years of his ministry, Muhammad experienced some success and a great deal of opposition and persecution. When he was invited to come from Mecca to Medina and lead the whole community, he saw this as an opportunity to establish the kind of society he was calling for. Instead of being a despised prophet, he was now both prophet and statesman, and believed that success in diplomacy and in war was a sign that God was establishing his kingdom on earth. Islam therefore finds it very difficult to accept the idea of suffering as having any place in the way God works (except in some of its forms—for example, Shiism). It has been said that Islam has a theology of *justice*, but has no theology of *suffering*.

TEN KEY THINKERS

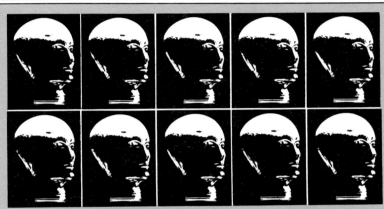

THOMAS AQUINAS

(c.1225–74)

Thomas Aquinas was an Italian friar who became the greatest Catholic theologian of the Middle Ages. He attempted to use many of the ideas of the Greek philosopher, Aristotle, and to work out a complete system of Christian theology.

The most important aspect of his thought which concerns us here is that he made a clear distinction between truths which could be deduced by *reason* (for example, the existence of God and the moral law), and truths which must be given by *revelation* (for example, the way of salvation):

It was necessary for man's salvation that there should be a doctrine revealed by God, besides the philosophical disciplines investigated by human reason . . . Hence it was necessary for the salvation of man that certain truths which exceed human reason should be made known to him by divine revelation. . .

Therefore, in order that the salvation of men might be brought about more fitly and more surely, it was necessary that they should be taught divine truths by divine revelation. It was therefore necessary that, besides the philosophical disciplines investigated by reason, there should be a sacred doctrine by way of revelation.

Thomas Aquinas

Although those things which are beyond man's knowledge may not be sought for by man through his reason, nevertheless, what is revealed by God must be accepted through faith.

This distinction, which seems relatively insignificant in itself was to have far-reaching consequences, because it came to be accepted as a basic assumption of Western thought throughout the Renaissance in the fourteenth century and the Enlightenment in the eighteenth century. It was

Aquinas who formulated the so-called 'proofs' for the existence of God. His many writings have been described as 'the highest achievement of medieval theological systematization and the accepted basis of modern Roman Catholic theology'.

RENE DESCARTES

(1596–1650)

René Descartes, a French philosopher, has been called 'the father of modern philosophy'. His two important works, *Discourse on Method* (1637) and *Meditations* (1641), marked a new departure in European thought, because they concentrated on the consciousness of the individual as the source and criterion of truth. This was the starting point of European rationalism.

His method of reaching truth was by systematic doubt:

My first rule was to accept nothing as true which I did not clearly recognize to be so; to accept nothing more than what was presented to my mind so clearly and distinctly that I could have no occasion to doubt it.

One thing, however, which he could not doubt was his own existence:

Cogito, ergo sum. I think, therefore I am.

He was also aware that he was finite. And if he was finite, this

René Descartes

implied that there must be an infinite Being. He himself was aware that he was imperfect, and this awareness implied that a perfect Being must exist.

It is inconceivable that God should deceive us by giving us ideas of this kind if they are not true. Therefore God must exist.

His principle of systematic doubt made him question even the existence of the external universe. The only way in which he could solve the problem for himself was to say that we all feel that the material world really exists outside of ourselves. And it

is inconceivable that God should give us this feeling if it is not in accordance with the truth, since God would not deceive us. Therefore, the external world must exist.

Descartes thus uses God as a guarantee that the universe exists.

This is how HANNAH AREND sums up the dilemma of the agnostic in the modern world, which is part of the legacy which we have inherited from Descartes:

Descartes' philosophy is haunted by two nightmares which in a sense became the nightmares of the whole modern age, not because this age was so deeply influenced by Cartesian philosophy, but because their emergence was almost inescapable once the true implications of the modern world view were understood. These nightmares are very simple and very well known. In the one, reality, the reality of the world as well as of human life, is doubted; if neither the senses nor common sense nor reason can be trusted, then it may well be that all that we take for reality is only a dream. The other concerns the general human condition as it was revealed by the new discoveries and the impossibility for man to trust his senses and his reason.

JOHN LOCKE

(1632–1704)

John Locke was an English philosopher who, instead of following the rationalism of Descartes and others on the continent, redeveloped the school of philosophy known as empiricism. This approach to knowledge emphasizes that it is not just reason but experience which plays an important part in all knowledge. One of his most influential books was *An Essay Concerning Human Understanding* (1690). The following are some of the basic ideas of his philosophy:

● The mind is like a blank piece of paper which receives all its impressions from outside. It is like 'white paper void of all characters, without any ideas':

In bare naked perception the mind is, for the most part, merely passive.

● All human knowledge is either '*ideas*' (which are impressions on the mind from external objects—such as yellow, white, heat, cold, soft, hard, bitter, sweet, and all those which we call sensible qualities) or the *reflection* of the mind on these ideas.

Human knowledge therefore hath no other immediate object but its own ideas.

● Reason and faith are totally different:

Reason is the discovery of the certainty or probability of such propositions or truths, which the mind arrives at by deduction made from such *ideas*, which it has got by the use of its natural faculties, *viz.* by sensation or reflection.

Faith, on the other hand, is the assent to any proposition not thus made out by the deductions of reason, but upon the credit of the proposer, as coming from God, in some extraordinary way of communication. This way of discovering truths to men we call *Revelation*.

John Locke

As an example of a truth of reason, he gives the existence of God.

The works of nature everywhere sufficiently evidence a Deity.

The existence of God is 'the most obvious truth that reason discovers'; 'its evidence,' he says, is 'equal to mathematical certainty'. The existence of one God is according to reason; the existence of more than one God contrary to reason; the resurrection of the dead, above reason.

● Any truth of revelation must be tested by truths of reason. If it does not contradict what we know by reason, then it can be accepted. But if it does, it must be rejected. Revelation must be totally subordinated to reason:

Revelation is natural *reason* enlarged by a new set of discoveries communicated by God immediately, which *reason* vouches the truth of by the testimony and proofs that they come from God.
    No principle can be received for divine revelation, or obtain the assent due to such, if it be contrary to our clear intuitive knowledge.

This is how two writers describe the revolutionary impact of Locke's philosophy:

John Locke epitomized the intellectual outlook of his own age and shaped that of the next. For over a century he dominated European thought ... The spirit in which he dealt with Christianity is more important than what he actually said about it. He made a certain attitude to religious faith almost universal.
G.R. CRAGG

Locke it was who turned the attention of thinkers to psychological truths, truths present in the mind, living, constant, and indefectible ...
    An Essay concerning Human Understanding. Whatever may be said of it by those who care only for the high flights of philosophy, the date marks a definite change, a new orientation. Henceforth man's sphere of exploration was the mind of man and its unfathomable riches. Let us

have done, said Locke, with these metaphysical conjectures; do we not realize how fruitless they are? Are we not tired of asking and always asking in vain? ...

The certitude which we need resides in the mind. Let us look therein and cease to probe those infinite spaces which do but breed deceiving visions; thereon let us concentrate our attention. Clearly recognizing that our understanding is limited, let us accept its limitations ... Putting aside the hope of attaining any perfect and absolute knowledge of the things around us as something beyond the range of finite beings, let us content ourselves with being what we are, with doing what we can, and with knowing what we can know.
PAUL HAZARD

The influence of ideas of this kind are clearly seen in the *American Declaration of Independence* of 1776:

We hold these truths to be self-evident, that all men are created equal, and that they are endowed by their Creator with certain inalienable rights ...

DAVID HUME
(1711–76)

David Hume was a Scottish philosopher who could well be described as the father of modern scepticism. He questioned not only traditional Christian beliefs (for example, miracles), but also basic assumptions which most of us take for granted (for example, the principle of cause and effect) and held that:

● We perceive the data of our senses; and we cannot hope to go beyond our senses or to know anything beyond what they tell us.

Let us fix our attention out of ourselves as much as possible: let us chase our imagination to the heavens, or to the utmost limits of the universe; we never really advance a step beyond ourselves, nor can we conceive any kind of existence, but those perceptions, which have appear'd in that narrow compass. This is the universe of the imagination, nor have we any idea by what is there produc'd.

● The idea that every like cause produces a like effect is a product of our own thinking. It cannot be inferred from the data of our senses. If cause *a* always seems to produce effect *b*, we have no justification for saying that *a* has *caused b*, it is only habit or custom which makes us think that this is so. All that we are entitled to say is that *a* generally seems to be followed by *b*.

There is nothing in any object, considered by itself, which can afford us a reason for drawing a conclusion beyond it.

'Tis not, therefore, reason, which is the guide of life, but custom. That alone determines the mind, in all instances, to suppose the future conformable to the past. However easy this step may seem, reason would never, to all eternity, be able to make it.

● Hume believed that the idea of miracles violate the principle of the uniformity of natural causes, and must therefore be ruled out as impossible. He suggested that the greatest miracle is that one can believe.

● He realized that his questioning of everything could lead eventually to total scepticism. He therefore kept his philosophical ideas for his study, and enjoyed life as if he had no doubts at all:

Carelessness and inattention alone can afford us any remedy. For this reason I rely entirely upon them; and take it for granted, whatever may be the reader's opinion at this present moment, that an hour hence he will be persuaded there is both an external and an internal world.

Most fortunately it happens, that since reason is incapable of dispelling these clouds, Nature herself suffices to that purpose, and cures me of this philosophical melancholy and delirium, either by relaxing this bent of mind, or by some avocation and lively impression of my senses, which obliterate all these chimeras. I dine, I play a game of backgammon, I converse, and am merry with my friends; and when, after three or four hours' amusement, I would return to these speculations, they appear so cold, and strained and ridiculous, that I cannot find in my heart to enter into them any further.

Thus the sceptic still continues to reason and believe, though he asserts that he cannot defend his reason by reason, and by the same rule, he must assent to the principle concerning the existence of the body, though he cannot pretend by any argument of philosophy to maintain its veracity.

This is how two modern writers describe this obvious inconsistency in his philosophy:

Among great philosophers, Hume, who hung his nose as far as any over the nihilistic abyss, withdrew it sharply when he saw the psychological risks involved and advised dilution of metaphysics by playing backgammon and making merry with his friends. The conclusion of Hume's philosophising was indeed a radical scepticism, which left no convincing logical grounds for believing anything natural, let alone supernatural, was there at all, and he saved his 'reason' or, as we might say, his 'philosophical personality' ... by refusing to take the implications of his philosophy to heart.
KATHLEEN KNOTT

Peculiar people, psychologically, these scholars. They will set a fuse to the most daring ideas, apparently unaware or regardless of what they are doing. It is their successors who, in the fulness of time, realise the implications of their legacy. Meanwhile, they

David Hume

themselves still cling to tradition.
PAUL HAZARD

For some people in the twentieth century Hume's scepticism is not just a philosophical theory to imagine or to play with; it has become their own world-view. This is how the atmosphere of Sartre's novel *Nausèa* is described by COLIN WILSON:

In the Journal, we watch the breaking-down of all Roquentin's values. Exhaustion limits him more and more to the present, the here-now. The work of memory, which gives events sequence and coherence, is failing, leaving him more and more dependent for meaning on what he can see and touch. It is Hume's scepticism becoming instinctive, all destroying. All he can see and touch is unrecognizable, unaided by memory; like a photograph of a familiar object taken from an unfamiliar angle. He looks at a seat, and fails to recognize it: 'I murmur: It's a seat, but the

word stays on my lips. It refuses to go and put itself on the thing ... Things are divorced from their names. They are there, grotesque, stubborn, huge, and it seems ridiculous to call them seats, or to say anything at all about them. I am in the midst of things—nameless things.'

JEAN JACQUES ROUSSEAU

(1712–78)

This French philosopher laid great emphasis on the *heart* and the *emotions*, claiming that feeling is a much more reliable guide than reason:

Whatever I feel to be right is right. Whatever I feel to be wrong is wrong. The conscience is the best of all casuists ... Reason deceives us only too often and we have acquired the right to reject it only too well but conscience never deceives.

His book *The Social Contract* (1762) had a considerable influence and helped to pave the way for the French Revolution in 1789. These are three summaries of the significance of this development in the eighteenth century:

Jean-Jacques Rousseau

As the eighteenth century wore on, it was discovered that the 'Nature' of man was not his 'reason' at all, but his instincts, emotions and 'sensibilities', and what was more, people began to glory in this discovery, and to regard reason itself as an aberration from 'Nature'. *Cogito ergo sum* is superseded by *je sens, donc je suis* associated with Rousseau. Shaftesbury, Hutcheson, and Hume had prepared the way by proclaiming that our moral judgements, like our aesthetic judgements, are not the offspring of Reason at all but proceed from an inner sentiment or feeling which is unanalysable.
BASIL WILLEY

He stressed the part played by the emotions, not only in religion, but in literature, politics, and philosophy. He offered a broad and original treatment of all fields on the basis of his new sensibility. The result to a large extent of his work was the so-called Romantic Movement. This is the essential content of Rousseau, the 'outsider', who fathered the romantic sensibility and opposed it to the dominant rationalism of his time.
BRONOWSKI AND MAZLISH

By the 1760s the scientific and philosophical speculation of the Enlightenment seemed to have ended in an impasse.

Chance, or the blind determinism of matter in regular but aimless motion, appeared to regulate the operations of the universe and the destiny of man. If metaphysical speculation had any meaning at all—which the sceptics denied—it served merely to open a window on to the blank wall of necessity. A brilliant and inquisitive age was not likely to be content for long with such a prospect, and in response to the challenge new attitudes were evolved that transformed the terms in which men thought of themselves and of the order of the universe. One of the most significant of these attitudes ... was the acceptance of the heart as legitimate consort of the head. It is important ... to realize what this new assumption did *not* imply. To present it as a revolt against an age of arid intellectualism seems to me to betray extraordinary insensitivity towards the vigour of eighteenth-century life and the excitement of its speculative thought. What happened was not that the artist usurped the position formerly occupied by the scholar, but that both turned to the emotions for the guidance they had previously expected of their reason.

Sentiment came to be accepted as the source of a kind of knowledge to which intelligence could not aspire, and as the arbiter of action. But if feeling became pilot, reason remained in command, except for a few extremists whose shipwreck discouraged imitation. The definition of their respective roles could never be established with finality but there was no question of the elimination of reason. However dramatically this new attitude may have seemed to challenge the urbanity of the Enlightenment, both grew from a common stock and both were rooted in the same intellectual soil . . .

In so far as one can ascribe a definite starting-point to a change in attitude, the most appropriate date would be 1749, when Rousseau wrote his prize essay on the subject set by the Dijon Academy: *Whether the restoration of the arts and sciences has contributed to the refinement of morals.* In other words, the 'reaction' against the Enlightenment preceded most of the major works of the Enlightenment itself!
NORMAN HAMPSON

IMMANUEL KANT

(1724–1804)

Immanuel Kant was a German professor of philosophy who took the nationalism and empiricism of the eighteenth century one stage further, and profoundly influenced the philosophy of the nineteenth century.

He agreed with Hume and the empiricists in saying that 'all knowledge begins with experience'. He acknowledged his debt to Hume and said that it was the reading of his works which awoke him from his 'dogmatic slumbers'.

But at the same time, 'it does not follow that it all arises out of experience'. The mind also plays a part, and is therefore not a complete *tabula rasa*. In this he disagrees with Locke. The mind does not perceive things precisely as they are: it conditions everything it perceives.

He then asks: if this is the case, what are the proper limits of human thought and knowledge? And his answer is to make a distinction between *knowledge* which has to do with *phenomena* (everything that can be seen) and *faith* which has to do with *noumena* (truths beyond space and time). These are two completely different ways of knowing, and they are another

Immanuel Kant

example of the dichotomy which we have already seen in Aquinas and Locke.

FAITH
KNOWLEDGE

Faith is concerned with *noumena* above the line, truths beyond space and time, things 'in themselves', reality as it is, the truths of religion (such as the existence of God, free will, immortality). Knowledge, *phenomena*, is truth which can be perceived by the senses, that is through science, truth about the external world of space and time.

Because of this distinction, therefore, we must accept the fact that we cannot know anything for certain beyond our direct experience of this world. Religious beliefs have their origin in the moral consciousness, but they cannot be classed as knowledge. This limitation of knowledge ensures the possibility of religious faith, because it makes it impervious to the attacks of sceptics.

I have therefore found it necessary to deny *knowledge* to make room for *faith*.

GEORGE FREDERICK HEGEL

(1770–1831)

Hegel was also a German professor of philosophy. He is particularly important for us today because of the elements of his philosophy which were taken over by Karl Marx.

● For Hegel God is no longer to be thought of as a Personal Being distinct from the universe. His idea amounted to a kind of philosophical pantheism:

We define God when we say, that He distinguishes Himself from Himself, and is an object for Himself, but that in this distinction He is purely identical with Himself, is in fact Spirit. This notion or conception is now realised, consciousness knows this content and knows that it is itself absolutely interwoven with this content; in the Notion which is the process of God, it is itself a moment. Finite consciousness knows God only to the extent to which God knows Himself in it; thus God is Spirit, the Spirit of His Church in fact, i.e. of those who worship Him. This is the perfect religion, the Notion become objective to itself. Here it is revealed what God is; He is no longer a Being above and beyond this world, and Unknown, for He has told men what He is, and this is not merely in outward history, but in consciousness.

● Hegel accepted Kant's distinction between faith and knowledge.

● He thought of truth as the 'synthesis of opposing

viewpoints'. Nothing is true in any absolute sense. All that we can expect is that one idea (*thesis*) will be challenged by an opposite idea (*antithesis*), and that this will in turn be superseded by an idea which transcends the two contradictory ideas (*synthesis*). This means that in discussions about truth, the basic rule of logic no longer applies. For in the dialectical process, views which are mutually incompatible can be held together.

● The basic idea of his philosophy of 'idealism' is that *everything* (the natural world, history, religion, ideas, etc.) is to be understood in terms of 'Spirit'. Everything is to be seen as the Absolute Spirit of the universe becoming self-conscious:

G.F. Hegel

Spirit is alone Reality. It is the inner being of the world, that which essentially is, and is *per se*; it assumes objective, determinate form, and enters into relations with itself—it is externality (otherness), and exists for itself; yet in this determination, and in its otherness, it is still one with itself—it is self-contained and self-complete, in itself and for itself at once . . .

LEOPOLD SENGHOR, the West African philosopher and statesman, explains the significance of Hegel's dialectical philosophy which was later taken over by Karl Marx:

What, then, is dialectics? . . . Today, we define dialectics by opposing it to logic. Classical logic rests on three principles: identity (A is A); non-contradiction (A is not non-A); and exclusion (A cannot be A and not be A at the same time). Hegel, with Marx following in his footsteps, opposes these principles, and proposes in their stead the principles of dialectics, which are: contradiction, reciprocal action, and change. For Hegel, the dialectical process is composed of three steps: affirmation, negation, and conciliation. For Marx, it consists of 'position, opposition, composition . . . We have thesis, antithesis, and synthesis . . . (or) affirmation, negation, and negation of the negation'. But that is only the beginning. The synthesis or 'new idea' is developed 'in two contradictory thoughts that blend in turn into a new synthesis' or 'groups of thoughts'. This group, continuing the process and developing into two groups of contradictory thoughts, ends in a 'series of thoughts'. The entire series of ideas forms the 'system' or body of doctrine.

In classical philosophy, which used logic, things and their concepts are objective realities placed one beside the other without any link or communication, fixed once and for all, immutable essences. They oppose each other in irreducible antitheses. Modern philosophy is quite different, for dialectics is its favourite instrument.

The dialectician can say at the same time: 'A is A' and 'A is not A', or 'A is not B' and 'A is B'.

SØREN KIERKEGAARD

(1813–55)

In order to understand the thinking of this Danish philosopher, it is helpful to note some of the ideas of Blaise Pascal, the French mathematician and philosopher (1623–62), whose ideas have something in common with those of Kierkegaard:

1. Pascal made a distinction between 'the heart' which he describes as 'the intuitive spirit' and 'the reason' or 'mind' which he describes as 'the geometric spirit':

The heart has its reasons which are unknown to reason ... It is the heart which is aware of God and not reason. This is what faith is: God perceived intuitively by the heart, not by reason.

What he did was to erect a dualism of his own in which two realms existed: one of the heart and one of the mind. In religion, unlike Descartes, he applied the logic of the heart. In mathematics and physics, however, Pascal used the same geometry as did Descartes.
BRONOWSKI AND MAZLISH

2. He put forward the idea of 'The Wager': Christianity cannot be proved conclusively by the reason, but neither can it be disproved. If it turns out that Christianity is true, we have everything to gain; but if it turns out to be false, we have nothing to lose. We should accept the inevitable risk of faith, and gamble on the truth of Christianity.

This was the essential step of Pascal: that doubt leads to faith, because doubt makes it certain that there is no answer to the question of self-consciousness. The view of Pascal was that the answer to the epistemological question is—that there is no rational answer. We must simply place our bet on faith.
BRONOWSKI AND MAZLISH

Kierkegaard was very much of an individualist in his philosophy and, like Pascal, had no following during his lifetime. But during this century he has suddenly become popular, and has become the source not only of secular existentialism, but also of Christian existentialism.

He built his ideas on the position reached by Hume and Kant; i.e. he accepted the impossibility of finding certain knowledge through the senses. And he accepted Kant's distinction between *noumena* and *phenomena*. He was very conscious, however, that he was breaking completely new ground:

My task is so new that there is literally no one in the 1800 years of Christianity from whom I can learn how I should proceed.

His position and the direction his views have taken can be summed up as follows:

● There is no point in asking 'What is "the truth"?' because it is impossible to know the truth objectively. The question we must ask is 'What is the truth *for me*? How am *I* to live my life?'

The thing is to understand myself, to see what God really wishes *me* to do; the thing is to find a truth which is true *for me*, to find *the idea for which I can live and die*.

● Reasoning will lead us only to paradox; and historical enquiry leads only to probability, which is without value for faith.

If from such a point of view we enquire about the truth

objectively, then we see that truth is a *paradox*.

If the contemporary generation had left nothing behind them but these words: 'We believed that in such and such a year God appeared among us in our community, and finally died,' it would be more than enough. The contemporary generation would have done all that was necessary: for this little advertisement, this *nota bene* on a page of universal history, would be sufficient to afford an occasion for a successor, and the most voluminous account can in all eternity do nothing more.

On the title page of *Philosophical Fragments or a Fragment of Philosophy* he puts the question:

Is an historical point of departure possible for an eternal consciousness; how can such a point of departure have any other than a merely historical interest; is it possible to base an eternal happiness upon historical knowledge?

● Christian beliefs are absurd; they are an offence to the reason. Christian faith, therefore, means believing *against* the reason, *against* the understanding.

... the paradox (of the Christian faith) cannot and shall not be understood ... the task is to hold fast to this and to endure the crucifixion of the understanding.
    A believer who believes, i.e. believes against the understanding, takes the mystery of faith seriously and is not duped by the pretence of understanding.
    Here is such a definition of truth: *objective incertitude, clung to and appropriated with passionate inwardness, is truth*, the highest truth that there can be, *for one who exists.*

● The emphasis in faith is on the *will* rather than on the intellect:

Christianity, ... or becoming a Christian, has nothing to do with a change in the intellect— but in the will. But this change is the most painful of all operations, comparable to vivisection ... And because it is so terrible, becoming a Christian in Christendom has long since ... been transformed into a change of the intellect.

Faith therefore depends entirely on the choice of the will. It is a huge risk. It is a 'leap of faith'.

And so I say to myself: I choose; that historical fact means so much to me that I decide to stake my whole life upon it. Then he lives; lives entirely full of the idea of risking his life for it: and his life is the proof that he believes. He did not have a few proofs, and so believed and then began to live. No, the very reverse.
    That is called risking; and without risk faith is an impossibility. *To be related to spirit means to undergo a test*; to believe, to wish to believe, is to change one's life into a trial; daily test is the trial of faith.

Faith must be existential faith:

From the Christian point of view faith belongs to the existential; God did not appear in the character of a professor who has some doctrines which must first be believed and then understood.
    No, faith belongs to and has its home in the existential, and in all eternity it has nothing to do with knowledge as a comparative or a superlative.
    Faith expresses a relation from personality to personality.
    Personality is not a sum of doctrines, nor is it something directly accessible ...

Personality is that which is within ... it is that which is within to which a man, himself in turn a personality, may be related in faith. Between person and person no other relation is possible. Take the two most passionate lovers who have ever lived, and even if they are, as is said, one soul in two bodies, this can never come to anything more than that the one believes that the other loves him or her.
    In this purely personal relation between God as personal being and the believer as personal being, in *existence*, is to be found the concept of faith.
    (Hence the apostolic formula, 'the obedience of faith' (e.g. Romans 1:5), so that faith tends to the will and personality, not to intellectuality—marginal note.)

This is how HERBERT READ, the English art historian, sums up Kierkegaard's position regarding the nature of Christian faith:

'Faith expresses a relation from personality to personality ... In this purely personal relation between God as personal being and the believer as personal being, in *existence*, is to be found the concept of faith.' The whole of Kierkegaard's philosophy revolves round this axiom ...
    What one realizes, in reading these late extracts from the *Journals*, is the absolute intransigence of the egoism which Kierkegaard made the basis of his faith.

H.J. BLACKHAM, the English humanist philosopher, sums up his philosophy in this way:

In rejecting Christianity, Kierkegaard had perceived the discontinuity between faith and reason, and in rejecting speculative philosophy he retained this perception and built his position upon it. He made it the effort of his life to renew the meaning of Christianity by compelling recognition of the permanent cleavage between faith and reason . . .

Kierkegaard's argument deals with the object of Christian faith and the manner of apprehending it.

That a man born and living in history says that he is God and dies in humiliation plunges into a dilemma those who would build their lives on him and his word. Nothing has happened since to enlighten by one scruple the strain on belief. The historical success of Christianity is worthless evidence. The present generation is exactly in the position of the contemporaries of Christ who witness his humiliation on the cross. Faith today, unless it is faith in the faith of the Apostles, is not other than their faith in the man who makes the most absurd of claims. The truth of this claim cannot in the nature of the case be made objectively certain, or even investigated; on the contrary the absolute discontinuity between the human and the divine which inheres in the conception of God makes it unthinkable, so that it cannot by any human mind be recognized as true, cannot be entertained as a possibility . . . If a man claims to be God, then all that reason can do is to take notice of this claim and give special attention to all the circumstances attending to it. Inquiry into the authenticity of the evidence (itself never finally conclusive) is beside the point, however, for if the historical facts were established beyond cavil the enquirer would be no nearer to making up his mind what to make of them. The incarnation

Søren Kierkegaard

is a paradox which can never be thought nor accepted by reason, and therefore the claim that it is the supreme truth imposes a limit on thought and throws the enquirer into a passion of uncertainty. If, by the grace of God he sets reason and experience aside and joins himself to the paradox in the passion of faith, he is 'out upon the deep, over 70,000 fathoms of water' and risks everything. The decision to take the risk cannot bring certainty. The intelligibility of the paradox remains absolute, incapable of being reduced or got round. Its acceptance by faith does nothing to reduce its offence to reason; it is a perpetual tension with the intelligence, a cause of suffering and passion, reducing the most powerful understanding to the level of the most simple, and both to nothing; for it poses itself as the limit of all thought, and the question at issue is eternal happiness.

Kierkegaard's ideas became the source of modern existential philosophy in writers such as Martin Heidegger and Jean-Paul Sartre. His ideas were first

introduced into theology by KARL BARTH, the Swiss theologian (1886–1968), who was probably the major influence in Western theology in the first half of the twentieth century.

For its introduction into theology, I myself must bear a good deal of unwitting responsibility, for I paid tribute to it in my commentary on the Epistle to the Romans (1921) and even in my well-known false start, the *Christliche Dogmatik in Entwurf* (1927). In the light of these works, and in respect of certain features of my theological thinking in its later development, I must admit that I have learned something from what Kierkegaard and his modern followers teach.

There were two particular ideas which he drew from Kierkegaard:

● He thought of God as 'Wholly Other', in reaction against the liberal tendency to make God so like man that he is hardly distinguishable from him. He maintained that there is an 'infinite qualitative difference between God and man':

The Gospel falls upon man as God's own mighty Word, questioning him down to the bottom of his being, uprooting him from his securities and satisfactions, and therefore tearing clean asunder all the relations that keep him prisoner within his own ideals in order that he may be genuinely free for God and for his wonderful new work of grace in Jesus Christ. The emphasis was quite definitely upon what became known as *diastasis*, the distance, the separation, between God's ways and man's ways, God's thoughts and man's thoughts, between Christianity and culture, between Gospel and humanism, between Word of God and word of man.

● The concept of 'indirect communication' between God and man:

In Jesus the communication of God begins with a rebuff, with the exposure of a vast chasm, with the clear revelation of a great stumbling-block. Remove from the Christian Religion, as Christendom has done, its ability to shock, and Christianity, by becoming a direct communication, is altogether destroyed. It then becomes a tiny, superficial thing, capable of neither inflicting deep wounds nor of healing them; by discovering an unreal and merely human compassion, it forgets the qualitative distinction between God and man.
KIERKEGAARD

In his Dogmatics, therefore, he refuses to discuss basic presuppositions like the existence of God and the possibility of revelation:

Really responsible, up-to-date theological thought, in genuine rapprochement with its contemporaries, will reveal itself to be such even today ... by refusing to discuss the basis of its ground, questions such as whether God is, whether there is such a thing as revelation, etc.

Thus, if we asked Barth, 'How can I know if Christianity is true?' his answer would be 'through *obedience*,' through complete surrender to the Word of God:

If faith is indeed the knowledge of the Creator then it cannot understand itself as acting creatively, but only as acting obediently. It is knowledge of the truth solely in virtue of the fact that the truth is *spoken* to us to which we respond in pure obedience.

KARL MARX

(1818–83)

Karl Marx was a German Jew, who was expelled from Germany and spent most of his life in London. His famous work, *Das Kapital*, published in 1867 four years after his death, was an analysis and critique of capitalism.

● Marx took over from Hegel the philosophical concept of the *dialectic* (i.e. the sequence of thesis, antithesis and synthesis) and turned it into a theory which explained the development of societies. He believed that every society must evolve through struggles between the different classes until it becomes a 'classless society'. Thus, for example, if we take the capitalist epoch in the history of any society, the owners (capitalists) can be thought of as the thesis, and the workers (proletariat) become the anti-thesis: as a result of the conflict between them, socialism emerges as the synthesis.
The Communist Manifesto (1848) begins with the words:

The history of all hitherto existing society is the history of class struggles.

It ends with the words:

The Communists disdain to conceal their views and aims. They openly declare that their ends can be attained only by the forcible overthrow of all existing conditions. Let the ruling classes tremble at a communist revolution. The proletarians have nothing to lose but their chains. They have a world to win. Working men of all countries, unite!

The tomb of Karl Marx in Highgate cemetery, London.

● He took over the philosophy of *materialism* from the German atheistic philosopher, Ludwig Feuerbach. This is the belief which denies everything supernatural, and claims that everything—including ideas, art, religion, politics etc.—can be explained in material terms and in the light of people's material conditions. This led him to claim that all 'gods' are no more than a 'projection' of the human mind, and that man creates the gods he wants 'in his own image'.

● He denounced religion because he saw it as an enemy of human progress:

Man makes religion, religion does not make man. Religion is indeed man's self-

consciousness and self-awareness as long as he has not found his feet in the universe. But man is not an abstract being, squatting outside the world. Man is the world of men, the State, and society. This State, this society, produce religion which is an inverted world consciousness, because they are in an inverted world ... Religious suffering is at the same time an expression of real suffering and a protest against real suffering. Religion is the sigh of the oppressed creature, the sentiment of a heartless world, and the soul of soulless conditions. It is the opium of the people. The abolition of religion, as the illusory happiness of men, is a demand for their real happiness.

● He also developed an economic theory of '*surplus-value*', which claimed the employers in all capitalist countries were enjoying the profits which could have been divided out among the workers. This theory led to the demand for the overthrow of bourgeois capitalists and the nationalization of the means of 'production, distribution and exchange', to enable the workers to obtain a fair share of the profits derived from their work.

● Marx thus provided the theory of Communism (though in his case it was through socialism), and it was left to Lenin, Stalin and others to put the theory into practice in Russia.

SIGMUND FREUD
(1856–1939)

Freud was an Austrian psychologist who developed the technique of 'psychoanalysis'.

● As a result of encouraging his patients to recount their dreams and talk freely about anything and everything which came into their minds, he came to make a distinction between the conscious mind and what he called the 'unconscious'. He believed that the unconscious plays a very important part in determining our everyday behaviour.

● He laid particular emphasis on the way in which sexual desires unconsciously influence human behaviour, especially when they are 'repressed' or put out of mind.

● He distinguished between three different parts of the human personality:
  1. the unconscious, which he called the *id*, i.e. the part concerned with basic drives and energy;
  2. the conscious mind, the *ego*;
  3. the *super-ego*, i.e. the part which includes the conscience and everything concerned with ideas of right and wrong.

● He summed up his attitude to religion in general in these words:

While the different religions wrangle with one another as to which of them is in possession of the truth, in our view the truth of religion may be altogether disregarded. Religion is an attempt to get control over the sensory world, in which we are placed, by means of the wish-world, which we have developed inside us as a result of biological and psychological necessities. But it cannot achieve its end. Its doctrines carry with them the stamp of the times in which they originated, the ignorant childhood days of the human race. Its consolations deserve no trust. Experience teaches us that the world is not a nursery. The ethical commands, to which religion seeks to lend its weight, require some other foundation instead, for human society cannot do without them, and it is dangerous to link up obedience to them with religious beliefs. If one attempts to assign to religion its place in man's evolution, it seems not so much to be a lasting acquisition as a parallel

Sigmund Freud

to the neurosis which the civilized individual must pass through on his way from childhood to maturity.

LESLIE PAUL describes the revolutionary effect of Freud's theory of the unconscious in this way:

Freud's concept of the unconscious is probably the most revolutionary change in thought which this century has produced ... The acceptance of the existence of the unconscious struck a blow at a fundamental humanist principle—the rationality of the mind. If the mind was subject to occult influences, never properly exposed to reason, let alone controlled by it, and if these occult influences determined to some extent the structure of the mind—what indeed became of the supremacy of human reason and therefore of the sovereignty of man?

This way of thinking is now so widely accepted that it is assumed everyone recognizes its truth. COLIN WILSON sums up the attitude of 'modern man':

Is modern man justified in believing in God on the basis of faith? There is, of course, no simple answer to this simple question; in the final analysis it appears to be more a question of emotional motivation than of rational argument.

MALCOLM JEEVES, a professor of psychology, points out that while Freud's theories have been strongly criticized by professional psychologists, they have been widely accepted by the man in the street:

One of the curious things about psychoanalytic theory is that, whilst it has been rejected in general by experts in the field of psychology and other behavioural sciences, it has

been readily accepted by the man in the street and by intelligent people in the arts. Since some of the main critics of psychoanalysis have been found amongst professional psychologists and anthropologists, it is important that we should ask ourselves why the man in the street has accepted it so readily. Some have suggested that, because the notions of psychoanalytic theory have a sufficiently close fit with what we might call 'common sense psychology' (the sort of psychology which attempts to give us some sort of understanding of ourselves and our fellow human beings) and therefore meets an immediate felt need, it is accordingly readily accepted. Others have pointed out that it is a lazy man's way of explaining, *post hoc*, almost any behaviour one can think of.

C.E.M. JOAD writes about the very practical consequences of Freud's psychological determinism which claims that all our rational thinking is little more than rationalizations of what is hidden in the unconscious mind:

The belief that men's views reflect their desires rather than their reason, has a number of harmful effects in practice. For example, it is destructive of good talk and inimical to fruitful discussion. Owing to the influence of psycho-analysis there prevails in modern society a refusal to discuss any view on its merits. If X expresses an opinion Y, the question discussed is not whether Y is true or at least reasonable, but the considerations which led X to believe it to be true. Objective truth being regarded as unobtainable, what alone is thought interesting are the reasons which led people to

formulate their particular brand of error.

MAURICE FRIEDMAN quotes some words of Martin Buber about the way in which such scepticism affects personal relationships:

This unmasking begins in the service of truth ... Yet it ends, paradoxically, by making all truth questionable and by undermining the foundations of existence between men. 'One no longer fears that the other will voluntarily dissemble', writes Martin Buber in a statement on 'existential mistrust'. One simply takes it for granted that he cannot do otherwise.

'I do not really take cognizance of his communication as knowledge ... Rather I listen for what drives the other to say what he says, for an unconscious motive, say, or a "complex" ... My main task in my intercourse with my fellow-man becomes more and more, whether in terms of individual psychology or sociology, to see through and unmask him. In the classical case this in no wise means a mask he has put on to deceive me, but a mask that has, without his knowing it, been put on him, indeed positively imprinted on him, so that what is really deceived is his own consciousness.'

THE LEGACY OF THESE THINKERS —'THE MODERN MIND'

The development of Western thought in the last eight centuries has produced a kind of consensus, which is often described by phrases like 'the modern mind' or 'modern secular man'.

This does not mean that *everyone* in the Western world has accepted *all* these beliefs. What it does mean, however, is that after centuries of Christian theism in the West, the *majority* of people in the Western world have come to accept certain beliefs and almost take them for granted. They have become part of their world-view, and are reflected in literature and the arts, and in the mass media.

The following writers all attempt to explain the basic difference between Christian theism which has dominated Western thinking for centuries and these new ways of thinking in the twentieth century.

The Western mind has turned away from the contemplation of the absolute and eternal to the knowledge of the particular and the contingent. It has made man the measure of all things and has sought to emancipate human life from its dependence on the supernatural. Instead of the whole intellectual and social order being subordinated to spiritual principles, every activity has declared its independence, and we see politics, economics, science and art organizing themselves as autonomous kingdoms which owe no allegiance to any higher power.
CHRISTOPHER DAWSON

Before the shift, the various religions had provided man with explanations of a kind which gave everything that happened to him meaning in the wider sense of transcendental causality and transcendental justice. But the explanations of the new philosophy were devoid of

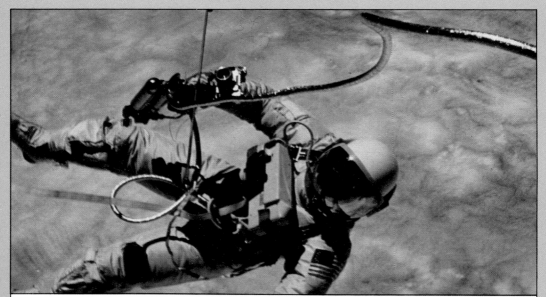

'Man's claim to be the centre of the universe has lost its foundation. Man is placed in an infinite space in which his being seems to be a single and vanishing point.' Ernst Cassirer.

Albert Camus

meaning in this wider sense ...
In a word, the old explanations,
with all their arbitrariness and
patchiness, answered the
question after 'the meaning of
life' whereas the new
explanations, with all their
precision, made the question
of meaning itself meaningless.
ARTHUR KOESTLER

Up till now, man derived his
coherence from his Creator.
But from the moment that he
consecrates his rupture with
Him, he finds himself delivered
over to the fleeting moment, to
the passing days, and to
wasted sensibility. Therefore
he must take himself in hand.
ALBERT CAMUS

ERNST CASSIRER, writing about
the legacy of thinkers like
Nietzsche, Freud and Marx:

Owing to this development our
modern theory of man lost its
intellectual centre. We
acquired instead a complete
anarchy of thought ... An
established authority to which
one might appeal no longer
existed. Theologians,
scientists, politicians,
sociologists, biologists,
psychologists, ethnologists,
economists all approached the
problem from their own
viewpoints ... Every author
seems in the last count to be
led by his own conception and
evaluation of human life.

He quotes MAX SCHELER:

In no other period of human
knowledge has man become
more problematical to himself
than in our own days ... We no
longer possess any clear and
consistent idea of man.

We have to accept the subtle
but closely woven evidence
that man is not different in kind
from other forms of life; that
living matter is not different in
kind from dead matter; and
therefore that a man is an
assembly of atoms that obeys
natural laws of the same kind
that a star does ...

The atoms in the brain as
much as those in the body
constitute a mechanism, which
ticks with the same orderly
regularity, and abides by
similar laws, as any other
interlocking constellation of
atoms. Men have uneasily
pushed this thought out of
their heads because they
wanted to avoid the conflict
with their rooted conviction
that man is a free agent who
follows only the promptings of
his own will. But we cannot
hide this contradiction for
ever.

My fundamental
assumption ... is that man is a
part of nature.

This simple proposition
seems innocent enough, and
neutral. Nearly all educated
men accept it now ... In the
latter half of the twentieth
century, it seems self-evident
to say that man is a part of
nature, in the same sense that
a stone is, or a cactus, or a
camel ... Yet this bland
proposition contains the
explosive charge which in this
century has split open the self-
assurance of western man.

We sense that there is no
break in the continuity of
nature. At one end of her range,
the star has been linked with
the stone; and at the other end,
man has been put among the
animals ... An unbroken line
runs from the stone to the
cactus and on to the camel, and
there is no supernatural leap in
it. No special act of creation, no
spark of life was needed to turn
dead matter into living things.
JACOB BRONOWSKI

ERNST CASSIRER describes how
new ways of thinking in the
fifteenth century called in
question the traditional Christian
belief:

All this is suddenly called into
question by the new
cosmology. Man's claim to
being the centre of the
universe has lost its
foundation. Man is placed in an
infinite space in which his
being seems to be a single and
vanishing point. He is
surrounded by a mute
universe, by a world that is
silent to his religious feelings
and to his deepest moral
demands.

He quotes some words of
Montaigne which, he says, give
the clue to the whole subsequent
development of the modern
theory of man.

Let man ... make me
understand by the force of his
reason, upon what foundation
he has built those great
advantages he thinks he has
over other creatures. Who has
made him believe that this
admirable notion of the
celestial arch, the eternal light
of those luminaries that roll so
high over his head, the
wondrous and fearful motions
of that infinite ocean, should be
established and continue so
many ages for his service and

convenience? Can anything be imagined so ridiculous, that this miserable and wretched creature, who is not so much as master of himself, but subject to the injuries of all things, should call himself master and emperor of the world, of which he has not power to know the least part, much less to command the whole?

'Whoever shall represent to his fancy, as in a picture, the great image of our mother nature, portrayed in her full majesty and lustre; whoever in her face shall read so general and so constant a variety, whoever shall observe himself in that figure, and not himself but a whole kingdom, no bigger than the least touch of a pencil, in comparison of the whole, that man alone is able to value things according to their true estimate and grandeur.'

Montaigne's words give us the clue to the whole subsequent development of the modern theory of man. Modern philosophy and modern science had to accept the challenge contained in these words. They had to prove that the new cosmology, far from enfeebling or obstructing the power of human reason, establishes and confirms this power. Such was the task of the combined efforts of the metaphysical systems of the sixteenth and seventeenth centuries. These systems go different ways, but they are all directed toward one and the same end. They strive, so to speak, to turn the apparent curse of the new cosmology into a blessing.

DIETRICH BONHOEFFER traces the development of thinking from the thirteenth to the twentieth century:

The movement beginning about the thirteenth century ... towards the autonomy of man (under which head I place the discovery of the laws by which the world moves and manages in science, social and political affairs, art, ethics, and religion) has in our time reached a certain completion. Man has learned to cope with all questions of importance without recourse to God as a working hypothesis. In questions concerning science, art, and even ethics, this has become an understood thing which one scarcely dares to tilt at any more. But in the last hundred years or so it has been increasingly true of religious questions also: it is becoming evident that everything gets along without 'God', and just as well as before. As in the scientific field, so in human affairs generally, what we call 'God' is being more and more edged out of life, losing more and more ground.

On the historical side I should say that there is *one* great development which leads to the idea of the autonomy of the world. In theology it is first discernible in Lord Herbert of Cherbury, with his assertion that reason is the sufficient instrument of religious knowledge. In ethics it first appears in Montaigne and Bodin with their substitution of moral principles for the ten commandments. In politics, Machiavelli, who emancipates politics from the tutelage of morality, and founds the doctrine of 'reasons of state'. Later, and very differently, though like Machiavelli tending towards the autonomy of human society, comes Grotius, with his international law as the law of nature, a law which would still be valid *etsi deus non daretur*. The process is completed in philosophy. On the one hand we have the deism of Descartes, who holds that the world is a mechanism which runs on its own without any intervention from God. On the other hand there is the pantheism of Spinoza, with its identification of God with nature. In the last resort Kant is a deist, Fichte and Hegel pantheists. All along the line there is a growing tendency to assert the autonomy of man and the world ...

There is no longer any need for God as a working hypothesis, whether in morals, politics, or science.

TEN '-ISMS'

We cannot call all of these '-isms' philosophies, because not all of them are complete systems of philosophy.
Several of them overlap with each other: for example, a deist is usually also a rationalist; a pantheist may or may not be a mystic; Jean-Paul Sartre called himself both an atheist and an existentialist. It is helpful, however, to take each one separately, in order to understand how it can affect a person's world-view.

CATHOLIC SCHOLASTICISM

Scholasticism is the name given to the system of theology developed by medieval theologians, 'the schoolmen' who were deeply influenced by men like Thomas Aquinas (see *Ten Key Thinkers*).

Their attitude to the question about the truth of Christianity can be summed up in two statements:

1. Man can find out some Christian beliefs by his own reason.

2. The other Christian beliefs are *beyond* reason; they have been revealed by God and must be accepted by faith.

MAN CAN FIND OUT SOME CHRISTIAN BELIEFS BY HIS OWN REASON
Man is finite, and he is a fallen creature; but he is still able to arrive at *some* of the truth about God and the universe simply by using his own reason. In this way, for example, he can know:

● the existence of God: reason can prove *that* God exists, though it cannot tell us everything we need to know about God.

● the existence of the moral law, or natural law, in the conscience.

This answer led to traditional arguments for the existence of God. The three basic arguments in their simplest form can be formulated in this way:

1. The ontological argument. I have an idea of God as the Perfect Being, or as 'that than which nothing greater can be conceived'.

If the idea exists, then the thing itself must exist; the idea must correspond to something which is there outside my mind.

Therefore God must exist.

2. The cosmological argument. Every effect has a cause.

Therefore there must be a First Cause to create the universe, and God is by definition the First Cause.

Therefore God must exist.

3. The teleological argument. Anything which shows traces of design must have been designed by some intelligent being.

The universe shows signs of order and design; therefore there must be a Designer; and God is, by definition, the Creator and Designer.

Therefore God exists.

These arguments for the existence of God are still an official part of Roman Catholic teaching:

If anyone says that the one true God, our Creator and Lord, cannot be known with certainty by the natural light of human reason through those things which are made: let him be anathema.

TRUTHS WHICH ARE BEYOND REASON HAVE BEEN REVEALED BY GOD AND MUST BE RECEIVED BY FAITH

The knowledge which we can gain by the use of reason is not complete. We cannot, for example, deduce the Trinity, or belief in salvation through Christ simply by reason.

If these beliefs are beyond reason, we cannot test them in any way by reason. We can ask questions to test the authority which teaches us these truths; but once we have accepted that authority we accept the truth of what it teaches.

For example, Roman Catholicism gives certain reasons for the infallible authority of the church as the teaching institution: e.g. the words of Jesus to Peter; the development of the papacy at Rome. Once we have accepted this authority, we accept what it tells us.

CARDINAL HEENAN (1905–75), former Archbishop of Westminster, stated this conviction as follows:

This secret of this wonderful unity of our Church is Christ's promise that the Church will never fail to teach the truth. Once we know what the Church teaches we accept it. For we know it must be true ... All Catholic priests teach the same doctrine because they all obey the Vicar of Christ. The word 'vicar' means 'one who takes the place of another'. The Pope is the Vicar of Christ because he takes the place of Christ as Head of the Church on earth.

The Church remains one because all her members believe the same Faith. They believe it because the Church cannot teach what is false. This is what we mean when we say that the Church is infallible. Christ promised to guide his Church. One of the ways Christ chose to guide the Church was by leaving his Vicar on earth to speak for him. That is why we say the Pope is infallible. He is the Head of the infallible Church. God could not allow him to lead it into error.

WHERE DOES THIS DISTINCTION BETWEEN TWO KINDS OF TRUTH LEAD?

It holds that there are two completely different kinds of truth: truths of reason and truths of revelation. Francis Schaeffer pictures this as a dividing line, with supernatural, religious truth—revealed by God and received by faith—above it, and natural, scientific truth—discovered by man and tested by reason—below:

$$\frac{\text{GRACE}}{\text{NATURE}}$$

This dichotomy of truth became widely accepted by both Protestants and Catholics.

FRANCIS BACON (1561–1626):

It is therefore most wise soberly to render unto faith the things that are faith's.

Sacred theology must be drawn from the word and oracles of God, not from the light of nature, or the dictates of reason.

(To study theology) we must quit the small vessel of human reason, and put ourselves on board the ship of the Church, which alone possesses the divine needle for justly shaping the course.

We are obliged to believe the word of God, though our reason be shocked at it. For if we should believe only such things as are agreeable to our reason, we assent to the matter, and not to the author.

And therefore, the more absurd and incredible any divine mystery is, the greater honour we do to God in believing it; and so much the more noble the victory of faith.

THOMAS BROWNE (1605–82):

It is no vulgar part of Faith to believe a thing not only above but contrary to Reason, and against the arguments of our proper senses.

I can answer all the Objections of Satan and my rebellious reason with that odd resolution I learned of Tertullian, *certum est quia impossibile est*.

Many who adopted this approach did so with the best of motives, as BASIL WILLEY says of Francis Bacon:

What can be asserted with confidence, I think, is that Bacon's desire to separate religious truth and scientific truth was in the interests of science, not of religion. He wished to *keep science pure from religion*; the opposite parts of the process—keeping religion pure from science— did not interest him nearly so much ... Bacon was pleading for science in an age dominated by religion. Religious truth, then, must be 'skied', elevated far out of reach, not in order that so it may be more devoutly approached, but in order to keep it out of mischief.

In the long run, however, the results were disastrous. The

guide and arbiter of truth from
now on would be 'natural
instinct' and 'common notions'
which all men would accept.

LORD HERBERT OF CHERBURY
(1583–1648):

**Universal consent will be the
sovereign test of truth, and
there is nothing of so great
importance as to seek out
these common notions, and to
put them each in their place as
indubitable truths.**

These were some of Herbert's
'common notions':
   1. That there is a supreme
power.
   2. That this sovereign power
must be worshipped.
   3. That the good ordering or
disposition of the faculties of man
constitutes the principal or best
part of divine worship, and that
this has always been believed.
   4. That all vices and crimes
should be expiated and effaced
by repentance.
   5. That there are rewards
and punishments after this life.
   It was not long, therefore,
before others began to make
greater claims for man's reason,
and dispensed with revelation
altogether. This kind of answer
thus eventually led to the answer
of the rationalists.

WHAT IF THE TRADITIONAL ARGUMENTS FOR THE EXISTENCE OF GOD ARE NO LONGER CONVINCING?

While Thomas Aquinas' proofs
may carry some conviction to
those who already believe, they
mean very little to the real
unbeliever.

● The conclusion is implied in
the premise. If you accept the
first assumption (e.g. every effect
must have a cause), then the
conclusion must follow of
necessity. But this is a circular
argument. It is similar to this
kind of syllogism:

All men are mortal.
Socrates was a man.
Therefore Socrates must be
mortal.

● The arguments do not prove
enough. The cosmological
argument, for example, would
only prove the existence of a First
Cause. But it is far too big a jump
to move from the First Cause to
the God of the Bible. Similarly,
the teleological argument points
to the existence of a Creator God;
but it cannot possibly prove that
this Creator must be one God or
that he is loving or infinite. The
argument does not exclude the
possibility that there could be
many creator gods, or that God is
finite or evil.

● Many people today no longer
accept even the premise. Many
people today have the vaguest
possible idea of 'God', or have
never seriously believed that he
exists. For them therefore the
idea of a Perfect Being is not
obvious or self-evident. Similarly
the principle of causality (that
every effect has a cause) has been
seriously questioned by many
philosophers since Hume, and
for them this premise is not self-
evident. And while some say that
they see little or no evidence of
order or design in the universe,
many others are convinced that
evolution by natural selection
gives a satisfactory account of the
apparent order in nature. Others
again do not think of the universe
as being ordered; to them it is a
product of chance and is basically
chaotic and absurd. To them
therefore the argument from
design does not make sense.
   BRONOWSKI sums up the
widespread rejection of this
approach:

**These debates are scholastic
exercises in absolute logic.
They begin from concepts
which are held to be fixed
absolutely; they then proceed
by deduction; and what is**

**found in this way is subject to
no further test. The deductions
are true because the first
concepts were true: that is the
scholastic system.**

WHAT IF THE HUMAN MIND REJECTS AN AUTHORITARIAN APPROACH OF THIS KIND?

It is true that a large number of
people are not very interested in
thinking for themselves, and
therefore want to be *told* what
they should believe. When they
trust their teachers, they are very
willing to believe what they are
taught.
   This approach, however, is
likely to be questioned more and
more by those who *do* want to
think for themselves.
   The following extracts are
from writers who explain why
they reject any kind of
authoritarian approach.
   The movement of Roman
Catholic modernism at the
beginning of this century was
partly a reaction against the
dogmatic teaching of the Roman
Catholic Church. One such
writer said in 1905:

**The very idea of dogma is now
repugnant, and a source of
scandal.**

His arguments have been
summarized as follows by ALEC
VIDLER:

   **1. A dogma appeared to be
a proposition that was said to
be intrinsically true, neither
proved nor provable. But
nowadays men rightly want to
be shown that there are
reasonable grounds for belief.
   2. If reasons for accepting
dogmatic proportions are
forthcoming, they take the form
of an appeal to a transcendent
authority that is supposed, as
it were, to introduce the truth
into us from outside. A dogma
thus seems to be an external
fetter, a limit to thought, a sort**

of intellectual tyranny, denying man's need to be autonomous and sincere.

3. Allowing for the sake of argument that dogmas could be simply taught by a doctrinal authority, they would in that case have to be intelligible and unambiguous. But the trouble with traditional Christian dogmas was that they were expressed in philosophical terminology. 'In short, the first difficulty which numbers of people today find when confronted with dogmas is that they do not convey to them any intelligible meaning. These statements say nothing to them, or rather seem to them to be indissolubly bound up with a state of mind which is no longer theirs ... Many believers are implicitly of the same opinion and so prefer to abstain from reflecting on their faith.'

4. There is the grave objection that dogmas do not cohere with the rest of knowledge. Dogmas too are supposed to be immutable while thought is always progressive. Dogmas do not throw any light on scientific or philosophical problems. They do not connect.

DOSTOIEVSKY, the Russian novelist (1821–81), made a vigorous protest against authoritarian Christianity and was very well aware of the connection between authoritarian religion and authoritarian government. In his imaginary account of the Grand Inquisitor, the Inquisitor represents the authoritarianism of the Roman Catholic Church at the time of the Inquisition in the sixteenth century. This is how the Inquisitor speaks to Christ when he meets him face to face:

Why ... did you come to meddle with us? ... Tomorrow I shall condemn you and burn you at the stake as the vilest of heretics ... Have you the right to reveal to us even one of the mysteries of the world you have come from? ... No, you have not. So that you may not add anything to what has been said before and so as not to deprive men of the freedom which you upheld so strongly when you were here on earth. All that you might reveal anew would encroach on men's freedom of faith, for it would come as a miracle, and their freedom of faith was dearer to you than anything even in those days, fifteen hundred years ago. Was it not you who said so often in those days, 'I shall make you free'? But now you have seen those 'free' men ... Yes, this business has cost us a great deal ... but we've completed it at last in your name. For fifteen centuries we've been troubled by this freedom, but now it's over and done with for good ... These men are more than ever convinced that they are absolutely free, and yet they themselves have brought their freedom to us and humbly laid it at our feet ...

You did not come down from the cross when they shouted to you, mocking and deriding you: 'If you be the Son of God, come down from the cross.' You did not come down because ... you did not want to enslave man by miracles and because you hungered for a faith based on free will and not on miracles. You hungered for freely given love and not for the servile rapture of the slave before the might that has terrified him once and for all ...

There is a mystery here and we cannot understand it. And if it is a mystery, then we, too, were entitled to preach a mystery and to teach them that it is neither the free verdict of their hearts nor that love that matters, but the mystery which they must obey blindly, even against their own consciences. So we have done. We have corrected your great work and have based it on *miracle*, *mystery*, and *authority*. And men rejoiced that they were once more led like sheep and that the terrible gift which had brought them so much suffering had at last been lifted from their hearts ... Why, then, have you come to meddle with us now? And why are you looking at me silently and so penetratingly with your gentle eyes?

H.J. BLACKHAM wrote:

An open mind is vulnerable to evidence.

By comparison a religious faith may not be vulnerable. If the believer will not allow that any experience could falsify his belief, he does not have an open mind about it because it is not founded on rational grounds. His faith rests in something other than the reliability of tested evidence. His trust is likely to be in God, who is then at once the author and the object of the faith.

GEORGE HARRISON, formerly of the Beatles:

When you're young you get taken to church by your parents and you get pushed into religion at school. They're trying to put something into your mind. But it's wrong you know. Obviously because nobody goes to church and nobody believes in God. Why? Because religious teachers don't know what they're teaching. They haven't interpreted the Bible as it was intended.

This is the thing that led me into the Indian scene, that I didn't really believe in God as I'd been taught it. It was just like something out of a science fiction novel ... You're taught just to have faith, you don't have to worry about it, just believe what we're telling you.

Authoritarian approaches, however, are not by any means confined to one church, and it is not necessarily associated with the view that some truths can be proved by reason. Sometimes those who regard the Bible as the supreme authority use the authority of the Bible in the same way as the Catholic uses the authority of church. They make frequent use of the phrase 'the Bible says . . .', usually with the implication 'what the Bible says must, by definition, be true; and you have no alternative but to accept what it says'.

EMIL BRUNNER links together these two approaches in this way:

From the outset it is assumed that the Christian Faith is the true Faith, because this faith is taught either in the Bible or by the Church. But the fact that the doctrine of the Church, or of the Bible, is 'the truth', must be accepted as axiomatic. We believe in Jesus Christ, because we believe first of all either in the doctrinal authority of the Church, or in that of the Bible.

The kind of dilemma which these approaches often create in young people is well expressed by this *cri de coeur*, written by the twenty-four-year-old daughter of missionary parents:

I have been taught the Christian faith from childhood. I attended a Christian high school and college. According to the accepted pattern I should now be a stable, vibrant Christian ... I wish I could conform to that pattern. But I cannot ... I grew up praying, attending church, reading my Bible, witnessing and giving testimonies ...

Then came a series of events that stopped me cold. I began to wonder if I really owned all that I claimed. I started to ask the meaning of faith in Christ, salvation by grace, and many other phrases that I had tossed around all my life ... Realizing my faith was not truly my own, I then refused to give intellectual assent to forms of belief that I did not feel within myself. I could no longer accept without examination that which is supposed to meet man's deepest needs.

As I now stand facing adulthood, I am overwhelmed by the incomprehensibility of life. I often see myself as an unwelcome guest in a seemingly impersonal, deterministic universe. And I ask 'Why am I here anyway?' I am like many other twentieth-century young people whose 'blazing optimism' is tainted and dulled by fear.

I long to know God through an intimate relationship with Jesus Christ. I have gone through the act of accepting Christ as my personal Saviour, but how can he meet my deepest needs? The simple statement of 'Just trust the Lord' does not satisfy my intellectual restlessness nor my emotional turmoil. Such statements and phrases I have heard so often that they are trite and meaningless in the complexity of my individual context. I cannot accept 'pat' answers, for to me they are dead clichés and platitudes that do not meet my feelings ...

Occasionally I have suggested to my parents and evangelical friends that I must have opportunity to think and discover for my own satisfaction the form of faith that is to satisfy me. My parents accuse me of 'going away from the Lord', of

backsliding. They say my thinking is dangerous to my spiritual life. Perhaps so, but is it any less dangerous to be a robot responding to mechanical instructions?

I am putting this down on paper because I have found that I am not alone in the struggle. Others are searching, too, for a personal and satisfying relationship with God. I have talked with many other young people who have a deep desire for meaningful communication with Jesus Christ, though they have known 'the answers' all their lives. We wonder how can parents and other adults help us?

I believe you can help by giving us sympathy and understanding ... Most young people in this situation are in the process of trying to discover themselves as well, and we tend to rebel against any ideas that seem to be offered to us as a substitute for our thinking for ourselves ... Even quoting Scripture to us can be infuriating, because usually we are just as aware of these verses as you are, and we tend to wonder if they actually meet your needs any more than they meet ours ... Your concern for me as an individual will have far deeper effects than if you try to offer answers ... Parents will do well to try to understand the effects that modern psychological pressures have on the emotions of youth and why we are reacting in this manner, instead of throwing up their hands in horror at the attitudes we express. Patiently encourage us and give us the freedom to search for a meaningful relationship to God and to find a real expression for that relationship.

This approach encourages us to use our minds to prove the

existence of God, and to establish the supreme authority of the church which guarantees the truth of God's revelation. And once we have accepted this authority, everything else follows. We can ask questions about what the revelation means, and in certain matters there may be liberty in interpretation; but we cannot question the truth of the revelation.

In practice, therefore, this kind of authoritarian approach often leads to: either

1. a blind and unquestioning acceptance of what the church teaches; or

2. a rebellion against the authoritative teaching of the church even among those who stay within the church, and a refusal to accept all its teachings; or

3. a total rejection of the church as an authoritative teacher of the truth; or

4. a mysticism which allows the individual to sit loosely to the accepted formulae of the church, and at the same time to remain within the church.

DEISM

Deism is the name which describes the religious beliefs of many in Europe in the eighteenth century who did not deny the existence of God, but simply modified, ignored or denied certain aspects of traditional Christian teaching.

They found it convenient to hold onto their belief in God as Creator, because their understanding of the universe as a mechanical system needed a Creator who could create the universe, wind it up like a great clock, and then leave it to run by itself.

THEIR IDEAS OF GOD
These were gradually emptied of content, so that eventually hardly anything could be said about him.

VOLTAIRE, the famous French sceptic (1694–1778):

I shall always be convinced that a watch proves a watch-maker, and that a universe proves a God.

I believe in God, not the God of the mystics and the theologians, but the God of nature, the great geometrician, the architect of the universe, the prime mover, unalterable, transcendental, everlasting.

JOSEPH JOUBERT, French religious essayist and letter-writer (1754–1824):

God has withdrawn within himself and hidden within the bosom of his own being; withdrawn even as the sun, when it hides behind a cloud. The sun of the spirit is visible to them no more ... With nothing now to wake them to ecstasy, nothing to excite their lofty contemplation, able no more to gaze upon God, they busy themselves with the world.

THOMAS HOBBES was an English deist (1588–1679); this is how his idea of God has been summarized:

It is, then, the God of deism— first mover and designer of the world-machines—that Hobbes offers as a substitute for Zeus or Jehovah. But even to say that he 'offers' this is an overstatement. For him the word God is really little but a symbol of the philosopher's fatigue. In his quest for truth the investigator at last reaches the limits of human capacity;

Voltaire

then, in sheer weariness, he gives over, and says 'God' ... And it is noticeable that in speaking of God his main endeavour is to empty this conception of all content. Of that which has not reached us through the senses we can have no 'image', thus we can have no 'idea' or 'conception' of God. We can only speak of him in a series of negatives, such as 'infinite', 'immutable', 'incomprehensible', or in terms signifying his remoteness from our mortal state, such as 'omnipotent', 'most high', and the like. All these 'attributes' are really 'pseudo-statements', that is to say, the reality to which they point is just simply our own pious disposition.
BASIL WILLEY

THEIR UNDERSTANDING OF THE UNIVERSE

In order to understand how deism developed it is important to see how Christian ideas about the universe had been gradually contaminated by Greek ideas many centuries before.

HOOKYAAS describes the difference between the biblical view of the universe and that of the ancient Greeks:

There is a radical contrast between the deification of nature in pagan religion and, in a rationalized form, in Greek philosophy, and de-deification of nature in the Bible. By contrast with the nature-worship of its neighbours, the religion of Israel was a unique phenomenon. The God of Israel, by his word, brings forth all things out of nothingness. He is truly all-powerful: He was not opposed by any matter that had to be forced into order, and He did not have to reckon with eternal Forms; His sovereign will alone created and sustains the world. In the first chapter of Genesis it is made evident that absolutely nothing, except

God, has any claim to divinity; even the sun and the moon, supreme gods of the neighbouring peoples, are set in their places between the herbs and the animals and are brought into the service of mankind. The personal gods of the Greeks had an origin, in spite of their immortality. The God of the Bible is the only god who is immutable and eternal, unlike all created things which are liable to change and final destruction. Nothing else has divine power, not even by delegation: 'The Lord is one; there is no one but He.'

The New Testament proclaims again the message that there is no eternal cycle of nature or cycle of history. The history of the world moves towards its final destination and heaven and earth are destined to fall back into the nothingness from which they once emerged. Not only the creating, but also the upholding of the world belongs to God alone; that is to say, Jahveh is not a deistic supreme being who, after the creative act, leaves everything to the innate laws of nature, and He does not withdraw, like a platonic demiurge, into 'the way of being that belongs solely to Him.' He remains for ever the will and power behind all events ... In total contradiction to pagan religion, nature is not a deity to be feared and worshipped, but a work of God to be admired, studied and managed. When we compare pagan and biblical religions, we find a fundamental contrast between the ideas concerning God and man which have emerged. In the Bible God and nature are no longer both opposed to man, but God and man together confront nature. The denial that God coincides with nature implies the denial that nature is god-like.

BASIL WILLEY explains how some of these ideas from pagan religions were carried over into the thinking of many Christians in the Middle Ages:

Nature was considered as a semi-independent power, and when things happened according to nature, this meant that they followed a pattern that seemed rational to the human mind, one which had been discovered by Aristotle ... In the Middle Ages ... the biblical view was only superimposed on, and did not overcome, the Aristotelian conception. The regular order of nature was considered to be something instituted by God, but liable to be over-ruled by Him in a *super*-natural way (the term is significant) when performing a miracle. Thomas Aquinas considered one of the useful functions of natural philosophy to be to enable us to distinguish that which belongs only to God (for example miracles, or the origin of things) from that which belongs to nature.

He speaks of the medieval idea of science as 'the forbidden knowledge':

The Faustus legend testifies to the strength of the fascinated dread with which the Middle Ages had thought of natural science ... 'Nature' had, in quite a special sense, been consigned to the Satanic order.

For practical purposes ... we may perhaps take the later fifteenth and the sixteenth centuries as the epoch of the rebirth of confidence in 'Nature' ...

This recrudescence of confidence in Nature was immensely strengthened by the scientific movement of the Renaissance, which reclaimed the physical world from its traditional association with Satan.

When we come to deism in the seventeenth century, we find that as the Creator recedes more and more into the background, 'Nature' itself becomes almost like a god.

THEIR IDEA OF MAN

CARL BECKER, summarizing typical beliefs about man in the eighteenth century:

1. Man is not natively depraved;
2. The end of life is life itself, the good life on earth instead of the beatific life after death;
3. Man is capable, guided solely by the light of reason and experience, of perfecting the good life on earth; and
4. The first essential condition of the good life on earth is the freeing of men's minds from the bonds of ignorance and superstition, and of their bodies from the arbitrary oppression of the constituted social authorities.

WHERE DOES DEISM LEAD? WHAT DID IT IN FACT LEAD TO?

Deism in the eighteenth century represented a comfortable, but not very convincing, half-way house between Christian theism on the one hand, and atheism or agnosticism on the other:

The Deism which we meet with in the writings of the period attenuates the idea of God, but does not annihilate it. It makes God the object of a belief vaguely defined, perhaps, yet positive none the less, and intentionally so. It sufficed at all events to endow its adherents with a sense of superiority over their godless brethren; it enabled them to pray and to worship; it prevented them from feeling that they were alone in the world, lost and fatherless ... It is no easy matter to be an

'*I shall always be convinced that a watch proves a watchmaker, and that a universe proves a God.*' Voltaire.

Atheist and brutally to crush out belief in the divine; it is incomparably easier to be a Deist ... 'A Deist', Bonald will one day be telling us, 'is simply a man who hasn't had time to become an Atheist.' 'A man who doesn't want to be an Atheist', would be much nearer the mark.
PAUL HAZARD

HOW DOES DEISM ENABLE US TO DEFINE MORAL VALUES?

The eighteenth-century deists believed that nature and reason pointed to certain basic values and truths which were self-evident. Any reasonable person therefore should be able instinctively to recognize these values for himself.

The state of Nature has a law of Nature to govern it, which obliges every one, and reason, which is that law, teaches all mankind who will but consult it, that being all equal and independent, no one ought to harm another in his life, health, liberty or possessions.
JOHN LOCKE

But what if we no longer believe that 'nature' and 'reason' give us a clear guide in making moral choices?

WHAT HELP DOES THE GOD OF DEISM OFFER MAN IN HIS SEARCH FOR MEANING?

O God, I do not know if you exist ... I ask nothing in this world, for the course of events is determined by its own necessity if you do not exist, or by your decree if you do ... Here I stand, as I am, a necessarily organized part of eternal and necessary matter—or perhaps your own creation.
DIDEROT

RATIONALISM

Rationalism is the belief that man can find the truth through his reason alone; there is no need for any revelation from God.

Most of the philosophers who thought in this way were deists, not atheists. They did not deny the existence of God. They simply said that God had little or nothing to do with man's search after the truth.

ERNST CASSIRER says that in the early Italian Renaissance there were three major currents of philosophical thought: humanism (which was largely interested in classical studies, and was not opposed to Christianity or the church), Platonism, and Aristotelianism (which looked to Averroes as a guide, and eventually came to inspire the free-thinkers of the seventeenth century, especially in France). The following are some of the ideas of this third group:

The supremacy of natural reason, the denial of creation and personal immortality, with their theological consequences, and the unity of the intellect were taught in the universities and, we are told, accepted by many Venetian gentlemen. Such a philosophy expressed with precision the stage of scepticism towards the religious system, of anti-supernaturalism rather than of positive naturalism and humanism, which had been reached by the northern Italian cities in the fourteenth century.

As these ideas were being developed in the eighteenth century, many became conscious of a one-sided emphasis on reason, while others began to think that reason was incapable of finding the truth by itself. It was this awareness which led to the Romantic Movement, which stressed that truth must be sought through reason *and the heart* working together.

Rousseau, for example, laid more emphasis on the heart and the emotions as a guide to truth (see *Ten Key Thinkers*).

PAUL HAZARD describes the extent to which the rationalists of the seventeenth and eighteenth centuries enthroned reason and used it to challenge every religious belief:

And now Reason breaks loose and there's no holding her any longer. Tradition, authority are nothing to her; 'What harm,' she says, 'in wiping the slate clean and beginning things all over again?' ... Heaven was theirs, and earth was theirs; theirs was the whole domain of the knowable. There was nothing, they thought, nothing in the whole universe which the geometrical mind could not grasp. Theology, too, was their business ...

Descartes the geometrician had called the tune for the new era. But what if the geometrical mind collides head on with religion? What will happen if it is applied wholesale to matters of faith? It would mean putting the sponge over the religious slate; every religion would be wiped out.

He goes on to trace the connection between the thought of the seventeenth century and the Renaissance of the fourteenth century in this way:

This critical urge, whence came it ? Who fostered it? What made it at once so daring and so strong? Where, in a word, did it originate? The answer is that it came from afar, from very far indeed: it came from ancient Greece; from this, that, or another heretical doctor of the Middle Ages; from many other distant sources, but beyond all doubt or question it came from the Renaissance. Between the Renaissance and the period we have just been studying (i.e. 1680–1715), the family likeness is unmistakable. There is the same refusal on the part of the more daring spirits to subordinate the human to the divine. In both cases a like importance is assigned to man, to man who has no rival, man who limits the boundary of the knowable, resolves all problems that admit of solution, regarding the rest as null and void, man the source and centre of the hopes of the world. Now and then, Nature comes in, not very clearly defined, but powerful, Nature no longer regarded as the work of a Creator, but as the upsurge of life as a whole, and of human life in particular ... This age bears upon it all the characteristics of a second Renaissance but a Renaissance sterner, more austere, and, in a measure, disillusioned, a Renaissance without a Rabelais, a Renaissance without a smile ...

And so the trend of modern thought can be charted more or less accurately as follows: starting from the Renaissance, an eagerness for invention, a passion for discovery, an urge to play the critic, traits all so manifest that we may call them the dominant elements in the European mentality. Somewhere about the middle of the seventeenth century there was a temporary pause, when a truce, wholly unlooked for, was entered into by the opposing forces, an entirely unpredictable reconciliation. This phenomenon, which was nothing short of miraculous, was what is called the Revival of Learning, the revival of the classical spirit, and the fruit of it was peace and tranquil strength . . .

As soon as the classical ideal ceased to be a thing to aim at, a deliberated goal, a conscious choice, and began to degenerate into a mere habit, and an irksome one at that, the innovators, all ready for action, set to work with all the old zest and energy. And so, yet once again, the mind of Europe set out on the unending quest. Then came a crisis so swift and so sudden, so at least it seemed, that it took men completely by surprise; yet it had long been stirring in the womb of Time, and, so far from being a new thing, was in reality a very old one.

WHERE DID THIS KIND OF RATIONALISM LEAD?

● It led to a reduction of Christian beliefs. Any belief which did not seem to be supported by reason was rejected. Many philosophers and theologians presented what they thought was the essence of the Christian faith, a basic minimum which could be defended by reason.

Adolph von Harnack, the German theologian (1851–1930) reduced the essence of the teaching of Jesus to these three themes: the Kingdom of God and its coming; God the Father and the infinite value of the human soul; the higher righteousness and the commandment of love.

D.F. Strauss in his *Life of Jesus* (written in 1835–36) entirely denied the supernatural element in the Gospels:

All things are linked together by a chain of causes and effects, which suffers no interruption . . . This conviction is so much a habit of thought with the modern world, that in actual life, the belief in a supernatural manifestation, an immediate divine agency, is at once attributed to ignorance or imposture.

In the person and acts of Jesus no supernaturalism shall be allowed to remain. He who would banish priests from the Church must first banish miracles from religion.

● It led many others to an attitude of complete scepticism. When certain beliefs of Christianity have been denied, the critic begins to feel 'Why stop here? Why reject this, but accept that? What happens when "reason" and "nature" are unable to point unambiguously to the truth? What happens when the heart and the mind give very different answers?'

Many who saw that their questioning would lead them to a position of total doubt were unwilling to be utterly consistent. The attitude of Pierre Bayle, one of the most radical of the French free-thinkers (1647–1706), has been summed up as follows:

Did he reach the point of absolute scepticism? He would have done so had he suffered his mind to follow its natural bent. Nothing ever pleased him better than that interplay of *pro* and *con*. He would have floated away into that far-off void, where actions lose their significance and life its

purpose, had he followed logic to its final term, and taken cognizance only of his human experience, which day by day impressed him more and more. He might, nay, he must, have arrived at last at what Le Clerc calls metaphysical and historical scepticism, at universal doubt.

But this he resisted. His intrepid spirit, the feeling that he had a mission to fulfil, an abhorrence of error, more potent than any doubt he might have entertained about truth, a reasoning mind that would not willingly accept defeat, and above all his strength of will enabled him to stop short of the final step.

The most advanced unbelievers among the thinkers with whom we have been dealing called a halt when they came face to face with the Nihilism to which their scepticism seemed about to lead them.
PAUL HAZARD

ATHEISM

Most rationalists sooner or later reach the point of denying the existence of God. Whereas the agnostic says 'God *may exist*, but we can never know', the atheist says categorically 'God *does not exist*; there is no one there'.

THOMAS HARDY, the English novelist (1840–1928):

I have been looking for God for fifty years and I think if he had existed I should have discovered him.

A.J. AYER, the English philosopher:

I do not believe in God. It seems to me that theists of all kinds have largely failed to make their concept of a deity intelligible; and to the extent that they have made it intelligible they have given no reason to think that anything answers to it.

ARTHUR ADAMOV, the playwright, quoted in *The Theatre of the Absurd*:

The name of God should no longer come from the mouth of man. This word that has so long been degraded by usage no longer means anything ... To use the word God is more than sloth, it is refusal to think, a kind of short cut, a hideous shorthand.

One of the first philosophers who argued consistently that God does not exist and tried to build his whole philosophy on this assumption was FRIEDRICH NIETZSCHE, the German philosopher (1844–1900). He sought to deny the *whole* system of Christian beliefs:

Vast upheavals will happen in the future, as soon as men realise that the structure of Christianity is only based on assumptions ... I have tried to deny everything.

He began by proclaiming 'God is dead':

Have you not heard of the madman who lit a lamp in broad daylight and ran up and down the market place shouting incessantly, 'I'm looking for God! I'm looking for God!' But, because many of the people who were standing there did not believe in God, he aroused a good deal of mirth ... But the madman thrust in between them and fixed them with his eyes. 'Where is God?' he shouted. 'I'll tell you! We have killed him—you and I! We are all his murderers! But how have we done it? How could we drink the sea dry? Who gave us the sponge to wipe away the horizon? What did we do when we uncoupled the earth from its sun? Where is the earth moving to now? Where are we moving to? Away from all suns? Are we not running incessantly? Backwards, sideways and forwards, in all directions? Is there still an above and a below? Are we not wandering through an infinite nothing? Is not the void yawning ahead of us? Has it not become colder? Is it not more and more night? Do the lamps not have to be lit during the day? Do we hear nothing of the noise of the gravediggers who are burying God? Do we smell nothing of the decomposition of God? The gods are decomposing! God is dead! God is dead! And we have killed him! ... I have come too soon! My time has not yet come. This terrible event is still coming.'

He poured scorn on those who rejected Christian beliefs about God, but at the same time wanted to hold on to Christian values:

They have got rid of the Christian God, and now feel obliged to cling all the more firmly to Christian morality: that is *English* consistency, let us not blame it on little blue-stockings *à la* Eliot. In England, in response to every little emancipation from theology one has to reassert one's position in a fear-inspiring manner as a moral fanatic. That is the *penance* one pays there.—With us it is different. When one gives up Christian belief one thereby deprives oneself of the *right* to Christian morality. For the latter is absolutely *not* self-evident: one must make this point clear again and again, in spite of English shallowpates. Christianity is a system, a consistently thought out and *complete* view of things. If one breaks out of it a fundamental idea, the belief in God, one thereby breaks the whole thing to pieces: one has nothing of any consequence left in one's hands. Christianity presupposes that man does not know, *cannot* know what is good for him and what is evil: he believes in God, who alone knows. Christian morality is a command: its origin is transcendental; it is beyond all criticism, all right to criticize; it possesses truth only if God is truth—it stands or falls with the belief in God.—If the English really do believe they know, of their own accord, 'intuitively', what is good and evil; if they consequently think they no longer have need of Christianity as a guarantee of morality; that is merely the *consequence* of the ascendancy of the Christian evaluation and an expression of the *strength* and *depth* of this ascendancy: so that the origin of English morality has been forgotten, so that the highly conditional nature of its right to exist is no longer felt. For the Englishman morality is not yet a problem.

He tried to go beyond his philosophy of nihilism to a positive 'affirmation of the world':

The kind of *experimental philosophy* which I am living, even anticipates the possibility of the most fundamental Nihilism, on principle: but by this I do not mean that it remains standing at a negation, at a *no*, or at a will to negation. It would rather attain to the very reverse—to a *Dionysian affirmation* of the world, as it is, without subtraction, exception, or choice ...

To overcome pessimism effectively and, at last, to look with the eyes of a Goethe full of love and goodwill.

He believed that his atheism opened up new horizons:

The most important of more recent events—that 'god is dead', that the belief in the Christian God has become unworthy of belief—already begins to cast its first shadows over Europe ... In fact, we philosophers and 'free spirits' feel ourselves irradiated as by a new dawn by the report that the 'old God is dead'; our hearts overflow with gratitude, astonishment, presentiment and expectation. At last the

horizon seems open once more, granting even that it is not bright; our ships can at last put out to sea in face of every danger; every hazard is again permitted to the discerner; the sea, *our* sea, again lies open before us; perhaps never before did such an 'open sea' exist.

ALBERT CAMUS sums up the significance of Nietzsche's atheism in this way:

We sense the change of position that Nietzsche makes. With him, rebellion begins at 'God is dead' which is assumed as an established fact ... Contrary to the opinion of certain of his Christian critics, Nietzsche did not form a project to kill God. He found Him dead in the soul of his contemporaries. He was the first to understand the immense importance of the event and to decide that this rebellion among men could not lead to a renaissance unless it were controlled and directed.

IS IT POSSIBLE TO LIVE WITH A PHILOSOPHY OF TOTAL NIHILISM?

An atheist does not always become a nihilist. Nietzsche, however, is an example of a person who tried perhaps harder than any person to *live* his philosophy of meaninglessness to the end. This is how H.J. BLACKHAM describes the attempt Nietzsche made:

In his own case, he provided himself with no means of getting out of the nihilism into which he plunged himself, precisely because it was a deliberate plunge over the edge. He tried to say at the same time: nihilism must be surmounted; nihilism cannot be surmounted; nihilism is good, nihilism is best. He imprisoned himself within the

Friedrich Nietzsche

chalked circle of his own metaphysical assumptions.

His thinking was ancillary to the real philosophic task he set himself of experimentally *living* all the valuations of the past, together with the contraries, in order to acquire the right to judge them ... There are positions which can be thought but not lived, there are exploratory ventures from which there is no return. Nietzsche's thoughts were fascinated by unexplored forbidden regions of abysses, glaciers, and mountain peaks. One can look down into the bottom of an abyss refusing the possibility of throwing oneself over the edge, but one cannot explore the possibility by a tentative jump. One can examine in thought the possibility of nihilism (as an irresolvable conflict between human valuations and cosmic facts) and try to show that it is not the truth; but if one is determined to will and to live the possibility of nihilism, then one no longer has any independent standpoint under one's feet; worse than Kierkegaard 'out upon the seventy thousand fathoms of water', one is actually sucked down and engulfed: what from the independent standpoint of responsible freedom was regarded as the unavoidable ambiguity of good and evil in the world becomes, first, the ambiguity of one's own will, and then its abandonment to the eternal destruction and the eternal return and the dionysian ecstasy. No more than scepticism can be overcome by doubting it can nihilism be overcome by willing it.

COLIN WILSON describes what the philosophy of meaninglessness meant for others in the nineteenth century:

Most of these poets of the late nineteenth century were only 'half in love with easeful death'; the other half clung very firmly to life and complained about its futility. None of them, not even Thomson, goes as far as Wells in *Mind at the End of Its Tether*. But follow their pessimism further, press it to the limits of complete sincerity, and the result is a completely life-denying nihilism that is actually a danger to life. When Van Gogh's 'Misery will never end', is combined with Evan Strowde's 'Nothing is worth doing', the result is a kind of spiritual syphilis that can hardly stop short of death or insanity. Conrad's story *Heart of Darkness* deals with a man who has brought himself to this point; he dies murmuring: 'The horror, the horror' Conrad's narrator comments: '... I wasn't arguing with a lunatic either ... His intelligence was perfectly clear; concentrated ... upon himself with a horrible intensity, yet clear ... But his soul was mad. Being alone in the Wilderness, it had looked within itself, and ... it had gone mad: he had summed up; he had judged: the Horror.'

MICHAEL HARRINGTON writes of those who have passed beyond the exhilaration which Nietzsche felt to a profound pessimism. If Nietzsche believed that *God* is dead, many in the twentieth century have come to feel that *man* is dead also.

After God died, Man, who was supposed to replace Him, grew sick of himself. This resulted in a crisis of belief and disbelief which made the twentieth century spiritually empty.
   God died in the nineteenth century. Nietzsche announced the event as a fact, not as an argument, and his report has been taken as the starting point of most serious theology ever since ...
   But since God did not have any heir, the funeral has been going on for over a hundred years. The nineteenth century predicted often enough that the modern world would dispel faith. It did not, however, expect that it would subvert anti-faith as well.

JEAN-PAUL SARTRE emphasizes the need to draw the consequences of atheism 'right to the end':

And when we speak of 'abandonment'—a favourite word of Heidegger—we only mean to say that God does not exist, and that it is necessary to draw the consequences of his absence right to the end.

IF ATHEISM DOESN'T LEAD TO NIHILISM, WHERE ELSE CAN IT LEAD?

Atheism in itself can hardly be a complete world-view. All that the atheist claims is that there is no god, and he has to look in some other direction to find a satisfying world-view. The three most popular forms of atheism at the present time are Marxism, existentialism, and humanism.

JEAN-PAUL SARTRE describes very vividly the atmosphere in which he was brought up and how 'God' gradually 'died' for him. His existentialism was simply an attempt to take his atheism to its logical conclusion:

My family had been affected by the slow de-christianization which was born in the Voltaire-influenced *haute bourgeoisie* and took a century to spread to every stratum of Society: without this general slackening of faith, Louise Guillemin, a young Catholic lady from the provinces, would have made more fuss about marrying a Lutheran. Naturally, everyone at home believed: for reasons of discretion ... An atheist was an eccentric, a hot-head whom you did not invite to dinner lest he 'create a scandal', a fanatic burdened with taboos who denied himself the right to kneel in church, to marry his daughters or indulge in tears there, who took it on himself to prove the truth of his doctrine by the purity of his conduct, who injured himself and his happiness to the extent of robbing himself of his means of dying comforted, a man with a phobia about God who saw his absence everywhere and who could not open his mouth without saying His name: in short, a Gentleman with religious convictions. The believer had none: for two thousand years the Christian certainties had had time to prove themselves; they belonged to everyone, and they were required to shine in the priest's glance, in the half-light of a church, and to illumine souls, but no one needed to appropriate them to himself; they were the common patrimony. Polite society believed in God so that it need not talk of Him. How tolerant religion seemed! How convenient it was: the

Nihilism has been described as an abyss which one can plunge into, or pass by. There can be no such thing as a tentative dip.

said, 'he can do as he pleases.' It was reckoned, at the time, far harder to acquire faith than to lose it.

Deep down, it all bored me to death; I was led to unbelief not through conflicting dogma but through my grand-parents' indifference. Yet I believed: in my nightshirt, kneeling on my bed, hands folded, I said my daily prayer but thought less and less often about the good God ... For several years longer, I kept up public relations with the Almighty; in private, I stopped associating with Him. Once only I had the feeling that He existed. I had been playing with matches and had burnt a mat; I was busy covering up my crime when suddenly God saw me. I felt His gaze inside my head and on my hands; I turned round and round in the bathroom, horribly visible, a living target. I was saved by indignation: I grew angry at such a crude lack of tact, and blasphemed, muttering like my grandfather: '*Sacré nom de Dieu de nom de Dieu de nom de Dieu.*' He never looked at me again.

I have just told the story of a missed vocation; I needed God, he was given to me, and I received him without understanding what I was looking for. Unable to take root in my heart, he vegetated in me for a while and then died. Today, when he is mentioned, I say with the amusement and lack of regret of some ageing beau who meets an old flame: 'Fifty years ago, without that misunderstanding, without that mistake, without the accident which separated us, there might have been something between us.' Nothing happened between us ...

Atheism is a cruel, long-term business: I believe I have gone through it to the end.

Christian could abandon Mass and yet marry his children in church, smile at the religious 'art' of the Place Saint-Sulpice and shed tears as he listened to the Wedding March from Lohengrin; he was not obliged to lead an exemplary life or to die in despair, or even to have himself cremated. In our circle, in my family, faith was nothing but an official name for sweet French liberty; I had been baptized, like so many others, to preserve my independence: in refusing me baptism, they would have been afraid of doing harm to my soul; as a registered Catholic, I was free, I was normal. 'Later on,' they

AGNOSTICISM

Whereas the atheist says 'God *does not exist*', the agnostic says 'We *don't know* if God exists, and we *can't possibly know* for certain. No matter how hard we try to find the truth through reason or the heart, we cannot hope to find it. Our minds are finite, and we cannot solve the mysteries of the universe. We must be content to recognize the limits of our knowledge, and not hope to know anything beyond these limits.'

The word 'agnostic' was first coined by T.H. HUXLEY (1825–95), the grandfather of Aldous Huxley and Julian Huxley.

When I reached intellectual maturity, and began to ask myself whether I was an atheist, a theist, or a pantheist; a materialist or an idealist; a Christian or a freethinker, I found that the more I learned and reflected, the less ready was the answer; until at last I came to the conclusion that I had neither art nor part with any of these denominations, except the last. The one thing in which most of these good people were agreed was the one thing in which I differed from them. They were quite sure they had attained a certain 'gnosis'—had more or less successfully solved the problem of existence; while I was quite sure I had not, and had a pretty strong conviction that the problem was insoluble. And, with Hume and Kant on my side, I could not think myself presumptuous in holding fast by that opinion. This was my situation when I had the good fortune to find a place among the members of that remarkable confraternity of antagonists, long since deceased, but of green and pious memory, the Metaphysical Society. Every variety of philosophical and theological opinion was represented there, and expressed itself with entire openness; most of my colleagues were -ists of one sort or another and, however kind and friendly they might be, I, the man without a rag of a label to cover himself with, could not fail to have some of the uneasy feeling of the historical fox when, after leaving the trap in which his tail remained, he presented himself to his normally elongated companions. So I took thought, and invented what I conceived to be the appropriate title of 'agnostic'. It came into my head as suggestively antithetic to the 'gnostic' of Church history, who professed to know so much about the very things of which I was ignorant; and I took the earliest opportunity of parading it at our Society, to show that I, too, had a tail, like the other foxes. To my great satisfaction, the term took; and when the *Spectator* had stood god-father to it, any suspicion in the minds of respectable people that a knowledge of its parentage might have awakened was, of course, completely lulled.

CHARLES DARWIN (1809–82) gradually became an agnostic. At the time when he wrote the *Origin of Species* (published in 1859), he described himself as a 'Theist':

When thus reflecting, I feel compelled to look to a First Cause having an intelligent mind in some degree analogous to that of man; and I deserve to be called a Theist.

Disbelief, however, gradually crept over him, and in his *Autobiography* (written in 1876) he wrote:

The mystery of the beginning of all things is insoluble to us; and I for one must be content to remain an Agnostic.

His agnosticism had a profound effect on his way of thinking about the universe and the meaning of human life:

My theology is a simple muddle; I cannot look at the universe as the result of blind chance, yet I can see no evidence of beneficient design, or indeed of design of any kind, in details.

Believing as I do that man in the distant future will be a far more perfect creature than he now is, it is an intolerable thought that he and all other sentient beings are doomed to complete annihilation after such long-continued progress.

A man who has no assured and ever present belief in the existence of a personal God or of a future existence with retribution and reward, can have for his rule of life, as far as I can see, only to follow those impulses and instincts which are the strongest or which seem to him the best ones.

The horrid doubt always arises whether the convictions of man's mind, which has developed from the mind of the lower animals, are of any value

or at all trustworthy. Would anyone trust the conviction of a monkey's mind, if there are any convictions in such a mind?

My mind seems to have become a kind of machine for grinding general laws out of large collections of facts, but why this should have caused the atrophy of that part of the brain alone, on which the higher tastes depend, I cannot conceive.

In my Journal I wrote that whilst standing in the midst of the grandeur of a Brazilian forest, 'it is not possible to give an adequate idea of the higher feelings of wonder, admiration, and devotion which fill and elevate the mind'. I well remember my conviction that there is more in man than the mere breath of his body; but now the grandest scenes would not cause any such conviction and feelings to arise in my mind. It may be truly said that I am like a man who has become colour-blind.

The following are some twentieth-century examples of agnosticism:

Albert Einstein

To ponder interminably over the reason for one's own existence or the meaning of life in general seems to me, from an objective point of view, to be sheer folly.
ALBERT EINSTEIN

No man has a right to speak for any one except himself and those who happen to resemble him ... Every man has as good a right to his own particular world-view as to his own particular kidneys ...
ALDOUS HUXLEY

The universe in general must, I think, simply be accepted as a totally inexplicable mystery.
BARBARA WOOTON

In religion above all things the only thing of use is an objective truth. The only God that is of use is a being who is personal, supreme, and good, and whose existence is as certain as that two and two makes four. I cannot penetrate the mystery. I remain an agnostic, and the practical outcome of agnosticism is that you act as though God did not exist.
SOMERSET MAUGHAM

While I believe that there can be an explanation in mundane terms for anything that happens within the world, I do not think it makes sense to ask for an explanation of the existence or the characteristics of the world as a whole. In this sense, it is a matter of brute fact that the universe exhibits the patterns which it does.
A.J. AYER

Scientific enquiry presupposes the situation of human beings confronting objects in this world. Anything supposed outside these conditions is not open to its inquiry. Anything totally transcendent, encompassing both subject and object, for example, is

beyond such enquiry, and beyond conceptual thought ... Ultimately, everything as given is equally inscrutable and mysterious; there is nothing privileged in terms of which all the rest can be explained. This is what is meant by the renunciation of 'God-like knowledge'. Agnosticism, which is more fundamental and radical than atheism, is the only position warranted by experience: recognition of the permanent nature and conditions of human knowledge, with its open horizon of continuous progressive investigation.
H.J. BLACKHAM

ALBERT CAMUS shows that his philosophy begins from an attitude of 'passionate unbelief':

Contemporary unbelief does not rest on science as it did towards the close of the last century. It denies both science and religion. It is no longer the skepticism of reason in the presence of miracle. It is a passionate unbelief.

JEAN-PAUL SARTRE's philosophy of existentialism, similarly, begins with the scepticism of the agnostic whose attitudes are described by a character in the novel *Nausea*:

I am beginning to believe that nothing can ever be proved. These are reasonable hypotheses which take the facts into account: but I am only too well aware that they come from me, that they are simply a way of unifying my own knowledge.

WHERE DOES AGNOSTICISM LEAD?
● It leads to a frightening world in which there are no certainties. Novelists, playwrights and artists are more helpful than philosophers in enabling us to see where agnosticism leads.

MARTIN ESSLIN writing about the Theatre of the Absurd:

The Theatre of the Absurd ... can be seen as the reflection of what seems to be the attitude most genuinely representative of our own time.

The hallmark of this attitude is its sense that the certitudes and unshakable basic assumptions of former ages have been swept away, that they have been tested and found wanting, that they have been discredited as cheap and somewhat childish illusions.

The plays of Samuel Beckett, for example, present a world 'where there is no certainty':

Samuel Beckett

Language in Beckett's plays serves to express the breakdown, the disintegration of language. Where there is no certainty, there can be no definite meanings—and the impossibility of ever attaining certainty is one of the main themes of Beckett's plays. Godot's promises are vague and uncertain. In *Endgame*, an unspecified something is taking its course, and when Hamm anxiously asks, 'We're not beginning to ... to ... mean something?' Clov merely laughs. 'Mean something! You and I mean something!'
MARTIN ESSLIN

EUGENE IONESCO's plays convey the feeling of the absurdity and meaninglessness of life:

Absurd is that which is devoid of purpose ... Cut off from his religious, metaphysical, and transcendental roots, man is lost; all his actions become senseless, absurd, useless.

BUNUEL's film *Belle de Jour*, which appeared in 1968, portrays both the real world and a world of fantasy at the same time, in such a way that one can never be sure what is going on.

Most audiences will not find anything visually shocking about *Belle de Jour*. They will find instead a cumulative mystery: What is really happening and what is not? ... The film continues—switching back and forth between Severine's real and fantasy worlds so smoothly that after a while it becomes impossible to say which is which ... There is no way of knowing—and this seems to be the point of the film with which Bunuel says he is winding up his 40-year career. Fantasy, he seems to be saying, is nothing but the human dimension of reality that makes life tolerable, and sometimes even fun.

HAROLD PINTER's plays portray a world in which certainties about people have dissolved:

The desire for verification is understandable, but cannot always be satisfied. There are no hard distinctions between what is real and what is unreal, nor between what is true and what is false. The thing is not necessarily either true or false; it can be both true and false. The assumption that to verify what has happened and what is happening presents few problems, I take to be inaccurate. A character on the stage who can present no convincing argument or

Harold Pinter

information as to his past experiences, his present behaviour or his aspirations, nor give a comprehensive analysis of his motives is as legitimate and as worthy of attention as one who, alarmingly, can do all these things. The more acute the experience the less articulate its expression.

● Professional philosophers abandon their search for truth. Traditional philosophy has always been concerned with the pursuit of the truth. Now, however, philosophers generally have abandoned the search for truth in the older sense, and have been forced to limit the field of their enquiries to, for example, the study of concepts, and the study of the meaning of words.

Ernest Gellner takes up a sentence from the book *English Philosophy since 1900* by G.J. Warnock: 'The proper concern of philosophy is with concepts, with the ways and means by which we think and communicate.' He believes that this attitude in a professional philosopher amounts to a complete betrayal of what philosophy in the past has always tried to do. This is how his criticism is summed up by LESLIE PAUL:

This has given rise to a paradox worthy of *Beyond the Fringe* that not a few philosophers disbelieve in philosophy: they believe that philosophy is the pathology of language and their own role, as diagnosticians and therapists of linguistic mistakes, is to catch out the chaps who indulge in it. It is as if, the sociologist Ernest Gellner said, ... swimming instructors no longer believed it possible to swim. In an epigram not easily forgotten he wrote, 'A cleric who loses his faith abandons his calling, a philosopher who loses his, redefines his subject.'

The view that the needle *must* be in the haystack is extremely powerful, and operative in making philosophers seek it. The needle has not turned up. But the burrowing in this haystack has become habitual and established, and a cessation of it would leave men in a bewildered state. Some have no other skills. So, some alternative positions have emerged and are to be found: there *may* be needles in the haystack. Haystacks are interesting. We like hay.

DONALD KALISH, writing about the present state of moral philosophy:

There is no system of philosophy to spin out. There are no ethical truths, there are just clarifications of particular ethical problems. Take advantage of these clarifications and work out your own existence. You are mistaken to think that anyone ever had the answers. There are no answers. Be brave and face up to it.

● It affects the way we think about science. In the early period of modern science, it was confidently believed that the scientist was engaged in the pursuit of 'the truth' about the universe. By observation and experiment, he believed that he would eventually be able to formulate reliable theories about how the universe works. Scientists today, however, make a very much more limited claim about what they are doing:

It is not possible for the brain to arrive at *certain* knowledge. All those formal systems, in mathematics and physics and the philosophy of science, which claim to give foundations for certain truth are surely mistaken. I am tempted to say that we do not look for truth, but for knowledge. But I dislike this form of words, for two reasons. First of all, we do *look* for truth, however we define it; it is what we *find* that is knowledge. And second, what we fail to find is not truth but certainty; the nature of truth is exactly the knowledge that we do find ... No knowledge can be certain that continues to expand with us as we live inside the growing flesh of our experience.
BRONOWSKI

The modern theories are never more than models to suggest new lines of practical action, and therefore capable of being discarded at any time in favour of radically new models in a way which would be impossible if they were attempts to express the hidden truth behind phenomena. Experimental science succeeds by finding truth in experience, in action, and this is utterly incompatible with the traditional outlook on the world both logically and psychologically.
WREN-LEWIS

The following extract is from a review by DOUGLAS SPANNER of the book *The Survival of God in the Scientific Age* by Alan Isaacs:

Dr. Isaac's humanism has no place for Truth ... Science has often been regarded as 'the disinterested search for Truth'. To express it thus is simply to imply that in some sense truth is an absolute, already existent and awaiting the searcher; but this is too near to being a concession to the theologians to be acceptable to the rationalist. Science has been held to seek truth in two respects at least; with regard to its *facts*, and with regard to its *theories*.

However, as Dr. Isaacs rightly points out, 'the scientist no longer talks about facts as if there were fragments of the truth. The word "fact", the scientist now sees, involves highly emotional ideas which are of much greater use to lawyers and theologians.' Instead, 'science deals not with facts but with observations.' The difference? Simply facts are things conceived of as true in themselves, *i.e. absolutely*; observations, on the other hand, are *relative* to the observer, and the relationship conditions their validity. Thus we slip our moorings!

Dr. Isaacs reveals by the whole tenor of his argument, that truth is no longer his goal; what he seeks for is rather *validity for the moment*.

This is how C.S. LEWIS interpreted some of these developments in modern science:

Men became scientific because they expected Law in nature, and they expected Law in nature because they believed in a Legislator. In most modern scientists this belief has died: it will be interesting to see how their confidence in uniformity survives it. Two significant developments have already appeared—the hypothesis of a lawless subnature, and the surrender of the claim that science is true. We may be living nearer than we suppose to the end of the Scientific Age.

● It leads beyond itself to other philosophies. Most people find it very hard to be content with the bare answer of agnosticism. Their restlessness has usually led them *beyond* the point of pure agnosticism to existentialism, for example.

C.S. Lewis

BARON VON HUGEL, writing in 1916, summed up in some prophetic words how dissatisfaction with agnosticism would lead many to the answer of pantheism:

Agnosticism is going, going, gone. Not it, but Pantheism is now and will long be, the danger of religion.

MYSTICISM

The mystic generally starts from the same position as the agnostic: he denies the possibility of knowing God with his mind. But he believes that knowledge of God of a different kind *is* possible—and this is a knowledge based purely on the mystical experience of union with 'God'.

F.C. HAPPOLD gives this summary of the main characteristics of mystical states:

1. They defy expression in terms which are fully intelligible to those who have not had some analogous experience.

2. Though states of feeling, they are also states of knowledge, resulting in a deeper insight into the nature of things.

3. Except in the case of true contemplatives, when they can result in a permanent shift of consciousness, they are infrequent and of short duration.

4. They convey the sense of something 'given', not dependent on one's own volition.

5. There is a consciousness of the oneness of everything.

6. They also have a sense of timelessness.

7. There is forced on one the conviction that the familiar phenomenal *ego* is not the real *I*.

Mysticism has always been a basic element in the Eastern religions, especially in Zen Buddhism, which claims that mystical experience brings real knowledge:

The purpose of Zen is to pass beyond the intellect. All that we know, we know but about. The expert, a wit has said, learns more and more about less and less; Zen wearies of learning about it and about, and strives to *know*. For this a new faculty is needed, the power of immediate perception, the intuitive awareness which comes when the perceiver and the perceived are merged in one. All mystics use this faculty, and all alike are unable to make their knowledge known. But he who knows can only say that he knows; to communicate what he knows he has to descend to the realm of concepts, counters of agreed and common meaning. Such are words, but they are fallible means of making our knowledge known ... What *knows?* The answer is Buddhi, the faculty of direct awareness, as present in every human mind as the intellect which all possess but few have yet developed to the full.

All phrases, dogmas, formulas; all schools and codes; all systems of thought and philosophy, all 'isms', including Buddhism, all these are means to the end of *knowing*, and easily become and are not perceived as obstacles in the way. Zen technique is designed to develop the mind to the limits of thought and then to drive it to the verge of the precipice, where thought can go no further. And then? As Dr Graham Howe, the psychiatrist, oftens says to his patients, 'when you come to a precipice, why stop, or go round, or go back? Why not go over? For only then can we go on, and progress is a walking on and on to the Goal. It is true that at a later stage one learns that there is no walking and no Goal, but that is Zen ... Meanwhile, until we achieve the goal of purposelessness, let us have this purpose: Said the Master Ummon to his monks, 'If you walk, just walk; if you sit, just sit, but don't wobble!' ...

The vision may come quite suddenly or slowly arise. It is in no way to be confused with a psychic trance or the phantasy of the schizophrenic. Nor is it concerned with morality or any man-made code. It is a foretaste of the Absolute Moment, of Cosmic Consciousness, of the condition in which I and my Father are one ...

... Others who have tried to describe the reward of their years of tremendous effort speak of a sense of certainty, of serenity, of clarity, and of unity with nature and the universe around. Hui-neng described the serenity:

Imperturbable and serene the ideal man practises no virtue;

Self-possessed and dispassionate he commits no sin;

Calm and silent he gives up seeing and hearing;

Even and upright his mind abides nowhere.
CHRISTMAS HUMPHREYS

Mysticism, however, is not confined to any one religion. There have been many within the Christian tradition who have taught some kind of mystical approach to the knowledge of God. They claim that mystical theology is

an incommunicable and inexpressible knowledge and love of God or of religious truth received in the spirit without precedent, effort or reasoning.
DAVID KNOWLES

The Cloud of Unknowing (an anonymous work of the fourteenth century) speaks of 'love' as a way of knowing God:

All rational beings, angels and men, possess two faculties, the power of knowing and the power of loving. To the first, to the intellect, God who made them is forever unknowable, but to the second, to love, he is completely knowable, and that by every separate individual. So much so that one loving soul by itself, through its love, may know for itself him who is incomparably more than sufficient to fill all souls that exist.

Whoever hears or reads about all this, and thinks that it is fundamentally an activity of the mind, and proceeds then to work it all out along these lines, is on quite the wrong track ... Do not attempt to achieve this experience intellectually. I tell you truly that it cannot come this way ...

By 'darkness' I mean 'a lack of knowing'—just as anything that you do not know or may have forgotten may be said to be 'dark' to you, for you cannot see it with your inward eye. For this reason it is called 'a cloud', not of the sky, of course, but 'of unknowing', a cloud of unknowing between you and your God.

SIMONE WEIL, a French writer and philosopher (1909–43):

The mysteries of the faith are not a proper object of the intelligence, permitting affirmation or denial. They are not of the order of truth, but are above it. The only part of the human soul which is capable of any real contact with them is

the faculty of supernatural Love. It alone therefore is capable of an adherence in regard to them.

LIN YUTANG, a Chinese writer who contributed to an anthology of English essays in the 1960s, shows how ideas from the Chinese religion of Taoism can appeal to people in the Western world:

I believe that the only kind of religious belief left for the modern man is a kind of mysticism in the broadest sense of the word, such as preached by Lao-tse. Broadly speaking, it is a kind of reverence and respect for the moral order of the universe, philosophic resignation to the moral order, and the effort to live our life in harmony with this moral order. The *tao* in Taoism exactly means this thing. It is broad enough to cover the most advanced present and future theories of the universe. It is, for me, the only antidote against modern materialism.

ALDOUS HUXLEY explains how the mystic uses the technique of meditation as a way of perceiving 'ultimate spiritual reality':

Meditation is more than a method of self-education; it has also been used, in every part of the world and from the remotest periods, as a method for acquiring knowledge about the essential nature of things, a method for establishing communion between the soul and the integrating principle of the universe. Meditation, in other words, is the technique of mysticism ... Properly practised ... meditation may result in a state of what has been called 'transcendental consciousness'—the direct intuition of, and union with an ultimate spiritual reality that is perceived as simultaneously beyond the self and in some way within it.

He shows how mysticism arises out of scepticism:

To the mystics who are generally regarded as the best of their kind, ultimate reality ... appears as a spiritual reality so far beyond particular form or personality that nothing can be predicated of it.

'The atman is silence' is what the Hindus say of ultimate spiritual reality. The only language that can convey any idea about the nature of this reality is the language of negation, of paradox, of extravagant exaggeration. The pseudo-Dionysius speaks of the 'ray of the divine darkness' of 'the super-lucent darkness of silence' and of the necessity to 'leave behind the senses and the intellectual operations and all things known by sense and intellect'. 'If anyone', he writes, 'seeing God, understands what he has seen, he has not seen God.' 'Nescio, nescio,' was what St Bernard wrote of the ultimate reality; 'neti, neti,' was Yajnavalkya's verdict at the other side of the world. 'I know not, I know not: not so, not so.'

He says that in a mystical experience the mystic loses consciousness of his own individuality and personality, and feels himself part of 'an impersonal spiritual reality underlying all being':

They find that their visions disappear, that their awareness of a personality fades, that the emotional outpourings which were appropriate when they seemed to be in the presence of a person, become utterly inappropriate and finally give place to a state in which there is no emotion at all ...
    This new form of experience—the imageless and

emotionless cognition of some great impersonal force—is superior to the old and represents a closer approach to ultimate reality.

In one of his later books, *The Doors of Perception* (1954), he advocated the use of drugs such as mescalin to induce this kind of mystical experience:

What happens to the majority of the few who have taken mescalin under supervision can be summarized as follows:
    1. The ability to remember and to 'think straight' is little if at all reduced ...
    2. Visual impressions are greatly intensified and the eye recovers some of the perceptual innocence of childhood, when the sensum was not immediately and automatically subordinated to the concept ...
    3. Though the intellect remains unimpaired and though perception is enormously improved, the will suffers a profound change for the worse. The mescalin taker sees no reason for doing anything in particular and finds most of the causes for which, at ordinary times, he was prepared to act and suffer, profoundly uninteresting. He can't be bothered with them, for the good reason that he has better things to think about.
    4. These better things may be experienced (as I experienced them) 'out there', or 'in here', or in both worlds, the inner and the outer, simultaneously or successively. That they *are* better seems to be self-evident to all mescalin takers who come to the drug with a sound liver and an untroubled mind ...
Other persons discover a world of visionary beauty. To others again is revealed the glory, the infinite value and

meaningfulness of naked existence, of the given, unconceptualized event. In the final stage of ego-lessness there is an 'obscure knowledge' that All is in all—that All is actually each. This is as near, I take it, as a finite mind can ever come to 'perceiving everything that is happening everywhere in the universe' ...

From this ... excursion into the realm of theory we may now return to the miraculous facts—four bamboo chair legs in the middle of a room. Like Wordsworth's daffodils, they brought all manner of wealth—the gift beyond price, of a new direct insight into the very Nature of Things, together with a more modest treasure of understanding in the field, especially, of the arts.

In a conversation with his wife shortly before his death in 1963 he admitted that while imagining that he was experiencing release through taking drugs, he realized that 'when one thinks one's got beyond oneself one hasn't':

It (an inner discovery Huxley had just made) shows ... the almost boundless nature of the ego ambition. I dreamed, it must have been two nights ago ... that in some way I was in a position to make an absolute ... *cosmic* gift to the world ... Some *vast* act of benevolence was going to be done, in which *I* should have the sort of star role ... In a way it was absolutely terrifying, showing that when *one thinks one's got beyond oneself one hasn't*.

Some writers within the Christian tradition have been so greatly influenced by this trend towards mysticism in the Western world that they believe Christianity must become more of a mystical religion if it is to survive. F.C. HAPPOLD comes to the conclusion that the *only possible religion for twentieth-century man is a mystical religion and that all theological language must be recognized as a language of symbols.*

H.R. ROOKMAAKER, a Dutch professor of the history of art (1922–77), shows in his book *Modern Art and the Death of a Culture* how these mystical ideas were introduced into western 'pop' culture in the 1960s through music, drugs, meditation, or the traditional observance of Eastern religious faiths:

H.R. Rookmaaker

There is no age as mystical as ours. Yet it is mysticism with a difference: it is a nihilistic mysticism, for God is dead. Very old ideas are being revived: gnosticism, neo-platonic ideas of reality emanating from and returning to God, and Eastern religion, a religion with a god that is not a god but impersonal and universalist, a god which (not who!) is everything and therefore nothing, with a salvation that is in the end self-annihilation. In the quest for humanity man is even willing to lose his identity, his personality. It is like the creed that the Beatles sing (on their Sergeant Pepper Lonely Hearts Club Band record): 'When

you've seen beyond yourself ... the time will come when you see we're all one and life flows on within you and without you.'

The Beatles, the group which became famous all over the world after 1962, did a lot to draw both the LSD experience and Eastern mysticism together and to express it in their music. The first thing to do is to 'turn off your mind':

Turn off your mind relax and float down-stream,
it is not dying, it is not dying,
lay down all thought surrender to the void,
it is shining, it is shining.
That you may see the meaning of within,
it is speaking, it is speaking,
that love is all and love is ev'ryone,
it is knowing, it is knowing.
Without going out of my door.
I can know all things on earth.
Without looking out of my window
I could know the ways of heaven.

BRIAN WILSON of the Beach Boys group, writing in 1968:

My experience of God came from Acid; its the most important thing that's ever happened to me.

In his book *The Electric Kool-Aid Acid Test* (1968) TOM WOLFE describes the attitudes and experiences of Ken Kelsey and his group, The Merry Pranksters in the Haight-Asbury district of San Francisco where the drug cult became very popular in the 1960s:

Gradually the Prankster attitude began to involve the main things religious mystics have always felt, things common to Hindus, Buddhists, Christians, and for that matter Theosophists and even flying-saucer cultists. Namely, the *experiencing* of an Other World, a higher level of reality.

And a perception of the cosmic unity of this higher level. And a feeling of timelessness, the feeling that what we know as time is only the result of a naive faith in causality ...

There was something so ... *religious* in the air, in the very atmosphere of the Prankster life, and yet one couldn't put one's finger on it. On the face of it there was just a group of people who had shared an unusual psychological state, the LSD experience—

But exactly! The *experience*—that was the word! and it began to fall into place. In fact, none of the great founded religions, Christianity, Buddhism, Islam, Jainism, Judaism, Zoroastrianism, Hinduism, none of them began with a philosophical framework or even a main idea. They all began with an overwhelming *new experience*, what Joachin Wach called 'the experience of the holy', and Max Weber, 'possession of the deity', the sense of being a vessel of the divine, of the All-one.

Every vision, every insight of the ... original ... circle always came out of the *new experience* ... the *kairos* ... and how to tell it! How to get it across to the multitudes who have never had this experience for themselves? *You couldn't put it into words.* You had to create conditions in which they would feel an approximation of *that feeling*, the sublime *kairos.* You had to put them into ecstasy ... Buddhist monks immersing themselves in cosmic love through fasting and contemplations, Hindus zonked out in Bhakti, which is fervent love in the possession of God, ecstatics flooding themselves with Krishna through sexual orgies or plunging into the dinners of the Bacchanalia, Christians off in Edge City through gnostic onanism or the Heart of Jesus or the Child Jesus with its running sore—or—

THE ACID TESTS

And suddenly Kelsey sees that they, the Pranksters, already have the expertise and the machinery to create a mindblown state such as the world has never seen, totally wound up, lit up, amplified and ... controlled—plus the most efficient key ever devised to open the doors in the mind of the world: namely, Owlsley's LSD.

HOW CAN MYSTICAL KNOWLEDGE BE COMMUNICATED?

The mystic would answer that it *cannot* be communicated unless we have a mystical experience ourselves. Until and unless we have the experience, we cannot hope to know the truth. We cannot investigate anything with our minds first, and then decide whether we think it is true and whether we are going to commit ourselves to it. We cannot really begin to know what we are talking about until we have had the experience. And even when we ourselves have had the experience, we cannot hope to be able to describe or explain it adequately to others.

We are ... compelled to use the only language available, a language of symbol and paradox, which may be alien and incomprehensible to one not accustomed to it. The Divine Ground can be spoken of only in a language of polarity, a language of opposites, as non-personal and personal, supranatural and transnatural, other and not-other, without and within, transcendent and immanent, as Eternal Rest and yet evolving activity. All these descriptions are true in their different spheres and at their different levels of significance and awareness. None, alone, expresses the complete truth.
F.C. HAPPOLD

The problem, however, is that there can never be a 'true' interpretation of what a symbol means. It can mean different things to different people, and no one is in a position to say whether one person has grasped the truth more clearly than another. There is a profound ambiguity about symbols.

We can feel that a symbol has meaning, indeed most profound meaning, yet we cannot hope to put into words exactly how or why. Not only that, symbols are ambivalent, they act differently on and convey different meanings to different people. A symbol acts on the hearer or seer in such a way that it arouses in him feelings of awe or fear or love; it shifts his centre of awareness, so that things are perceived in a different light; it changes his values. It has thus a dynamic quality.
F.C. HAPPOLD

DO WORDS ANY LONGER HAVE ANY VALUE?

Mystics tend to say that when we have some experience, we discover that all the differences between good and evil, truth and falsehood as we know them, are overcome or transcended. Things that appear to us to be contradictory are brought together and seem both to be true.
NICHOLAS OF CUSA (1401–64):

I have learnt that the place where Thou (i.e. God) art found unveiled is girt round with the coincidence of contradictories, and this is the wall of Paradise wherein Thou dost abide, the door whereof is guarded by the proud spirit of Reason, and, unless he is vanquished, the way will not be open. Thus 'tis beyond the coincidence of contradictories Thou mayest be seen and nowhere this side thereof.

DIONYSIUS THE AREOPAGITE, a Syrian writer who probably lived in the sixth century AD:

... neither does anything that is, know Him as He is; ... neither can the reason attain to Him, nor name Him, nor know Him; neither is He darkness, nor light, nor the false nor the true; nor can any affirmation or negation be applied to Him, for though we may affirm or deny the things below Him, we can neither affirm nor deny Him, inasmuch as the all-perfect and unique Cause of all things transcends all affirmation, and the simple pre-eminence of His absolute nature is outside of every negation—free from every limitation beyond them all.

Surely we must conclude that words begin to mean very little when modern mystics like F.C. HAPPOLD bring together ideas and beliefs which seem so totally different from each other.

The Something, within and beyond the polarities of human perception, which simply *is* has been called by many names with various shades of meaning. In general terms it is spoken of as Ultimate Reality or Ultimate Truth. Some philosophers call it the Absolute. For the religious it is God. Chinese metaphysicians call it Tao, Plotinus the One. For Hinduism it is the Everlasting Spirit. For others Ultimate Reality is conceived as Mind, though in a much wider sense than our finite minds. Scientists use the concept of Energy, which cannot be known in itself, but only through its effects.

This Something which is the Is-ness of everything, is, however, in its completeness,

The Maharishi Mahesh Yogi has brought mysticism to many in the West. In the 1960s, with the Beatles, it was accompanied by psychedelia. In the 1980s it has the more restrained form of TM.

concealed from human perception. It is the *Unknowable*, the *Inexpressible*, the *Unconditioned*. It is the *Mystery* which can only be known, at least intellectually, as an *image*, a *model*, an *approximation*.

We are thus led on to draw a distinction between *Truth* and *truths*. Each partial *truth* may be true within its own sphere, but be only a fragment of *Truth* in its fullness; and, owing to the limitations of human perception, there is not seldom a conflict between different *truths*.

To India was given the vision of the spiritual foundation of the universe and the immanence of God in it; to Palestine the vision of the significance of the material world and of the historical process; to Greece the vision of order and reason.

Each of these visions of reality can be seen as complementary, each as a fragment of the full truth, each supplementing the other. All are necessary if one is to grasp the full significance of the Christ . . .

If you have stood in a Buddhist temple and gazed up at a beautiful statue of the Buddha above the flower-decked altar, you cannot, if you are spiritually sensitive, but have been impressed by the calm serenity of the face gazing down on you. This was the teacher who taught the way of the ending of the world's sorrow and an all-embracing compassion towards every sentient being. Here before you is the Buddhist 'God-image'. And, as you gazed, there may have come before you another symbol, another God-image, the image of the Man of Sorrows who took upon himself the world's sorrow and showed forth the love of God on a cross on a desolate hill. Are the two images incompatible; or are they complementary; two sides of the face of the Divine Totality?

PANTHEISM

Pantheism is the belief that 'God is everything' or 'everything is God'. It is one of the basic assumptions of the Eastern religions.

When people reach a point of complete atheism or agnosticism, certain conclusions seem to follow:

● that what we have in the universe is all there is; there is nothing beyond what we can see or touch—no unseen supernatural world;

● that death is the end of the individual; there is no life beyond.

Many are consistent and build their philosophies on these assumptions—for example, communism, existentialism and humanism. Others, however, are only too conscious of the vacuum created by the 'death' of God and the supernatural. They are anxious to find some belief which will account for their sense of awe and mystery as they look at the universe, and give it some meaning.

Those who take this course tend to retain the word 'God' and words such as 'divinity' and 'transcendence', but they give them different meanings. This position has many different forms of expression, but they all have certain features in common:

● 'God' does not mean a Personal Being who is distinct from the universe and was there 'before' the universe was created.

● 'God' is identified in some way with the universe as a whole or with some part or aspect of it

Australian sculptor William Ricketts expressed a pantheistic faith in his work, merging human figures with nature.

(e.g. the spirit or consciousness of man, the 'personal' aspect of the universe).

ROBERT BROW distinguishes four variations on this basic theme:

1. 'Everything there is is God.' (Absolute Pantheism)
2. 'God is the reality or principle behind nature.' (Modified Pantheism)
3. 'God is to nature as soul is to body.' (Modified Monism)
4. 'Only God is reality. All else is imagination.' (Absolute Monism).

The nearest word to 'God' in Hinduism is 'Brahman', the Universal Spirit. In the *Upanishads* he is described as the one Divine Being . . .

hidden in all beings, all-pervading, the self within all beings, watching over all works, dwelling in all beings, the witness, the perceiver, the only one, free from all qualities. He is the one ruler of many who (seem to act, but really) do not act; he makes the one seed manifold.

In the *Bhagavad Gita*, the Brahman 'speaks' to Arjuna through Krishna in these words:

Listen and I shall reveal to thee some manifestations of my divine glory . . .

I am the soul, prince victorious, which dwells in the heart of all things. I am the beginning, the middle, and the end of all that lives . . .

Among the sons of light I am Vishnu, and of luminaries the radiant sun. I am the lord of the winds and storms, and of the lights in the night I am the moon.

Of the Vedas I am the Veda of songs, and I am Indra, the chief of the gods. Above man's senses I am the mind, and in all living beings I am the light of consciousness.

Among the terrible powers I am the god of destruction . . .

I am time, never-ending time. I am the Creator who sees all. I am death that carries off all things, and I am the source of things to come.

And know, Arjuna, that I am the seed of all things that are; and that no being that moves or moves not can ever be without me...

Know thou that whatever is beautiful and good, whatever has glory and power is only a portion of my own radiance.

But of what help is it to thee to know this diversity? Know that with one single fraction of my Being I pervade and support the Universe, and know that I AM.

In the many traditions of Hindu philosophy, 'God' may be *either* personal *or* impersonal: or 'God' may be *both* personal *and* impersonal.

All that can be said is that the scriptures provide grist for the mills of both theistic and monistic interpretations which come later in Hindu story, with more grist, perhaps, for the monist than for the theist.
H.D. LEWIS

Pantheism has always been foreign to the Christian tradition of the West which emphasizes the distinction between God and the universe.

In the seventeenth century, however, the Dutch philosopher BARUCH SPINOZA (1632–77) introduced pantheistic ideas into Western philosophy. Some of his ideas have been summarized in this way:

The *Ethic*, which appeared posthumously in 1667, introduced us to a sort of palace, a palace wrought of concepts so aspiring they seem like a vaulted roof soaring up as though to mingle with the heavens. Geometrical, no doubt, but tremulous throughout with the breath of life itself, the *Ethic* is woven of tissues both human and divine, making the two a single category, and over its portals are engraven the words, God is

All and All is God ... All that is, is in God, and nothing can be, or be conceived, apart from God. God is thought; God is extension, and man, body, and soul, is a mode of Being.
PAUL HAZARD

Some theologians in the twentieth century have been deeply influenced by the Eastern religions. They maintain that they are not *departing from* the historic Christian understanding of God, but are merely *reinterpreting* the traditional ideas in a form that is more intelligible and acceptable today. These restatements, however, seem to come very close to pantheism, or else represent an uneasy compromise between pantheism and Christianity.

PAUL TILLICH (1886–1965) described God as 'Being Itself', rather than 'A Being':

The God who is *a* being is transcended by the God who is Being itself, the ground and abyss of every being. And the God who is *a* person is transcended by the God who is the Personal—Itself, the ground and abyss of every person.

God does not exist, He is being-itself beyond essence and existence. Therefore, to argue that God exists is to deny him.

This is how TILLICH explained his concept of God in a more popular form:

The name of this infinite and inexhaustible depth and ground of all being is *God*. That depth is what the word *God* means. And if that word has not much meaning for you, translate it, and speak of the depths of your life, of the source of your being, of your ultimate concern, of what you take seriously without any reservation. Perhaps, in order to do so, you must forget

everything traditional that you have learned about God, perhaps even that word itself. For if you know that God means depth, you know much about him. You cannot then call yourself an atheist or unbeliever. For you cannot think or say: Life has no depth! Life is shallow. Being itself is surface only. If you could say this in complete seriousness, you would be an atheist; but otherwise you are not. He who knows about depth knows about God.

TEILHARD DE CHARDIN wrote:

As early as in St. Paul and St. John we read that to create, to fulfil and to purify the world is, for God, to unify it by uniting it organically with himself. How does he unify it? By partially immersing himself in things, by becoming 'element', and then, from this point of vantage in the heart of matter, assuming the control and leadership of what we now call evolution. Christ, principle of universal vitality because sprung up as a man among men, put himself in the position (maintained ever since) to subdue under himself, to purify, to direct and superanimate the general ascent of consciousness into which he inserted himself. By a perennial act of communion and sublimation, he aggregates to himself the total psychism of the earth. And when he has gathered everything together and transformed everything, he will close in upon himself and his conquests, thereby rejoining, in a final gesture, the divine focus he has never left. Then, as St. Paul tells us, *God shall be in all*. This is indeed a superior form of 'pantheism' without trace of the poison of adulteration or annihilation: the expectation of perfect unity, steeped in which each element will reach its consummation at the same time as the universe.

The universe fulfilling itself in a synthesis of centres in perfect conformity with the laws of union. God, the centre of centres.

He described his position as 'a superior form of "pantheism"'. But he identified God so closely with the universe that it was difficult for him to maintain at the same time that God is transcendent and distinct from the universe:

To put an end once and for all to the fears of 'pantheism', as regards evolution, how can we fail to see that, in the case of a *converging universe* . . . the universal centre of unification . . . must be conceived as pre-existing and transcendent. A very real 'pantheism' if you like (in the etymological meaning of the word) but an absolutely legitimate pantheism—for if, in the last resort, the reflective centres of the world are effectively 'one with God', this state is obtained not by identification (God becoming all) but by the differentiating and communicating action of love (God all *in everyone*). And that is essentially orthodox and Christian.

JOHN ROBINSON, an Anglican theologian and bishop, in a controversial book called *Honest to God* published in 1963, tried to go beyond a mere 'restating of traditional orthodoxy':

I believe we are being called, over the years ahead, to far more than a restating of traditional orthodoxy in modern terms. Indeed, if our defence of the Faith is limited to this, we shall find in all likelihood that we have lost out to all but a tiny religious remnant. A much more radical recasting, I would judge, is

demanded, in the process of which the most fundamental categories of our theology—of God, of the supernatural, and of religion itself—must go into the melting.

Like Tillich, he rejected the idea of God as 'a Being'. In doing so he was not merely rejecting certain caricatures of God (as in deism), but vital elements of historic Christian belief:

The conception of God as *a* Being, a Person—like ourselves but supremely above and beyond ourselves—will, I believe, come to be seen as a human projection.

I believe, with Tillich, that we should give up speaking of 'the existence' of God. For it belongs to a way of thinking that is rapidly ceasing to be ours.

Unless we can represent him (God) in functional rather than ontological terms, he will rapidly lose all reality. As a Being he has no future.

He agreed with some words written by Julian Huxley in his book *Religion without Revelation*:

The sense of spiritual relief which comes from rejecting the idea of God as a superhuman being is enormous.

He vigorously rejected the accusation that he was propounding pantheism. He described his position by the word 'panentheism'. Writing about his earlier book *Honest to God* he said:

I was concerned not to abolish transcendence (for without transcendence God becomes indistinguishable from the world, and so superfluous), but to find a way of *expressing* transcendence which would not tie God's reality to a supernaturalistic or mythological world-view which, if not actually falsifying,

was largely meaningless for twentieth century man.

If one had to find a label to replace that of traditional 'theism' I would fall back on one that has a respectable pedigree but has never quite succeeded in establishing itself in orthodox Christian circles—namely, 'panentheism'. This is defined by *The Oxford Dictionary of the Christian Church* as 'the belief that the Being of God includes and penetrates the whole universe, so that every part of it exists in him, but (as against pantheism), that his Being is more than, and is not exhausted by, the universe.' It is the view that God is in everything and everything is in God.

He explained that the starting-point of his belief was:

. . . the awareness of the world as 'Thou'—and . . . the meeting through it of 'the Eternal Thou'.
. . . the overmastering, yet elusive, conviction of the 'Thou' at the heart of everything.

This seems to amount to saying: 'The universe is not impersonal. There is a kind of personal x, a personal quality in the universe over and above matter.' He used the word 'God' as a kind of pointer to this feeling that the universe is personal:

To use the famous image of Lao Tzu, it is the hole in the middle that makes the wheel. The word 'God' is useful not because it fills in what is in the middle, but precisely because it witnesses to that which can never be filled in. In itself the word is expendable, it 'says' nothing. But *something like it* is an indispensable necessity if we are to refer to the hole at all. Since there is in fact nothing quite like it—no word that can replace it as a direct substitute—I am convinced that we must be able to go on using it, if only as shorthand. And this means that we must try to redeem it.

To assert that '*God* is love' is to believe that in love one comes into touch with the most fundamental reality in the universe, that Being itself ultimately has this character.

To affirm that 'the Lord is my rock' is to affirm that there is a bottom, an utterly reliable and unshakable basis to living.

God-language does not describe a Thing-in-Itself or even a Person-in-Himself . . . It points to an ultimate relatedness in the very structure of our being from which we cannot get away. It is a way of keeping guard over the irreducible, ineffable mystery at the heart of all experience.

WHY KEEP THE NAME 'GOD'?

Why keep the name 'God'? If there is no personal Being called God, why not dispense with the name altogether? If we still need some name to describe the mystery of the universe, why not find a new and less confusing one?

PETER DUMITRIU describes a kind of mystical experience in which he sees that the sense and meaning of the universe is 'love'. He then wonders what *words* he should use:

What name was I to use? 'God', I murmured, 'God'. How else should I address Him. O Universe? O Heap? O Whole? As 'Father'? or 'Mother'? I might as well call Him 'Uncle'. As 'Lord'? I might as well say, 'Dear Sir', or 'Dear Comrade'. How could I say 'Lord' to the air I breathed and my own lungs which breathed the air? 'My child'? But he contained me, preceded me, created me. 'Thou' is His name, to which

'God' may be added. For 'I' and 'me' are no more than a pause between the immensity of the universe which is Him and the very depth of our self, which is also Him.

Dumitriu thinks it is obvious that he should use the name of 'God'. But is it so obvious and self-evident? Would not words like 'O Universe' 'O Heap' and 'O Whole' be very much more consistent? Is there anything more than convention and sentiment to justify choosing 'God'?

IS IT REALLY POSSIBLE AND HONEST TO IMPORT THESE IDEAS INTO A CHRISTIAN WORLD-VIEW?

There is bound to be an element of deception (whether conscious or unconscious) in continuing to use the word 'God' (which most people associate with a personal Being) and at the same time denying that such a personal Being exists. All these answers, therefore, contain an element of linguistic cheating, as the following three reactions from humanists to John Robinson's *Honest to God* point out:

(Robinson) is surely wrong in making such statements as that 'God is ultimate reality'. God is a hypothesis constructed by man to help him understand what existence is all about. The God hypothesis asserts the existence of some sort of supernatural person or supernatural being, exerting some kind of purposeful power over the universe and its destiny. To say that God is ultimate reality is just semantic cheating, as well as being so vague as to become effectively meaningless (and when Dr. Robinson continues by saying 'and ultimate reality must exist', he is surely running round a philosophically very vicious circle.)

Dr. Robinson, like Dr. Tillich and many other modernist theologians, seems to me, and indeed to any humanist, to be trying to ride two horses at once, to keep his cake and eat it. He wants to be modern and meet the challenge of our new knowledge by stripping the image of God of virtually all its spatial, material, mythological, Freudian, and anthropomorphic aspects. But he still persists in retaining the term *God*, in spite of all its implication of supernatural power and personality; and it is these implications, not the modernists' fine-spun arguments, which consciously or unconsciously affect the ordinary man and woman. Heads I win, tails you lose: humanists dislike this elaborate double-talk.
JULIAN HUXLEY

The disappearance of a personal deity does not . . . dispose of the riddle of the universe and of man's place therein. Nor can this riddle be solved by such verbal tricks as those which the Bishop of Woolwich (Robinson) proceeds to employ. According to him, 'God is by definition ultimate reality. And one cannot argue whether ultimate reality *exists*. One can only ask what ultimate reality is like.' Such statements, I submit, are purely semantic exercises, which, strictly interpreted, are devoid of all meaning. If God and ultimate reality are identical, then the statement that God is ultimate reality amounts to neither more nor less than an assertion that ultimate reality is ultimate reality.
BARBARA WOOTON

ALASDAIR MACINTYRE comments:

What is striking about Dr. Robinson's book is first and foremost that he is an atheist

... Yet ... he is unwilling to abandon the word 'God' and a great many kindred theological words. Yet I think that we might well be puzzled by this strong desire for a theological vocabulary; for the only reason given for preserving the name 'God' is that 'our being has depths which naturalism whether evolutionary, mechanistic, dialectical or humanistic, cannot or will not recognize'. But this is to say that all atheists to date have described 'our being' inadequately ... His book testifies to the existence of a whole group of theologies which have retained a theistic vocabulary but acquired an atheistic substance.

He points out that while the new theologies disown historic Christianity, they still depend on all the associations which surround the traditional language:

The formulas of the new theology seem to me to derive both such sense and such emotional power as they have by reason of their derivation from and association with the much more substantial faith of the past. Without that derivation and association these formulas, far from providing modern man with a faith rewritten in terms that he can understand, would be even more unintelligible than the theology they seek to correct. Thus the new theologians are in a fundamentally false position. They in fact depend on the traditionalism which they proclaim that they discard.

Writing about Paul Tillich:

Belief in God has been evacuated of all its traditional content. It consists now in moral seriousness and nothing more.

MARXISM

The theory of Marxism is derived largely from the writings of Karl Marx (see *Ten Key Thinkers*) and some of his closest associates, including Engels. It was Lenin who first saw that a truly socialist society in Russia would never come about by gradual, natural evolution, but that Marxists must take matters into their own hands and create a Marxist society through revolution.

He therefore set about planning revolutionary activity—for example, by urging his followers in the trade unions to use any method to achieve their goals:

If need be resort to all sorts of devices, manoeuvres, and illegal methods, to evasion and subterfuge ... in order to penetrate into the trade unions, to remain in them and to carry on Communist work in them at all costs.

As a result of the Bolshevik Revolution, the Czar's regime was overthrown, and the Soviet Union inaugurated in July 1918.

The Marxist Revolution in China was led by Mao Tse-tung, who defeated the Nationalist Government of Chiang Kai-shek in 1949 and established the People's Republic of China. Mao's new form of Marxism, called Maoism, emphasized the role of the peasants rather than the proletariat in the social revolution; and he encouraged guerilla warfare as a means of forwarding the revolution in other countries. China has done much in recent years to help less developed countries in the Third World, encouraging them in their struggle against the rich countries.

Marxists of all kinds are committed to work for socialist revolution all over the world.

HOW DOES THE MARXIST DECIDE HUMAN VALUES?
If we cannot base moral values on 'God' or on 'reason' or 'nature', there are only two alternatives: either
   1. total moral anarchy in which every individual behaves as he wishes;
or
   2. some powerful individual or group imposes its values on the rest of society.

Morality is determined by what is in the interests of the socialist revolution, which in practice means the leaders of the communist party.

NORMAN HAMPSON describes how this dilemma appeared to thoughtful minds at the time of the Enlightenment in the eighteenth century:

The escape from moral anarchy was already beginning to point towards a new totalitarian nightmare.

An attempt to base a code of ethics on purely human values was likely to lead, not to the emancipation of the individual, but to his immolation on the altar of society.

DOSTOIEVSKY realized in the nineteenth century that anarchy would sooner or later lead to a totalitarian government:

Starting from unlimited liberty, I arrive at unlimited despotism.

Marxism has therefore pointed to two sources for morality:

1. The morality which emerges from the economic system. In each epoch in history a set of moral values evolves as a direct result of the economic processes during that epoch. Moral values therefore vary according to the economic structure—for example, the capitalist structure produces capitalist moral values.

2. The morality which emerges from the development of a communist society. In this epoch man enjoys a good relationship with his neighbour, with the world and with himself. This final set of moral values seems suspiciously close to that of the Judaeo-Christian tradition!

HOW DO MARXIST VALUES WORK OUT IN PRACTICE?

LESLIE PAUL describes how Marxist moral values have been applied in practice by Marxist revolutionary governments:

If moral indignation is the motivator of Marxist parties in opposition, it disappears from their baggage once they attain power. There is a clear conflict between this morality in opposition and the immorality in power which has nothing to do with the ordinary process of corruption by office . . .

It was the moral passion of Marxism, and its principal child, Communism, which commended Marxism to so many social consciences in the interwar years and it was the disillusion with its moral consequences which has done so much to tarnish its image since. All over the world it has behaved with a moral indifference to human rights and sufferings. Its penal camps in Russia, which operated over at least a generation, probably succeeded in killing as many people as the Nazi extermination camps for the Jews. In lying, terror, secrecy, judicial murder, there has been little to choose between Nazi and Communist dictatorships.

A book called *The God that Failed*, published in 1950, consisted of essays written by six people in different European countries who had all at one time

In 1949 Mao Tse-tung established the Marxist People's Republic of China.

been members of the communist party, or very sympathetic to it. In the introduction RICHARD CROSSMAN pointed out that it was 'a despair of western values' which led each one of them towards communism:

The only link ... between these six very different personalities is that all of them—after tortured struggles of conscience—chose Communism because they had lost faith in democracy and were willing to sacrifice 'bourgeois liberties' in order to defeat Fascism. Their conversion, in fact, was rooted in despair—a despair of western values.

WHAT HAPPENS TO TRUTH?

In Marxist thinking any distortion of the facts of any situation is justified if it helps the aims of a Marxist group or government:

In Marxist doctrine there is no such thing as truth—at least not in the absolute sense— there is only relative truth.
ANDRE GIDE

GEORGE ORWELL, in his book *Nineteen Eighty-Four*:

Doublethink means the power of holding two contradictory beliefs simultaneously, and accepting both of them. The party intellectual knows that he is playing tricks with reality, but by the exercise of doublethink he also satisfies himself that reality is not violated.

This approach to truth in communism has some very practical consequences. It means, for example, that the authorities feel perfectly free to tell any lies they want if it serves their purpose. IGNAZIO SILONE, who was for many years a member of the Italian

George Orwell

Communist Party, describes an incident which took place at a meeting of the International in Moscow:

They were discussing one day, in a special commission of the Executive, the ultimatum issued by the central committee of the British trade unions, ordering its local branches not to support the Communist-led minority movement, on pain of expulsion. After the representative of the British Communist Party had explained the serious disadvantages of both solutions, because one meant the liquidation of the minority movement and the other the exit of the minority from the trade unions, the Russian delegate Piatnisky put forward a suggestion which seemed as obvious to him as Columbus' egg: 'The branches', he suggested, 'should declare that they submit to the discipline demanded, and then, in practice, should do exactly the contrary.' The English Communist interrupted: 'But that would be a lie.' Loud laughter greeted this ingenuous objection, frank, cordial, interminable laughter,

the like of which the gloomy offices of the Communist International had perhaps never heard before. The joke quickly spread all over Moscow, for the Englishman's entertaining and incredible reply was telephoned at once to Stalin and to the most important offices of State, provoking new waves of mirth everywhere.

NIKITA STRUVE, writing about contemporary Russia and its attitude to Christianity:

What impresses me ... is that atheism today seems to have given up the search for truth. Facts and arguments which tell against it are dismissed in silence.

WHAT KIND OF FUTURE DO WE HAVE TO LOOK FORWARD TO?

When ADAM SCHAFF asks the question 'what is the aim of life?' he expresses his Marxist understanding of the goal for which he is working:

Marxist theory ... leads to the general position that may be called 'social hedonism'—the view that the aim of human life is to secure the maximum happiness for the broadest mass of the people, and that only within the compass of this aim can personal happiness be reached.

ARTHUR KOESTLER'S novel *Darkness at Noon* was based on his knowledge of people involved in the Moscow Trials in the early 30s. The main character, Rubashov, has been condemned to death for crimes against the state and at any moment he expects the final summons. His feelings express the reaction of those who are not content to pin their hopes on a glorious future which they themselves will never see, and of which they see little evidence at the present time. The book ends with these words:

What happened to those masses, to this people? For forty years it had been driven through the desert, with threats and promises, with imaginary terrors and imaginary rewards. But where the Promised Land?

Did there really exist any such goal for this wandering mankind? That was a question to which he would have liked an answer before it was too late. Moses had not been allowed to enter the land of promise either. But he had been allowed to see it, from the top of the mountain, spread at his feet. Thus it was easy to die, with the visible certainty of one's goal before one's eyes. He, Nicolai Salmanowitch Rubashov, had not been taken to the top of a mountain; and wherever his eye looked, he saw nothing but desert and the darkness of night.

Arthur Koestler

EXISTENTIALISM

It is impossible to give a precise definition of existentialism, because it is not a precise philosophy. One of its basic ideas is that there can be no complete philosophical system which answers all our questions. It insists that instead of talking about 'objective truth', which can never be obtained, we should begin with the actual individual and his experience as a human being—with his freedom, his despair and his anguish. The following extracts give some idea of what existentialism stands for.

E.L. ALLEN defines it as:

the attempt to philosophize from the standpoint of the actor rather than from that of the detached spectator.

A proposition or truth is said to be *existential* when I cannot apprehend or assent to it from the standpoint of a mere spectator but only on the ground of my total existence. KARL HEIM

The Humanist Glossary, under existentialism:

Kierkegaard and Heidegger, who are religious existentialist philosophers, and Sartre, who is an atheist, all share certain fundamental ideas. The starting point of their philosophy is the plight of the individual, thrust, as it were, into a world without authority, system of values, of law or human nature. Their basic tenet is that there is an inescapable tension between thought and existence; existence cannot be thought and thought departs from
existence into abstraction. Man, being both thinker and in existence, has to live this tension, which he can never resolve once for all. Similarly, there are other oppositions which man has to live and cannot resolve because they make the human condition, e.g. faith and reason, the other and myself as persons. Human beings are always finding ways to escape from instead of living by, the conditions of the human situation.

Existentialism is nothing else but an attempt to draw the full conclusions from a consistently atheistic position.

Atheistic existentialism, of which I am a representative, declares with greater consistency that if God does not exist there is at least one being whose existence comes before its essence, a being which exists before it can be defined by any conception of it. That being is man or, as Heidegger has it, the human reality. What do we mean by saying that existence precedes essence? We mean that man first of all exists, encounters himself, surges up in the world—and defines himself afterwards. If man as the existentialist sees him is not definable, it is because to begin with he is nothing ... Man is nothing else but that which he makes of himself. That is the first principle of existentialism.

The first effect of existentialism is that it puts every man in possession of

himself as he is, and places the entire responsibility for his existence squarely upon his own shoulders. And, when we say that man is responsible for himself, we do not mean that he is responsible only for his own individuality, but that he is responsible for all men.
JEAN-PAUL SARTRE

The peculiarity of existentialism ... is that it deals with the separation of man from himself and from the world, which raises the questions of philosophy ... The main business of this philosophy therefore is not to answer the questions which are raised but to drive home the questions themselves until they engage the whole man and are made personal, urgent, and anguished ... Existentialism goes back to the beginning of philosophy and appeals to all men to awaken from their dogmatic slumbers and discover what it means to become a human being ...
The second business of philosophy ... is to cure the mind of looking for illusory objective universal answers, and to aid the person in making himself and getting his experience.
H.J. BLACKHAM

WHO OR WHAT AM I AS AN INDIVIDUAL?
The Humanist Glossary explains that existentialist philosophy *starts* with 'the plight of the individual':

Kierkegaard and Heidegger, who are religious existentialist philosophers, and Sartre, who is an atheist, all share certain fundamental ideas. The starting point of their philosophy is the plight of the individual, thrust, as it were, into a world without authority, system of values, of law or human nature.

The individual thus has to begin with himself and his own experience in approaching all the other basic human questions: for example each individual must affirm meaning in life; life has no meaning in itself—it only has the meaning that *I give* to it. There are no objective moral standards which can show me the difference between right and wrong—the individual must work out values for himself and cannot impose them on anyone else. It is in ways such as these that the individual seeks to 'authenticate' himself and to 'be' himself.

Some existentialist writers express vividly the loss of personality and individuality felt by many people. The character Roquentin in SARTRE's novel *Nausea* expresses these feelings in this way:

Now when I say 'I', it seems hollow to me. I can no longer manage to feel myself, I am so forgotten. The only real thing left in me is some existence which can feel itself existing. I give a long, voluptuous yawn. Nobody. Antoine Roquentin exists for Nobody. That amuses me. And exactly what is Antoine Roquentin? An abstraction. A pale little memory of myself wavers in my consciousness. Antoine Roquentin ... And suddenly the I pales, pales, and finally goes out ...

WHAT IS THE MEANING OF LIFE?
ALBERT CAMUS was not an existentialist in the strict sense of the term, but many of his ideas are close to those of existentialist writers:

I do not know whether this world has a meaning that is beyond me. But I know that I am unaware of this meaning and that, for the time being, it is impossible for me to know it. What can a meaning beyond

my condition mean to me? I can understand only in human terms. I understand the things I touch, things that offer me resistance.

It is plain that absurdist reasoning ... recognizes human life as the single necessary good, because it makes possible that confrontation, and because without life the absurdist wager could not go on. To say that life is absurd, one must live. How can one, without indulging one's desire for comfort, keep for oneself the exclusive benefits of this argument? The moment life is recognized as a necessary good, it becomes so for all men.
... the living warmth that gives forgetfulness of all ...

Everything which exalts life adds at the same time to its absurdity.

His character Mersault, in *The Outsider*, reminds himself, while waiting for his trial, that 'it's common knowledge that life isn't worth living':

Then all day there was my appeal to think about. I made the most of this idea, studying my effects so as to squeeze out the maximum of consolation. Thus I always began by assuming the worst; my appeal was dismissed. That meant, of course, I was to die. Sooner than others, obviously. 'But,' I reminded myself, 'it's common knowledge that life isn't worth living anyhow.' And, on a wide view, I could see that it makes little difference whether one dies at the age of thirty or three-score and ten—since in either case, other men and women will continue living, the world will go on as before. Also, whether I died now or forty years hence, this business of dying had to be got

Jean-Paul Sartre

through, inevitably. Still, somehow this line of thought wasn't as consoling as it should have been; the idea of all those years of life in hand was a galling reminder! However, I could argue myself out of it, by picturing what would have been my feelings when my term was up, and death had cornered me. Once one's up against it, the precise manner of one's death has obviously small importance.

SARTRE's novel *Nausea* conveys the feeling of meaninglessness in the experience of Roquentin:

His judgement pierced me like a sword and called in question my very right to exist. And it was true, I had always realized that: I hadn't any right to exist. I had appeared by chance, I existed like a stone, a plant, a microbe. My life grew in a haphazard way and in all directions. Sometimes it sent me vague signals; at other times I could feel nothing but an inconsequential buzzing.

I was just thinking ... that here we are, all of us, eating and drinking, to preserve our precious existence, and that there's nothing, nothing, absolutely no reason for existing.

One aspect of Roquentin's Nausea is the awareness of the bare existence of everything.

So this is the Nausea: this blinding revelation? To think how I've racked my brains over it! To think how much I've written about it! Now I know: I exist—the world exists—and I know that the world exists. That's all. But I don't care. It's strange that I should care so little about everything: it frightens me. It's since that day when I wanted to play ducks and drakes. I was going to throw that pebble, I looked at it and that was when it all began; I felt that it *existed*. And then, after that, there were other Nauseas; every now and then objects start existing in your hand.

But these things lose their names and their identity, and everything appears with a 'frightening, obscene nakedness':

Things have broken free from their names. They are there, grotesque, stubborn, gigantic, and it seems ridiculous to call them seats or say anything at all about them: I am in the midst of Things, which cannot be given names. Alone, wordless, defenceless, they surround me, under me, behind

me, above me. They demand nothing, they don't impose themselves, they are there ...

All of a sudden, there it was, as clear as day: existence had suddenly unveiled itself ... the diversity of things, their individuality, was only an appearance, a veneer. This veneer had melted, leaving soft monstrous masses, in disorder— naked, with a frightening, obscene nakedness.

He experiences the feeling that there are no fixed natural laws: 'anything could happen'.

It is out of laziness, I suppose, that the world looks the same day after day. Today it seemed to want to change. And in that case, *anything, anything* could happen.

The idiots. It horrifies me to think that I am going to see their thick, self-satisfied faces again. They make laws, they write Populist novels, they get married, they commit the supreme folly of having children. And meanwhile, vast, vague Nature has slipped into their town, it is infiltrated everywhere, into their houses, into their offices, into themselves. It doesn't move, it lies low, and they are right inside it, they breathe it, and they don't see it, they imagine that it is outside, fifty miles away. I *see* it, that Nature, I *see* it ... I know that its submissiveness is laziness, I know that it has no laws, that what they consider its constancy doesn't exist. It has nothing but habits and it may change those tomorrow.

An absolute panic took hold of me. I no longer knew where I was going. I ran along the docks, I turned into the deserted streets of the Beauvoisis district: the houses watched my flight with their mournful eyes. I kept saying to myself in anguish: 'Where shall I go? Where shall I go? *Anything* can happen.' ...

MARTIN ESSLIN speaks of the 'terrible stability of the world' as seen in Samuel Beckett's plays, where time loses all meaning.

Waiting is to experience the action of time, which is constant change. And yet, as nothing real ever happens, that change is in itself an illusion. The ceaseless activity of time is self-defeating, purposeless, and therefore null and void. The more things change, the more they are the same. That is the terrible stability of the world. 'The tears of the world are a constant quantity. For each one who begins to weep, somewhere else another stops.' One day is like another, and when we die, we might never have existed.

ALBERT CAMUS points out the contradiction in the absurdist position:

I proclaim that I believe in nothing and that everything is absurd, but I cannot doubt the validity of my own proclamation and I am compelled to believe, at least, in my own protest.

A literature of despair is a contradiction in terms ... In the darkest depths of our nihilism I have sought only for the means to transcend nihilism.

Today meaning can be found, if at all, only through the attitude of the man who is willing to *live* with the absurd, to remain open to the mystery which he can never pin down.
MAURICE FRIEDMAN

For many, the only way to *live* with the absurd is to *write* about it. The very fact that one feels the meaninglessness of life and yet is able to give artistic expression to it is a kind of defiance.

André Malraux

The greatest mystery is not that we have been flung at random among the profusion of the earth and the galaxy of the stars, but that in this prison we can fashion images of ourselves sufficiently powerful to deny our nothingness.
ANDRÉ MALRAUX

Everything happens as though I were only one of the particular existences of some great incomprehensible and central being ... Sometimes this great totality of life appears to me so dramatically beautiful that it plunges me into ecstasy. But more often it seems like a monstrous beast that penetrates and surpasses me and which is everywhere, within me and outside me ... And terror grips me and envelopes me more powerfully from moment to moment ... My only way out is to write, to make others aware of it, so as not to have to feel all of it alone, to get rid of however small a portion of it.
ARTHUR ADAMOV

WHAT BASIS IS THERE FOR MORAL VALUES?
ALBERT CAMUS believed that man's natural impulse to

rebellion should be the source from which values can be derived:

Rebellion is the common ground on which every man bases his first values. I *rebel*—therefore we *exist*.

The excesses to which rebellion has led in the last few centuries, he argued point to certain 'limits' or a new 'law of moderation'. It is up to the individual to perceive what these limits are, because they should be almost self-evident.

We know at the end of this long inquiry into rebellion and nihilism that rebellion with no other limits but historical expediency signifies unlimited slavery. To escape this fate, the revolutionary mind, if it wants to remain alive, must therefore return again to the sources of rebellion and draw its inspiration from the only system of thought which is faithful to its origins; thought which recognizes limits.

SARTRE was critical of French radicalism towards the end of the nineteenth century because it held on to traditional values long after their basis had dissolved:

Towards 1880, when the French professors endeavoured to formulate a secular morality, they said something like this: God is a useless and costly hypothesis, so we will do without it. However, if we are to have morality, a society and a law-abiding world, it is essential that certain values should be taken seriously; they must have an *a priori* existence ascribed to them. It must be considered obligatory *a priori* to be honest, not to lie, not to beat one's wife, to bring up children and so forth; so we are going to do a little work on this subject, which will enable us to show that these values exist all

the same, inscribed in an intelligible heaven although, of course, there is no God. In other words—and this is, I believe, the purport of all that we in France call radicalism—nothing will be changed if God does not exist; we shall rediscover the same norms of honesty, progress and humanity and we shall have disposed of God as an out-of-date hypothesis which will die away quietly of itself.

Sartre wanted to make his understanding of values completely consistent with atheism:

When we speak of 'abandonment'—a favourite word of Heidegger—we only mean to say that God does not exist, and that it is necessary to draw the consequences of his absence right to the end. The existentialist is strongly opposed to a certain type of secular moralism which seeks to suppress God at the least possible expense. The existentialist, on the contrary, finds it ... embarrassing that God does not exist, for there disappears with Him all possibility of finding values in an intelligible heaven. There can no longer be any good *a priori*, since there is no infinite and perfect consciousness to think it. It is nowhere written that 'the good' exist, that one must be honest or must not lie, since we are now upon the plane where there are only men.

He went on to argue that freedom is the foundation of all values:

Dostoievsky once wrote 'If God did not exist, everything would be permitted'; and that, for existentialism, is the starting point. Everything is indeed permitted if God does not exist, and man is in consequence forlorn, for he cannot find anything to depend upon either within or outside himself. He discovers forthwith, that he is without excuse. For if indeed existence precedes essence, one will never be able to explain one's action by reference to a given and specific human nature; in other words, there is not determinism—man is free, man *is* freedom. Nor, on the other hand, if God does not exist, are we provided with any values or commands that could legitimise our behaviour. Thus we have neither behind us, nor before us in a luminous realm of values, any means of justification or excuse. We are left alone, without excuse. That is what I mean when I say that man is condemned to be free.

My freedom is the unique foundation of values. And since I am the being by virtue of whom values exist, nothing—absolutely nothing—can justify me in adopting this or that value or scale of values. As the unique basis of the existence of values, I am totally unjustifiable. And my freedom is in anguish at finding that it is the baseless basis of values.

This freedom does not mean that the individual can be irresponsible; on the contrary it places on man an even heavier burden of responsibility. 'In fashioning myself', says Sartre, 'I fashion man.'

This means, in practice, that the individual must 'create' his values. His freedom is similar to the free creativity of the artist:

Moral choice is comparable to the construction of a work of art.

We are in the same creative situation. We never speak of a work of art as irresponsible ... There is this in common between art and morality, that in both we have to do with creation and invention. We cannot decide *a priori* what it is that should be done.

Albert Camus

To follow this out consistently could lead to a position in which all morals are arbitrary. If we cannot point to any firm standard of values, we have no right to protest when each individual *does* decide what is right for himself. If we are completely free in this sense, we have no right to expect others to accept our values, no right to say 'You *ought* to do this . . .' or 'you *ought not* to do that.'

To the ordinary reader Sartre's position sounds like this summary by COLIN WILSON:

His philosophy of 'commitment' . . . is only to say that since all roads lead nowhere, it's as well to choose any of them and throw all the energy into it . . .
. . . Any purpose will do provided it is altruistic.

JOHN D. WILD, writing about the weaknesses of the existential understanding of man, speaks of:

the supposed arbitrariness of human choice, and the lack of any firm grounds. For Sartre, the whole effort to justify an act is a cowardly abandonment of freedom and responsibility, the turning of myself into a thing. Whether I decide to die for justice or drink at a bar, the matter is indifferent.

In practice this approach means that the individual has to rely on his own instincts. SARTRE himself makes this admission:

If values are uncertain, if they are still too abstract to determine the particular, concrete case under consideration nothing remains but to trust in our instincts.

One can never hope to *know* for certain whether one's values are good or bad. His extreme agnosticism becomes evident at this point:

Who, then, can prove that I am the proper person to impose,

by my own choice, my conception of man upon mankind? I shall never find any proof whatever; there will be no sign to convince me of it. If a voice speaks to me, it is still I myself who must decide whether the voice is or is not that of an angel. If I regard a certain course of action as good, it is only I who choose to say that it is good and not bad.

No state can function on a philosophy of complete freedom. Here Sartre himself is inconsistent. As ADAM SCHAFF points out, Sartre the existentialist was committed to total freedom, while Sartre the communist sympathiser paid tribute to a political system which restricts the freedom of the individual in the interests of the state:

Does the individual create society, by choosing the manner of his behaviour in complete spontaneity and freedom of choice? Or is it society that creates the individual and determines his mode of behaviour?—These questions lie at the heart of the antagonism between Existentialism and Marxism.
There is a contradiction between the Sartre who clings to traditional Existentialism and the Sartre who pays tribute to the philosophy of Marxism. The contradiction can be overcome only by abandoning one or other of the two antagonistic views he now holds.

WHAT IS LOVE?

Many modern writers question the possibility of finding love. ALBERT CAMUS speaks of friendship, and love between a man and a woman, as perhaps the only thing that can have meaning in an otherwise absurd universe:

If there is one thing one can always yearn for, and

sometimes attain, it is human love.
The world is beautiful and, outside it, there is no salvation.
There is but one love in this world. To embrace a woman's body is also to retain, close to one, that strange joy which descends from the sky to the sea . . . I love this life with abandon and I want to speak of it freely; it fills me with pride at my human fate.

This incident in his novel *The Outsider* reveals what many think and feel about love and marriage:

Marie came that evening and asked me if I'd marry her. I said I didn't mind; if she was keen on it, we'd get married.
Then she asked me again if I loved her. I replied, much as before, that her question meant nothing or next to nothing—but I supposed I didn't.
'If that's how you feel', she said, 'why marry me?'
I explained that it had no importance really but, if it would give her pleasure, we could get married right away. I pointed out that anyhow the suggestion came from her; as for me, I'd merely said 'Yes'.
Then she remarked that marriage was a serious matter.
To which I answered: 'No'.
She kept silent after that, staring at me in a curious way. Then she asked:
'Suppose another girl had asked you to marry her—I mean, a girl you liked in the same way as you like me— would you have said "Yes" to her, too?'
'Naturally.'
Then she said she wondered if she really loved me or not. I, of course, couldn't enlighten her as to that. And, after another silence, she murmured something about my being 'a queer fellow'. 'And I dare say that's why I love you', she added. 'But maybe that's

Existentialism believes that each individual is alone in a hostile world, responsible to, and reliant on, himself alone.

why one day I'll come to hate you.'

To which I had nothing to say, so I said nothing.

SARTRE's picture of love is much blacker. In *Nausea*, Roquentin speaks of his disgust at the way in which a man and a woman are behaving with each other—disgust simply because there is no such thing as love any more:

I stop listening to them: they annoy me. They are going to sleep together. They know it. Each of them knows that the other knows it. But as they are young, chaste, and decent, as each wants to keep his self-respect and that of the other, and as love is a great poetic thing which mustn't be shocked, they go several times a week to dances and restaurants, to present the spectacle of their ritualistic, mechanical dances . . .

After all, you have to kill time. They are young and well built, they have another thirty years in front of them. So they don't hurry, they take their time, and they are quite right. Once they have been to bed together, they will have to find something else to conceal the enormous absurdity of their existence. All the same . . . is it absolutely necessary to lie to each other? I look around the room. What a farce!

MARTIN ESSLIN speaks about 'the tragic nature of all love relationships' depicted in Samuel Beckett's plays:

The experience expressed in Beckett's plays is of a far more profound and fundamental nature than mere autobiography. They reveal his experience of temporality and evanescence; his sense of the tragic difficulty of becoming aware of one's own self in the merciless process of renovation and destruction that occurs with change in

time; of the difficulty of communication between human beings; of the unending quest for reality in a world in which everything is uncertain and the borderline between dream and waking is ever shifting; of the tragic nature of all love relationships and the self-deception of friendship . . .

HOW ARE WE TO FACE SUFFERING AND DEATH?

The existentialist faces the absurdity of suffering and evil with a profound despair. In his determination to protest and rebel and fight suffering and evil he comes near to the Christian attitude.

ALBERT CAMUS, addressing a Christian audience:

I share with you the same horror of evil. But I do not share your hope, and I continue to struggle against this universe where children suffer and die.

Writing in *The Rebel*:

The words which reverberate for us at the confines of this long adventure of rebellion, are not formulae for optimism, for which we have no possible use in the extremities of our unhappiness, but words of courage and intelligence which, on the shores of the eternal seas, even have the qualities of virtue.

No possible form of wisdom today can claim to give more. Rebellion indefatigably confronts evil, from which it can only derive a new impetus. Man can master, in himself, everything that should be mastered. He should rectify in creation everything that can be rectified. And after he has done so, children will still die unjustly even in a perfect society. Even by his greatest effort, man can only propose to diminish, arithmetically, the sufferings of the world. But the injustice and the suffering of the world will remain and, no matter how limited they are, they will not cease to be an outrage. Dmitri Karamazov's cry of 'Why?' will continue to resound through history; art and rebellion will only die with the death of the last man on earth.

Camus' novel *The Plague* gives a vivid picture of what this rebellion in the face of suffering must mean. Rieux, the doctor, sees his work in the plague as 'fighting against creation as he found it'.

I have no idea what's awaiting me, or what will happen when all this ends. For the moment I know this; there are sick people and they need curing. Later on, perhaps, they'll think things over; and so shall I. But what's wanted now is to make them well. And I defend them as best I can, that's all . . .

Have you ever heard a woman scream 'Never!' with her last gasp? Well, I have. And then I saw that I could never get hardened to it. I was young then, and I was outraged by the whole scheme of things, or so I thought. Subsequently, I grew more modest. Only, I've never managed to get used to seeing people die. That's all I know . . .

At this moment he suffered with Grand's sorrow, and what filled his breast was the passionate indignation we feel when confronted by the anguish all men share.

BUT: this rebellion means fighting against the order of things without knowing why, and without hope and at this point there is a significant

When left-wing forces overthrew the Portuguese regime in 1974, Jean-Paul Sartre was keen to see how the new proletariat leadership was faring.

difference from the Christian attitude. Rieux, the doctor in CAMUS' *The Plague*, expresses this dilemma:

For nothing in the world is it worth turning one's back on what one loves. Yet that is what I'm doing—though *why* I do not know ... That's how it is ... and there's nothing to be done about it. So let's recognize the fact, and draw the conclusions ... a man can't cure and *know* at the same time. So let's cure as quickly as we can. That's the more urgent job.

He knew that the tale he had to tell could not be one of a final victory. It could be only the record of what had had to be done, and what assuredly would have to be done again in the never-ending fight against terror and its relentless onslaughts, despite their personal afflictions, by all who, while unable to be saints but refusing to bow down to pestilences, strive their utmost to be healers.
    And, indeed, as he listened to the cries of joy rising from the town, Rieux remembered that such joy is always imperilled.

JEAN-PAUL SARTRE described the tension he felt between the absurdity of life and his desire to live:

I felt superfluous so I had to disappear. I was a sickly bloom under constant sentence of extinction. In other words, I was condemned, and the sentence could be carried out at any time. Yet I rejected it with all my strength: not that my life was dear to me—quite the contrary, for I did not cling to it: the more absurd life is, the less tolerable death.

HUMANISM

Humanism is defined in *The Glossary of Humanism* as follows:

In broad terms contemporary Humanism subscribes to a view of life that is centred on man and his capacity to build a worthwhile life for himself and his fellows here and now. The emphasis is placed on man's own intellectual and moral resources, and the notion of supernatural religion is rejected.
    One of the most important trends in modern Humanism is its reliance on the application of scientific enquiry and its evaluation of truth, reality and morals in purely human terms.

We may take each of these main elements and illustrate them in turn.

● **The autonomy of man.** Humanism proceeds from the assumption *that* man is on his own and this life is all and an assumption *of* responsibility for one's own life and for the life of mankind.

The simple theme of humanism is self-determination, for persons, for groups and societies, for mankind together.
H.J. BLACKHAM

Men have become like gods. Isn't it about time that we understood our divinity? Science offers us total mastery over our environment and over our destiny, yet instead of rejoicing we feel deeply afraid ... All of us need to understand that God, or Nature, or Chance, or Evolution, or the Course of History, or whatever you like to call it, can't be trusted any more. We simply must take charge of our own fate ... It has ceased to be true that nature is governed by inevitable laws external to ourselves. We ourselves have become responsible.
EDMUND LEACH

● **Progress and improvement of man's condition.**

Humanism is a faith, a faith by which it is possible to live. To sum it up very briefly, I believe that this life is the only one of which we have any knowledge, and it is our job to improve it.
LORD WILLIS

● **Reliance on reason.**

Humanism is the effort of men to think, to feel, and to act for themselves, and to abide by the logic of results ... A new method is suddenly apprehended, tested, and carried firmly to its conclusion. Authority, habit, orthodoxy, are disregarded or defied. The argument is pragmatic, realistic, human. The question, 'Has this new thing a value?' is decided directly by the individual in the court of his experience; and there is no appeal. That is good which is seen to satisfy the human test, and to have brought an enlargement of human power.
GEOFFREY SCOTT

I do not like to think of Humanism as a religion

because one of its great merits, one of the things that has attracted me to it and caused me to become a Humanist, is its lack of dogma. One of the fundamental positions taken by Humanists is that men should have freedom to think out for themselves how they ought to live, to think out their own principles.
A.J. AYER

Each must think and decide for himself on important questions concerning the life he has and his conduct of it; and, most general, that nothing is exempt from human question. This means that there is no immemorial tradition, no revelation, no authority, no privileged knowledge (first principles, intuitions, axioms) which is beyond question because beyond experience and which can be used as a standard by which to interpret experience. There is only experience to be interpreted in the light of further experience, the sole source of all standards of reason and value, for ever open to question. This radical assumption is itself, of course, open to question, and stands only in so far as it is upheld by experience.
H.J. BLACKHAM

● Reliance on science.

This new idea-system, whose birth we of the mid twentieth-century are witnessing, I shall simply call *Humanism*, because it can only be based on our understanding of man and his relations with the rest of his environment ...

Science has attained a new and very real unity and firmness of organization and is giving us a scientifically-based picture of human destiny and human possibilities. For the first time in history, science can become the ally of religion instead of its rival or its enemy,

for it can provide a 'scientific' theology, a scientifically-ordered framework of belief, to whatever new religion emerges from the present idealogical disorder.
JULIAN HUXLEY

CAN WE BE SURE THE INDIVIDUAL HAS ANY VALUE?

If I am not a creature created in the image of God and therefore having meaning and value as an individual, what reason do I have for holding on to the feeling that my personality is unique and individual?

PEARL BUCK, the American novelist (1892–1973), saw no difficulty in asserting the freedom and uniqueness of the individual:

I believe we are born free—free of inheritance in that we can by our wills determine to be free of it, free of environment because no environment can shape one who will not be shaped. We are born free, in other words, of every sort of predestination. In each of us there is a little germ of individual being, compounded, it may be, of everything, inheritance, environment and all else, but the compound itself is new. It is forever unique. This *I* is never *You* or *He*. And this *I* is free, if I only know it and act upon that freedom.

Does this make a philosophy? Such as it is, it is all I have.

E.M. FORSTER, the English author (1878–1970), felt the problem more keenly, but had the optimistic hope that the individual could hold on to the feeling of his own individuality:

These are the reflections of an individualist and a liberal who has found liberalism crumbling beneath him and at first felt ashamed. Then, looking

around, he decided there was no special reason for shame, since other people, whatever they felt, were equally insecure. And as for individualism—there seems no way out of this, even if one wants to find one ...

Until psychologists and biologists have done much more than seems likely, the individual remains firm and each of us must consent to be one, and to make the best of the difficult job.

FRED HOYLE, the astronomer, found it harder to argue for the uniqueness of each individual because of his philosophy of evolution:

Only the biological processes of mutation and natural selection are needed to produce living creatures as we know them. Such creatures are no more than ingenious machines that have evolved as strange by-products in an odd corner of the Universe ... Most people object to this argument for the not very good reason that they do not like to think of themselves as machines.

JULIAN HUXLEY believed that the individual only has meaning because he is involved in the evolution of the human race:

In the light of the evolutionary vision the individual need not feel just a meaningless cog in the social machine, nor merely the helpless prey and sport of vast impersonal forces. He can do something to develop his own personality, to discover his own talents and possibilities, to interact personally and fruitfully with other individuals, to discover something of his own significance. If so, in his own person he is realizing an important quantum of evolutionary possibility: he is contributing his own personal quality to the fulfilment of human destiny; and he has assurance of his own significance in the vaster and more enduring whole of which he is a part.

WHAT IS THE MEANING OF LIFE?

H.J. BLACKHAM, who is an optimistic humanist, starts from the position of 'recognizing the pointlessness of it all':

There is no end to hiding from the ultimate end of life, which is death. But it does not avail. On humanist assumptions, life leads to nothing, and every pretence that it does not is a deceit. If there is a bridge over a gorge which spans only half the distance and ends in mid-air, and if the bridge is crowded with human beings pressing on, one after another they fall into the abyss. The bridge leads to nowhere, and those who are pressing forward to cross it are going nowhere. It does not matter where they think they are going, what preparations for the journey they may have made, how much they may be enjoying it all ... such a situation is a model of futility.

COLIN WILSON believes that the philosophy of evolution can give birth to 'a new kind of purpose *inside* man':

He (man) is not yet a 'spiritual being', for spiritual, in its ultimate sense, means capable of exercising freedom, and freedom without ultimate purpose ... The one thing that is required to complete the transition from ape to man is the birth of a new kind of purpose *inside* man. Sir Julian Huxley is right in calling this sense of evolutionary purpose a 'new religion'.

He suggests as his answer what he calls 'evolutionary phenomenology':

What has been suggested is that the answer is to be sought in the idea of evolution, as described by Shaw, Wells, or Sir Julian Huxley ... What if science *could* replace that sense of individual meaning, the feeling of having a direct telephone line to the universal purpose? For this is precisely the aim of evolutionary phenomenology: to change man's conception of himself and of the *interior forces* he has at his command, and ultimately to establish the new evolutionary type, foreshadowed by the 'outsiders'.

JOHN WREN-LEWIS believes that 'a positive vision of human good in concrete experience' can lead to the emergence of 'a deeper humanism':

The Renaissance failed precisely in so far as society failed to push the revolt against the traditional outlook right through, and here too it seems to me that we are today witnessing the gradual emergence of a new vision which fulfils the Renaissance promise because it *does* complete the revolution. We are witnessing, that is to say, the emergence of a deeper humanism based on a positive vision of human good in concrete experience, and it springs from the same discipline of psychological analysis that has exposed the neurotic character of mankind's traditional moral and social orientations.

Just what practical expression can be given to this faith is something which still remains to be worked out.

The vast majority of writers who have considered the subject have reached a pessimistic answer:

If one puts aside the existence of God and the possibility of

Somerset Maugham

survival as too doubtful to have any effect on one's behaviour, one has to make up one's mind what is the meaning and use of life. If death ends all, if I have neither to hope for good to come nor to fear evil, I must ask myself what I am here for, and how in these circumstances I must conduct myself. Now the answer to one of these questions is plain, but so unpalatable that most men will not face it. There is no reason for life, and life has no meaning.
SOMERSET MAUGHAM

Here we are in this wholly fantastic Universe with scarcely a clue as to whether our existence has any real significance.
FRED HOYLE

COLIN WILSON, writing about Ernest Hemingway:

The key sentence, 'most men die like animals, not like men', is his answer to the humanist notion of the perfectibility of man ... There is nothing that man cannot lose. This doesn't mean that life is of no value; on the contrary, life is the only value; it is ideas that are valueless.

Nikos Kazantzakis, the Greek novelist, author of *Zorba the Greek*, writing to a friend in 1947:

To conquer illusion and hope, without being overcome by terror: this has been the whole endeavour of my life these past twenty years; to look straight into the abyss without bursting into tears, without begging or threatening, calmly, serenely preserving the dignity of man; to see the abyss and work as though I were immortal . . .

Man now realises that he is an accident, that he is a completely futile being, that he has to play out the game without reason. I think that even when Velasquez was painting, even when Rembrandt was painting, they were still, whatever their attitude to life, slightly conditioned by certain types of religious possibilities, which man now, you could say, has had cancelled out for him. Man now can only attempt to beguile himself for a time, by prolonging his life—by buying a kind of immortality through the doctors. You see, painting has become—all art has become—a game by which man distracts himself. And you may say that it always has been like that, but now it's entirely a game.
Francis Bacon

I feel as if I am at a dead end and so I am finished. All spiritual facts I realize are true but I never escape the feeling of being closed in and the sordidness of self, the futility of all that I have seen and done and said.
Allen Ginsberg

(i) *Sweeney:* Nothing to hear but the sound of the surf. Nothing at all but three things.
Doris: What things?
Sweeney: Birth, and copulation and death. That's all, that's all, that's all, that's all. Birth, and copulation, and death.
Doris: I'd be bored.
Sweeney: You'd be bored. Birth, and copulation, and death.
Doris: I'd be bored.
Sweeney: You'd be bored. Birth, and copulation, and death. That's all the facts when you come to brass tacks: Birth, and copulation, and death. I've been born, and once is enough. You don't remember, but I remember. Once is enough.

(ii) *Doris:* That's not life, that's no life. Why I'd just as soon be dead.
Sweeney: That's what life is. Just is.
Doris: What is? What's that life is?
Sweeney: Life is death.
T.S. Eliot

Many who reach the point of saying that human life is meaningless find it difficult, if not impossible, to *live* with this conclusion. They feel compelled to cast around for a way to create at least some measure of meaning somewhere.

T. S. Eliot

HOW DOES THE HUMANIST FIND A BASIS FOR MORAL VALUES?

Somerset Maugham based his values on 'nature':

What then is right action? For my part the best answer I know is that given by Fray Luis de León. To follow it does not look so difficult that human weakness quails before it as beyond its strength. With it I can end my book. The beauty of life, he says, is nothing but this, that each should act in conformity with his nature and his business.

C.E.M. Joad, writing in 1942 when he was still an agnostic, expressed the hope that the Christian code of ethics could be maintained even when Christian beliefs had been dismissed. But he realized that this might be nothing more than a temporary solution, since Christian values could not survive without some firm basis. He then wondered if it is possible to hold on to them not because they are *true*, but because they prove to be *useful*:

I have been led to place a new value upon the Christian code of ethics and the way of life that is based on their acceptance,

Allen Ginsberg

and to see that this value remains, even if the metaphysical foundations upon which Christianity bases the codes are thought to be dubious or dismissed as untenable. But then comes the question: 'Can the code endure without the supernatural foundation, any more than a flower can endure that is cut from its roots?' That the Christian code and the Christian way of life may so endure *for a time* is clear. Plato has an interesting passage about the substitution of habit for principle in a society. He gives a vivid description of the power of habit, describing how men and women will continue to cultivate certain virtues and practise restraints, when the principles which would alone have justified the cultivating and the practising have ceased to be held. They may do this, he points out, for a time, even, if the times are quiet, for a long time, in ignorance that the basis of principle is no longer there; but the structure of habit lacking foundation collapses at the first impact of adversity.

Is it not doing so now? Is it well that it should do so? And if

C. E. M. Joad

it is not well, is it wise to continue to erode the foundations in history and metaphysics upon which the Christian faith is based? If we can't accept them ourselves, may it not, nevertheless, be well that we should at least pretend, remembering in our emergency Plato's hint about the social beneficence of the useful lie?

JULIAN HUXLEY believed that through what he calls 'the evolutionary vision', a sense of right and wrong can evolve to meet the needs of each new generation:

The evolutionary vision is enabling us to discern, however incompletely, the lineaments of the new religion that we can be sure will arise to serve the needs of the coming era. Just as stomachs are bodily organs concerned with digestion, and involving the biochemical activity of special juices, so are religions psychological organs concerned with the problems of human destiny, and involving the emotion of sacredness and the sense of right and wrong. Religion of some sort is probably necessary. But it is not necessarily a good thing.

H.J. BLACKHAM follows the Utilitarian Principle which was first expounded by J.S. Mill (1806–73), which is that an action is right if it promotes the greatest happiness of the greatest number:

The humanist's system of morality is a consecration of the actual facts of life as men live it. He proceeds in the reverse direction from that taken by the super-humanist; for, instead of passing from the arbitrary imperative to the corresponding fantastic indicative, he moves from the

indicative of the observed and experienced facts to the imperative of a realistic morality and a rational legislation.

J. S. Mill

The problem with this approach is that happiness is generally a by-product of action pursued for other reasons than the attainment of happiness, as J.S. Mill recognized later in life:

I never, indeed, wavered in the conviction that happiness is the test of all rules of conduct, and the end of life. But now I thought that this end was only to be attained by not making it the direct end. Those only are happy (I thought) who have their minds fixed on some subject other than their own happiness; on the happiness of others, on the improvement of mankind, even on some art or pursuit, followed not as a means, but as itself an ideal end. Aiming thus at something else, they find happiness by the way.

A second weakness is that it is not possible, logically, to derive an 'ought' statement from an 'is' statement.

We cannot move from a simple statement about a state of

affairs (how things actually are) to make a further statement about an obligation (how things ought to be). If we say 'people *do in fact act* like this . . .' we have no right to base a moral judgement on this and say 'therefore people *ought to act* as follows . . .' For example, not even the most exhaustive study of the sexual habits and customs of a particular society would enable us to say what customs people ought to accept or reject.

H.J. BLACKHAM also appeals to the principle that values can be based on 'social agreement'. This means that we base moral principles on a study of how people actually live:

Humanism is rooted in two historical quests of universal import: free inquiry and social agreement.
   Only too obviously there is precious little agreement in the world outside the province of the natural sciences—and perhaps less inside than is popularly supposed. Nevertheless, agreement is the ultimate criterion for values as well as for facts, some humanists would hold, and at any rate for rules which concern everybody in a society . . .
   All humanists want to see a consensus on the secular *foundations* of society fully prevail.

The problem here, however, is to know *how* any society can reach this kind of agreement. One could hardly hope for 100 per cent agreement on a code of values. Failing such a consensus, what kind of majority vote would be acceptable—80 per cent or 51 per cent? In many situations, a society would be at the mercy of individual experts who would claim to *know* what is best for society. And in this case the concept of agreement cannot mean 'agreement of the majority'

but rather 'agreement of the experts'.
   Even if it were possible to find 100 per cent agreement, how would this agreement make some things right and others wrong? How could agreement itself be the ultimate criterion of values?

ALVIN TOFFLER in his book *Future Shock* suggests that the development of electronics in the future will enable millions of people all over the world to take part in games which could 'help us formulate goals for the future':

While televised players act out the role of high government officials attempting to deal with a crisis—on ecological disaster, for example— meetings of trade unions, women's clubs, church groups, student organizations and other constituencies might be held at which large numbers could view the program, reach collective judgments about the choices to be made, and forward those judgments to the primary players. Special switchboards and computers could pick up the advice or tabulate the yes—no votes and pass them on to the 'decision-makers'. Vast numbers of people could also participate from their own homes, thus opening the process to unorganized, otherwise non-participating millions. By imaginatively constructing such games, it becomes not only possible but practical to elicit futural goals from previously unconsulted masses.
   Such techniques, still primitive today, will become fantastically more sophisticated in the years immediately ahead, providing us with a systematic way to collect and reconcile conflicting images of the preferable future, even from people unskilled in academic

debate or parliamentary procedure.

In his vision of the future, however, he has not given the slightest hint of *how* individuals or groups should discuss moral values. We are not given any hint about any possible *basis* for morality. If the leaders don't make all the vital decisions themselves, it will only be the consensus of public opinion which will decide.

JACOB BRONOWSKI believes that science can actually 'create' values:

The values of science derive neither from the virtues of its members, nor from the finger-wagging codes of conduct by which every profession reminds itself to be good. They have grown out of the practice of science, because they are the inescapable conditions for its practice . . .
   Like the other creative activities which grew from the Renaissance, science has humanized our values. Men have asked for freedom, justice, and respect precisely as the scientific spirit has spread among them . . .
   The inspiration of science . . . has created the values of our intellectual life and, with the arts, has taught them to our civilization.

These are some of the values which he believes have been 'created' by science:

Independence and originality, dissent and freedom and tolerance: such are the first needs of science; and these are the values which, of itself, it demands and forms . . .
   In societies where these values do not exist, science has had to create them.

From these basic conditions, which form the prime values, there follows step by step a range of values: dissent, freedom of thought and speech, justice, honour, human dignity and self-respect.

Our values since the Renaissance have evolved by just such steps.

This, therefore, is the principle which he puts forward as the scientific basis for values:

We OUGHT to act in such a way that what IS true can be verified to be so.

BUT: making scientific values our 'absolute' creates some problems. In the first place, it is a confusion of language to say that science can 'create' values. Science is a human activity pursued by individual scientists. 'Science' cannot create values any more than other human activities like art or sport. Science may proceed more effectively if scientists recognize certain values; but the values which are said to have been created by science were recognized and practised long before the development of modern science.

Second, there are certain values which have little or nothing to do with science.

JACOB BRONOWSKI admits in the preface to the later edition of his book, that there are values

which are not generated by the practice of science—the values of tenderness, of kindliness, of human intimacy and love.

Third, when it comes to particular moral problems, it will always be particular scientists or groups of scientists who will have to make the choices and point out the values. The tyranny of scientists could be just as frightening as the tyranny of soldiers or politicians.

ARTHUR KOESTLER recognizes the moral dilemma of the twentieth century very clearly:

The logic of expediency leads to the atomic disintegration of morality; a kind of radioactive decay of all values.

He cherishes the hope that science can somehow 'heal the neurotic flaw in us':

Can science heal the neurotic flaw in us? If science cannot, then nothing can. Let us stop pretending. There is no cure in high moral precepts ... The

insight of science is not different from that of the arts. Science will create values, I believe, and discover virtues, when it looks into man and not an animal, and makes his societies human and not animal packs.

At the same time he is well aware of the possible consequences of reliance on science, which he describes as 'the new Baal,

The humanist ideal of social improvement has greatly influenced city-centre architecture.

lording it over the moral vacuum with his electronic brain':

Within the foreseeable future, man will either destroy himself or take off for the stars ...

   Our hypnotic enslavement to the numerical aspects of reality has dulled our perception of non-quantitative moral values; the resultant end-justifies-the-means ethic may be a major factor in our undoing.

HOW DOES THE HUMANIST THINK ABOUT DEATH?

FRED HOYLE believes that we have 'not the smallest clue to our own fate':

Perhaps the most majestic feature of our whole existence is that while our intelligences are powerful enough to penetrate deeply into the evolution of this quite incredible Universe, we still have not the smallest clue to our own fate.

The Humanist Manifesto II of 1973 is agnostic about any life after death:

As far as we know, the total personality is a function of the biological organism transacting in a social and cultural context. There is no credible evidence that life survives the death of the body.

JOHN UPDIKE, the American novelist, paints a very black picture of one person's vision of death:

Without warning, David was visited by an exact vision of death: a long hole in the ground, no wider than your body, down which you are drawn while the white faces recede. You try to reach them but your arms are pinned. Shovels pour dirt in your face. There you will be forever, in an upright position, blind and

silent, and in time no one will remember you, and you will never be called. As strata of rock shift, your fingers elongate, and your teeth are distended sideways in a great underground grimace indistinguishable from a strip of chalk. And the earth tumbles on, and the sun expires, an unaltering darkness reigns where once there were stars.

TOM STOPPARD expresses this view of death in his play *Rosencrantz and Guildenstern are Dead*:

No-one gets up after *death*— there is no applause—there is only silence and some second-hand clothes, and that's— *death*—

   ... Dying is not romantic, and death is not a game which will soon be over ... Death is not anything ... death is not ... It's the absence of presence, nothing more ... the endless time of never coming back ... a gap you can't see, and when the wind blows through it, it makes no sound ...

WHAT IS THE HUMANIST VISION OF THE FUTURE?

Some humanists look forward to the future with considerable optimism.

I prefer to concentrate my powers upon that which is within my reach to do: to make this world with its tremendous, with its incredible potentialities for beauty and happiness—a place in which every man, woman, and child will be truly able to say, 'We are grateful that we are alive, for life is food!'

   Today that sounds like mocking blasphemy. A hundred centuries hence, it will make sense. For by then man will have acquired the courage necessary to see himself as he really is—as a being equipped

with a power of intellect which will eventually allow him to penetrate into every secret of nature until he will truly be the master of all he surveys, and endowed with such a complete freedom of will that he himself—and no one else—is the true master of his fate and therefore dependent for his ultimate happiness upon no one but *himself*.

H.W. VAN LOON

H.J. BLACKHAM rejects the pessimism and despair which he sees in Francis Bacon and Jean-Paul Sartre, and believes that these are 'distorted and immature forms of humanist expression'. He then goes on to ask:

But can humanism really and justifiably maintain equanimity in the face not only of probable ultimate annihilation but also of actual human suffering and stupidity and brutality on the present scale? Is there any satisfaction at all to be found in the general behaviour of mankind or in the trends and tendencies that can be discerned? There is no answer to such a question, or no general answer, for there is no general behaviour of mankind. Everybody must balance his own account here. In any such reckoning, the ready money of daily cheerfulness and unalloyed pleasures is not too small to count. One dimension of finality is here and now. On the public fronts, defeatism may sometimes be the part of reason acting as prudence, but who will responsibly say that the time is not? So long as there are better or worse possibilities there is time for action. Today the better and the worse are better and worse than they have ever been. That is the summons to humanists and the summons of humanism.

JULIAN HUXLEY believed that the course of evolution itself would lead to a better future for mankind:

Evolution ... is the most powerful and the most comprehensive idea that has ever risen on earth. It helps us to understand our origins, our own nature, and our relations with the rest of nature. It shows us the major trends of

Julian Huxley

evolution in the past and indicates a direction for our evolutionary course in the future.

From the specifically religious point of view, the desirable direction of evolution might be defined as the divinization of existence—but for this to have operative significance, we must frame a new definition of 'the divine', free from all connotations of external supernatural beings.

This new point of view that we are reaching, the vision of evolutionary humanism, is essentially a religious one, and ... we can and should devote ourselves with truly religious devotion to the cause of ensuring greater fulfilment for

the human race in its future destiny.

ARTHUR KOESTLER diagnoses the problem of man in this way:

When one contemplates the streak of insanity running through human history, it appears highly probable that *homo sapiens* is a biological freak, the result of some remarkable mistake in the evolutionary process ... somewhere along the line of his ascent something has gone wrong.

The cause underlying these pathological manifestations is the split between reason and belief—or more generally, insufficient co-ordination between the emotive and discriminating faculties of the mind ... between instinct and intellect, emotions and reason.

He believes that science alone can provide a solution:

Biological evolution has let us down; we can only hope to survive if we develop techniques which supplant it by inducing the necessary changes in human nature.

He believes that a 'New Pill' could be developed which could change human nature by acting as a mental stabilizer:

The psycho-pharmacist cannot *add* to the faculties of the brain—but he can, at best, *eliminate* obstructions or blockages which impede their proper use. He cannot aggrandise us—but he can, within limits, normalise us; he cannot put additional circuits into the brain, but he can, again within limits, improve the coordination between existing ones, attenuate conflicts, prevent the blowing of fuses, and ensure a steady power supply. That is all the help we can ask for—but if we were able to obtain it, the benefits to

mankind would be incalculable; it would be the 'Final Revolution' in a sense opposite to Huxley's—the break-through from maniac to man.

Other humanists have a very pessimistic outlook for the future. This description by D.R. DAVIES of the despair he

Arthur Koestler

experienced in the 1930s expresses very well what many people feel about the 1980s:

As the significance of each group ... of events became clear to my mind, my whole being underwent a most painful process of disintegration. I became oppressed with a dreadful sense of futility. As I came to realise the failure to establish peace; as the utter irrationality of the whole economic life of Europe gradually broke in upon me; and the meaning of Fascism gradually dawned upon me; and finally, as the illusion of Russia broke in upon me, I suffered a despair I had never previously known.

Bertrand Russell

BERTRAND RUSSELL wrote:

That man is the product of causes which had no prevision of the end they were achieving; that his origin, his growth, his hopes and fears, his loves and his beliefs, are but the outcome of accidental collocations of atoms; that no fire, no heroism, no intensity of thought and feeling, can preserve an individual life beyond the grave; that all the labour of the ages, all the devotion, all the inspiration, all the noonday brightness of human genius, are destined to extinction in the vast death of the solar system, and that the whole temple of man's achievement must inevitably be buried beneath the debris of a universe in ruins—all these things, if not quite beyond dispute, are yet so nearly certain, that no philosophy which rejects them can hope to stand. Only within the scaffolding of these truths, only on the firm foundation of unyielding despair, can the soul's habitation henceforth be safely built.

Brief and powerless is man's life; on him and all his race the slow, sure doom falls pitiless and dark. Blind to good and evil, reckless of destruction, omnipotent matter rolls on its relentless way; for man, condemned today to lose his dearest, tomorrow himself to pass through the gate of darkness, it remains only to cherish, ere yet the blow fall, the lofty thoughts that ennoble his little day; disdaining the coward terrors of the slave of Fate, to worship at the shrine that his own hands have built; undismayed by the empire of chance to preserve a mind free from the wanton tyranny that rules his outward life; proudly defiant of the irresistible forces that tolerate, for a moment, his knowledge and his condemnation, to sustain alone, a weary but unyielding Atlas, the world that his own ideals have fashioned despite the trampling march of unconscious power.

I think we may hope that liberation from the load of fear, private economic fear and public fear of war, would cause the human spirit to soar to hitherto undreamt of heights. Men, hitherto, have always been cramped in their hopes and aspiration and imagination by the limitations of what has been possible ... There is no need to wait for Heaven. There is no reason why life on earth should not be filled with happiness. There is no reason why imagination should have to take refuge in a myth. In such a world as men could now make, it could be freely creative within the framework of our terrestrial existence ... If our present troubles can be conquered. Man can look forward to a future immeasurably longer than his past, inspired by a new breadth

of vision, a continuing hope perpetually fed by a continuing achievement. Man has made a beginning creditable for an infant—for, in a biological sense, man, the latest of the species, is still an infant. No limit can be set to what he may achieve in the future. I see in my mind's eye, a world of glory and joy, a world where minds expand, where hopes remain undimmed, and what is noble is no longer condemned as treachery to this or that paltry aim. All this can happen if we let it happen. It rests with our generation to decide between this vision and the end decreed by folly.

FOCUSSING ON JESUS OF NAZARETH

Ask God to show you how Jesus' life, body and soul, was the only fully human life that has ever been lived and keep looking at Jesus, as you meet him in the Gospels, till you can see it. Then the prospect of being like him—that, and no less—will seem to you the noblest and most magnificent destiny possible and by embracing it you will become a true disciple.
JAMES PACKER

'I'm ready to accept Jesus as a great moral teacher, but I don't accept his claim to be God'. That is the one thing we must not say. A man who was merely a man and said the sort of things Jesus said would not be a great moral teacher. He would either be a lunatic—on a level with the man who says he is a poached egg—or else he would be the Devil of Hell. You must make your choice. Either this was, and is, the Son of God; or else a madman or something worse. You can shut him up for a fool, you can spit at him and kill him as a demon, or you can fall at his feet and call him Lord and God. But let us not come with any patronizing nonsense about his being a great human teacher. He has not left that open to us. He did not intend to.
C.S. LEWIS

There are words that I have never quite understood, such as sin.
ALBERT CAMUS

How can the guilt of one man be expiated by the death of another who is sinless—if indeed we may speak of a sinless man at all? What primitive notions of guilt and righteousness does this imply? And what primitive idea of God? The rationale of sacrifice in general may of course throw some light on the theory of the atonement, but even so, what a primitive mythology it is, that a divine Being should become incarnate, and atone for the sins of men through his own blood!
RUDOLPH BULTMANN

The need for God I could understand, and the need for religion; I could even sympathize with the devotees like Suso or St. Francis, who weave fantasies around the Cross, the nails, and all the other traditional symbols. But ultimately I could not accept the need for redemption by a Saviour. To pin down the idea of salvation to one point in space and time seemed to me a naive kind of anthropomorphism.
COLIN WILSON

I have never been interested in an historical Jesus. I should not care if it was proved by someone that the man called Jesus never lived, and that what was narrated in the Gospels was a figment of the writer's imagination. For the Sermon on the Mount would still be true for me.
MAHATMA GANDHI

The question at issue is ... for me not so much a question of proving that the Christian record of fact is false or that the Christian revelation in the matter of the Resurrection cannot be substantiated; to a mind awake to the new knowledge of science these time-honoured claims you continue to make seem to be those of a man talking in his sleep.

To ascribe a central position to Jesus in the history of mankind may have accorded well enough with the narrow world picture of the Middle Ages, with its few thousand years of human history and its expectation of Christ's Return in the comparatively near future to put an end to the universe. But to me and to any modern this whole way of thinking is as unintelligible as it is impertinent. The framework of assumptions required for an understanding of the modern universe has been so widened that the old Christian hypothesis is lost sight of. And that, I suppose, is why, to return to your oft-reiterated complaint, we simply cannot be bothered to give the Christian hypothesis the attention which you seem to think it still deserves.
C.E.M. JOAD

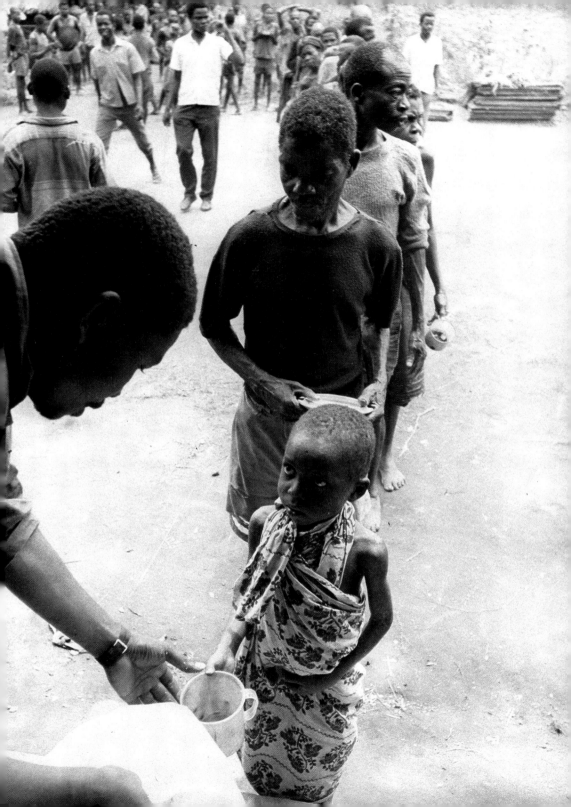

Our approach to this section will depend largely on whether our sympathies lie more with Packer and Lewis—or with Camus, Wilson, Gandhi and Joad.

If we already have some idea of who God is, and are willing to discuss who Jesus was, we are probably ready to look more closely at the accounts of the life of Jesus.

If, however, words such as 'sin' and 'salvation' make as little sense to us as they did to Camus, Bultmann and Wilson, there's little point in discussing the details of the life and teaching of Jesus.

If we share Gandhi's understanding of history and truth, then Jesus' teaching about himself, and the story of his death will be largely irrelevant.

If our ideas about the universe rule out the possibility of a Creator God at work in the universe

he has made, we will no doubt be as impatient as Joad, and not even bother to consider the evidence for the resurrection.

This does not mean that the discussion between the 'believer' and the 'unbeliever' must end at this point. All it means is that the discussion should *turn to basic assumptions* before it can focus on questions about Jesus.

We may need to express more fully our difficulties and disagreements with the Christian assumptions about man and God, about the universe, truth and salvation (*Section 3*).

Or we may need to spend most of our time discussing the alternatives to Christian beliefs (*Section 5*), and then testing them as rigorously as we have tried to test Christian beliefs (*Section 4*).

Outline

PRELIMINARY QUESTIONS
What historical evidence is there concerning Jesus from non-biblical sources?
How reliable are the documents relating to the life of Jesus?

HOW WAS JESUS RELATED TO GOD?
EVIDENCE
His birth
His character: compassion, anger, humility, goodness
His claims about himself
   His claim to be the Son
   His claim to be the fulfilment of the Old Testament
   His indirect claims
His miracles
POSSIBLE ANSWERS
He was fully human and fully divine
He was a created being from heaven
He was a prophet sent by God
He was a man and nothing more

WHAT WAS THE MEANING OF HIS DEATH?
EVIDENCE
How Jesus thought about his death
The circumstances of his death
POSSIBLE ANSWERS
His death achieved something—he was bearing our sins
He died as an example
The cross is merely a symbol
His death on the cross disproves any claim that he was the Messiah
Jesus did not die on the cross
His death has no special meaning

DID JESUS RISE FROM THE DEAD?
EVIDENCE
The accounts of the empty tomb
The appearances
The existence of the church
POSSIBLE ANSWERS
We can be reasonably certain
It's improbable
   How account for the empty tomb?
   How account for the appearances?
   How account for the existence of the church?
It's impossible
We don't know and it doesn't matter

PRELIMINARY QUESTIONS

WHAT HISTORICAL EVIDENCE IS THERE CONCERNING JESUS FROM NON-BIBLICAL SOURCES?

● The earliest piece of evidence can be dated with certainty to between AD 40 and 50. It consists of two inscriptions on ossuaries (caskets containing bones of the dead) which were found in a burial chamber in Talpioth, a suburb of Jerusalem, in 1945 by Professor E.L. Sukenik, a Jewish archaeologist:

'Ιησους ιου—**which probably means 'Jesus woe!' or 'Jesus, help!' (i.e. a short prayer addressed to Jesus).**

'Ιησους ἀλωθ—**which probably means 'Jesus, let him (who rests here) arise!'**

These two inscriptions suggest that even at this early date people were praying to Jesus—assuming this was Jesus of Nazareth—and that followers of Jesus were looking forward to a future resurrection.

● Another inscription which may be relevant was found in Nazareth. It records an edict of the EMPEROR TIBERIUS (AD 14–37) or the EMPEROR CLAUDIUS (AD 41–54), about the robbing of graves:

Ordinance of Caesar. It is my pleasure that graves and tombs remain undisturbed in perpetuity for those who have made them for the cult of their ancestors or children or members of their house. If however any man lay information that another has either demolished them, or has in any other way extracted the buried, or has maliciously transferred them to other places in order to wrong them, or has displaced the sealing of other stones, against such a one I order that a trial be instituted, as in

**respect of the gods, so in regard to
the cult of mortals. For it shall be
much more obligatory to honour the
buried. Let it be absolutely
forbidden for anyone to disturb
them. In case of contravention I
desire that the offender be
sentenced to capital punishment on
charge of violation of sepulture.**

Obviously we cannot be certain there is any
connection between this inscription and the disappearance of the body of Jesus from the tomb. But it
does suggest, at the very least, that reports had
reached the emperor about bodies being removed
from tombs, perhaps in Palestine itself. This edict
may represent the official reaction to such reports.

● JOSEPHUS, the Jewish historian, writing about
AD 93 or 94 in his *Antiquities of the Jews*, speaks
about the ministry, death and resurrection of
Jesus. This version is based on the Greek text,
which dates from the fourth century:

**About this time there arose Jesus, a
wise man, if indeed it be lawful to
call him a man. For he was a doer of
wonderful deeds, and a teacher of
men who gladly receive the truth.
He drew to himself many both of the
Jews and of the Gentiles. He was
the Christ; and when Pilate, on the
indictment of the principal men
among us, had condemned him to
the cross, those who loved him at
the first did not cease to do so, for
he appeared to them again alive on
the third day, the divine prophets
having foretold these and ten
thousand wonderful things about
him. And even to this day the race
of Christians, who are named after
him, has not died out.**

Josephus was not a Christian, and some scholars
have argued that some clauses (e.g. 'he was the
Christ') could not have been written by Josephus,
and must have been interpolated in an early text by
a Christian. But others, including scholars who
have no Christian bias, see no reason for doubting
that Josephus could have written these words.
They argue that this is exactly how a slightly
cynical Jew might refer to Christian beliefs about
Jesus.

Further light has been shed on this text by
Professor Shlomo Pines of the Hebrew University
in Jerusalem, who has discovered an Arabic version of the same text which he believes to be older
than the Greek one. It was found in a church
history written by BISHOP AGAPIUS, an Arab
bishop in Baghdad. This is what the Arabic text
says:

**At this time there was a wise man
who was called Jesus. And his
conduct was good and (he) was
known to be virtuous. And many
people from among the Jews and
from the other nations became his
disciples. Pilate condemned him to
be crucified and to die.
And those who had become his
disciples did not abandon his
discipleship. They reported that he
had appeared to them three days
after his crucifixion and that he was
alive. Accordingly he was perhaps
the Messiah of whom the prophets
have recounted wonders.**

Professor Pines believes that medieval Christian
censorship was probably responsible for the differences between the two versions: The Arabic
version is less Christian in character than the
traditional Greek one. Because of this it may be an
earlier version than the traditional one.

In another passage in the *Antiquities*, JOSEPHUS
writes about the martyrdom of James, the brother
of Jesus:

**(Ananus) assembled the sanhedrin
of the judges, and brought before
them the brother of Jesus, who was
called Christ, whose name was
James, and some others, and when
he had formed an accusation
against them as breakers of the law,
he delivered them to be stoned.**

● PLINY, a Roman pro-consul in Bithynia (modern
Turkey) wrote the following letter to the Emperor
Trajan in AD 110 about the way in which he had
been dealing with Christians. This gives some idea
of Christian beliefs and practices, and their reactions to persecutions:

**This is the course that I have
adopted in the case of those**

brought before me as Christians. I ask them if they are Christians. If they admit it I repeat the question a second and a third time, threatening capital punishment; if they persist I sentence them to death. For I do not doubt that, whatever kind of crime it may be to which they have confessed, their pertinacity and inflexible obstinacy should certainly be punished. There were others who displayed a like madness and whom I reserved to be sent to Rome, since they were Roman citizens.

Thereupon the usual result followed: the very fact of my dealing with the question led to a wider spread of the charge, and a great variety of cases were brought before me. An anonymous pamphlet was issued, containing many names. All who denied that they were or had been Christians I considered should be discharged, because they called upon the gods at my dictation and did reverence, with incense and wine, to your image which I had ordered to be brought forward for this purpose, together with the statues of the deities; and especially because they cursed Christ, a thing which, it is said, genuine Christians cannot be induced to do. Others named by the informer first said that they were Christians and then denied it; declaring that they had been but were so no longer, some having recanted three years or more before and one or two as long ago as twenty years. They all worshipped your image and the statues of the gods and cursed Christ. But they declared that the sum of their guilt or error had amounted only to this, that on an appointed day they had been accustomed to meet before daybreak, and recite a hymn antiphonally to Christ, as to a god, and to bind themselves by an oath, not for the commission of any crime but to abstain from theft, robbery, adultery and breach of faith, and not to deny a deposit when it was claimed....

● TACITUS, the Roman historian, writing in about AD 115, speaks about Nero's persecution of Christians in the year AD 64:

But all the endeavours of men, all the emperor's largesse and the propitiations of the gods, did not suffice to allay the scandal or banish the belief that the fire had been ordered. And so, to get rid of this rumour, Nero set up as the culprits and punished with the utmost refinement of cruelty a class hated for their abominations, who are commonly called Christians. Christus, from whom their name is derived, was executed at the hands of the procurator Pontius Pilate in the reign of Tiberius. Checked for the moment, this pernicious superstition again broke out, not only in Judaea, the source of the evil, but even in Rome, that receptacle for everything that is sordid and degrading from every quarter of the globe, which there finds a following.

● SUETONIUS, the Roman historian, refers to 'Chrestus' (which is probably a confusion of 'Christus', i.e. Christ) in his *Life of Claudius* (the emperor from 41–54), which was written about AD 120. He is probably referring to quarrels between Jews and Christians about Jesus:

Since the Jews were continually making disturbances at the instigation of Chrestus, he (Claudius) expelled them from Rome.

● The *Talmud* is a collection of Jewish traditions which dates from the third century:

On the eve of Passover they hanged Yeshu of Nazareth, and the herald went before him for forty days saying, Yeshu of Nazareth is going forth to be stoned in that he hath practised sorcery and beguiled and

led astray Israel. Let everyone knowing aught in his defence come and plead for him. But they found naught in his defence and hanged him on the eve of the Passover.

HOW RELIABLE ARE THE DOCUMENTS RELATING TO THE LIFE OF JESUS?

WHO WERE THE AUTHORS AND WHAT WERE THEIR SOURCES?

The first Gospel was probably that of *Mark*, written between AD 50 and 60. The author was probably John Mark, who came from Jerusalem. There is an early tradition, recorded by PAPIAS (around AD 140) that Mark gathered most of his material from Peter, one of the disciples:

Mark, who was the interpreter of Peter, wrote down accurately all that he remembered, whether of sayings or doings of Christ, but not in order. For he was neither a hearer nor a companion of the Lord; but afterwards, as I have said, he accompanied Peter, who adapted his instruction as necessity required, not as though he were making a compilation of the Lord's oracles. So then Mark made no mistake when he wrote down thus some things as he remembered them; for he concentrated on this alone—not to omit anything that he had heard, nor to include any false statement among them.

The Gospel according to *Matthew* includes some material from Mark's Gospel, as well as material from other sources. The earliest traditions say that the author was Matthew the disciple, but his name is not mentioned in the Gospel. It could have been written at any time between AD 50 and 100.

The third Gospel was almost certainly written by *Luke*, a Greek-speaking doctor who ac-companied Paul on several of his journeys. The other book he wrote, the *Acts of the Apostles*, continues the story of the spread of Christianity up until the early 60 s when Paul was in prison. In the introduction to the Gospel he explains how he has gathered his material:

Dear Theophilus: Many people have done their best to write a report of the things that have taken place among us. They wrote what we have been told by those who saw these things from the beginning and who proclaimed the message. And so, your Excellency, because I have carefully studied all these matters from their beginning, I thought it would be good to write an orderly account for you. I do this so that you will know the full truth about everything which you have been taught.
ACTS 1:1–4

The fourth Gospel was probably written by *John*, the disciple, around AD 90 in Asia Minor.

There are two reasons why we can be fairly confident that the Gospels give us a reliable account of the life and teaching of Jesus:

● Jesus seems to have used some of the teaching methods of the Jewish rabbis, who took great care to ensure that their disciples understood and remembered their teaching. For example, some of his teaching was in parables which would easily be remembered. Much of his teaching was in poetical form and could easily be memorized. Many of the important sayings of Jesus arose out of particular events or questions put to him, and eye-witnesses would therefore be able to associate particular sayings with the events.

● The disciples would have been brought up as orthodox Jews, and would have known the ninth commandment which warns against any kind of false testimony. They would also have been brought up to believe that all men are sinners, and would have assumed that Jesus was just an ordinary person like themselves. Since they were in close touch with him for three years, they must have had some very good reasons for claiming, as Peter did, 'he committed no sin, and no one ever heard a lie come from his lips', or as John did, 'there is no sin in him'.

Manuscripts of the Gospels, like this papyrus fragment, have been found dating from within a hundred years of Jesus' death.

None of the writers goes out of his way to paint an impressive picture of the character of Jesus. All that we learn about his character is from his actions and his words; there are no passages which set out to describe what kind of person he was.

The accusations of his critics and enemies are fully reported: for example, they accused him of blasphemy, of keeping bad company, of not being strict enough in his religious observance, of breaking the sabbath. The writers make no deliberate attempt to defend Jesus from any of these charges. They simply leave the accounts to speak for themselves.

If the disciples and the writers *were* conscious of weaknesses or faults in his character, they have been very clever in suppressing them—and very much cleverer than the followers and admirers of other great men have been. None of the founders and leaders of the great religions—for example, Muhammad or Buddha or Confucius—ever claimed that he was perfect or sinless, and their followers generally have never made this claim for them.

CAN WE TRUST THE MANUSCRIPTS OF THE GOSPELS?

The earliest manuscript of any part of the New Testament so far discovered consists of a small papyrus fragment of some verses in John's Gospel (18:31–33, 37, 38). It was found in the sands in Egypt, and can be dated fairly accurately to around AD 125—i.e. about ninety years after the death of Jesus, and about thirty years after the Gospel was written. It is written in Greek, and the text is the same as in other Greek manuscripts from a later period.

Another papyrus manuscript containing most of John's Gospel dates from around AD 200, and another containing large parts of Luke and Mark, and a few parts of Matthew and John, dates from about AD 250.

The earliest manuscripts of the whole of the Bible date from the fourth century, and were written on parchment. Two of the most famous of these are the Codex Sinaiticus and the Codex Vaticanus, both probably written in Egypt.

Where there are small differences between all these different manuscripts, scholars are able to compare them and are in a good position to find out which text is most likely to be closest to the original.

HOW DO THE GOSPELS COMPARE WITH OTHER DOCUMENTS RELATING TO THE LIFE OF JESUS?

There is a very striking difference between the Gospels and the so-called 'Apocryphal' Gospels of a later period which report other stories about the life of Jesus. For example, THE GOSPEL OF THOMAS includes the following stories in which the boy Jesus works miracles largely to get himself out of awkward situations:

> Now on a day, when Jesus climbed up upon an house with the children, he began to play with them; but one of the boys fell down through the door out of the upper chamber and died straightway. And when the children saw it they fled all of them, but Jesus remained alone in the house. And when the parents of the child which had died came they spake against Jesus saying: Of a truth thou madest him fall. But Jesus said: I never made him fall: nevertheless they accused him still. Jesus therefore came down from the house and stood over the dead child and cried with a loud voice, calling him by name: Zeno, Zeno, arise and say if I made thee fall. And on a sudden he arose and said: Nay, Lord. And when his parents saw this great miracle which Jesus did, they glorified God, and worshipped Jesus.
>
> And when Jesus was six years old, his mother sent him to draw water. And when Jesus was come unto the well there was much people there and they brake his pitcher. But he took the cloak which he had upon him and filled it with water and brought it to Mary his mother. And when his mother saw the miracle that Jesus did she kissed him and said: Lord, hearken unto me and save my son.

The following is another story about the boyhood of Jesus. While some might believe that something like this *could* easily have happened and been remembered, others might say it is merely a harmless story created by someone's imagination. Whichever opinion we prefer, a story like this has no bearing on our understanding of Jesus:

> Now in the month of Adar, Jesus assembled the boys as if he were their king; they strewed their garments on the ground and he sat upon them. Then they put on his head a crown wreathed of flowers and like attendants waiting on a king they stood in order before him on his right hand and on his left. And whoever passed that way the boys took him by force saying, Come hither and adore the King and then proceed upon thy way.

RODERIC DUNKERLEY gives this assessment of the value of these other sources:

> As regards the conventionally called 'apocryphal Gospels' . . . it does not take very much examination to convince us that they are almost entirely fiction not fact. They deal mostly with the nativity and boyhood of Jesus on the one hand, and with his passion and resurrection on the other. Many fantastic miracles are attributed to the child Jesus, as for example that he made birds of clay and then they flew away, and again that another boy who accidentally ran against him dropped down and died . . .

The events of the New Testament are reflected in these contemporary coins of the emperors Augustine and Tiberius.

HOW WAS JESUS RELATED TO GOD?

Was he anything more than an ordinary man? If he was related to God in some special way, how are we to describe this relationship?

EVIDENCE

The main evidence we have to consider in the four Gospel accounts concerns his birth, his character, his claims about himself, and his miracles.

His birth

Two of the Gospels begin with an account of the birth of Jesus. His birth is described as a perfectly natural birth, but his conception as the work of the Holy Spirit.

MATTHEW describes the events from the point of view of Joseph, who was at this time engaged to Mary:

Now the birth of Jesus Christ took place in this way. When his mother had been betrothed to Joseph, before they came together she was found to be with child of the Holy Spirit; and her husband Joseph, being a just man and unwilling to put her to shame, resolved to divorce her quietly. But as he considered this, behold, an angel of the Lord appeared to him in a dream, saying, 'Joseph, son of David, do not fear to take Mary your wife, for that which is conceived in her is of the Holy Spirit; she will bear a son, and you shall call his name Jesus, for he will save his people from their sins.' . . . When Joseph awoke from sleep, he did as the angel of the Lord commanded him; he took his wife, but knew her not until she had borne a son; and he called his name Jesus.

LUKE describes the events from the point of view of Mary:

In the sixth month the angel Gabriel was sent from God to a city of Galilee named Nazareth, to a virgin betrothed to a man whose name was Joseph, of the house of David;

**and the virgin's name was Mary.
And he came to her and said, 'Hail,
O favoured one, the Lord is with
you! . . . Do not be afraid, Mary, for
you have found favour with God.
And behold, you will conceive in
your womb and bear a son, and you
shall call his name Jesus . . .' And
Mary said to the angel, 'How can
this be, since I have no husband?'
And the angel said to her, 'The Holy
Spirit will come upon you, and the
power of the Most High will
overshadow you; therefore the
child to be born will be called holy,
the Son of God.'**

There are hints in other parts of the New Testament that something was known about the unusual
circumstances of his birth.

When the JEWS objected to the way in which
Jesus called himself 'the Son', they taunted him
with these words:

**We were not born of fornication; we
have one Father, even God.**

The implication may well be 'We were not born of
fornication—*as you were.*'

PAUL speaks of the entrance of Jesus into the
world in these words:

**When the time had fully come, God
sent forth his Son, born of woman,
born under the law . . .**

In the early days of the church, the story of the
death and resurrection of Jesus would have over-
shadowed the story of his birth. The story might
therefore have remained a secret tradition, known
only to a small number.

The only direct evidence for belief in the virgin
birth in the New Testament is contained in the two
passages from Luke and Matthew. If the belief is
important, why do the other Gospels not record the
story?

From the very nature of the case, we would not
expect the story to be common knowledge in the
early days of the church.

At first only Mary and Joseph would have
known the circumstances of the conception of
Jesus. They would hardly be likely to tell the story
to others inside or outside the family!

Joseph must have died at some time before

Jesus began his public ministry. Mary would have
no compelling motive for publishing the story,
since she herself seems to have had doubts about
him during this period. LUKE gives the impression
that Mary kept the secret to herself, and that he
heard the story about Jesus' birth and childhood
from her own mouth:

**. . . and all who heard it wondered at
what the shepherds told them. But
Mary kept all these things,
pondering them in her heart.
    And he (Jesus) went down with
them and came to Nazareth, and
was obedient to them; and his
mother kept all these things in her
heart.**

The question has often been asked: why is there so
little about the early life of Jesus? A normal
biography would describe a person's background
and childhood. The only details given in the
Gospels are:

● Joseph and Mary took Jesus to Egypt while he
was still a baby because of the threat to his life from
Herod. After the death of Herod, they returned to
Nazareth, and it was here that he was brought up
(Matthew 2:13–15).

● Jesus had brothers and sisters who were born to
Mary and Joseph (this is the most natural and
obvious interpretation of the references to the
'brothers' of Jesus):

**Many who heard him (Jesus) were
astonished, saying, 'Where did this
man get all this? . . . Is not this the
carpenter, the son of Mary and
brother of James and Joses and
Judas and Simon, and are not his
sisters here with us?'**

Similarly, Paul speaks of

James, the Lord's brother . . .

The interpretation that the 'brothers' were in fact
cousins and not blood-brothers first appears in
Christian writings in the third century. This
tradition seems to have been associated with the
belief that Mary remained a virgin after her
marriage to Joseph and after the birth of Jesus; but
there is no basis for this belief in the New
Testament itself.

● Jesus first visited Jerusalem at the age of twelve.
After a long search his parents found him 'in the

temple, sitting among the teachers, listening to them and asking them questions' (Luke 2:41–51).
● Joseph, his foster-father, was a carpenter, and it appears that Jesus learned this trade from him. Joseph must have died before Jesus left home for his public ministry. Being the eldest son, Jesus would have had the responsibility for the home (Matthew 13:55).

If we ask why the writers of the Gospels do not tell us more about the early life of Jesus, the simplest answer is that they were not intending to write full biographies of Jesus. Their main concern was with his public ministry, his death and resurrection.

His character

There are at least four features which stand out clearly: compassion and anger, humility and goodness.

COMPASSION
Jesus' compassion shows in his attitude towards the crowds:

> They went away in the boat to a lonely place by themselves. Now many saw them going, and knew them, and they ran there on foot from all the towns, and got there ahead of them. As he landed he saw a great throng, and *he had compassion on them*, because they were like sheep without a shepherd; and he began to teach them many things.

towards children:

> They were bringing children to him, that he might touch them; and the disciples rebuked them. But when Jesus saw it he was indignant, and said to them, 'Let the children come to me, do not hinder them; for to such belongs the kingdom of God ...' And he took them in his arms and blessed them, laying his hands upon them.

Jesus' ministry was characterized by his compassion for the poor and needy.

towards the sick:

> And a leper came to him beseeching him, and kneeling said to him, 'If you will, you can make me clean.' *Moved with pity,* he stretched out his hand and touched him, and said to him, 'I will; be clean.' And immediately the leprosy left him and he was made clean.

towards the bereaved:

> As he drew near to the gate of the city, behold, a man who had died was being carried out, the only son

of his mother, and she was a widow;
and a large crowd from the city was
with her. And when the Lord saw
her, *he had compassion* on her and
said to her, 'Do not weep.' And he
came and touched the bier, and the
bearers stood still. And he said,
'Young man, I say to you, arise.'
And the dead man sat up, and
began to speak.

towards the socially unacceptable:

Now the tax collectors and sinners
were all drawing near to hear him.
And the Pharisees and the scribes
murmured, saying, 'This man
receives sinners and eats with
them.'

ANGER

Jesus had many angry words to say to the religious
leaders who, by their teaching and behaviour, were
distorting or denying the truth for which Jesus had
such deeply-felt concern:

Well did Isaiah prophesy of you
hypocrites ... You leave the
commandment of God, and hold
fast the tradition of men ... You
have a fine way of rejecting the
commandment of God, in order to
keep your tradition!

Woe to you, scribes and Pharisees,
hypocrites! because you shut the
kingdom of heaven against men; for
you neither enter yourselves, nor
allow those who would enter to go
in ...

Woe to you, blind guides ... you
blind fools!

Woe to you, scribes and Pharisees,
hypocrites! for you cleanse the
outside of the cup and of the plate,
but inside they are full of extortion
and rapacity ... You ... outwardly
appear righteous to men, but within
you are full of hypocrisy and
iniquity.

He entered the temple and began to
drive out those who sold and those
who bought in the temple, and he
overturned the tables of the money-
changers and the seats of those
who sold pigeons; and he would not
allow any one to carry anything
through the temple. And he taught,
and said to them, 'Is it not written,
"My house shall be called a house
of prayer for all the nations"? But
you have made it a den of robbers.'

HUMILITY

Jesus' humility before God:

I can do nothing on my own
authority ... I seek not my own will
but the will of him who sent me.

I have come down from heaven, not
to do my own will, but the will of him
who sent me.

His humility before men. LUKE describes this
incident at the Last Supper:

A dispute also arose among them,
which of them was to be regarded
as the greatest. And he said to
them, 'The kings of the Gentiles
exercise lordship over them; and
those in authority over them are
called benefactors. But not so with
you; rather let the greatest among
you become as the youngest, and
the leader as one who serves. For
which is the greater, one who sits at
table, or one who serves? Is it not
the one who sits at table? But I am
among you as one who serves.

After the supper, he demonstrated in action something of what he meant by the outlook of the
servant:

Jesus, knowing that the Father had
given all things into his hands, and
that he had come from God and was
going to God, rose from supper,
laid aside his garments, and girded
himself with a towel. Then he
poured water into a basin, and
began to wash the disciples' feet,
and to wipe them with the towel with
which he was girded ...
    When he had washed their feet,

and taken his garments and resumed his place, he said to them, 'Do you know what I have done to you? You call me Teacher and Lord; and you are right, for so I am. If I then, your Lord and Teacher, have washed your feet, you also ought to wash one another's feet. For I have given you an example, that you also should do as I have done to you.'

GOODNESS

People acknowledged the positive goodness of what Jesus was doing:

And they were astonished beyond measure, saying, 'He has done all things well; he even makes the deaf hear and the dumb speak.'

He himself claimed to be without sin:

Which of you convicts me of sin?

His disciples claimed that he was sinless:

He committed no sin; no guile was found on his lips. When he was reviled, he did not revile in return; when he suffered, he did not threaten; but he trusted to him who judges justly.

If we say we have no sin, we deceive ourselves ... He appeared to take away sins, and in him there is no sin.

His claims about himself

HIS CLAIM TO BE THE SON

He spoke of himself as 'the Son' and of God as 'the Father' or 'my Father'.

Of that day or that hour (the day of judgement) no one knows, not even the angels of heaven, nor *the Son*, but only *the Father*.

All things have been delivered to me by *my Father*; and no one knows *the Son* except *the Father*, and no one knows *the Father* except *the*

Son and any one to whom *the Son* chooses to reveal him.

Whoever does the will of *my Father* in heaven is my brother.

The Son of man is to come with his angels in the glory of *his Father*.

I and *the Father* are one.

The Father judges no one, but has given all judgement to *the Son*, that all may honour *the Son*, even as they honour *the Father*. He who does not honour *the Son* does not honour *the Father* who sent him.

No one comes to *the Father*, but by me. If you had known me, you would have known *my Father* also.

HIS CLAIM TO BE THE FULFILMENT OF THE OLD TESTAMENT

The time is fulfilled (i.e. the time spoken about by the prophets), and the kingdom of God is at hand.

The Son of man also came ... to serve, and to give his life as a ransom for many.
(These are allusions to the Son of man described in Daniel 7 and the Suffering Servant in Isaiah 42–53.)

This is my blood of the covenant, which is poured out for many.
(An allusion to the blood of the Old Testament sacrifices, the covenant which God made with the nation at Sinai, and the 'new covenant' spoken of by Ezekiel and Jeremiah.)

The high priest asked him, 'Are you the Christ, the Son of the Blessed?' And Jesus said, 'I am; and you will see the Son of man sitting at the right hand of Power, and coming with the clouds of heaven.'
(Another reference to the Son of man in Daniel.)

He opened the book and found the place where it was written, 'The Spirit of the Lord is upon me ...' And he began to say to them,

'Today this scripture has been fulfilled in your hearing.'
(He was reading from a passage in Isaiah.)

**Everything written about me in the law of Moses and the prophets and the psalms must be fulfilled ...
Thus it is written, that the Christ should suffer and on the third day rise from the dead.**

The scriptures ... bear witness to me.

If you believed Moses, you would believe me, for he wrote of me.

HIS INDIRECT CLAIMS

Jesus claimed to be able to do things which, according to Jewish belief, only God could do.

He forgave sins:

Jesus ... said to the paralytic, 'My son, your sins are forgiven.' Now some of the scribes were sitting there, questioning in their hearts, 'Why does this man speak thus? It is blasphemy! Who can forgive sins but God alone?' And ... Jesus ... said ... '... the Son of man has authority on earth to forgive sins.'

He claimed to be able to give eternal life:

As the Father raises the dead and gives them life, so also the Son gives life to whom he will.

I am the resurrection and the life; he who believes in me, though he die, yet shall he live.

He claimed to teach the truth with authority:

You have heard that it was said to the men of old, 'You shall not kill ...' But I say to you ...

Heaven and earth will pass away, but my words will not pass away.

For this I have come into the world, to bear witness to the truth. Every one who is of the truth hears my voice.

He said he would one day judge the world:

When the Son of man comes in his glory, and all the angels with him, then he will sit on his glorious throne. Before him will be gathered all the nations, and he will separate them one from another as a shepherd separates the sheep from the goats.

The Father judges no one, but has given all judgement to the Son, that all may honour the Son, even as they honour the Father.

He claimed to be able to satisfy the deepest needs of men, and he invited them to follow him and give him their allegiance:

Come to me, all who labour and are heavy laden, and I will give you rest. Take my yoke upon you, and learn from me; for I am gentle and lowly in heart, and you will find rest for your souls.

If any one comes to me and does not hate his own father and mother ... and even his own life, he cannot be my disciple.

If any one thirst, let him come to me and drink.

This is the work of God, that you believe in him whom he has sent.

Believe in God, believe also in me.

Why did Jesus appear at times to conceal his identity?

Why was he so indirect in his claims about himself? If he really was God the Son, why did he not say so directly and openly from the beginning, so as to leave no shadow of doubt in people's minds? When some *did* think of him as 'the Christ' or as 'the Son of God', why did he tell them not to tell others?

And whenever the unclean spirits beheld him, they fell down before him and cried out, 'You are the Son of God.' And he strictly ordered them not to make him known.

Jesus was careful not to allow hysterical hero-worship.

And he (Jesus) asked them (the disciples), 'But who do you say that I am?' Peter answered him, 'You are the Christ.' And he charged them to tell no one about him.

● A political reason

Jesus would have been well aware of the confused and misleading ideas about the Messiah which were circulating at the time (e.g. the idea of the warrior king who would lead the Jews to drive out the Romans, or the heavenly Son of man who would descend from the clouds in glory).

If he had repeatedly used titles like 'Messiah', he would have identified himself in the eyes of the people and the Roman authorities with the extreme nationalists, and he might well have been taken as a purely political figure.

● A theological reason

Jesus would also have been aware of the Jewish emphasis on the oneness of God: 'The Lord our God is one Lord . . .' If he had made direct and unmistakable claims from the beginning, his hearers might not have been willing even to give him a hearing. A certain indirectness would force people to think for themselves and to come gradually to understand the full implications of what he claimed. We must add, however, that although the claims of Jesus may seem very indirect and subtle to us today, they would have sounded *less* so to the well-taught Jew who heard him. No Jew would fail to see what was implied when Jesus claimed authority to forgive sins—he would immediately accuse him of blasphemy.

● A moral reason

When Jesus spoke indirectly about himself, he was not simply encouraging his hearers to think with their minds. He was at the same time presenting a challenge to their wills and their consciences. On one occasion he refused to be more direct simply because he could see that his questioners were ignoring the moral challenge in what they already knew.

As he was walking in the temple, the chief priests and the scribes and the elders came to him, and they said to him, 'By what authority are

you doing these things, or who gave you this authority to do them?' Jesus said to them, 'I will ask you a question; answer me, and I will tell you by what authority I do these things. Was the baptism of John from heaven or from men? Answer me.' And they argued with one another, 'If we say, "From heaven," he will say, "Why then did you not believe him?" But shall we say, "From men"?'—they were afraid of the people, for all held that John was a real prophet. So they answered Jesus, 'We do not know.' And Jesus said to them, 'Neither will I tell you by what authority I do these things.'

● The time factor

When the disciples came to realize that he was the Christ, the Son of God, he told them not to tell anyone openly:

And he asked them, 'But who do you say that I am?' Peter answered him, 'You are the Christ.' And he charged them to tell no one about him.
　　And he began to teach them that the Son of man must suffer many things ... and be killed, and after three days rise again.

Very soon after this three of the disciples witnessed the transfiguration, and Jesus gave a similar command:

As they were coming down the mountain, he charged them to tell no one what they had seen, until the Son of man should have risen from the dead. So they kept the matter to themselves, questioning what the rising from the dead meant.

This suggests that Jesus expected that what was hidden and obscure *during* his lifetime would be proclaimed openly to all *after* his death and resurrection.

● Direct answers

On some occasions when he was presented with a direct question, he gave a direct answer:

The high priest said to him, 'I adjure you by the living God, tell us if you are the Christ, the Son of God.' Jesus said to him, 'You have said so ...' (or 'the words are yours', New English Bible) ... Then the high priest tore his robes, and said, 'He has uttered blasphemy ...'

His miracles

Three different kinds of miracle are recorded.

1. Nature miracles: e.g. stilling the storm (Mark 4:35–41); feeding the 5,000 with five loaves and two fishes (Mark 6:30–44); walking on the water (Mark 6:45–52); changing the water into wine (John 2:1–11).

2. Healing miracles: e.g. healing of fever, leprosy, blindness, demon possession, etc.

3. Raising from death: e.g. the son of the woman of Nain (Luke 7:11–17); Lazarus of Bethany (John 11:1–53).

The Gospels record Jesus' motives in performing the miracles.

● Compassion:

As they went out of Jericho, a great crowd followed him. And behold, two blind men sitting by the roadside, when they heard that Jesus was passing by, cried out, 'Have mercy on us, Son of David!' ... Jesus stopped and called them, saying, 'What do you want me to do for you?' They said to him, 'Lord, let our eyes be opened.' And Jesus in pity touched their eyes, and immediately they received their sight and followed him.

In those days, when again a great crowd had gathered, and they had nothing to eat, he called his disciples to him, and said to them, 'I have compassion on the crowd, because they have been with me now three days, and have nothing to eat ...'

● The glory of God. Many of the miracles led people to give glory to God:

> ... so that the throng wondered, when they saw the dumb speaking, the maimed whole, the lame walking, and the blind seeing; and they glorified the God of Israel.

● Evidence to support his claims:

> And immediately Jesus, perceiving in his spirit that they thus questioned within themselves, said to them, 'Why do you question thus in your hearts? Which is easier, to say to the paralytic "Your sins are forgiven," or to say, "Rise, take up your pallet and walk"? But that you may know that the Son of man has authority on earth to forgive sins'— he said to the paralytic—'I say to you, rise, take up your pallet and go home.' And he rose, and immediately took up the pallet and went out before them all ...

> When John heard in prison about the deeds of the Christ, he sent word by his disciples and said to him, 'Are you he who is to come, or shall we look for another?' And Jesus answered them, 'Go and tell John what you hear and see: the blind receive their sight and the lame walk, lepers are cleansed and the deaf hear, and the dead are raised up, and the poor have good news preached to them.

> If I am not doing the works of my Father, then do not believe me; but if I do them, even though you do not believe me, believe the works, that you may know and understand that the Father is in me and I am in the Father.

There were times, however, when people pressed him to work miracles not out of a genuine desire to be convinced, but out of a defiant scepticism. And on these occasions, Jesus refused to work miracles to order:

> The Pharisees came and began to argue with him, seeking from him a sign from heaven, to test him. And he sighed deeply in his spirit, and said, 'Why does this generation seek a sign? Truly, I say to you, no sign shall be given to this generation.' And he left them.

Matthew's version of this saying (Matthew 12:39–40) adds an exception which points forward to the resurrection as the one and only sign which he would give these proud Pharisees.

BELIEF AND UNBELIEF

It is significant that the miracles of Jesus did not always compel people to believe. Several of the miracles played an important part in bringing individuals and groups to believe in Jesus. For example, after the turning of the water into wine, we are told 'his disciples believed in him'. As a result of the healing of the son of the official at Capernaum, we are told that the boy's father 'and all his family believed'.

There is no suggestion, however, that the miracles persuaded vast numbers of people. All the Gospels speak of the ill-feeling, misunderstanding and opposition aroused by many of the miracles. After healing a man with a withered arm,

> the Pharisees left and made plans to kill Jesus.

The miracle of the feeding of the 5,000 was misunderstood by the crowd:

> Jesus knew that they were about to come and seize him in order to make him king by force; so he went off again to the hills by himself.

After healing a paralyzed man, his defence of what he had done:

> made the Jewish authorities all the more determined to kill him; not only had he broken the Sabbath law, but he had said that God was his own Father and in this way had made himself equal with God.

The raising of Lazarus from the dead led to the final plot to kill Jesus:

> From that day on the Jewish authorities made plans to kill Jesus.

POSSIBLE ANSWERS

How did people react to the man Jesus? These are some of the earliest reactions to Jesus, as recorded by MARK:

> ... they were astonished at his teaching, for he taught them as one who had authority ...

> ... they were all amazed and glorified God, saying, 'We never saw anything like this!'

> ... they said, 'He is beside himself.'

> ... they were filled with awe, and said to one another, 'Who then is this, that even wind and sea obey him?'

> ... they were afraid ... and they began to beg Jesus to depart from their neighbourhood.

> ... many who heard him were astonished, saying, 'Where did this man get all this? What is the wisdom given to him? What mighty works are wrought by his hands! Is not this the carpenter, the son of Mary and brother of James and Joses and Judas and Simon, and are not his sisters here with us?'

> they were astonished beyond measure, saying, 'He has done all things well; he even makes the deaf hear and the dumb speak.'

In our study of the evidence about Jesus, we have to get beyond these initial reactions and make up our minds about the deeper issue: what was the relationship of this man Jesus to God?

There are basically only four possible answers that can be given.

He was fully human and fully divine. He was a real human being; but at the same time he was God the Son

The first disciples could not have expressed their beliefs about Jesus in these terms *during* his lifetime. But they spoke of him as God's Messiah, i.e. God's Anointed Agent for working out his purposes in the world. And they used words and titles for him which a Jew would reserve exclusively for the one true God:

PETER said:

'You are the Christ'.

THOMAS said:

'My Lord and my God!'

THE DISCIPLES said:

'We have believed and have come to know, that you are the Holy One of God.'

'We believe that you came from God.'

The words which they used *after* his lifetime do not go beyond these claims. They identify him fully *both* with man *and* with God:

> Since therefore the children share in flesh and blood, he himself likewise partook of the same nature, that through death he might destroy him who has the power of death.

> We have not a high priest who is unable to sympathize with our weaknesses, but one who in every respect has been tempted as we are, yet without sinning.

> ... the Lord of glory ...

> ... the ... man ... from heaven ...

> ... Christ Jesus, who, though he was in the form of God, did not count equality with God a thing to

The events of the Gospels were rooted in a real place at a real time. This is Bethlehem, scene of Jesus' birth.

> be grasped, but emptied himself,
> taking the form of a servant, being
> born in the likeness of men. And
> being found in human form he
> humbled himself and became
> obedient unto death, even death on
> a cross. Therefore God has highly
> exalted him and bestowed on him
> the name which is above every
> name, that at the name of Jesus
> every knee should bow, in heaven
> and on earth and under the earth,
> and every tongue confess that
> Jesus Christ is Lord, to the glory of
> God the Father.

Certain conclusions follow from this belief about Jesus:

● If Jesus is both God and man, he can be a perfect revelation of God to men. He can reveal God adequately because he himself is fully divine:

> No one has ever seen God; the only
> Son, who is in the bosom of the
> Father, he has made him known.

This revelation is in a form that can be grasped fully by men; they can perceive it through hearing, through sight and through touch:

> That which was from the beginning,
> which we have heard, which we
> have seen with our eyes, which we
> have looked upon and touched with
> our hands, concerning the word of
> life—the life was made manifest,
> and we saw it, and testify to it, and
> proclaim to you the eternal life
> which was with the Father and was
> made manifest to us—that which we
> have seen and heard we proclaim
> also to you, so that you may have
> fellowship with us . . .

● If Jesus is both God and man, he is in a position to deal with the moral problem of man. As a man, he lived a life of complete obedience to the Father, and he was obedient right to the point of death.

His life of obedience can therefore be the reversal of the disobedience of Adam. His complete obedience has the effect of undoing the consequences of the sin of Adam:

> . . . sin came into the world through
> one man and death through sin, and

> so death spread to all men because
> all men sinned . . . But the free gift is
> not like the trespass. For if many
> died through one man's trespass,
> much more have the grace of God
> and the free gift in the grace of that
> one man Jesus Christ abounded for
> many. . . . If, because of one man's
> trespass, death reigned through
> that one man, much more will those
> who receive the abundance of grace
> and the free gift of righteousness
> reign in life through the one man
> Jesus Christ. Then as one man's
> trespass led to condemnation for all
> men, so one man's act of
> righteousness leads to aquittal and
> life for all men. For as by one man's
> disobedience many were made
> sinners, so by one man's obedience
> many will be made righteous.

Because he himself is fully divine, what *he* does, *God* does in him:

> All is from God, who through Christ
> reconciled the world to himself . . .
> God was in Christ reconciling the
> world to himself, not counting their
> trespasses against them . . .

Because he is fully human, he can identify himself with men and the guilt of their sin:

> There is one God, and there is one
> mediator between God and men, the
> man Christ Jesus, who gave himself
> as a ransom for all . . .

● The fact that Jesus is both divine and human can mean something in the present experience of the Christian. Jesus is still fully human in heaven. He did not discard his humanity as if it were a garment which he could take off. There is therefore no need for any further mediator (such as Mary or the saints). There can be no one in heaven who is 'more human' and tender and compassionate than Jesus himself.

> He had to be made like his brethren
> in every respect, so that he might
> become a merciful and faithful high
> priest in the service of God . . . For
> because he himself has suffered

and been tempted, he is able to help those who are tempted.

We have not a high priest who is unable to sympathize with our weaknesses, but one who in every respect has been tempted as we are, yet without sinning. Let us then with confidence draw near to the throne of grace, that we may receive mercy and find grace to help in time of need.

● When the Christian puts his faith in Jesus Christ as the one who is fully God and fully man, he is united with him in the closest possible union. It is not a union in which the believer is absorbed into God, but a union in which he retains his identity and even experiences the love that there is between the Father and the Son. This was the kind of union for which Jesus prayed before his arrest. It is possible because Jesus is perfectly one *both* with God *and* with man.

I do not pray for these only, but also for those who are to believe in me through their word, that they may all be one; even as thou, Father, art in me, and I in thee, that they also may be in us, so that the world may believe that thou hast sent me. The glory which thou hast given me I have given to them, that they may be one even as we are one, I in them and thou in me, that they may become perfectly one, so that the world may know that thou hast sent me and hast loved them even as thou hast loved me. Father, I desire that they also, whom thou hast given me, may be with me where I am, to behold my glory which thou hast given me in thy love for me before the foundation of the world. O righteous Father, the world has not known thee, but I have known thee; and these know that thou hast sent me. I have made known to them thy name, and I will make it known, that the love with which thou hast loved me may be in them and I in them.

He was a created being from heaven

That is to say, Jesus was more than an ordinary man; but he was not God in any sense. He was the 'Son of God' in the sense that he was a supernatural being from heaven—but a created being.

This answer has taken several different forms throughout the course of history. It was, for example, the teaching of Arius of Alexandria in the fourth century.

In our own day, JEHOVAH'S WITNESSES teach that Jesus was a created spirit from heaven:

That Jesus might save his people from their sin, it was necessary that the Son of God be born as a human creature and grow to become 'the man Christ Jesus' ... None of Adam's offspring being sinless or having the right life to offer as a redemptive price, it was necessary for the Son of God to lay aside his spirit existence and become the needed perfect man, no more, no less. Thus Jesus could die, not as a spirit creature, but as a perfect human creature, for humankind needing redemption. For these and other reasons Jesus was not a 'God-man', for that would be more than the required price of redemption. Had he been immortal God or an immortal soul he could not have given his life. According to the Scriptural facts, he was mortal on earth ...

The primary purpose of the Son of God in coming to earth was to meet and decisively answer Satan's false charge that God cannot put on earth a creature who will keep his integrity and abide faithful till death under the test of persecution from the Devil and his demons ...

They believe that Jesus was appointed to be the Son of God at the time of his baptism:

John heard God's voice announcing Jesus as His Son. This proves that God there begot Jesus by his Spirit or active force, by virtue of which Jesus now became the spiritual Son of God, possessing the right to spirit life in heaven. God so begot him, because Jesus' right to human life was henceforth to be dedicated to redeeming humankind...

God's prophecy, at Psalm 2:7, was directed to Jesus: 'Thou art my Son; this day I have begotten thee.' When Jehovah begot the baptized Jesus and made him the spiritual Son of God with right to life in the heavenly spirit realm, Jesus became a 'new creature'.

He thus became immortal after his death on the cross:

In due time, after proving his faithfulness to death and providing redemption from sin, the Son was rewarded with immortality.

This answer, however, is based on a very selective reading of the New Testament. It makes some sense of verses which speak of Jesus' dependence on the Father and his humility before the Father. But it ignores all the other evidence which points to a much closer relationship with the Father.

● The verses which are claimed to support this interpretation can hardly bear the weight that is put on them, as the three following examples show.

1. The Father is greater than I.

These words must be understood in the light of all the other sayings of JESUS in *John's Gospel*, for example:

I and the Father are one.

He who has seen me has seen the Father; how can you say, 'Show us the Father'? Do you not believe that I am in the Father and the Father in me?

These words therefore point to the way in which the eternal Son humbled himself before the Father,

for the work of revelation and salvation. PAUL writes about the humbling and self-emptying of the Son in this way:

... Christ Jesus ... though he was in the form of God, did not count equality with God a thing to be grasped, but emptied himself, taking the form of a servant, being born in the likeness of men ...

2. Why do you call me good? No one is good but God alone:

JESUS gave this answer in reply to the person who asked him:

Good Teacher, what shall I do to inherit eternal life?

Jesus was probably testing the man to see whether his words were a casual compliment, or whether he had realized who Jesus was. Or he could be saying, 'If you think I am no more than an ordinary human teacher, why do you call me good?' Whatever the exact interpretation of these words, JESUS goes on to make a very big claim for himself. He does not argue with the man when he claims that he has kept all the commandments. Instead he takes it upon himself to tell the man where he is still falling short, and tells him to become a disciple:

One thing you still lack. Sell all that you have and distribute to the poor, and you will have treasure in heaven; and come, follow me.

3. He is the image of the invisible God, the first-born of all creation...

The remaining verses of this passage show that the writer did *not* believe that Jesus was a created being. On the contrary, *everything* both in heaven and on earth was created through him:

He is the image of the invisible God, the first-born of all creation; for in him all things were created, in heaven and on earth, visible and invisible, whether thrones or dominions or principalities or authorities—all things were created through him and for him. He is before all things, and in him all things hold together...

C.F.D. MOULE explains the two possible interpretations of the word 'first-born':

/ **(i) Translate the 'first—' as a time-metaphor ... Translated thus, it may allude to Christ's priority to the created world: he was born (or, as more considered theology would say, begotten, not born) before any created thing ...**
(ii) Take 'firstborn' not as a temporal term so much as in the sense of *supreme*— 'the one who is supreme over all creation' ... If one must choose, there is, perhaps, a little more to be said in favour of (ii) ... But possibly (i) and (ii) are to be combined: 'prior to and supreme over'.

● Other passages of the New Testament expressly reject this kind of interpretation. The writer of the letter to the HEBREWS, for example, was aware of beliefs which made Jesus an exalted being, but a being created by God. He emphasizes the gulf which separates Jesus, the Son, from all the created angels in heaven:

In many and various ways God spoke of old to our fathers by the prophets; but in these last days he has spoken to us by a Son, whom he appointed heir of all things, through whom also he created the world. He reflects the glory of God and bears the very stamp of his nature, upholding the universe by his word of power. When he had made purification for sin, he sat down at the right hand of the Majesty on high, having become as much superior to angels as the name he has obtained is more excellent than theirs.

This kind of answer makes Jesus a mediator who is less than God. Being less than God, he cannot do anything more than reveal messages from God, and he cannot deal with the guilt of man before the holy God. He can act to some extent on behalf of men if he is fully man, but he cannot take it upon himself to forgive sin. Since it is God himself who has been wronged, and God himself whose laws have been broken, *only God* can forgive the wrong and the

disobedience. If Jesus were less than God, he could not act on behalf of God in dealing with the moral problem of man.

He was a prophet sent by God

Many Jews recognize that Jesus was a godly man who brought a real message from God to his fellow men.

In the first few centuries after the death of Jesus, although most Jews did not recognize Jesus as Messiah, they were not totally unsympathetic to him. Later, however, more critical attitudes were expressed.

HERBERT DANBY, writing about the Jewish traditions recorded in the *Talmud*:

Here is the sum-total of all that the Talmud is *alleged* (sometimes rightly, but more often wrongly) to say of Christianity's Founder:
A certain Yeshu, called the Notsri, or the Son of Stada, or the Son of Pantera, was born out of wedlock. His mother was called Miriam. She was a woman's hairdresser (the word here is *M'gadd'la*, a pun on the name Mary Magdalen). Her husband was Pappus, the son of Yehudah, and her paramour a Roman soldier, Pantera. She is said to have been the descendant of princes and rulers. This Yeshu had been to Egypt, whence he brought back the knowledge of many tricks and sorcery. He was just a sorcerer, and so deceived and led astray the people of Israel; he sinned and caused the multitude to sin. He made a mock of the words of the learned men and was excommunicated. He was tainted with heresy. He called himself God and said that he would go up to heaven. He was tried before the Court at Lud on a charge of being a deceiver and teacher of apostasy.

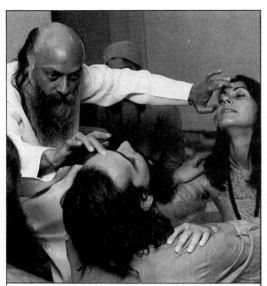

If Jesus was just a good teacher, he was no different in kind from present-day 'prophets' such as Baghwan Rajneesh.

Evidence was produced against him by concealing witnesses to hear his statements, and a lamp was so placed that his face could be seen, but so that he could not see the witnesses. He was executed in Lud on the Eve of Passover, which fell on the eve of a Sabbath. During forty days a herald proclaimed that Yeshu was to be stoned, and evidence was invited in his favour, but none was forthcoming. He was stoned and hanged. Under the name of Balaam he was put to death by 'Pinhas the Robber' (supposed to refer to Pontius Pilate). At the time he was thirty-three years old. He was punished in Gehenna by means of boiling scum. He was 'near to the kingdom' (whatever that may mean). He had five disciples: Mattai, Naqai, Netser, Buni and Today. Under the name of Balaam he was excluded from the world to come.

ABOUT THE DOCUMENTS

Because the Gospels, while containing valuable material, are all written in a polemical spirit and for the purpose of substantiating the claim of the Messianic spirit and superhuman character of Jesus, it is difficult to present an impartial story of his life.

The following articles from the *Jewish Encyclopedia* sum up the attitude of many Jews in the twentieth century to Jesus.

HIS BIRTH

The supernatural in the life of Jesus according to the Gospels is restricted to the smallest dimensions, consisting mainly of incidents and characteristics intended to support these prophecies (from the Old Testament) and the dogmatic positions of Christianity. This applies especially to the story of the virgin-birth, a legend which is common to almost all folk-heroes as indicating their superiority to the rest of their people.

HIS CLAIMS

The prophets spoke with confidence in the truth of their message, but expressly on the ground that they were declaring the word of the Lord. Jesus adopted equal confidence, but he emphasised his own authority apart from any vicarious or deputed authority from on high. Yet in doing so he did not—at any rate publicly— ever lay claim to any authority as attaching to his position as Messiah.

The most striking characteristic of the utterances of Jesus, regarded as a personality, were the tone of authority adopted by him and the claim that spiritual peace and salvation were to be found in the mere acceptance of his leadership. Passages like Matthew 11:29, 8:35, 25:40 indicate an assumption of power which is certainly unique in Jewish history, and indeed account for much of modern Jewish antipathy to Jesus, so far as it exists. On the other hand, there is little in any of these utterances to show that they were meant by the speaker to apply to anything more than personal relations with him; and it might well be that in his experience he found that spiritual relief was often afforded by simple human trust in his good-will and power of direction.

This ... raises the question whether Jesus regarded himself as in any sense a Messiah or spiritual ruler; and there is singularly little evidence in the synoptic Gospels to carry out this claim. These assert only that the claim was made to some of the disciples, and then under a distinct pledge of secrecy. In the public utterances of Jesus there is absolutely no trace of the claim (except possibly in the use of the expression 'Son of man'). Yet it would almost appear that in one sense of the word Jesus regarded himself as fulfilling some of the prophesies which were taken among contemporary Jews as applying to the Messiah. In other words, Jesus regarded himself as typically human, and claimed authority and regard in that respect.

HIS MIRACLES

It is difficult to estimate what amount of truth exists in the accounts of these cures, recorded about forty years after their occurrence; but doubtless the mental excitement due to the influence of Jesus was often efficacious in at least partial or temporary cures of mental illness. This would tend to confirm the impression, both among those who witnessed the cures and among his disciples, of his possession of supernatural powers. He himself occasionally deprecated the exaggeration to which such cures naturally led.

Other Jews have expressed an attitude which is considerably more sympathetic.

The most important Jew who ever lived, one who exercised a greater influence upon mankind and civilization than any other person, whether within the Jewish race or without it ... A Jew whose life and character have been regarded by almost all the best and wisest people who have heard or read of his actions and his words, as the greatest religious exemplar of every age.

God's nearness was felt by Jesus directly with a vivid intensity unsurpassed by any man.

CLAUDE MONTEFIORE

What was quite new in the teaching of Jesus was that for the first time there appeared in Israel a teacher who, while in agreement with the law of Moses, did not derive his authority from that law ... He appealed to an authority which had been entrusted to his keeping ... The Jews were bound to the authority which had been given to Moses on Sinai, and which they had recognized with their promise of obedience. They could not pass to the new authority without the sign which should proclaim that the old had been cancelled and the new one validated ... The first coming of the Messiah was not for us but for the Gentiles.

SHOLEM ASCH

It is only right to admit that it was the shameful way in which Christians began to treat the Jews that made Jews take a more hostile attitude to Jesus. It is Christians who are largely responsible for preventing Jews from getting a fair and accurate picture of Jesus.

We are forced to the conclusion that so long as Pharisaic Judaism (which, we must remember, was the only form of Judaism which survived the destruction of Jerusalem)—so long as it records

personal or almost personal
reminiscence of our Lord, the
surviving record is not viciously
hostile (as later became the case);
but the farther the Jews were
removed from the time of our Lord's
earthly life, and the more dependent
they became for knowledge of
Jesus upon later generations of
Christians, then so much worse
became the Jewish characterization
of Jesus.
HERBERT DANBY

Writing about the Jewish *Talmud:*

In the main the Jews had already
begun the process which has
characterized a great part of
Judaism even to the present day—
the process of slamming the door,
and locking, barring and bolting his
mind against the whole subject of
Christianity.
HERBERT DANBY

Where there *is* a willingness to open the door and
discuss the Gospel accounts, these are some of the
questions which might be raised in response to the
Jewish estimates of Jesus:

1. How could orthodox Palestinian Jews introduce elements from pagan legends to describe the
birth of Jesus, knowing that by doing so they
denied the most fundamental article of their faith,
the oneness of God?

2. Is it really true to say that Jesus never
claimed any authority deputed by the Father?
What of his claims to be 'the Son'? Granted that he
did not claim openly to be the Messiah; did he not
make many other direct and indirect claims in
which he identified himself with God himself!

3. How could a Jew invite fellow Jews to find
comfort in personal relations with him by using
language which associated him so closely with
God, and which ignored the difference between the
creature and the Creator?

● Islam recognizes Jesus as one of the great
prophets sent by God.

The *Qur'an* has its own accounts of the life of
Jesus, who is known as 'Esa, son of Mary'.

HIS BIRTH

'I am the messenger of your Lord,'
he (Gabriel) replied, 'and have come
to give you a holy son.'

'How shall I bear a child,' she
answered, 'when I am a virgin,
untouched by man?'

'Such is the will of your Lord,' he
replied. 'This is no difficult thing for
Him. "He shall be a sign to
mankind," says the Lord, "and a
blessing from Ourself. That is Our
decree."' Thereupon she conceived . . .

And remember the angel's words to
Mary. He said: 'Allah has chosen
you. He has made you pure and
exalted you above all women . . .'

HIS CHARACTER

There are many references to Jesus, but it is not
possible to build up any picture of his character.
Islam, however, seems to share the belief that Jesus
was sinless. Although it speaks of the sins of all the
other great prophets—Adam, Noah, Abraham,
Moses, and Muhammad—it nowhere attributes
any sin to Jesus. This conclusion is expressed in
one of the *Traditions:*

Every child born of Adam is
touched by Satan the day his
mother is delivered of him with the
exception of Mary and her son.

HIS CLAIMS

None of Jesus' claims for himself are quoted. But
the *Qur'an* gives the following titles to Jesus:

'the Messiah'
'the Word of God'
'the Sure Saying'
'a spirit sent from God'
'the Messenger of God', or 'the Apostle of God'
'the Servant of God'
'the Prophet of God'

The Messiah, Jesus the son of
Mary, was no more than Allah's
apostle and His Word which he cast
to Mary: a spirit from Him.

To these titles we can add two further claims made
about Jesus in the *Traditions:* He will be an

Intercessor in heaven. The *Qur'an* says of Jesus 'God took him to himself', implying that Jesus is now alive in heaven. Another verse describes Jesus as 'worthy of regard in this world and in that to come'.

BEIDHAWI, an authoritative commentator, interprets these words in this way:

> In this world as Prophet, in the next as an Intercessor.

He will be a judge.

> There is no doubt that the Son of Mary, on whom be blessing and peace, shall descend in the midst of you as a righteous judge.

HIS MIRACLES
Jesus, while still a baby, defends his mother against those who think she has been immoral and had a child out of wedlock:

> Then she took her child to her people, who said to her: 'This is indeed a strange thing! Sister of Aaron, your father was never a wicked man, nor was your mother a harlot.'
>
> She made a sign to them, pointing to the child. But they replied: 'How can we speak with a new-born infant?'
>
> Whereupon he spoke and said: 'I am the servant of Allah. He has given me the Gospel and ordained me a prophet. His blessing is upon me wherever I go, and He has commanded me to be steadfast in prayer and to give alms to the poor as long as I shall live . . .'

This miracle of the table spread with food sent from heaven contains echoes of the miracle of the feeding of the 5,000 as recorded in the *Gospels:*

> 'Jesus, son of Mary,' said the disciples, 'can Allah send down to us from heaven a table spread with food?'
>
> He replied: 'Have fear of Allah, if you are true believers.'
>
> 'We wish to eat of it,' they said, 'so that we may reassure our hearts and know that what you said to us is true, and that we may be witnesses of it.'
>
> 'Lord,' said Jesus, the son of Mary, 'send to us from heaven a table spread with food, that it may mark a feast for us and our sustenance; You are the best Giver.'
>
> Allah replied: 'I am sending one to you. But whoever of you disbelieves hereafter shall be punished as no man has ever been punished.'

This summary of his miracles refers to the story, found also in one of the apocryphal gospels, of Jesus making clay birds come to life:

> Allah will say: 'Jesus, son of Mary, remember the favour I have bestowed on you and on your mother: how I strengthened you with the Holy Spirit, so that you preached to men in your cradle and in the prime of manhood; how I instructed you in the Scriptures and in wisdom, in the Torah and in the Gospel; how by My leave you fashioned from clay the likeness of a bird and breathed into it so that, by My leave, it became a living bird; how, by My leave, you healed the blind man and the leper, and by My leave restored the dead to life; how I protected you from the Israelites when you brought them veritable signs: when the unbelievers among them said: "This is nothing but plain magic"; how when I enjoined the disciples to believe in Me and in my Apostle they replied: "We believe; bear witness that we submit to You utterly."'

From the above passages it is obvious that the *Qur'an* puts Jesus in a unique position. This is a position not shared by any of the other prophets, not even by Muhammad who is said to be the last and greatest of the prophets:

1. The birth of Jesus was a miraculous virgin birth; the words of annunciation addressed to Mary are not paralleled by any similar words addressed to Amina, the mother of Muhammad.

2. No sin of any kind is attributed to Jesus; but all the other five great prophets need to seek forgiveness from God.

3. Of the titles given to Jesus, some are exactly the same as the titles given to Muhammad: 'the Messenger of God', 'the Servant of God', 'the Prophet of God'. But the other titles given to Jesus are given to no other prophet: 'the Messiah', 'the Word of God', 'the Sure Saying', 'a spirit sent from God'. Whereas Jesus can be thought of as an intercessor, Muhammad explicitly disclaims the right to intercede for sinners before God. And whereas Jesus is said to have been raised to heaven, Muhammad is dead and has not yet been raised to be with God in heaven.

4. Later traditions attributed miracles to Muhammad. But according to the *Qur'an*, he consistently disclaimed power to work miracles. When he was challenged to produce his credentials and to prove that he was a prophet sent from God, he pointed to the *Qur'an* as being sufficient miracle in itself.

But why is Jesus so unique if Muhammad is the greatest prophet and the final messenger from God?

And what of the many questions left unanswered in the *Qur'an*? Why is Jesus called 'the Messiah'? Why his miraculous birth? What precisely was his Message, his Ingil? The Jesus of the *Qur'an* remains something of an enigma.

HENRI MICHAUD in his study of Jesus according to the *Qur'an*:

> **After having tried to understand what the Qur'an says about Jesus, we shall ask our brothers of Islam with very great anxiety: 'Is this indeed what you believe about Jesus?' If there is a reply without ambiguity, then an irenical dialogue can be begun.**

● The *Qur'an*'s rejection of the Christian understanding of Jesus is based to some extent on a misunderstanding.

It may be that the Trinity which Muhammad rejected was a Trinity consisting of the Father, Jesus and Mary:

> **Then Allah will say: 'Jesus, son of Mary, did you ever say to mankind: "Worship me and my Mother as gods beside Allah?"'**

The relationship between the Father and the Son is thought of as a purely physical relationship:

> **He is the Creator of the heavens and the earth. How should He have a son when he had no consort?**

> **Never has Allah begotten a son, nor is there any other god beside him.**

The Christian rejects these ideas as vigorously as the Muslim.

● It may be, however, that in the end we must move from the details of the picture of Christ in the *Qur'an* and the Gospels and talk about fundamental assumptions.

The original disciples of Jesus were as firmly convinced as any Muslim that God is one. This was their basic creed, their basic assumption. However, through their contact with Jesus over a period of three years they were gradually forced by what they saw and heard and experienced to revise their understanding of the oneness of God. They did not reject it; they simply revised their idea of 'oneness' in the light of the inescapable evidence which confronted them. If you are not willing even to consider the possibility of revising your assumption about the oneness of God in the light of the evidence of the life of Jesus, then the discussion must turn on rather basic questions arising out of the Muslim understanding of God.

He was a man and nothing more

1. This is to say, Jesus was simply a man. He was not divine in the sense that he shared the nature of a supernatural God. And he was not a created being from heaven. He may have been a very exceptional person, and he may help us to find the meaning of life. But he was not in any sense more than an ordinary human being.

HUGH SCHONFIELD explains the Christian belief as being the result of

> **... the intrusion into early Christianity of a pagan assessment of his worth in terms of deity.**

Jesus has been described as merely 'the symbol of martyrdom and the aspirations of man'. This would put him on a level with John Lennon, who was murdered in New York in 1980.

In spite of this he is able to see some deeper meaning in the person of Jesus:

> **We find in him the symbol both of the martyrdom and the aspirations of man, and therefore we must cling to him as the embodiment of an assurance that our life has meaning and purpose.**

PAUL VAN BUREN interprets the life of Jesus through the concept of 'freedom':

> **Jesus of Nazareth was a singular individual. His characteristics seem to have impressed his followers so that he stands out as a remarkably free man in the records of remembered parable, saying or incident, and in the way in which the early Christian community spoke of him ...**
>
> **He followed the religious rites and obligations of his people, but he also felt free to disregard them. In miracle stories he is even presented mythologically as being free from the limitations of natural forces.**
>
> **He was called rabbi, teacher, but his teaching broke down the limitations of this title ... He simply spoke and acted with the authority of a singular freedom.**

> **The content of his teaching reveals this same freedom ... Perhaps the most radical expression of this freedom is found in an incident in which Jesus forgave a sick man his sins, and then demonstrated his right to do so by healing him ... His freedom, finally, is evident in his making no claims for himself. He seems to have been so free of any need for status that he was able to resist all attempts by others to convey status on him ...**
>
> **If we would define Jesus by his freedom, however, we must emphasize its positive character. He was free from anxiety and the need to establish his own identity, but was above all free for his neighbour ... He was free to be compassionate for his neighbour, whoever that neighbour might be, without regard to himself ...**
>
> **We have summed up the characteristics of Jesus around the one concept, freedom ...**

2. Another version of this answer is to say that he was an ordinary man; he was not related personally to a supernatural God, for no such God exists. However, if we redefine the word 'God', we can

see in Jesus a revelation of the true meaning of 'God'.

> **What the early Christians saw in Jesus, implicitly if not explicitly, was a full and perfect pattern of divinity, so far as divinity could be shown forth in man. This divinity, moreover, was inherent in each one of them. For Jesus was Representative Man, Archetypal Man, Man as he might be if he could become that which in his essential nature he really is: or, as a Hindu would put it, if he could realize his Greater Self.**
>
> F.C. HAPPOLD

EARLY CHRISTIAN BELIEFS
Both of these answers have to attempt to explain the further question:

How was it that the early Christians came to believe that he was more than an ordinary man?
● If the Gospels do give a substantially reliable account of his life, what do you make of his claims about himself? In the final analysis there are only two possible answers. Either

1. he was *deceived* and *misled* about his own identity; he was wrong about his claims, but did not know it. Therefore, at best he was mentally unbalanced, at worst he was out of his mind, completely mad. Or

2. he *deceived* and *misled* others consciously and deliberately; he was wrong about his claims, and he knew it; but he spoke and acted in this way to get people to believe in his teaching and in what he stood for. Therefore, at best he was a teacher with ideals, who used unscrupulous methods; at worst he was a dishonest rogue.
● If the Gospels are not a reliable account of the life of Jesus, how are we to account for the distortion? The first Gospel was probably written thirty to forty years after the death of Jesus; and the process of distortion must already have begun at this stage. There are three possible answers: Either

1. the disciples and/or the writers were *deceived* and *misled*; they completely misunderstood Jesus themselves, and passed on their misunderstanding to others.

BUT: are we to imagine that Jesus spent the best part of three years with the disciples and allowed them to misunderstand him so completely?

And how can we explain this misunderstanding in the light of the vast difference between Jewish beliefs about the one God and pagan beliefs about many gods? The first disciples were all Palestinian Jews; is it likely that they would make Jesus out to be a demi-god? Or

2. the disciples and/or the writers were *deceiving* and *misleading* their readers deliberately, although they may have had the best of motives. Somewhere along the line there were those who knew that Jesus was an ordinary man, but they made him out to be more than a man in order to convince others of the importance of his message.

BUT: how could a religion based on a lie, or even on an 'honest' deception make so much of truthfulness and honesty?

And what possible motive could they have had? Jews would find it very difficult to accept a new understanding of the oneness of God. And non-Jews would not easily accept the claims about the uniqueness of Jesus. Or

3. the disciples and/or the writers were not misled or misleading; it is *we* who are misled if we read the Gospels as a straightforward account of what Jesus said and did. The Gospels tell us about the inward *experience* and *faith* of the first disciples, and cannot be taken as reliable evidence about the *events* behind that faith.

BUT: if we are to be agnostic about what it was that created the faith of the disciples, Christian faith ceases to be faith in the Jesus of history, and becomes faith in the faith of the first disciples. And why not carry the agnosticism one stage further and be agnostic about the *faith* of the disciples as well as the *events*?

BASIC ASSUMPTIONS
Sooner or later the discussion must turn on basic assumptions rather than on detailed points of interpretation. One of the basic assumptions which is evident in answers of this kind is that a 'God-man' is inconceivable and incredible.

HUGH SCHONFIELD sets out to examine the evidence about Jesus without any bias or prejudice. In his Introduction to *The Passover Plot* he begins with a claim to be unbiassed and unprejudiced:

Most books about him (Jesus) have been devotional, apologetic or polemical, and I wished mine to be

none of these. What I aimed at was to shed all dispositions to make use of Jesus and allow him from his own time to explain himself to me.

But on the very next page he writes:

> The traditional portraiture no longer satisfies; it is too baffling in its apparent contradiction of the terms of our earthly existence. The God-man of Christianity is increasingly incredible, yet it is not easy to break with centuries of authoritative instruction and devout faith, and there remains embedded deep in the subconscious a strong sense of the supernatural inherited from remote ages.

One of his basic assumptions, therefore, is that the Christian interpretation of Jesus can be safely ruled out from the start because it no longer satisfies and appears increasingly incredible.

Even as a historian he cannot approach the enquiry without any assumptions. In this case he declares that it was the Christians who made Jesus God; therefore none of the evidence of the New Testament can be taken at its face value.

PAUL VAN BUREN indicates that he begins his study accepting the basic assumptions of 'secular man'. His interpretation is determined by the methods of linguistic analysis:

> How can the Christian who is himself a secular man understand his faith in a secular way? ... The answer will be reached by analysing what a man means when he uses the language of faith, when he repeats the earliest Christian confession: 'Jesus is Lord'.
>
> The question is whether a Christian is to be distinguished from an 'unbeliever' by a different logic or thinking ... We shall conduct this study on the assumption that 'being a Christian' does not deny one's involvement in the secular world and its way of thinking. This assumption will govern our attempt to understand the Christian conviction that 'Jesus is Lord'.

He admits that Jesus is not unique in having freedom:

> Having spoken of him as an exceptionally liberated individual, we should point out that we might say this of other men.

F.C. HAPPOLD begins with an understanding of the meaning of the word 'God' which is very different from the Christian understanding. He assumes that all the religions have basically the same vision of 'God' and 'man', even though they use different words and symbols.

> Eternal and essential God-man-unity; this is what these men saw and what they were determined to express, even though, with their inherited idea of God, it seemed to involve contradictions. In doing so they expressed the supreme significance of the Christian revelation. For the Incarnation of Jesus Christ was not only a diaphany of the Divine, but also a diaphany of the human.
>
> Though they express it in different ways according to their different theologies and philosophies, the mystics of all religions are at one in asserting the inherent divinity of man's real self. This inner deity is, however, hidden. It exists at the level of human existence as a potentiality. For it to become an actuality a 'divine birth' must take place in the soul, so that a man is raised to a higher state of consciousness. In Christianity this divine birth is thought of as the birth of Jesus Christ, the eternal Son or Logos (Word) of God, in the centre of the soul.

If we approach the Gospels with assumptions of this kind, no amount of detailed study of the Gospels is likely to make us change our minds. It is the assumption itself which needs to be tested and challenged.

WHAT WAS THE MEANING OF THE DEATH OF JESUS?

How Jesus thought about his death

When Jesus went up to Jerusalem he knew he was going to die. On three different occasions he told his disciples what would happen to him:

And they were on the road, going up to Jerusalem, and Jesus was walking ahead of them; and they were amazed, and those who followed were afraid. And taking the twelve again, he began to tell them what was to happen to him, saying, 'Behold, we are going up to Jerusalem; and the Son of man will be delivered to the chief priests and the scribes, and they will condemn him to death, and deliver him to the Gentiles; and they will mock him, and spit upon him, and scourge him, and kill him; and after three days he will rise.

Jesus did not give a detailed explanation of why he was going to die. But he gave certain important indications or clues as to what it would mean.

● He identified himself with the Suffering Servant described in Isaiah. In his predictions of his sufferings there are echoes of the description of the suffering of the Servant. Compare, for example, Mark 8:31, 'The Son of man must suffer many things, and be rejected . . . and be killed . . .' with Isaiah 53:3,8, 'He was despised and rejected by men. . . By oppression and judgement he was taken away. . .' And Mark 10:15, 'The Son of man . . . came not to be served but to serve, and to give his life as a ransom for many' with Isaiah 53:10, 'It was the will of the Lord to bruise him . . . he makes himself an offering for sin' ('ransom' is another possible translation for 'offering for sin' here).

● Jesus saw his death as part of the good news which would be spread throughout the world. At a party in Bethany a short time before his death a woman anointed Jesus with expensive ointment, and there were complaints about the waste:

> **But Jesus said, 'Let her alone; why do you trouble her? She has done a beautiful thing to me . . . She has done what she could; she has anointed my body beforehand for burying. And truly, I say to you, wherever the gospel is preached in the whole world, what she has done will be told in memory of her.'**

● He connected the meaning of his death with the Passover. When he celebrated the Passover with his disciples, just before his arrest—commemorating the deliverance of Israel from Egypt—he gave some parts of the meal a new significance:

> **And as they were eating, he took bread, and blessed, and broke it, and gave it to them, and said, 'Take; this is my body.' And he took a cup, and when he had given thanks he gave it to them, and they all drank of it. And he said to them, 'This is my blood of the covenant, which is poured out for many. Truly, I say to you, I shall not drink again of the fruit of the vine until that day when I drink it new in the kingdom of God.'**

● Jesus connected his death with the judgement of God on human sin. He thought of the suffering and death before him as 'a cup' held out to him by the Father:

> **And going a little farther he fell on his face and prayed, 'My Father, if it be possible, let this cup pass from me; nevertheless, not as I will, but as thou wilt.'**

> **Again, for the second time, he went away and prayed, 'My Father, if this cannot pass unless I drink it, thy will be done.'**

There is an echo here of the many passages in the Old Testament which speak of the cup of the wrath of God—for example:

> **For in the hand of the Lord there is a cup,
> with foaming wine, well mixed;
> and he will pour a draught from it,**

> **and all the wicked of the earth
> shall drain it down to the dregs.**

> **Thus the Lord, the God of Israel, said to me: 'Take from my hand this cup of the wine of wrath, and make all the nations to whom I send you drink it. They shall drink and stagger and be crazed because of the sword which I am sending among them.**

> **Rouse yourself, rouse yourself, stand up, O Jerusalem,
> you who have drunk at the hand of the Lord
> the cup of his wrath,
> who have drunk to the dregs
> the bowl of staggering.**

In approaching his death, therefore, he was not only shrinking from the physical agony involved; he had come to feel that in his death God was holding out to *him*—not 'the wicked of the earth'— the cup of his wrath. It was a cup that *he* must drink. He knew also how his fellow-Jews would think of such a death on the cross, because he knew from the Old Testament law that a hanged person was regarded as being under a curse from God:

> **If a man has committed a crime punishable by death and he is put to death, and you hang him on a tree, his body shall not remain all night upon the tree; but you shall bury him the same day, for a hanged man is accursed by God.**

The circumstances of his death

The last week of Jesus' life is reported in all four Gospels in much greater detail than any other period of his life; this suggests that the writers saw a great deal of significance in the actual events which led up to his death.
● He went to his death voluntarily. The words and actions of Jesus provoked opposition from the religious authorities at a very early stage in his ministry. And when Jesus made his final journey to

On the night before he died, Jesus took bread, broke it and said, 'This is my body, given for you.'

Jerusalem he knew that he was going to die.

He must have known what was involved in scourging and execution at the hands of the Romans. They would use a flagellum, a whip of leather thongs, to which small pieces of metal or bone were tied. People sometimes died under the scourge. The procedure for crucifixion was this: the two hands were nailed to the cross-beam while the victim was still on the ground; the cross-beam would then be drawn up by ropes and fastened to the upright part of the cross. The feet would then be nailed to the upright. The victim rarely died in less than thirty-six hours, but could be put out of his misery at any time by having his legs broken with a hammer, which would soon lead to suffocation; or his side could be pierced by a sword.

Right up to the moment before his arrest, Jesus was aware that he could avoid this kind of death if he wanted to. He did not believe he was caught in a trap from which he could not escape.

They went to a place which was called Gethsemane ... And he took with him Peter and James and John, and began to be greatly distressed and troubled. And he said to them,

'My soul is very sorrowful, even to death ...' And going a little farther, he fell on the ground and prayed that, if it were possible, the hour might pass from him. And he said, 'Abba, Father, all things are possible to thee; remove this cup from me; yet not what I will, but what thou wilt.'

Thus, when Peter starts to fight to defend Jesus:

Jesus said to Peter, 'Put your sword in its sheath; shall I not drink the cup which the Father has given me?'

● He had done nothing to deserve the death penalty. The Jewish authorities realized that their own charge of blasphemy would mean nothing according to Roman law. They therefore handed him over to Pilate, the Roman governor, on a charge of treason against the state. They accused him of claiming to be 'the king of the Jews' and thereby posing a threat to the authority of Caesar:

And Pilate asked him, 'Are you the King of the Jews?' And he

answered him, 'You have said so.'
... Pilate again said to them, 'Then what shall I do with the man you call the King of the Jews?' And they cried out again, 'Crucify him.' And Pilate said to them, 'Why, what evil has he done?' But they shouted all the more, 'Crucify him.' So Pilate, wishing to satisfy the crowd, released for them Barabbas; and having scourged Jesus, he delivered him to be crucified.

Pilate tried in three ways to avoid passing the sentence of death which the Jewish authorities wanted him to pass:

1. he tried to pass the responsibility over to Herod, the puppet king;

2. he offered to punish Jesus simply with a flogging and then to release him;

3. and finally he offered to release Jesus as a gesture of goodwill during the Passover feast.

But the Jewish authorities and the crowd were not satisfied, and in the end Pilate passed the sentence of death on Jesus simply to satisfy their demands and avoid a riot.

It was obvious to at least four people that he had done nothing to deserve the death penalty:

PILATE:

I find no crime in him.

HEROD:

Nothing deserving death has been done by him.

ONE OF THE CRIMINALS crucified with Jesus:

We are receiving the due reward of our deeds; but this man has done nothing wrong.

THE ROMAN CENTURION who watched him dying:

Certainly this man was innocent!

● Jesus' last words were recorded.

His attitude towards those who killed him was an expression of God's willingness to forgive:

And when they came to the place which is called The Skull, there they crucified him, and the criminals, one on the right and one on the left. And Jesus said, 'Father forgive them; for they know not what they do.'

He made provision for one of his disciples to look after his mother:

When Jesus saw his mother, and the disciple whom he loved standing near, he said to his mother, 'Woman behold your son!' Then he said to the disciple, 'Behold your mother!'

One of the criminals being crucified beside him began mocking him but later came to change his mind. Jesus assured him that he would be entering into his royal triumph through his death:

And he said, 'Jesus, remember me when you come in your kingly power.' And he said to him, 'Truly, I say to you, today you will be with me in Paradise.'

He felt as if he was forsaken by God; but it was more than a feeling—it was a reality, because in his death he was experiencing a complete separation from God:

At the ninth hour Jesus cried with a loud voice, 'Eloi, Eloi, lama sabachthani?' which means, 'My God, my God, why hast thou forsaken me?'

His last words express the conviction that something had been achieved through all his suffering and agony. He was not only conscious that his life was ending, but also that he had accomplished something of a permanent and lasting nature:

Then Jesus, crying with a loud voice, said, 'Father, into thy hands I commit my spirit!'

After this Jesus, knowing that all was now finished, said (to fulfil the scripture), 'I thirst.' A bowl full of vinegar stood there; so they put a sponge full of the vinegar on hyssop and held it to his mouth. When Jesus had received the vinegar, he said, 'It is finished'; and he bowed his head and gave up his spirit.

POSSIBLE ANSWERS

His death achieved something—he was bearing our sins

This is to say, Jesus was bearing the guilt and consequences of human sin. He was dying in our place and enduring what we deserve for our proud rebellion against our Creator. His death can deal with the guilt of our past, and can bring us into a new relationship with God in the present. We can enjoy increasing deliverance from the power of sin in our lives and all the other positive benefits of his death.

Almost every writer of the New Testament gives an explanation of *how* the death of Jesus achieved something. They take as their starting-point that the death of Jesus deals with the sin of men:

JOHN records John the Baptist's description of Jesus:

> Behold, the Lamb of God, who *takes away* (i.e. bears) *the sin* of the world.

> ... Jesus Christ the righteous; and he is the *expiation for our sins*, and not for ours only but also for the sins of the whole world.

LUKE records some of the last words of Jesus before his ascension:

> Thus it is written, that the Christ should suffer and on the third day rise from the dead, and that repentance and *forgiveness of sins* should be preached in his name to all nations ...

PETER:

> He himself *bore our sins* in his body on the tree.
> Christ ... *died for sins* once for all,

the righteous for the unrighteous,
that he might bring us to God.

PAUL:

Christ died *for our sins*.

THE WRITER TO THE HEBREWS:

... he ... *made purification for sins* ...

● This answer makes sense of the Old Testament background.

It takes seriously both the *personal* aspect of the relationship between God and man, and also the *legal* aspect. There is through the cross, both forgiveness for the personal injury to God and for the disobedience to his laws:

And you, who were dead in trespasses and the uncircumcision of your flesh, God made alive together with him, having forgiven us all our trespasses, having cancelled the bond which stood against us with its legal demands; this he set aside, nailing it to the cross.

It does justice both to the *wrath* of God and to the *love* of God towards the sinner. It is the love of God which turns aside the wrath of God and all its consequences:

God shows his love for us in that while we were yet sinners Christ died for us. Since, therefore, we are now justified by his blood, much more shall we be saved by him from the wrath of God.

In this is love, not that we loved God but that he loved us and sent his Son to be the propitiation for our sins.

The word propitiation conveys the idea of turning aside the wrath of God.

It fits in with the close connection which the Old Testament sees between *sin* and *death*.

The death he died he died to sin, once for all, but the life he lives he lives to God.

The wages of sin is death, but the

free gift of God is eternal life in Christ Jesus our Lord.

It explains how the system of sacrifices, which were said to 'bear sin', has been fulfilled:

When Christ had offered for all time a single sacrifice for sins, he sat down at the right hand of God, then to wait until his enemies should be made a stool for his feet. For by a single offering he has perfected for all time those who are sanctified.... Where there is forgiveness ..., there is no longer any offering for sin.

It explains the sense in which Jesus could be under a *curse* from God as he hung on the cross:

Christ redeemed us from the curse of the law, having become a curse for us—for it is written, 'Cursed be every one who hangs on a tree' ...

● This interpretation also makes sense of the many different metaphors which the New Testament writers used to describe what Jesus achieved by his death. It also shows how these different metaphors are related to each other, because it provides a basic link which binds them together.

The metaphor of *justification* comes from the law court and means simply 'acquittal'. If Jesus was bearing the judgement of God on human sin, then for those who believe in Jesus and accept for themselves the benefits of his death, there is complete acquittal before God. The verdict of 'guilty' no longer stands against them, and they can now enjoy fellowship with God without fear or shame.

Therefore, since we are justified by faith, we have peace with God through our Lord Jesus Christ ... God shows his love for us in that while we were yet sinners Christ died for us.

The metaphor of *redemption* or *ransom* comes from the Old Testament idea of the kinsman redeemer and from the slave-market, where a person could be redeemed through the payment of a fee. This metaphor, therefore, emphasizes that the forgiveness God offers on the basis of the death of Jesus

cost him something. There was no simple announcement of forgiveness. It shows that if it costs men something to forgive each other, the cost for God in forgiving rebellious man is infinitely greater.

You know that you were ransomed from the futile ways inherited from your fathers, not with perishable things such as silver or gold, but with the precious blood of Christ ...

The metaphor of *victory* emphasizes that in the death of Jesus a decisive victory was won over sin and death and over the supernatural powers of evil which lie behind the rebellion of the human race against God. By this victory he had liberated men who were held prisoners of sin, death and the devil. If Jesus was bearing the sins of men when he died on the cross, we have an explanation as to *why* and *how* Jesus was able to gain the victory over the devil.

... You, who were dead in trespasses and the uncircumcision of your flesh, God made alive together with him, having forgiven us all our trespasses, having cancelled the bond which stood against us with its legal demands; this he set aside, nailing it to the cross. He disarmed the principalities and powers and made a public example of them, triumphing over them in him.

The metaphor of *reconciliation* stresses that man has broken off relations with God, and also that God cannot turn a blind eye to man's rebellion against him and act as if nothing had happened. If we understand that Jesus was dying in our place on the cross, this metaphor stresses that God himself has taken the initiative in doing something to win men back into fellowship with himself.

God shows his love for us in that while we were yet sinners Christ died for us ... For if while we were enemies we were reconciled to God by the death of his Son, much more, now that we are reconciled, shall we be saved by his life. Not only so, but we also rejoice in God through our Lord Jesus Christ, through whom

**we have now received our
reconciliation.**

The metaphor of *salvation* comes from the many
occasions in the Old Testament when the children
of Israel were delivered or saved from a desperate
situation. If we think of the death of Jesus as the
remedy for the guilt and power of sin, then the
word 'salvation' stresses the completeness of the
deliverance from the consequences and the power
of sin which is available through the death of
Christ. If Christ was bearing sins on the cross, this
is the means by which the deliverance has been
achieved.

**Since, therefore, we are now
justified by his blood, much more
shall we be saved by him from the
wrath of God.**

● This answer provides us with a starting-point
from which we can go on to see what the death of
Jesus must mean in the experience of the individual Christian. To say that Jesus was bearing the
sins of men when he died on the cross by no means
exhausts all that can or should be said about the
death of Jesus. But without this basic starting-
point, anything else that we may say lacks an
adequate foundation and leaves many questions
unanswered.

The way in which Jesus reacted to undeserved
abuse and suffering is an example which the
Christian is bound to follow:

**Christ ... suffered for you, leaving
you an example, that you should
follow in his steps. He committed
no sin; no guile was found on his
lips. When he was reviled, he did
not revile in return; when he
suffered, he did not threaten; but he
trusted him who judges justly.**

**... rejoice in so far as you share
Christ's sufferings, that you may
also rejoice and be glad when his
glory is revealed.**

The way in which Jesus renounced self-interest
and went to the cross for the sake of others shows
the Christian that he too must say no to his self-
centredness and be willing to be closely identified
with Jesus in the eyes of the world. He must also be
prepared to receive the same kind of treatment that
Jesus received.

**If any man would come after me, let
him deny himself and take up his
cross daily and follow me ... For
whoever is ashamed of me and of
my words, of him will the Son of
man be ashamed when he comes in
his glory and the glory of the Father
and of the holy angels.**

This is how PAUL longs to be identified fully with
Jesus; he wants to receive his righteousness, to
share his sufferings and be like him in his denial of
self in death:

**... whatever gain I had, I counted as
loss for the sake of Christ. Indeed I
count everything as loss because
of the surpassing worth of knowing
Christ Jesus my Lord. For his sake I
have suffered the loss of all things,
and count them as refuse, in order
that I may gain Christ and be found
in him, not having a righteousness
of my own, based on law, but that
which is through faith in Christ, the
righteousness from God that
depends on faith; that I may know
him and the power of his
resurrection, and may share his
sufferings, becoming like him in his
death...**

Jesus' willingness to die to self when he went to the
cross is the strongest possible plea that we should
die to self and live for him and not ourselves:

**... the love of Christ controls us,
because we are convinced that one
has died for all; therefore all have
died. And he died for all, that those
who live might live no longer for
themselves but for him who for
their sake died and was raised.**

The way that Jesus went willingly to death, the
death of the worst kind of criminal, is a powerful
incentive to an attitude of humility:

**Have this mind among yourselves,
which you have in Christ Jesus,
who, though he was in the form of
God, did not count equality with
God a thing to be grasped, but
emptied himself, taking the form of
a servant, being born in the**

Paul wrote, 'By the death of Christ we are set free, that is, our sins are forgiven.'

likeness of men. And being found in human form he humbled himself and became obedient unto death, even death on a cross . . .

Jesus' death for all men must affect our attitude to others as we realize their value before God. We are not to despise any individual, for he is

. . . the brother for whom Christ died.

When the Christian shares the suffering of Christ, he can also experience the comfort and consolation of Christ. And this in turn can be shared with all Christ's people:

Blessed be the God and Father of our Lord Jesus Christ, the Father of all mercies and God of all comfort, who comforts us in all our affliction, so that we may be able to comfort those who are in any affliction, with the comfort with which we ourselves are comforted by God. For as we share abundantly in Christ's sufferings, so through Christ we share abundantly in comfort too. If we are afflicted, it is for your comfort and salvation; and

if we are comforted, it is for your comfort, which you experience when you patiently endure the same sufferings that we suffer. Our hope for you is unshaken; for we know that as you share in our sufferings, you will also share in our comfort.

HOW CAN THE DEATH OF ONE MAN DEAL WITH THE SINS OF THE WHOLE HUMAN RACE?

The three aspects of this question are:
● How can the death of one man have this effect for all men?

The answer must lie in the identity of the person who died. The death of an ordinary man could not have this effect for all men. But when the person who dies is the eternal Son of God, his death is unique and has unique effects. For if Jesus was the eternal Son of God, then what Jesus did, God did. We must not think of Jesus merely as a neutral third party coming between God and man. This is why PAUL links God the Father so closely with Christ when he says:

God was in Christ reconciling the world to himself, not counting their trespasses against them . . .

The biblical understanding of the solidarity of the human race helps further to explain how the action of Jesus can affect all men. Adam is seen as the first man and the 'head' of the human race. All his descendants are thought of as being 'in Adam', and inherit his fallen human nature. Jesus, on the other hand, is seen as the 'second Adam' who reverses the effects of Adam's disobedience. All who believe in Christ are now no longer 'in Adam' and doomed to condemnation, but are 'in Christ' and enjoy a new relationship with God. And just as the disobedience of the one man Adam affected all men, so the obedience of the one man Jesus affects all who trust in him. This is how PAUL draws out the parallel between Adam and Christ:

... sin came into the world through one man and death through sin, and so death spread to all men because all men sinned ... But the free gift is not like the trespass. For if many died through one man's trespass, much more have the grace of God and the free gift in the grace of that one man Jesus Christ abounded for many. And the free gift is not like the effect of that one man's sin. For the judgement following one trespass brought condemnation, but the free gift following many trespasses brings justification. If, because of one man's trespass, death reigned through that one man, much more will those who receive the abundance of grace and the free gift of righteousness reign in life through the one man Jesus Christ.

● How can suffering and death deal with sin?

The answer to the second question similarly hinges on the identity of the man who suffered and died. It was not the intensity of the suffering which had the effect of dealing with sin, but its quality and value. It was not how much he suffered which makes the difference; it is rather who suffered, and the fact that death is so closely associated with sin in the Bible.

Moreover, the suffering and death of Jesus must not be isolated from his whole life. Sin came into the world through the disobedience of Adam, and the consequences of this disobedience could

therefore only be undone through obedience—obedience exemplified not only in an isolated act, but throughout a life. In this way the willingness of Jesus to go to the cross is seen as the climax of a life which was utterly obedient to God. PAUL writes:

Then as one man's trespass led to condemnation for all men, so one man's act of righteousness leads to acquittal and life for all men. For as by one man's disobedience many were made sinners, so by one man's obedience many will be made righteous.

● How can his death then deal with my sins now?

We must not think of the death of Jesus simply as a transaction carried out in the past. The New Testament writers speak of something that was accomplished when Jesus died on the cross. But the benefits of what he achieved do not pass to us automatically; we have to receive them by a conscious and deliberate act of faith. The fact that Jesus died so many years ago is hardly relevant; all that is relevant is that he died at a particular time in history, and that his death achieved salvation once and for all. His death does not need to be repeated in each generation, even if it could be.

He has appeared once for all at the end of the age to put away sin by the sacrifice of himself.

When Christ had offered for all time a single sacrifice for sins, he sat down at the right hand of God ... For by a single offering he has perfected for all time those who are sanctified.

What Jesus achieved in the past has to be appropriated by each person in the present; and it is simply faith and trust in Jesus which makes the connection between the death and resurrection of Jesus in the past and our experience in the present. PAUL writes:

Since we are justified by faith, we have peace with God through our Lord Jesus Christ. Through him we have obtained access to this grace in which we stand, and we rejoice in our hope of sharing the glory of God.

He died as an example—his death shows us something about God and man

The meaning of Christ's death is to be seen primarily in what it teaches us and in how it influences us. His death is an example of self-sacrifice, of non-resistance in the face of evil and injustice, and of patient endurance of undeserved suffering. His attitude and behaviour in facing death give a demonstration of the love of God, and give us an example to follow when we face suffering ourselves.

On this view, it is not important to ask whether Jesus actually achieved anything at the time when he died on the cross; his death achieves something only when it moves me here and now. In his life he proclaimed the willingness of God to forgive sin; and his death is simply a further demonstration of the love of God, because it shows us the lengths to which Jesus was prepared to go to win us back to God. His death is also a demonstration of the sinfulness of man, because it exposes the pride and selfishness of human nature. Evil is shown up in its true colours when it comes face to face with the holy Son of God.

The message of the death of Jesus, therefore, is this: 'This is what God is like—look how far love was prepared to go for us. And this is what human nature is like—look and see what you are by nature.' As we look at the crucified Jesus, therefore, we ought to be moved to turn to him in repentance and faith. We ought to come to God to ask for forgiveness and to put our faith in Jesus as the one who shows us that we are accepted by God.

J.W.C. WAND explains what theologians have called the 'Exemplarist Theory' of the atonement:

This is the view that we are changed in conformity with the example of Jesus. That example is so beautiful, so overwhelming in its beauty, that it has the power to transform anyone who sincerely considers it and is prepared to yield to it. 'We needs must love the highest when we see it', and living it be changed by it.

The typical illustration of this divine alchemy is the incident of the penitent thief on Calvary. In the midst of his sufferings he had evidently been so moved by the patience and calmness of the Person who hung between him and his blaspheming fellow bandit that he attained some kind of belief in the crucified Messiah and prayed to be taken into his kingdom. The contrast between the two robbers has stirred the imagination of Christians all down the ages, and change in the penitent thief has always been taken as an indication of what the example of Christ can do.

DAVID EDWARDS writes:

The Creator of the universe was willing to suffer everything in order that the nails which harpooned and bloodily smashed the human life in which he was expressing himself might also pin down our wandering thoughts and stab our consciences awake.

● This answer contains many important aspects of the first answer 'His death achieved something—he was bearing our sins', but it leaves many important questions unanswered. For example, how and why can the death of Jesus on a criminal's cross become a demonstration of the love of God? One could make out a good case for seeing it as a demonstration not so much of the love of God, but of the cruelty or callousness or weakness of God. For how could God the Father 'stand by' and do nothing while God the Son was being tortured to death? If a man stands by and does nothing while he watches his wife being beaten to death, this does not prove his love either for his wife or for anyone else.

The problem therefore can be stated in this way: how can the death of Jesus be a demonstration of the love of God unless it actually achieves something? If a woman is in danger of drowning in a river and a man jumps in at considerable risk to save her, he is certainly demonstrating his concern for her. But if he fails to rescue her, the mere demonstration of his concern doesn't help her at all. The death of Jesus certainly shows the self-sacrifice, the humility and the courage of Jesus, and it may move men to pity and repentance. But how can we speak about the cross as a demonstration of the love of God if we can give no clue as to how or why it rescues men from their terrible condition?

● This answer has nothing to say to the person who is not in the least moved by imagining Jesus dying a cruel death on a cross. If the picture of Jesus being slowly tortured to death doesn't appeal to him or move him, he may say, 'It leaves me cold; I don't see what it has to do with me or with anyone else.' This answer could be open to the charge that it uses the death of Jesus to make a purely emotional appeal. And if this is so, the sceptic has every right to say, 'Why are you trying to pull at my heart strings in this way? Of course there is something repulsive and revolting about his death. But so what? What does it prove? Even if he is the Son of God, why should his death by itself move me to repentance any more than the deaths of other innocent people who have died even more horribly?'

● Whenever the New Testament writers speak of the cross as a demonstration of the love of God, they give a clue as to *why* this is so. They speak of the death of Christ as God's way of dealing with sin, and averting the consequences of sin:

God so loved the world that he gave his only Son, that whoever believes in him should not perish but have eternal life.

God is love. In this the love of God was made manifest among us, that God sent his only Son into the world, so that we might live through him. In this is love, not that we loved God but that he loved us and sent his Son to be the expiation for our sins.

God shows his love for us in that while we were yet sinners Christ died for us. Since, therefore, we are now justified by his blood, much more shall we be saved by him from the wrath of God.

The New Testament teaches that out of love, Jesus gave himself for the world.

PETER speaks of the example that Christians can see in the way Jesus faced suffering and death. But while he sees this as part of the meaning of the death of Jesus, he does not see it as the only meaning, or as the heart of its meaning. For in the same paragraph he goes on to speak about the death of Jesus as God's way of dealing with sin.

> **For what credit is it, if when you do wrong and are beaten for it you take it patiently? But if when you do right and suffer for it you take it patiently, you have God's approval. For to this you have been called, because Christ also suffered for you, leaving you an example, that you should follow in his steps. He committed no sin; no guile was found on his lips. When he was reviled, he did not revile in return; when he suffered, he did not threaten; but he trusted to him who judges justly. He himself bore our sins in his body on the tree, that we might die to sin and live to righteousness. By his wounds you have been healed ...**

● The root of the difficulty may well be that this answer rests on the assumption that man's basic problem is his ignorance about himself and God, and his lack of feeling towards God and Christ. What we need therefore is not someone to deal with our guilt, but rather someone to show us the truth and to melt our hard hearts. And this assumption is different in certain important respects from the biblical assumption that man's most fundamental need is for his guilt before a holy God to be dealt with.

For many, an answer like this may prove to be the starting-point for genuine Christian faith. But it is hardly adequate as a complete answer, because it leaves many questions unanswered. If we can go one step further and believe that Jesus died as a sin-bearer, then there is an adequate answer to these questions. And it becomes clear why ISAAC WATTS, the hymn-writer could say:

> **Were the whole realm of nature mine,**
> **That were an offering far too small;**
> **Love so amazing, so divine,**
> **Demands my soul, my life, my all.**

The cross is merely a symbol—any interpretation is 'myth'

This is to say, Jesus did not actually achieve anything when he died on the cross. We must look at the cross from our own standpoint, and see it as a symbol of what is true in human experience or what is true for us as individuals.

RUDOLPH BULTMANN puts all the emphasis on what the cross must mean in the experience of the individual:

> **To believe in the cross of Christ does not mean to concern ourselves with a mythical process wrought outside of us and our world, or even an objective event turned by God to our advantage, but rather to make the cross of Christ our own, to undergo crucifixion with him. .... The cross is not just an event of the past which can be contemplated in detachment, but the eschatological event in and beyond time, for as far as its meaning—that is, its meaning for**

As a symbol, the cross can become no more than a piece of jewellery.

faith—is concerned, it is an ever-present reality.

The cross and passion are ever-present realities ... The abiding significance of the cross is that it is the judgement of the world, the judgement and the deliverance of man ... The real meaning of the cross is that it has created a new and permanent situation in history. The preaching of the cross as the event of redemption challenges all who hear it to appropriate this significance for themselves, to be willing to be crucified with Christ.

For us the cross cannot disclose its own meaning; it is an event of the past. We can never recover it as an event in our lives.

Cross and resurrection form a single, indivisible cosmic event which brings judgement to the world and opens up for men the possibility of authentic life.

According to Bultmann, the language of the *New Testament* about Jesus dying for our sins is mythological language. What we must do, therefore, is to translate it into existential language which will mean something to modern man. The preaching of the cross in this way becomes a challenge to existential decision. And if we respond to the challenge in the appropriate way, we gain a deep understanding of ourselves and of the human predicament, and we can begin to enjoy authentic existence.

DIETRICH BONHOEFFER sees the cross as a symbol of 'the suffering of God in the life of the world' and of 'the participation in the power-lessness of God in the world'.

The God who makes us live in this world without using him as a working hypothesis is the God before whom we are ever standing. Before God and with him we live without God.

God allows himself to be edged out of the world and on to the cross. God is weak and powerless in the world, and that is exactly the way, the only way, in which he can be

with us and help us. Matthew 8:17 makes it crystal clear that is it not by his omnipotence that Christ can help us, but by his weakness and suffering. This is the decisive difference between Christianity and all religions. Man's religiosity makes him look in his distress to the power of God in the world; he uses God as a *deus ex machina*. The Bible, however, directs him to the powerlessness and suffering of God; only a suffering God can help.

PAUL VAN BUREN interprets the death of Jesus in accordance with his understanding of existential 'freedom':

What can it mean to say, 'He *died* for our sins'? The emphasis is on his death, but we need to remember that theology, as well as the New Testament, speaks of the 'cross' or the death of Jesus as the consequence of his life. 'The cross' and other references to Jesus' death became summary ways of speaking of his whole history, as indeed his end seemed to his disciples, after the fact, to have been foreshadowed in all of his life. Since his life was one of solidarity with men, compassion for them, mercy towards their weakness and wrong, it is not surprising that his death, which was the consequence of his freedom to be related to men in this way, was spoken of as a death 'for us'. His death ... was regarded as the measure of the freedom for which he set other men free. The man for whom the history of Jesus and his liberation of his disciples on Easter is a discernment situation of prime importance will say, 'He died for me, for my forgiveness and freedom'. When the New Testament says that he died not only for 'our' sins, 'but also for the sins of the whole world', it reflects the fact that Jesus was free for every man, those who did not acknowledge him as well as those that did, and it articulates a perspective by which all men, not just believers, are seen.

DAVID EDWARDS writes:

> The cross is the Christian symbol not only because it marked the end of the public life of Jesus of Nazareth, but also because it stands for truths of continuing experience.

As examples of these truths of experience he mentions 'inevitable suffering', 'the evil corruption of our very ideals', 'the great suffering of the innocent individual'.

NIKOS KAZANTZAKIS' novel *Christ Recrucified* describes the life of a village as it prepares to perform a Passion Play. The events of the year turn out to be a strange re-enactment of the events leading to the death of Jesus, and towards the end of the Christ-figure, Manolios, is killed.

> He (Pope Fotis) extended his hand and tenderly caressed the face of Manolios.
>
> 'Dear Manolios, you'll have given your life in vain,' he murmured; 'they've killed you for having taken our sins upon you; you cried: "It was I who robbed, it was I who killed and set things on fire; I, nobody else!" so that they might let the rest of us take root peacefully in these lands ... In vain, Manolios, in vain will you have sacrificed yourself ...'
>
> Pope Fotis listened to the bell pealing gaily, announcing that Christ was coming down on earth to save the world ... He shook his head and heaved a sigh: 'In vain, my Christ, in vain,' he muttered; 'two thousand years have gone by and men crucify You still. When will you be born, my Christ, and not be crucified any more, but live among us for eternity?'

THOMAS MANN writes about the novel:

> The novel *Christ Recrucified* is without doubt a work of high artistic order formed by a tender and firm hand and built up with strong dynamic power. I have particularly admired the poetic tact in phrasing the subtle yet unmistakable allusions to the Christian Passion story. They give the book its mythical background which is such a vital element in the epic form of today.

● This answer hardly does justice to the whole of the New Testament teaching. For the New Testament writers it was not a case of either an event which achieved something in the past *or* a truth of present experience. It was rather a case of both/and. The death of Jesus meant something to them in present experience because it had already achieved something for them.

● Is there any criterion for deciding the meaning of symbols? To some it is the very ambiguity of symbols which commends them as a means of religious communication:

> The religious symbol when examined is seen to have an ambivalent quality. It is an indefinite expression which conveys different meanings to different people. People react to religious symbols in different ways, according to their particular mental and psychological make-ups. The symbols point to something beyond themselves which is not intellectually definable, and therefore cannot be fully rationally known or described. They make perceptible what is invisible, ideal and transcendent, giving it a sort of objectivity, and so allowing it to be better apprehended.
> F.C. HAPPOLD

If we treat the cross in this way, therefore, we are in effect saying, 'If the cross means something to you and something completely different to me, then it doesn't matter—because its truth is indefinable, and cannot properly be described in words. There is no such thing as "the true interpretation" of the death of Jesus; any interpretation can be true if it is true to me.'

● Those who do not share or do not understand the basic assumptions about truth on which this answer is based, tend to react to the language of symbols with indifference or impatience:

> I have never been able to make anything of symbolism. A symbol I understand to be a sign for something else. Either the symbolist knows what the something else is, in which case I cannot see why he should not tell us what it is straight out, instead of obscurely hinting at it in symbols, or he does not, in which case not knowing what the symbols stand for he cannot expect his readers to find out for him. Usually, I suspect, he does not, and his symbolism is merely a device to conceal his muddled thinking.
>
> C.E.M. JOAD

● If we regard the death of Jesus on the cross as merely a symbol, we cannot at the same time claim that it is unique. Why should we not attach the same significance to the deaths of great men like Socrates or Gandhi?

● If salvation has not been worked out in history at a particular place and at a particular time, then the Christian message ceases to be good news about what God *has done* for man. If the saving work of Christ is extracted from history and made completely independent of history, Christian faith changes its character completely.

J. GRESHAM MACHEN outlines the alternatives in this way:

> If the saving work of Christ were confined to what He does now for every Christian, there would be no such thing as a Christian gospel—an account of an event which put a new face on life. What we should have left would be simply mysticism, and mysticism is quite different from Christianity ...
>
> If religion be made independent of history there is no such thing as a gospel. For 'gospel' means 'good news', tidings, information about something that has happened. A gospel independent of history is a contradiction in terms.

His death on the cross disproves any claim that he was the Messiah

The Jewish Encyclopedia sums up the answer of Judaism:

> 'My God, my God ...' which showed that even his resolute spirit had been daunted by the ordeal. This last utterance was in all its implications itself a disproof of the exaggerated claims made for him after his death by his disciples. The very form of his punishment would disprove those claims in Jewish eyes. No Messiah that Jews could recognize could suffer such a death; for 'He that is hanged is accursed of God' (Deut. 21: 23), 'an insult to God' (Targum, Rashi).

> It is an impossible article of belief, which detracts from God's sovereignty and absolute otherness—an article which, in fact, destroys the world ... It is the same passionate belief which can be heard in an admittedly late homiletical midrash: 'It is not permitted for a human mouth to say, "The Holy One—blessed be he—has a son." If God could not look on in anguish while Abraham sacrificed his son, would he then have suffered his own son to be killed, without destroying the entire world?'
>
> HANS JOACHIM SCHOEPS

This was probably PETER's feeling when he protested at the suggestion of Jesus having to suffer and die:

> And Peter took him and began to rebuke him, saying, 'God forbid, Lord! This shall never happen to you.'

It is clear from the Gospels that *Jesus* himself felt the full force of this kind of thinking. He must have felt its attraction very keenly, but rejected it because he knew that it was a purely human way of thinking which was not in accordance with the mind of God. He answered Peter very sternly:

> Then Jesus turned and said to Peter, 'Away with you, Satan; you are a stumbling-block to me. You think as men think, not as God thinks.'

When Jesus realized what kind of death lay ahead of him, he knew that it was possible for him to appeal to God for deliverance; but he firmly rejected the idea:

> Now is my soul troubled. And what shall I say, 'Father, save me from this hour'? No, for this purpose I have come to this hour ...

When Peter began using a sword to protect Jesus, Jesus rebuked him and explained why he rejected the use of force to defend himself and why he refused to ask for a miraculous deliverance:

> Then Jesus said to him, 'Put your sword back into its place; for all who take the sword will perish by the sword. Do you think that I cannot appeal to my Father, and he will at once send me more than twelve legions of angels? But how then should the scriptures be fulfilled, that it must be so?'

After his resurrection JESUS explained to the disciples that it was *necessary* for him to suffer in this way:

> 'O foolish men, and slow of heart to believe all that the prophets have spoken! Was it not necessary that the Christ should suffer these things and enter into his glory?' And beginning with Moses and all the prophets, he interpreted to them in all the scriptures the things concerning himself.

> Then he opened their minds to understand the scriptures, and said to them, 'Thus it is written, that the Christ should suffer and on the third day rise from the dead, and that repentance and forgiveness of sins should be preached in his name to all nations ...'

The many Old Testament passages from which Jesus explained the need for his suffering and death must have been the main source of understanding for the New Testament writers.

Jesus did not die on the cross

The *Qur'an* has generally been interpreted by Muslims as denying that Jesus was crucified:

> They denied the truth and uttered a monstrous falsehood against Mary. They declared: 'We have put to death the Messiah Jesus the son of Mary, the apostle of Allah.' They did not kill him, nor did they crucify him, but they thought they did.
>
> Those that disagreed about him were in doubt concerning his death, for what they knew about it was sheer conjecture; they were not sure that they had slain him. Allah lifted him up to his presence; He is mighty and wise.

We need to be clear as to what precisely the *Qur'an* denies and what it does not deny:
● It does not deny that men wanted to kill Jesus.
● It does not deny that Jesus was willing to suffer and die.
● It does deny that Jesus was finally killed on the cross.
KENNETH CRAGG explains the background to this belief, and the traditional interpretations in Islam:

> The context of controversy and dispute here referred to may reflect certain docetic tendencies in early heretical Christianity which, for various mainly metaphysical reasons, questioned the possibility of the Messiah being literally and actually a sufferer. The attitudes of Islam reproduce many of these misgivings and may derive from them historically ...
>
> The prevailing view is that at some point, undetermined, in the

course of the final events of Christ's arrest, trial and sentence, a substitute person replaced Him while Jesus Himself was, in the phrase, raised or raptured into Heaven, from whence, unscathed and uncrucified, He returned to His disciples in personal appearances in which He commissioned them to take His teachings out into the world. The Gospel they were thus to preach was a moral law only and not the good tidings of a victorious, redemptive encounter with sin and death. Meanwhile, the substitute sufferer bore the whole brunt of the historical crucifixion, having been sentenced and condemned *as if he were the Christ*.

The Muslim believes it is unthinkable that God should allow his prophet to suffer such a shameful death. If a man is sent from God as a prophet, he has the authority of God behind him, and he represents God to the people. Is it conceivable that God should allow his messenger to undergo such humiliation and rejection? Surely God would intervene to save his representative from such a degrading fate.

The Muslim also argues that the death of Jesus is totally unnecessary from God's point of view. The Christian therefore needs to explain as far as possible why it was necessary for Jesus to suffer. If the Muslim can understand the reason for the death of Christ, he may be more open to accept the fact of his death.

● Forgiveness by its very nature involves suffering. The essence of forgiveness is that you accept an injury or an offence without wanting to punish or to fight back. You simply bear the injury and accept all the consequences. If this is true on the human level, the Christian would say that it is also true when we think about God forgiving men. When he forgives men the wrongs and injuries they have done to him, he himself is bearing the personal affront. In a sense he is taking the consequences upon himself. The Muslim, on the other hand, feels that God's forgiveness has little in common with forgiveness between men, and is more like the pardon extended by an all-powerful ruler to his subjects.

● If we can say that 'Christ . . . died for sins once for all . . . that he might bring us to God . . .' (1 Peter 3:18), then it is possible to be sure that if we repent, we have been forgiven. Assurance of forgiveness is therefore based on what Jesus has already accomplished through his death. According to the Muslim way of thinking forgiveness depends entirely on our repentance and on God's mercy, which in turn depends on what happens on the Day of Judgement, when our good deeds are weighed in the balance against our bad deeds. This means we cannot be sure, here and now, of God's forgiveness, or of our final acceptance by him.

● If Jesus did not die, then he ceased to be identified with men at the point which men fear and dread most of all. And if Jesus did not die, he could not in any sense defeat and overcome death. If there was no death, there can have been no resurrection. Yet the writer of the letter to the HEBREWS speaks in the clearest terms of Jesus destroying the power of death through his own death:

Since . . . the children share in flesh and blood he himself likewise partook of the same nature, that through death he might destroy him who has the power of death, that is, the devil, and deliver all those who through fear of death were subject to lifelong bondage.

His death has no special meaning

This answer takes a number of different forms.

● He died as a martyr; his death was not unique. On this view, the meaning of Christ's death is simply that it shows us how far he was prepared to go to uphold his cause. He was willing to suffer and die a cruel death rather than deny what he stood for. Just as people have died for social and political causes, so in the same way Jesus died as a martyr in his own cause. His willingness to die in this way shows how sincerely he believed in his message, and how concerned he was that others should know it.

BUT: what precisely was the cause that he died for? Did he die merely to uphold the ideal of an unselfish life or the idea of the brotherhood of man? Did he die merely to convince others that it is a good thing to love one's neighbour?

The Gospels make it clear that what the Jews objected to was not the moral teaching of Jesus, but rather his claims about himself and his relationship with God the Father. If Jesus had died merely as a martyr advocating love, it is difficult to see how the cross could ever have come to be regarded as 'good news'.

The view that Jesus died as a martyr, therefore, ignores a great deal of the evidence about how Jesus thought about his death, and how his disciples came to interpret it.

Certain other answers which have been given by Christians come into this category, because they play down or deny the unique significance of his death.

● It is the incarnation (i.e. the Son of God becoming man in the person of Jesus Christ), not the death of Christ, which is the heart of the Christian message. The mere fact that God became man and lived the kind of life he lived reveals what God is like. There was no need or necessity for Jesus to die on the cross; his incarnation and life are themselves an adequate revelation of the character of God. The way he died does not add anything to what his life achieved.

BUT: it is difficult to reconcile this answer with the teaching of the New Testament as a whole. The main centre of interest in both the Gospels and the Epistles is the crucifixion and resurrection.

This answer is sometimes based on the assumption that the material world is somehow infected with sin and needs to be redeemed. But this is contrary to the biblical view of the universe.

● It is not the laying down of Christ's life in death which was the significant factor in procuring salvation for men, but rather his offering of his risen life to the Father in heaven. We are saved in so far as we participate in his present offering of his life to the Father.

BUT: the New Testament nowhere suggests that Jesus continues to offer any sacrifice in heaven—even the sacrifice of his life. On the contrary it stresses the finality and completeness of Jesus' sacrifice.

When Christ had offered for all time a single sacrifice for sins, he sat down at the right hand of God, then to wait until his enemies should be made a stool for his feet. For by a single offering he has perfected for all time those who are sanctified.

This idea of Jesus offering his risen life to the Father is based on the assumption that in the sacrificial system of the Old Testament it was the offering of the blood of the animal to God that was the important thing, because the offering of the blood signified the offering of the life of the animal. However, the way in which the word 'blood' is used throughout the Bible would suggest rather that it signifies not so much the life that is offered to God but rather the life that is laid down in death. The offering of life cannot deal with the guilt of sin; it can only be dealt with when life is surrendered in death, which is the ultimate penalty for sin.

● It is not the death of Jesus as such which saves men, but his 'repentance' on our behalf. Jesus felt our sins *as if* they were his own, and was able to repent for them on our behalf. The sympathetic or vicarious repentance of Christ and its influence on men therefore enables God to forgive men.

BUT: however sympathetically Jesus could enter into our condition, how could he repent for sins which he had not committed?

According to this view, our forgiveness and salvation are dependent on our own repentance and faith. Our repentance and faith become the grounds on which God forgives us. In this way we can be said to earn our salvation through repentance and faith. But the New Testament writers speak about what God has already done in the death of Jesus; and they invite us to repent and believe on these grounds. In this way our repentance and faith are our response to what God has done.

PETER writes:

You know that you were ransomed from the futile ways inherited from your fathers, not with perishable things such as silver or gold, but with the precious blood of Christ, like that of a lamb without blemish or spot ... Through him you have confidence in God, who raised him from the dead and gave him glory, so that your faith and hope are in God.

DID JESUS RISE FROM THE DEAD?

The question we are asking here is a question about historical fact. Did Jesus rise from the dead or did he not? Did the resurrection really happen?

EVIDENCE

The accounts of the empty tomb

CHRIST'S DEATH

Jesus was nailed to the cross at about 9 a.m. on the Friday. Many were present when he died at about 3 p.m. (Mark 15:21–37). John (19:31–37) records that a Roman soldier 'stabbed his side with a lance, and at once there was a flow of blood and water.'

HIS BURIAL

Soon after he died, Joseph of Arimathea, a member of the Jewish Council, received permission from Pilate, the Roman governor, to take the body off the cross. He and Nicodemus (also a member of the Council) wrapped it with spices in strips of linen cloth and laid it in Joseph's unused tomb, which had been cut out of the rock in a garden very close to the site of the crucifixion. The women who had followed Jesus watched all this being done (Mark 15:40–47, John 19:38–42).

THE GUARD

On the Saturday morning, the chief priests and Pharisees went to Pilate to ask him to have the tomb guarded, in case the disciples stole the body. Pilate agreed to this, and the tomb was then sealed and guarded by (Matthew 27:62– 66).

THE WOMEN AT THE TOMB

Very early on the Sunday morning some of the women came to the tomb bringing more spices to anoint the body of Jesus, and they found that the stone had been rolled away from the entrance to the tomb. When they went inside they saw two angels who explained that Jesus had risen from the dead, and told them he would meet them again in Galilee (Mark 16:1–8; Luke 24:1–11).

THE DISCIPLES AT THE TOMB

The women hurried back to tell the disciples, and Peter and John ran to the tomb to see for themselves. John records that they saw 'the linen cloths lying, and the napkin, which had been on his head, not lying with the linen cloths but rolled up in a place by itself' (John 20:1–10).

The accounts of the appearance of the risen Jesus

● Mary returned to the tomb with Peter and John, and remained there after they had gone back. She stooped to look into the tomb again, and after speaking to the two angels, she turned round and saw Jesus, though at first she did not recognize him. He told her not to cling to him and gave her a message for the disciples (John 20:11–18).

● On the same day, when two of the disciples were on their way to a village called Emmaus, about seven miles from Jerusalem, 'Jesus himself drew near and went with them. But their eyes were kept from recognizing him.' They talked with him about all that had happened and invited him to spend the night with them. As he broke the bread at table, 'they recognized him; and he vanished out of their sight'. They immediately returned to Jerusalem to tell the other disciples (Luke 24:13–33).

● When they got back to the disciples, they were told that Jesus had appeared to Peter, and they gave their account of how Jesus had appeared to them on the road (Luke 24:34–35).

● While they were talking about all this, 'Jesus himself stood among them. But they were startled and frightened and supposed that they saw a spirit. And he said to them, "Why are you troubled, and why do questionings rise in your hearts? See my hands and my feet, that it is I myself; handle me, and see; for a spirit has not flesh and bones as you see that I have."' They were still unconvinced, and to give them further evidence he took a piece of fish and ate it in front of them (Luke 24:36–49).

● On the following Sunday he appeared to them again in the upper room. Thomas had not been present the previous week and was still sceptical about what the others told him; but now he was with them. 'The doors were shut, but Jesus came and stood among them.' He invited Thomas to touch his hands and his side (John 20:24–29).

● Some time later he appeared to the disciples beside the Lake of Galilee, where he had spent much of the three years of his ministry. He had prepared a charcoal fire at the lakeside and had breakfast with them (John 21:1–9).

● He appeared to them on another occasion on a mountain in Galilee, and gave them the commission, 'Go therefore and make disciples of all nations' (Matthew 28:16–20).

● During this period also 'he appeared to more than 500 brethren at one time . . . then he appeared to James, then to all the apostles' (1 Corinthians 15:3–8; Paul writing in about AD 57).

● The last occasion on which the disciples saw him was on the Mount of Olives in Jerusalem, about forty days after the resurrection (Acts 1:6–11).

This is LUKE's summary of the period after the resurrection:

He showed himself to these men after his death, and gave ample proof that he was alive: over a period of forty days he appeared to them and taught them about the kingdom of God.

The existence of the Christian church

The writer of the Acts of the Apostles describes the origin and spread of the Christian church. According to his account, the very fact that Christianity became a separate religion is part of the evidence for the resurrection.

THE TRANSFORMATION OF THE DISCIPLES

When Jesus was arrested at night in the Garden of Gethsemane, the disciples all forsook him and fled. Peter followed at a distance while Jesus was led away for trial, and disowned him three times; he was apparently too ashamed or too afraid to be identified with Jesus now that he was being tried as a criminal. After the public execution of Jesus, the disciples all hid for a time in a locked room in Jerusalem, because they were still afraid of the Jewish authorities.

Seven weeks after the death of Jesus, however, a dramatic change came over the disciples. They were no longer ashamed to be identified with Jesus, but were speaking about him boldly in public. When this brought them into open conflict with the Jewish authorities, they were prepared to be imprisoned and flogged rather than be forced to disown Jesus or to keep quiet (Acts 2–4).

THE SEPARATION OF CHRISTIANITY FROM JUDAISM

When the disciples first began to speak boldly about Jesus on the Day of Pentecost, they laid special emphasis on the resurrection and the implications of the resurrection. They never ceased to think of themselves as Jews, but it was their persistent teaching of this message about Jesus and the resurrection which led to persecution from the Jewish authorities (Acts 4:1–22).

This same pattern was repeated in the life of *Paul*, who had been brought up as a devout Jew and thoroughly trained in the school of the Pharisees. He took an active part in the persecution of Christians, but in about AD 34 or 35 he himself became a Christian and his preaching about Jesus and the resurrection soon brought him into conflict with the Jewish authorities.

LUKE, the author of Acts, was writing for a Roman called Theophilus, who probably wanted to know how Christianity had come into being, how it differed from Judaism, and in particular why Paul was on trial in Rome. He therefore describes in considerable detail how he came to be a prisoner in Rome, and in doing so illustrates the final breach between Christianity and Judaism.

He tells us that in many places Jews opposed Paul and his message and often actively persecuted him. Eventually some of them plotted to murder him, and were about to kill him during a disturbance in the temple area in Jerusalem, when he was rescued by Roman soldiers. The Roman authorities, arranged for him to be tried before the Jewish Council, the same Council which had condemned Jesus and handed him over for execution about thirty years before. In the course of the trial he argued:

The true issue in this trial is our hope of the resurrection of the dead.

What he was saying to them in effect was this: 'Those of you who are Pharisees believe in the future resurrection; and you who are Sadducees say that the resurrection is impossible. We Christians believe in a future resurrection, and we also believe that Jesus has already been raised from the dead. The basic issue in this trial therefore is simply this: did it happen or did it not? Was Jesus raised from the dead or was he not?'

Luke clearly wanted his readers to understand that it was belief in the resurrection of Jesus which was the basic issue dividing Christianity from Judaism, and for which Paul was on trial (Acts 21:27–28:31).

LUKE also tells us that it was Paul's insistence on the resurrection which roused the curiosity and the scorn of the philosophers in Athens:

Some said, 'What would this babbler say?' Others said, 'He seems to be a preacher of foreign divinities'—because he preached Jesus and the resurrection ... Now when they heard of the resurrection of the dead, some mocked; but others said, 'We will hear you again about this.'

Since we are asking a historical question (did Jesus rise from the dead or did he not?), we need to approach the above evidence in the same way as we would for other historical questions.

But since we are dealing with something unique, it is essential to be aware of our own assumptions. It is not quite as simple as a Sherlock Holmes detective case. Our assumptions will play an important part in our estimate of what is possible or impossible in history. If we approach the evidence with our minds *already made up* that miracles *cannot* happen, no amount of evidence will convince us that the resurrection *did* happen. If on the other hand we are prepared to believe that there is a God who can work miracles in the universe he has made, then we may be willing to be convinced—provided, of course, the evidence is good enough.

POSSIBLE ANSWERS

We can be reasonably certain Jesus rose from the dead

If we give this answer, the next obvious step is to consider what the resurrection means. If the event has no significance there is no point in pursuing the enquiry any further. We might just as well conclude that it did not happen.

These are some of the conclusions which the early Christians drew from the resurrection:

● It provides conclusive evidence about the identity of Jesus. All that Jesus had claimed about himself is vindicated by the resurrection.

PETER speaking to the crowds in Jerusalem on the Day of Pentecost:

> This Jesus God raised up, and of that we all are witnesses ... Let all the house of Israel therefore know assuredly that God has made him both Lord and Christ, this Jesus whom you crucified.

● It vindicates the work of Jesus and demonstrates that his death achieved something. If he had not been raised from death, his death would have been evidence of the failure of his mission. This is how the risen JESUS himself interpreted the meaning of his death:

> These are my words which I spoke to you, while I was still with you, that everything written about me in the law of Moses and the prophets and the psalms must be fulfilled ... Thus it is written, that the Christ should suffer and on the third day rise from the dead, and that repentance and forgiveness of sins should be preached in his name to all nations.

● It makes Jesus the perfect mediator who brings us into fellowship with the Father. The risen Christ gives us the right to come to the Father with boldness and confidence.

> Through him (Jesus) we ... have access in one Spirit to the Father.

> He is able for all time to save those who draw near to God through him, since he always lives to make intercession for them.

● It can mean something in everyday experience. For the Christian the resurrection is not simply an event in the past to which he looks back. It also has implications for the present.

The person who puts his trust in Jesus is united with him; and this union and identification with him offers a real deliverance from the power of sin, and an opportunity of enjoying here and now a 'newness of life' which flows from Christ's own risen life. If we are now 'in Christ' and are willing to die to self as he did, all the benefits of his death and resurrection are available to us:

> We were buried therefore with him by baptism into death, so that as Christ was raised from the dead by the glory of the Father, we too might walk in newness of life. For if we have been united with him in a death like his, we shall certainly be united with him in a resurrection like his. We know that our old self was crucified with him so that the sinful body might be destroyed, and we might no longer be enslaved to sin. For he who has died is freed from sin. But if we have died with Christ, we believe that we shall also live with him. For we know that Christ being raised from the dead will never die again; death no longer has dominion over him. The death he died he died to sin, once for all, but the life he lives he lives to God. So you also must consider yourselves dead to sin and alive to God in Christ Jesus.

> I count everything as loss because of the surpassing worth of knowing Christ Jesus my Lord. For his sake I have suffered the loss of all things, and count them as refuse, in order that I may gain Christ ... that I may know him and the power of his

resurrection, and may share in his sufferings, becoming like him in his death, that if possible I may attain the resurrection from the dead.

None of us lives to himself, and none of us dies to himself. If we live, we live to the Lord, and if we die, we die to the Lord; so then, whether we live or whether we die, we are the Lord's. For to this end Christ died and lived again, that he might be Lord both of the dead and of the living.

The power by which God raised Jesus from death is available still. In desperate situations the Christian can have confidence that God is still able to work in the same dynamic way. PAUL makes it plain that this confidence is no mere wishful thinking:

... we do not want you to be ignorant, brethren, of the affliction we experienced in Asia; for we were so utterly, unbearably crushed that we despaired of life itself. Why, we felt that we had received the sentence of death; but that was to make us rely not on ourselves but on God who raises the dead; he delivered us from so deadly a peril, and he will deliver us; on him we have set our hope that he will deliver us again.

It's improbable that Jesus rose from the dead

This is to say, it is not impossible that something extraordinary happened, but the evidence is far from convincing. There are other possible and far more plausible explanations of what is recorded in the Gospels.

The Jewish Encyclopedia suggests that the belief in the resurrection is

... due to two psychic forces that never before had come so strongly into play: (1) the great personality

of Jesus, which had so impressed itself upon the simple people of Galilee as to become a living power to them even after his death; and (2) the transcendentalism, or other-worldliness, in which those penance-doing, saintly men and women of the common classes, in their longing for godliness lived ... In an atmosphere of such perfect naiveté the miracle of the Resurrection seemed as natural as had been the miracle of the healing of the sick.

HUGH SCHONFIELD has put forward his theory of the 'Passover Plot'. He suggests that Jesus planned secretly with a few friends (but not with his disciples) that he should be taken down from the cross before he died, so that he could be revived later. They were to give the impression, however, that he was really dead. In the event, the plot failed; for although he was not completely dead when he was taken down from the cross; he died soon afterwards before he could be revived. In spite of the failure of the plot, SCHONFIELD sees a profound meaning in these events:

He had schemed in faith for his physical recovery, and what he expected had been frustrated by circumstances quite beyond his control. Yet when he sank into sleep, his faith was unimpaired, and by an extraordinary series of contributory events, partly resulting from his own planning, it proved to have been justified. In a manner he had not foreseen resurrection had come to him ... Whenever mankind strives to bring in the rule of justice, righteousness and peace, there the deathless presence of Jesus the Messiah is with them.

Many of those who say that the story is highly improbable refuse to work out a detailed alternative. But some who do, recognize how tentative it must be.

We are nowhere claiming for our reconstruction that it represents what actually happened, but that on

After the crucifixion, Jesus' body was laid in a rock tomb, like this one at Bethphage. On the following Sunday the tomb was found empty, with the huge stone rolled away from the door.

the evidence we have it may be fairly close to the truth . . .

Naturally it cannot be said that this is a solution to the puzzle (about the alleged appearances of Jesus after his death). . . . There is room for other theories, such as that the man concerned (i.e. the man who collaborated with Jesus in the Passover Plot), if there was one, was a medium, and that Jesus, rising from the dead into the After Life in the spiritualist sense, spoke through him in his own voice which enabled his presence to be recognized . . . Too little is told, and that little quickly became too legendary, and too contradictory, for any assured conclusion. The view taken here does seem to fit the requirements and is in keeping with what has been disclosed of the Passover Plot. The planning of Jesus for his expected recovery created the mystery of the empty tomb.

HUGH SCHONFIELD

If we give this answer, we need to find convincing answers to questions like these:

HOW ARE WE TO ACCOUNT FOR THE STORY OF THE EMPTY TOMB?
These are all the theories which have been suggested:

● **Jesus was not really dead.** The theory goes that Jesus was not really dead when he was taken down from the cross. Some time after being placed in the cool tomb he revived and got out of the tomb.

BUT: after being scourged and hanging on the cross for six hours, Jesus would have needed considerable medical treatment. Is it likely that a person in such a condition (with his back lacerated by a scourging that often proved fatal, with wounds in his hands and feet and a sword-thrust in his side) could appear to people who had known him well, *and* give the impression that he had been raised from death?

We are told that the body of Jesus was wrapped in long pieces of cloth and covered with a large amount of spices. He would have had to extricate

himself from these grave-clothes, roll aside the heavy stone which several women feared they would be unable to move and escape the notice of the guard.

If he didn't really die at this time, what happened to him afterwards? How did he finally die?

● **The women came to the wrong tomb.** It is argued that in the dim light of the early morning the women went to a different tomb, which was empty.

BUT: we are told that the women watched Joseph and Nicodemus taking the body and putting it in the tomb on the Friday evening.

The disciples went to the tomb after hearing the report of the women; are we to assume that they were all misled, and that they did nothing to check up on the facts?

When Joseph of Arimathea heard the rumours about the resurrection, wouldn't he have taken the trouble to check the facts for himself, since he had put the corpse in his own tomb in his private garden?

What about the detailed description of the way in which the grave-clothes were lying? Must we assume this was invented?

● **The body could have been stolen.**
BUT: who would have stolen it? And what motive could there be?

It could have been the Roman authorities or the guards: but what possible motive could they have? It was in their own interests to see that the Jesus affair was closed.

It could have been the Jewish authorities: but again, what was the motive? If they knew (as Matthew tells us) that Jesus had prophesied that he would rise from the dead, they would want to ensure that the body did *not* disappear from the tomb, in case the disciples might claim that he had risen. Indeed, Matthew tells us that it was the Jewish authorities who asked for the guard to be placed at the tomb.

It could have been an unknown person or group of people: but what was the motive? If the body was stolen by anyone who was not a disciple, could he not have produced the remains of the body as soon as the Christians began preaching about the resurrection? If he couldn't produce the remains, could he not at least come forward and provide enough evidence to convince many people that there was a perfectly natural explanation for what the disciples were talking about? Or must we fall back on the suggestion that it was done by an unknown person without any particular motive; that he let no one know what he had done, and left Jerusalem soon after stealing the body? No one can deny that this is a possible explanation; but is it likely?

It could have been the disciples or some friends of Jesus (e.g. Joseph of Arimathea); but what possible motive was there? And does this tally with the rest of the account which tells us that the disciples were not expecting anything to happen? Would they not be putting themselves in a dangerous position with the authorities, who might give them the same treatment they had given Jesus? And if one or more of the friends of Jesus stole the body, how could they have concealed it from the others? If those who stole it remained Christians for the rest of their lives, their whole faith would have been based on a lie. We would also have to say that the other disciples were extraordinarily gullible in believing the story of the resurrection without checking up on the facts for themselves, and in being prepared to die for this incredible story.

● **The story has been exaggerated.** On this theory, something miraculous may have happened, and the story may have some basis in fact. But we cannot accept all the details of the story, since there must have been some elaboration somewhere along the line.

BUT: how are we to decide what is fact and what is fiction in the accounts? By what principles are we to decide what really happened and what was added later on? Most of the suggested rules are very subjective and the dividing line is bound to be very delicate. The sceptic will naturally want to say, 'Why do you draw the line here? If you reject so much, why do you stop here and not reject some more?'

No vast period of time elapsed between the death of Jesus and the first written record which speaks about the resurrection—i.e. Paul's letter to the Corinthians, which was written about twenty-six years after the event.

It is natural to assume that the disciples and followers of Jesus would have gone to the tomb to check up on the rumours for themselves. And the more eyewitnesses there are to any event, the greater the safeguard against individuals elaborating the story.

The story was not passed on through a large number of people between the original eyewitnesses and the writers. It is not a fair comparison to say 'Look how much a story can get twisted and distorted when it passes from mouth to mouth. It comes out very different by the time it reaches the fiftieth person.'

When the first accounts were written, many of the original eyewitnesses would still have been alive, and could easily have confirmed the details of the story or cast doubt on them and discredited them. Luke, for one, specifically claims to have obtained information directly from eyewitnesses (Luke 1:2).

● **The whole story has been invented.** Nothing like this ever happened, so the argument goes. The body remained in the tomb, and the first disciples knew it. However, in the course of time they, and/or other Christians, came to express their faith in Jesus in terms of a story describing events. The story was not intended to be an historical account of what happened, but was merely intended as a way of expressing their beliefs about Jesus. Some would say that the stories were invented deliberately and consciously to convince others about the identity of Jesus. Others say that there was nothing dishonest about what they did, and that it would have been very natural for them to express their personal beliefs and experiences in this way.

BUT: if there was no event which led the disciples to their faith in the victory of Jesus over death, how did they come to believe this in the first place? If it was the faith of the early Christians which produced the story of the empty tomb, what gave them that faith?

One can imagine a person composing a myth to teach something or to stir the imagination; but why compose such a story (even with the best of motives) and present it as sober fact rather than as pure fantasy?

Even if the disciples had the very best motives in inventing the story, would they really be prepared to go on teaching it to others as simple fact when they found that it was just this which led to ridicule, persecution and suffering?

If the early Christians who used the story of the empty tomb understood it simply as myth and nothing more, why should anyone want to oppose their message?

What about the question of honesty? When is a lie not a lie? At some stage in the process there would inevitably have been many Christians (followers of one who claimed to be 'the truth') who knew perfectly well that the story of the empty tomb was not true, but went on telling the story which led others to believe that something objective really did happen.

HOW ARE WE TO ACCOUNT FOR THE STORIES OF THE APPEARANCES OF THE RISEN JESUS?

● **Hallucination.** There was never anyone there; the disciples were simply experiencing some kind of hallucination.

BUT: although individuals can experience hallucination, a group of people who have very different personalities normally do not. It is virtually unheard of for 500 people to experience the same kind of hallucination at the same time.

These experiences were reported over a period of seven weeks and were not confined to one day; and they occurred at different places and at different times of the day.

Hallucination often takes the form of seeing things one would like to see; but there is no evidence that the disciples were expecting or looking for these appearances.

● **Exaggeration.** There was something there, but the details have been exaggerated.

BUT: as before, how are we to decide what happened? How are we to pare away the additions from the accounts as they stand?

● **Nothing really happened.** Nothing actually happened in the objective world; the disciples either saw visions communicated to them by God or had experiences which were purely subjective. Eventually they came to express these experiences and their new beliefs about Jesus in terms of stories about seeing, hearing and touching the risen Jesus. They were so conscious of the continuing influence of his personality and teaching, that they came to express this in terms of 'myth'—i.e. the stories looked as if they were about real events in the external world, but in fact they were merely a convincing way of expressing personal beliefs about Jesus.

BUT: exactly the same problems arise as before.

● **The accounts are factual and reliable.** The documents together give us an account of what the disciples actually witnessed—what they saw with their eyes, heard with their ears and touched with their hands. The accounts are not exhaustive; they do not tell us, for instance, what the risen Christ was wearing. But they are detailed enough to rule out the idea that the appearances were purely inward, subjective experiences, or that the disciples were merely seeing some kind of ghost.

HOW ARE WE TO ACCOUNT FOR THE EXISTENCE OF THE CHRISTIAN CHURCH?

If we discount the evidence of the New Testament about the origin of the Christian church, how did it come into existence?

● How are we to explain the transformation of the small group of frightened disciples?

● How are we to account for the separation of Christianity from Judaism?

According to the Gospels and Acts, it was the resurrection which transformed the disciples. Because of their conviction about the risen Christ, they had the courage to abandon their defensive position and to tell the world the good news of his death and resurrection. The records imply that if they had been content to speak about Jesus simply as a good man or a prophet or teacher, they would never have brought on themselves such fierce opposition and suffering. The Jews would never have had any reason to persecute the Christians, and they would probably have remained as a small sect within Judaism. In this case, Christianity would never have become a separate religion.

It's impossible for Jesus to have risen from the dead

That is, it is inconceivable that any human being should be raised from death. In the light of all that science has discovered about the workings of the universe, it is simply not possible for a dead man to be raised to life.

DAVID HUME, the philosopher, is well known for the way he formulated this argument, which has been used by many others since in different

The resurrection of Jesus completely remade his dispirited disciples. With boldness they confronted an often hostile world. Worship of the Roman emperor was promoted at this temple at Ephesus, built for the Emperor Hadrian. Ephesus itself typified the splendour and vigour of contemporary hellenistic culture.

forms. His arguments can be summarized in these stages:

1. The uniformity of natural causes within a closed system is an established fact.

2. No testimony about any miracle has ever been sufficiently convincing.

3. Therefore we cannot hope to prove that any miracle has actually taken place.

> A miracle is a violation of the laws of nature; and as a firm and unalterable experience has established these laws, the proof against a miracle from the very nature of the fact, is as entire as any argument from experience can possibly be imagined.... It is a miracle, that a dead man should come to life; because that has never been observed in any age or country. There must therefore be a uniform experience against every miraculous event, otherwise the event would not merit that appellation. And as a uniform experience amounts to proof, there is here a direct and full *proof*, from the nature of the fact, against the existence of any miracle; nor can such a proof be destroyed, or the miracle rendered credible, but by an opposite proof, which is superior.
>
> The plain consequence is ... that no testimony is sufficient to establish a miracle, unless the testimony be of such kind, that its falsehood would be more miraculous, than the fact, which it endeavours to establish ... When anyone tells me, that he saw a dead man restored to life, I immediately consider with myself, whether it be more probable, that this person should either deceive or be deceived, or that the fact, which he relates, should really have happened. I weigh the one miracle against the other; and according to the superiority, which I discover, I pronounce my decision, and always reject the greater miracle.

After discussing the evidence for certain miracles outside the Bible, but without discussing in detail the evidence for the resurrection, he concludes:

> **Upon the whole, then, it appears, that no testimony for any kind of miracle has ever amounted to a probability, much less to a proof; and that even supposing it amounted to a proof, it would be opposed by another proof ... We may establish it as a maxim, that no human testimony can have such force as to prove a miracle, and make it a just foundation for any such system of religion.**

There is little point in urging a sceptic like Hume to examine the accounts of the resurrection in the New Testament if he comes to the question with his mind already made up that miracles cannot happen. No amount of evidence is likely to convince him.

The discussion should therefore turn to the assumptions of the sceptic and his world view: is it consistent with itself? Is it consistent with the real world? (See *Ten Key Thinkers: David Hume*.)

'We don't know whether or not Jesus rose from the dead—and it doesn't matter'

That is to say, it is impossible to be certain whether the resurrection happened or not; but in any case, it doesn't really matter. Faith in Jesus Christ does not depend on the results of historical enquiry. For it is a personal faith, independent of questions about what actually happened.

To this way of thinking, therefore, in spite of the uncertainty, either:

1. we accept the resurrection by a leap of faith, knowing that it is contrary to reason; or:

2. we accept the resurrection as symbol or myth; or:

3. we remain content simply to experience what 'resurrection' means in our own lives.

The resurrection is not an event of past history. All that historical criticism can establish is the fact that the first disciples came to believe in the resurrection. The historian can perhaps to some extent account for that faith from the personal intimacy which the disciples had enjoyed with Jesus during his earthly life, and so reduce the resurrection appearances to a series of subjective visions. But the historical problem is scarcely relevant to Christian belief in the resurrection. For the historical event of the rise of the Easter faith means for us what it meant to the first disciples, namely, the self-manifestation of the risen Lord, the act of God in which the redemptive event of the cross is completed.

RUDOLPH BULTMANN

HARVEY COX is prepared to accept the assumptions of naturalistic science—i.e. the universe is a system in which there can be no divine intervention. He therefore admits that on these assumptions, the resurrection is not possible. He believes, however, that Christian faith can survive in spite of this contradiction:

We will have to live the rest of our lives both with the affirmation that in some way the Christ lives among us and with the gnawing doubt that this really isn't possible. If we want to escape this kind of ambiguity, we are looking for a perfection which will not be available in this life.

I personally do not believe that we shall have any *personal* experience of the deep mystery ... (of the resurrection) until we are ready to identify our lives with these people (the poor, the rejected, the despised, the sick and the hurt) in our time. Then and only then I think do we have the kind of experience on the basis of which we can talk about the reality of the resurrection.

As historians, and indeed as proper users of the English language, we would prefer not to speak of the Easter event as a 'fact' at all, not in the ordinary sense of the word. We can say something about the situation before Easter, and we can say other things about the consequences of the Easter event, but the resurrection does not lend itself to being spoken of as a 'fact', for it cannot be described. We can say that Jesus died and was buried, and that his disciples were then discouraged and disappointed men. That was the situation before Easter ... On the other side of Easter, we can say that the disciples were changed men. They apparently found themselves caught up in something like the freedom of Jesus himself, having become men who were free to face even death without fear. Whatever it was that lay between, and which might account for this change, is not open to our historical investigation. The evidence is insufficient. All we can say is that something happened.

PAUL VAN BUREN

The important thing about a myth or a fiction is the direction in which it points us, and for me the Christian myth of resurrection is important because it represents a vision of the possibility of building a world where love shall be all in all.

There is a real possibility ... that the idea of resurrection might well be an expression of the ultimate achievements of technology.

JOHN WREN-LEWIS

If we reach this kind of conclusion, no amount of historical evidence is likely to change our minds. As long as we assume that historical events are irrelevant to faith, the discussion must turn not on the accounts of the empty tomb and so on, but on our understanding of truth and faith.

RUDOLPH BULTMANN states very clearly his assumptions about the meaning of faith:

The resurrection of Jesus cannot be a miraculous proof by which the sceptic might be compelled to believe in Christ. The difficulty is not simply the incredibility of a mythical event like the resuscitation of a corpse—for that is what the resurrection means ... Nor is it merely the difficulty of establishing the objective historicity of the resurrection no matter how many witnesses are cited, as though once it was established it might be believed beyond question and might have its unimpeachable guarantee. No; the real difficulty is that the resurrection is itself an article of faith, and you cannot establish one article of faith because it is far more than the resuscitation of a corpse— it is an eschatological event. And so it cannot be a miraculous proof. The resurrection is not a mythological event adduced in order to prove the saving efficacy of the cross, but an article of faith just as much as the meaning of the cross itself. Indeed, faith in the resurrection is really the same thing as faith in the saving efficacy of the cross, faith in the cross as the cross of Christ.

The real purpose of myth is not to present an objective picture of the world as it is, but to express man's understanding of himself in the world in which he lives. Myth should be interpreted not cosmologically, but anthropologically, or better still, existentially.

These attitudes are all derived in different ways from Kierkegaard's understanding of faith, and we ought to turn back to the section on existentialism to see the implications of the existentialist understanding of truth.

SECTION 7

SEEING
AND BELIEVING

I talked about things I did not understand,
about marvels too great for me to know.
You told me to listen while you spoke
and to try to answer your questions.
Then I knew only what others had told me,
but now I have *seen* you with my own
eyes.
JOB

O Lord, open his eyes and let him *see*.
ELISHA

THOMAS answered him,
'My Lord and my God!' Jesus said to him,
'Do you *believe* because you *see* me? How
happy are those who *believe* without
seeing me!'

The Word became a human being and, full
of grace and truth, lived among us. We *saw*
his glory, the glory he received as the
Father's only Son.
We write to you about the Word of life,
which has existed from the very beginning.
We have heard it, and we have *seen* it with
our own eyes; yes, we have *seen* it, and our
hands have touched it.
JOHN

What we *see* now is like a dim image in a
mirror; then we shall *see* face to face.
PAUL

For Job, seeing meant looking at the universe in a different light and finding in it evidence of an all-powerful and loving God who knows what he is doing.

For Elisha, seeing meant experiencing the reality of the supernatural world all around him with such vividness that he prayed that his young servant would come to see it in the same way.

For Thomas, seeing meant actually setting eyes on the risen Jesus and touching him, so that his testimony would be there for all time to help those who would never see the resurrection body of Jesus.

For John, seeing meant watching the character of the unseen God being gradually revealed in the life of someone who was fully human and fully divine.

For Paul, seeing meant understanding all that God had accomplished in Jesus, and realizing that this was only a foretaste of what he would one day see and know in heaven.

WHERE HAS OUR ENQUIRY LED US?

● We began by trying to make sure that were talking the same language. Instead of speaking about God and about Jesus, we started with ourselves and our questions, our hopes and our fears. (section 1)

● We then saw how Christians begin answering these questions, in order to see if Christianity is relevant to life as we have to live it. (section 2)

● We tried to understand the assumptions on which these answers are based—to see what it feels like to be a creature created in the image of God, to live in a created universe, to explore the truth that God has revealed and to call him 'Father'. (section 3)

● This led us to ask if these beliefs can pass any of the tests of truth which have become part of our thinking in the twentieth century. (section 4)

● At this point we turned to consider other world-views. If we haven't got lost in the maze of conflicting religions and philosophies, the discipline of considering other ways of looking at the world may have helped to sharpen our understanding of the Christian world-view. On the other hand, it may have aroused the hope that another world-view offers much more satisfying answers to our basic questions! Or it may have made us more willing to consider Christian beliefs once again with a slightly more open mind. (section 5)

● As we have focussed our attention on Jesus of Nazareth, we've tried to face the problem of his identity: who was he and is he? We've tried to interpret the meaning of his death, and to deal with a question of historical fact on which everything in the Christian faith depends: did the resurrection happen or did it not? (section 6)

What we can*not* do at this stage is to express vague appreciation or admiration for Christian beliefs—because the Christian world-view is not like a work of art that is there to be admired.

And we can*not* start selecting particular Christian ideas which appeal to us—because Christian beliefs are not like items in a supermarket which we can choose according to our taste.

Throughout this enquiry we have probably felt—and ought to have felt—that *we* are in control of the situation. *We* have decided what to read and what to miss out; *we* have been asking the questions and finding the answers convincing or unconvincing as the case may be. *We*'ve been thinking what to make of it all, because *we* have been putting *Christianity* 'on trial'.

Sooner or later, however, it ought to dawn on us that *if* Christianity is true, then ultimately it's *us*—you and me—who are 'on trial'. God gives us every encouragement to ask our questions. ('Call to me and I will answer you' Jeremiah 33:3), to reason with him ('Come now, let us reason together' Isaiah 1:18), and to ask for evidence ('Put your fingers here, and look at my hands' John 20:27). But somewhere along the line we find the tables being turned, and it is *God* who starts asking *us* questions: 'Stand up now like a man and answer the questions I ask you. Where were you when I made the world? . . .' (Job 38:3–4).

We therefore have to come to the parting of the ways.

If we find ourselves totally uninterested in the Christian faith, we're still faced with the human questions with which we began. We can put God and Christ out of our minds, but if life means anything to us at all, we can hardly put these questions totally out of our minds, since some of them, whether we like it or not, are matters of life and death.

If we find we don't understand Christian beliefs, we need to be honest with ourselves and ask why it is that we don't understand. We may feel overwhelmed by a set of beliefs which sound so complicated and so deep. But this should not deter us, and we should work on any small area where we do feel there is a glimmer of light—like the idea of God as a loving Creator, or as the figure of Jesus of Nazareth. The experience of many Christians is that the light began to dawn for them when they understood *one* particular aspect of the gospel, such as the meaning of the death of Jesus, or the significance of the resurrection.

In many cases, however, we don't understand because we don't want to understand. We may be satisfied with whatever beliefs we have already, and cannot face the possibility of changing our minds and our way of life. Jesus emphasized the part played by the will when he said: 'Whoever is *willing* to do what God wants *will know* whether what I teach comes from God or whether I speak on my own authority.' (John 7:17)

If we reject the Christian world-view, we ought at least to go on testing the alternative that we have chosen, by seeing how it works out in practice and how it answers our questions. If at any stage we become disillusioned with our religion or philosophy, we have others to choose from—although there isn't an infinite number of possible world-views. All the main options have already been stated and explored, and every new idea is little more than a variation on an old theme. If we're still interested in finding the truth, we need to apply 'the simple but profound test of fact' to see if our belief is true.

If it turns out in the end that we're wrong, and that the Bible is right, then the further we move away from its world-view, the further we move away from the real world. We may think that we can 'see', that we know who we are and where we're going; but the Bible's description of our condition is much less flattering. For in PAUL's words:

They know God, but they do not give him the honour that belongs to him, nor do they thank him. Instead, their thoughts have become complete nonsense, and their empty minds are filled with darkness. They say they are wise, but they are fools . . . They exchange the truth about God for a lie; they worship and serve what God has created instead of the Creator himself . . .

Elsewhere he speaks of

the heathen, whose thoughts are worthless and whose minds are in the dark . . .

These blunt words are either an expression of unforgivable pride and arrogance, or else they are a sober description of people who think they know and see, but in fact are wandering in the dark.

If Christian beliefs are true, don't reject them, we won't have any excuse when we stand before the God who has given us our life—our minds and bodies. Apart from all that he has revealed to us in Jesus, he has given us very significant clues about himself both in the natural world and in our own human experience. We will have no excuse, no second chance, and there will be no court of appeal if the verdict goes against us.

But what if we find ourselves attracted to the Christian faith? What if some at least *does* make sense? What does it mean to see the Christian world-view—to hold it and believe it? Jesus told two parables which illustrate different ways by which people come to faith:

> **The Kingdom of heaven is like this. A man happens to find a treasure hidden in a field. He covers it up again, and is so happy that he goes and sells everything he has, and then goes back and buys that field.**
>
> **Also, the Kingdom of heaven is like this. A man is looking for fine pearls, and when he finds one that is unusually fine, he goes and sells everything he has, and buys that pearl.**

The first man who stumbles across the treasure hidden in a field is like the person who stumbles across the Christian faith. He hasn't been looking for anything. He hasn't been plagued with questions and doubts, and hasn't been desperately unhappy. But as soon as he discovers the gospel, he is willing to sacrifice everything he has to hold on to the truth that he has found.

The second man who is looking for fine pearls is like the seeker: he isn't satisfied with his present beliefs, and so he thinks and reads and discusses. When at last he sees what the gospel is all about, he is ready to make any sacrifice in order to enjoy the beauty and wonder of what he has found in Christ.

The process of coming to believe involves two very basic steps: repentance and faith. Repentance means realizing that in certain ways our world-view up till now has been wrong, and being willing to change our minds. It also means admitting the facts of our moral condition before God. Faith means *believing that* certain things are true: that there is a personal, infinite God, that Jesus had a special relationship with him and that he can bring him into focus for us; believing that Jesus defeated death and is now alive . . It also means *believing in*, trusting and surrendering to our Creator, and trusting Jesus as the one who deals with our guilt and our failure. Life then becomes a relationship in which we know God as Father, and have a right to enjoy his company through Jesus, the eternal Son. And just as we enter into this relationship by repentance and faith, so we grow to maturity through our daily experience of repentance and faith.

For some the experience of 'entering in' can happen in a moment of time; for others it's a slow process which lasts days, weeks or even years.

For some it is something that they *do*—very consciously and deliberately as they say to God: 'I believe that these things are true . . . I'm sorry for all the ways in which I've been wrong and done wrong . . . and I trust you and your Son Jesus . . .' For others, instead of *their* taking a deliberate step, it's as if something happens *to them*. It's not that they are forced to do something against their will, but rather that after all the reflection and (perhaps) wrestling they have been through, something—or rather someone—from outside takes over.

For AUGUSTINE, it happened in a garden in Rome after he had reached a point of despair over his past life and his inability to find the truth:

I probed the hidden depths of my soul and wrung its pitiful secrets from it, and when I gathered them all before the eyes of my heart, a great storm broke within me, bringing with it a great deluge of tears . . . For I felt that I was still enslaved by my sins, and in my misery I kept crying, 'How long shall I go on saying "Tomorrow, tomorrow"? Why not now? Why not make an end of my ugly sins at this moment?'

I was asking myself these questions, weeping all the while with the most bitter sorrow in my heart, when all at once I heard the sing-song voice of a child in a nearby house. Whether it was the voice of a boy or a girl I cannot say, but again and again it repeated the chorus, 'Take it and read, take it and read'. At this I looked up, thinking hard whether there was any kind of game in which children used to chant words like these, but I could not remember ever hearing them before. I stemmed my flood of tears and stood up, telling myself that this could only be God's command to open my book of Scripture and read the first passage on which my eyes should fall.

I seized it and opened it, and in silence I read the first passage on which my eyes fell: 'No orgies or drunkenness, no immorality or indecency, no fighting or jealousy. Take up the weapons of the Lord

Jesus Christ; and stop giving attention to your sinful nature, to satisfy its desires'. I had no wish to read more and no need to do so. For in an instant, as I came to the end of the sentence, it was as though the light of faith flooded into my heart and all the darkness of doubt was dispelled.

For C.S. LEWIS there were at least two decisive stages in his pilgrimage to faith. In the first he came to reject his previous world-view (which had been based on Hegel's Idealism), and came to believe in a personal God. (See section 2: *Truth*) The second stage was when, some time later, he came to believe that Jesus was the Son of God:

I know very well when, but hardly how, the final step was taken. I was driven to Whipsnade one sunny morning. When we set out I did not believe that Jesus Christ is the Son of God, and when we reached the zoo I did. Yet I had not exactly spent the journey in thought. Nor in great emotion. 'Emotional' is perhaps the last word we can apply to some of the most important events. It was more like when a man, after long sleep, still lying motionless in bed, becomes aware that he is now awake.

The truth of the gospel is for everyone to find and experience in his own way—whether he stumbles across it or goes out in search of it.

The person who finds it and believes it will soon be able to say—with the blind man whose sight was restored by Jesus:

One thing I do know: I was blind, and now I see.

INDEX

REFERENCES

SECTION 1

Page 13
Jacob Bronowski, *The Identity of Man*, Penguin 1967, pp. 14–15, 7–9
Thomas Mann, *I Believe*, p. 88

14
Aldous Huxley, *Brave New World Revisited*, Chatto and Windus 1966, p. 164, 156
Colin Wilson, *The Outsider*, Pan 1967, pp. 71–72

15
Ecclesiastes 7:23–25
Leo Tolstoy, 'Memoirs of a Madman'; in Colin Wilson, *The Outsider*, Pan 1967, p. 164
Somerset Maugham, *The Summing Up*, Penguin 1963, pp. 181–82
Adam Schaff, *A Philosophy of Man*, Lawrence and Wishart, London 1963, p. 34
Martin Esslin, *The Theatre of the Absurd*, Penguin 1968, p. 389

17
Marcel Proust, in Michael Harrington, *The Accidental Century*, p. 154
Arthur Koestler, 'What the Modern World is Doing to the Soul of Man'; essay in *The Challenge of Our Time*, Percival, Marshall, London 1948, pp. 15–17
Edmund Leach, in *The Listener*, 7 December 1967

18
Albert Camus, *The Rebel*, Penguin 1967, p. 57, 27–28
Jean-Paul Sartre, *Existentialism and Humanism*, tr. Philip Mairet, Methuen 1968, p. 269
Jean-Paul Sartre, 'Saint-Genet'; in *Sartre, A Collection of Critical Essays*, ed. Edith Kern, Prentice Hall 1962, p. 87
Alvin Toffler, *Future Shock*, Bantam Books 1970

20
C.E.M. Joad, *Is Christianity True?*, Eyre and Spottiswoode 1943, p. 97
C.E.M. Joad, *The Book of Joad*, Faber and Faber 1944, p. 213
Bertrand Russell, *The Problems of Philosophy*, Home University Library 1967, pp. 9–10
Paul Hazard, *The European Mind 1680–1715*, pp. 8–9

21
Michael Polanyi, *Knowing and Being*, Routledge 1969, p. 41
John Russell Taylor, *Anger and After*, p. 287

22
Bertrand Russell, *The Impact of Science on Society*, Allen and Unwin 1952, p. 114
Thomas Mann, *The Magic Mountain*, Penguin 1967, p. 716
Mother Theresa, in Malcolm Muggeridge, *Something Beautiful for God*, Collins Fontana 1972, pp. 73–74
William Goldman, *Marathon Man*, Pan 1975, p. 80
Robert Alley, *Last Tango in Paris: a novel based on the film*, 1973, p. 41

23
Edward Albee, *Who's Afraid of Virginia Woolf?* Coles Pub. Co., Canada, 1962, Act II

26
Psalm 22:1–2
Aldous Huxley, *Do What You Will*, Watts and Co. 1937, p. 189
Eugene Ionesco, 'L'orsque j'écris . . .'; in Martin Esslin, *The Theatre of the Absurd*, Penguin 1968, p. 132
Adam Schaff, *A Philosophy of Man*, Lawrence and Wishart 1963, p. 35

28
Ecclesiastes 3:18–22
James Packer, *I Want to Be a Christian*, Kingsway Publications 1978, pp. 47–48
Adam Schaff, *A Philosophy of Man*, p. 34

29
Raymond Chandler, *The Big Sleep*, 1939
Woody Allen, 'Death (a play)'; in *Without Feathers*, 1972

30
P.T. Forsyth, in David Bebbington, *Patterns in History*, Inter-Varsity Press 1979, p. 5
W.E. Hocking, 'Tentative Outlook for the State and Church'; in *This is My Philosophy*, ed. W. Burnett, Allen and Unwin 1958, pp. 304–5
Aldous Huxley, *Do What You Will*, Watts and Co. 1937, p. 180
Bertrand Russell, in Ved Mehta, *Fly and Fly-Bottle*, Penguin 1965, p. 41

31
Alvin Toffler, *Future Shock*, Bantam Books 1971, p. 2, 446, 447
Michael Harrington, *The Accidental Century*, Penguin 1965, p. 11
Franz Fanon, *The Wretched of the Earth*, Penguin 1967, pp. 251–55

33
Alvin Toffler, *Future Shock*, Bantam Books 1971, pp. 449–50
Peter L. Berger, *A Rumour of Angels*, Pelican 1971, p. 59
Hal Lindsey, *Satan is Alive and Well on Planet Earth*, Lakeland 1973, p. 29

35
Habakkuk 1:2–4, 12–13
Ecclesiastes 4:1–3
Martin Luther King Jr., *Why we can't wait*, 1964

36
Albert Camus, 'The Myth of the Sisyphus'; in Martin Esslin, *The Theatre of the Absurd*, Penguin 1968, p. 416
Albert Camus, *The Rebel*, Penguin 1967, p. 267

SECTION 2

Page 41
Luke 12:6–7
Psalm 139:13–16
Job 7:17–21
Lesslie Newbigin, *Honest Religion for Secular Man*, SCM Press 1966, p. 62

43
Ecclesiastes 3:12–13, 5:18–20, 12:13–14
Exodus 6:6–7
Ephesians 1:3–10

44
James Packer, *I Want to Be a Christian*, Kingsway Publications 1978, p. 147

45
1 Peter 1:15
Exodus 10:3–17
Isaiah 61:8
Malachi 3:5
Matthew 5:27–28, 37–40

46
Ephesians 5:15, 17
Justin Martyr, Introduction to the Sermon on the Mount, in *First Apology*
James Packer, *I Want to Be a Christian*, pp. 239–40
J.N.D. Anderson, 'Issues of Life and Death', in *London Lectures in Contemporary Christianity*, Hodder and Stoughton 1978, pp. 31–34

49
John 1:18
Deuteronomy 29:29
1 Corinthians 13:12, 2:12–13
Micah 6:8
Lactantius, *On the Anger of God*, Lactantius II

50
Lactantius, *Divine Institutes*, Lactantius V

51
Arthur Eddington, *Science and Religion*, Friends Home Service Committee 1931, p. 16
Donald MacKay, *The Clockwork Image: a Christian perspective on science*, Inter-Varsity Press 1974, p. 95

52
R. Hookyaas, *Religion and the Rise of Science*, Scottish Academic Press

1972, p. 161
C.S. Lewis, *Surprised by Joy*, Collins Fontana 1955, pp. 179, 181–82

53
1 John 4:7–12
Song of Solomon 4:1–7
Genesis 2:24

54
Ephesians 5:21–23, 25–28
Walter Trobisch, *I Loved a Girl*, Harper and Row 1965, p. 18
Jack Clemo, *The Invading Gospel*, 1958
James Packer, *I Want to Be a Christian*, p. 221

56
Genesis 1:31
Genesis 3:16, 17–19

57
Job 42:2–6
Luke 4:18–19
Luke 11:20–22
Luke 13:15–16

58
Luke 9:1–2
Luke 12:4–5
Isaiah 53:4–9
Revelation 21:1–4
Michel Quoist, *Prayers of Life*, Gill 1965, p. 66

60
C.S. Lewis, *The Problem of Pain*, Collins Fontana 1974, p. 8
Mother Theresa, in Malcolm Muggeridge, *Something Beautiful for God*, Collins Fontana 1972, p. 119

61
Dietrich Bonhoeffer, *Letters and Papers from Prison*, Collins Fontana 1959

62
Ecclesiastes 3:19–23
Ecclesiastes 11:9–12:7

63
2 Timothy 1:10
1 Peter 1:3–5

64
Hebrews 2:14–15
1 Corinthians 15:51–55
James Packer, *I Want to Be a Christian*, Kingsway Publications 1978, pp. 71–72
Bishop Festo Kivengere, *I Love Idi Amin*, Marshall Morgan and Scott 1977, p. 25

66
Luke 21:8–12, 25–28
David Bebbington, *Patterns in History*, Inter-Varsity Press 1979,

p. 169
Herman Dooyerweerd, *In the Twilight of Western Thought*, 1960, p. 111
1 Samuel 28:8, 11–15
Deuteronomy 18:10–12
Colossians 2:15
Ephesians 1:18–21
Os Guinness, *The Dust of Death*, Inter-Varsity Press 1973
Hal Lindsey, *Satan is Alive and Well on Planet Earth*, Lakeland 1972, p. 15
Mark 7:20–23
Psalm 96:11–13
Isaiah 42:1, 3–6
James Packer, *I Want to Be a Christian*, Kingsway Publications 1978, pp. 30–31
C.E.M. Joad, *The Recovery of Belief*, Faber and Faber 1952, p. 63
Stephen Neill, 'The Wrath of God and the Peace of God'; in Max Warren, *Interpreting the Cross*, SCM Press 1966, pp. 22–23

SECTION 3

Page 77
Exodus 3:14–15
Isaiah 55:8–9

78
Psalm 135:5–6
Hosea 11:8
Isaiah 57:13
Psalm 25:14
Isaiah 43:10
Psalm 90:2
Jeremiah 23:23–24
Psalm 139:1–2
Isaiah 46:9–10
Job 23:13–14

79
Habakkuk 1:12
Genesis 1:1
Psalm 148:3–5
Psalm 33:6–9

80
Hebrews 11:3
Isaiah 40:28–31
Psalm 104:1–2, 14, 20
Psalm 147:8–9
Nehemiah 9:6

81
Jeremiah 31:3
Ezekiel 33:11

Isaiah 55:6–7
Lamentations 3:22–23
Hosea 11:1–4
John 3:16
Romans 5:8
John 5:20
John 17:24
Habakkuk 1:13
Psalm 5:4

82
Jeremiah 9:23–24
Genesis 17:1
Leviticus 19:2
Psalm 11:7
Deuteronomy 13:4–5
Psalm 7:9, 11
Jeremiah 5:7–9
Jeremiah 5:26–30
Exodus 34:6–7
Isaiah 54:7–8

83
Romans 5:8–9
1 John 4:10
Deuteronomy 6:4–5
Isaiah 45:5–6
Isaiah 45:22–23
Matthew 11:27
John 17:5
John 15:26
Acts 1:8

84
Acts 2:1–4
Galatians 5:22–23
Ephesians 3:14–17
Psalm 95:6
Psalm 5:7
Psalm 9:1–2
Psalm 84:1–2
Psalm 18:1
Psalm 28:7

85
Genesis 1:26–27
Genesis 5:1–3

86
Genesis 1:31

87
Genesis 2:16–17
Romans 5:12
1 John 3:4
Romans 1:18–21
Romans 2:1–3
Romans 3:9, 23

88
Isaiah 65:1–3, 6–7
Ephesians 2:3
2 Thessalonians 1:9
Isaiah 1:18
Romans 5:6–11
John 1:12–13
Ephesians 5:1–2

90
Genesis 1:1–4

92
Psalm 104:10–15
Genesis 8:22
Psalm 104:5–9
Jeremiah 51:15–16
Genesis 3:17–19

93
Romans 8:19–23
2 Peter 3:10–13
Psalm 104:1–3
Matthew 6:25–30
Genesis 1:27–30

94
Psalm 19:1–4
Job 26:8–9, 14

95
Romans 1:18–20
Romans 2:1, 14–15

96
Matthew 11:27
John 14:6–10
John 1:18
Hebrews 1:1–2
John 14:26
John 16:12–13
1 Corinthians 2:12–13
Matthew 5:17–19

97
John 5:39
Mark 12:35–36
Matthew 19:3–5
Luke 24:44
Exodus 33:11
Amos 3:7
Exodus 24:3–4
Jeremiah 1:9–11
Jeremiah 36:4

98
Genesis 15:5–8
Genesis 15:13–16
Exodus 4:1–9
Exodus 7:17
Exodus 8:10, 22
Deuteronomy 4:9–14

99
1 Kings 18

100
Deuteronomy 18:21–22
Isaiah 41:20
Isaiah 48:3–5
Ezekiel 6:7
John 6:68–69
John 2:11
John 20:26–28

101
Acts 2:22–36
1 Corinthians 15:3–8
Luke 1:1–4

102
Jeremiah 5:7–9

104
Hosea 11:8–9
B.B. Warfield, 'Modern Theories of
the Atonement'; in *The Person and
Work of Christ*, Presbyterian and
Reformed Publishing Co. 1950,
p. 386
Genesis 2:16–17

105
Romans 5:12
Romans 6:23
James 1:15
Luke 15:20–24
Leviticus 10:17
Leviticus 16:21–22

106
Isaiah 53:4–6
Romans 7:18–25

SECTION 4

Page 111
Pieter Geyl, *Napoleon: For and
Against*, Penguin 1965, pp. 15–18

113
C.S. Lewis, *Surprised by Joy*, Collins
Fontana 1959, pp. 178–79
Frank Morison, *Who Moved the
Stone?*, Faber pp. 11–12
N.P. Williams (and W. Sanday),
*Form and Content in the Christian
Tradition*, 1916; in A.R. Vidler,
*Twentieth Century Defenders of the
Faith*, SCM Press 1965, p. 90
Ronald Gregor Smith, *Secular
Christianity*, Collins 1966, p. 103

114
Paul van Buren, *The Secular Meaning
of the Gospel*, Penguin, pp. 132–33
Eduard Schweitzer, *Jesus*, SCM
Press 1971, pp. 49–51
T.W. Fowle, *Nineteenth Century
Opinion*, ed. Michael Goodwin,
Pelican 1951, p. 117

116
J.S. Bezzant, in *Objections to
Christian Belief*, Constable 1963, pp.
90–91

117
Alasdair MacIntyre, *Difficulties in
Christian Belief*, SCM Press 1959,
p. 31

Bertrand Russell, *Human Knowledge:
Its Scope and Limitations*, Allen and
Unwin 1948, p. 448, 148

118
C.E.M. Joad, *The Recovery of Belief*,
Faber and Faber 1952, pp. 13–14,
16, 46

119
Jacob Bronowski, *Science and Human
Values*, Penguin 1964, pp. 33–34,
38–40, 66, 72

122
Richard Wurmbrand, *Tortured for
Christ*, Hodder and Stoughton 1967,
p. 23

123
Jacob Bronowski, *Science and Human
Values*, Penguin 1964, pp. 49, 52–53,
57

125
C.F. Von Weizacker, *The Relevance
of Science*, Collins 1964, p. 163
Donald MacKay, *Science and
Christian Faith Today*, CPAS, pp.
18–19, 20

126
Derek Kidner, *Genesis*, Tyndale
Press 1967, p. 30
Genesis 1:1
Genesis 1:21, 27

127
Genesis 1:20
Genesis 2:7
James Packer, *I Want to Be a
Christian*, Kingsway Publications
1978, pp. 32–33
Genesis 2:4
Genesis 5:1
Genesis 6:9
Genesis 10:1
Matthew 19:3–5

128
Luke 3:23–38
Roman 5:12–19

129
Professor W.R. Thompson,
*Introduction to the Origin of the
Species*, Everyman Library No. 811,
1956
Julian Huxley, *Essays of a Humanist*,
Penguin 1966
Professor W.R. Thompson,
Introduction to the Origin of the Species

130
Professor D.S.M. Watson, in
C.E.M. Joad *Recovery of Belief*,
Faber and Faber 1952
John Stott, in *The Church of England
Newspaper*, 7 June 1968

131
Professor W.R. Thompson,
Introduction to the Origin of the Species
John Habgood, *Religion and Science*,
Mills and Boon 1964, pp. 69–70

132
Julian Huxley, *Essays of a Humanist*,
pp. 24–25
Teilhard de Chardin, *Phenomenon of
Man*, Collins Fontana 1965, p. 241
Thomas Altizer, *Radical Theology
and the Death of God*, Penguin 1968,
p. 131

SECTION 5

Page 139
Robert Brow, *Religion, Origins and
Ideas*, Tyndale Press 1966, pp. 10–11

140–42
John Mbiti, *African Religions and
Philosophy*, Heinemann 1969, pp. 29,
35, 38, 56–57, 213–14, 99, 165, 209,
38, 214–15, 169–70

143
Robert Brow, *Religions, Origins and
Ideas*, pp. 37, 13–14
Professor Zaehner, *Foolishness to the
Greeks*, in H.D. Lewis and R.L.
Slater, *The Study of Religions*,
Penguin 1969, p. 145
K.M. Sen, *Hinduism*, Penguin 1969,
p. 19
Christmas Humphreys, *Buddhism*,
Penguin 1967, pp. 157, 85

144
Wilfred Cantwell-Smith, *The Faith of
Other Men*, Mentor 1965, pp. 25–26
Radhakrishnan, *The Hindu View of
Life*, Allen and Unwin 1960, pp. 48–
49, 51
Rabindranath Tagore, *Fruit
Gathering*, Macmillan 1922, pp. 82–
83

145
Christmas Humphreys, *Buddhism*,
p. 128
Jacob Bronowski, *Science and Human
Values*, Penguin 1964, p. 50
C.E.M. Joad, *Recovery of Belief*,
Faber and Faber 1952, p. 174
Radhakrishnan, *The Hindu View of
Life*, Allen and Unwin 1960, pp. 55,
56
D.T. Suzuki, *Mysticism, Christian*

and Buddhist, Collier Books, New York 1962, p. 58

146
Radhakrishnan, in Buddhism by Christmas Humphreys, Penguin 1967, p. 122
Francis Schaeffer, The God Who Is There, Hodder and Stoughton 1968, p. 101
Radhakrishnan, The Hindu View of Life, p. 20
Radhakrishnan, The Hindu View of Life, p. 28
K.M. Sen, Hinduism, Penguin 1969, p. 37
Wilfred Cantwell-Smith, Questions of Religious Truth, p. 74

148
Christmas Humphreys, Buddhism, Penguin 1967, pp. 79–80
Arnold Toynbee, in Ved Mehta, Fly and Fly-Bottle, Penguin 1965, p. 124
Wildred Cantwell-Smith, Questions of Religious Truth, p. 74

149
Arthur Koestler, The Ghost in the Machine, Hutchinson 1967, p. 262
G.T. Manley; in The World's Religions, ed. J.N.D. Anderson, p. 65
Lesslie Newbigin, Honest Religion for Secular Man, SCM Press, 1966, p. 27

150
Radhakrishnan, The Hindu View of Life, p. 88
Christmas Humphreys, Buddhism, p. 123

151
Roy A. Stewart, Rabbinic Theology, Oliver and Boyd 1961, p. 20
Isidore Epstein, Judaism, Epworth Press 1939, p. 80; in J.N.D. Anderson, The World's Religions, IVF 1965, p. 32
J.H. Hertz, The Pentateuch and the Haftorahs; in J.N.D. Anderson, pp. 32, 523–24
Roy A. Stewart, Rabbinic Theology, pp. 173–74
Herbert Danby, The Jew and Christianity, Sheldon Press 1927, pp. 83–85

154
The Koran, tr. N.J. Dawood, Penguin 1964, Sura 2:255; 59:23–24
The Koran, Sura 38:71–72; 2:30
Basic Principles of Islam: Introduction, Minaret House, Croydon

155
H.A.R. Gibb, Mohammedanism, Oxford University Press 1964, p. 70

C.C. Adams, Islam and Modernism in Egypt, A Study of the Modern Reform Movement Inaugurated by Mohammad Abduh, OUP 1933, p. 147
Al-Junayd, in S.M. Zwemer, A Moslem Seeker After God (Al-Ghazzali), Revell 1920, p. 182
Reynold Nicholson, The Mystics of Islam, Khayyats 1966 reprint, pp. 21–22, 22–23
The Koran, Sura 19:93–95; 28:88

156
The Koran, Sura 81:27–29
R.A. Nicholson, The Mystics of Islam, Khayyats, Beirut reprint 1966, pp. 167–68
W. Cantwell-Smith, Questions of Religious Truth, Gollancz 1967, pp. 48–49
The Koran, Sura 29:50
Sura 2:2–4, 23–24
Sura 13:27–28
Sura 42:35
Sura 3:2–3
Sura 46:7–9

157
The Koran, Sura 7:203–4
Sura 3:7–8

159
J.N.D. Anderson, The World's Religions, IVF 1965, p. 85
The Koran, Sura 59:23, p. 263
Beidhawi; in S. Zwemer, The Moslem Doctrine of God, American Tract Society 1905, pp. 58–59
Al-Ghazzali; in S. Zwemer, The Moslem Doctrine of God, pp. 55–56
Ahmad Galwash, The Religion of Islam, The Supreme Council for Islamic Affairs, Cairo 1966, Vol. 2, pp. 341–42
The Koran, Sura 51:56; 76:4–22

160
Muhammad Abduh; in C.C. Adams, Islam and Modernism in Egypt, p. 153
The Koran, Sura 13:11; 4:79

161
Thomas Aquinas, Summa Theologica, 1, Question 1; in Historical Selections in the Philosophy of Religion, ed. Ninian Smart, SCM Press 1962, p. 62

162
René Descartes, Everyman Discourse 15
Hannah Arend, The Human Condition, University of Chicago 1969, p. 252

163
John Locke, An Essay Concerning Human Understanding, 2:IX:1; in

Willey, The Seventeenth Century Background, p. 259; John Locke, 4:I:1; 4:XVIII:2
John Locke, in Willey, The Eighteenth Century Background, p. 32
John Locke, An Essay Concerning Human Understanding, 4:XIX:4
G.R. Cragg, The Church and the Age of Reason (1648–1789), Pelican 1960, p. 75
Paul Hazard, The European Mind 1680–1715, pp. 278, 282–83

164
David Hume, Treatise of Human Nature, 1:II:6, in Basil Willey, The Eighteenth Century Background, p. 113
David Hume, Treatise of Human Nature, 1:III:12
David Hume, An Abstract of a Treatise of Human Nature; in Bronowski and Mazlish, Western Intellectual Tradition, Penguin 1963, p. 528
David Hume, Treatise of Human Nature, 1:IV:2; 1:IV:7; 1:V:1

165
Kathleen Knott, Objections to Humanism, Penguin 1967, p. 62
Paul Hazard, The European Mind in the Eighteenth Century, p. 82
Colin Wilson, The Outsider, Pan 1967, pp. 23–24

166
Rousseau; in Norman Hampson, The Enlightenment, Penguin 1968, p. 195
Basil Willey, The Eighteenth Century Background, Chatto and Windus 1946, p. 107
Jacob Bronowski and Bruce Mazlish, The Western Intellectual Tradition, Penguin 1963, p. 330
Norman Hampson, The Enlightenment, Penguin 1968, pp. 186–87

167
Kant; in Reardon, Religious Thought in the Nineteenth Century, CUP 1946, Introduction to chapter on Kant

168
Hegel, in The Philosophy of Religion, Vol. 2, ed. N. Smart, SCM Press, p. 327
Hegel, The Phenomenology of the Mind, Allen and Unwin, 1931
Leopold Senghor, on African Socialism, tr. Mercer Cook, Praeger 1964, pp. 41, 123

169
Blaise Pascal, Pensées, tr. Martin Turnell, Harvill Press 1962, p. 163

Bronowski and Mazlish, *The Western Intellectual Tradition*, pp. 276, 278
S. Kierkegaard, *Journals* (1854); in H. Diem, *Kierkegaard's Theology of Existence*, Oliver and Boyd 1959, p. 202
S. Kierkegaard, *Journals*, selected and tr. by Alexander Dru, Fontana 1958, p. 44
S. Kierkegaard, in Diem, *Kierkegaard's Theology of Existence*, p. 49

170
S. Kierkegaard, *Philosophical Fragments*, tr. David F. Swenson, Oxford and New York 1936, p. 87
Title page of S. Kierkegaard, *Philosophical Fragments*, Princeton 1957 edition
S. Kierkegaard, *Concluding Unscientific Postscript*, Princeton 1944, pp. 500, 503
S. Kierkegaard, in Diem, *Kierkegaard's Theology of Existence*, p. 49
S. Kierkegaard, *Philosophical Fragments*, pp. 358–59
S. Kierkegaard, *Journals*, ed. A. Dru, pp. 185–86
S. Kierkegaard, *The Last Years: Journals 1853–1855*, ed. and tr. Ronald Gregor Smith, Collins 1965, pp. 99–100
Herbert Read, Review of the above in *The Listener*
H.J. Blackham, *Six Existential Thinkers*, Routledge and Kegan Paul 1965, p. 4

171
T.F. Torrance, *Karl Barth*, pp. 143, 49

172
T.F. Torrance, *Karl Barth*, pp. 44–45
Karl Barth, *The Doctrine of the Word of God, Church Dogmatics*, 1:1, p. 31
T.F. Torrance, *Karl Barth*, p. 164
K. Marx and F. Engels, *Manifesto of the Communist Party*, 1948
K. Marx, *Economic and Philosophical Manuscripts*, 1884, in *Karl Marx: Selected Writings in Sociology and Social Philosophy*, ed. T.B. Bottomore and M. Rubel, Pelican 1965

173
S. Freud, *New Introductory Lectures on Psycho-Analysis*, Penguin 1973

174
Leslie Paul, *Alternatives to Christian Belief*

Colin Wilson, *Religion and the Rebel*, Gollancz 1957, p. 177
M.A. Jeeves, *Psychology and Christianity: the view both ways*, IVP 1976
C.E.M. Joad, *The Book of Joad*, Faber and Faber 1944, p. 103
Maurice Friedman, *To Deny Our Nothingness*, Gollancz 1967, pp. 223–24

175
Christopher Dawson, 'Christianity and the New Age', in *Essays in Order*, 1931; in Basil Willey, *The Seventeenth Century Background*
Arthur Koestler, *The Sleepwalkers*, Penguin 1968, p. 540

176
Albert Camus, *The Rebel*, Penguin 1967, p. 47
Ernst Cassirer, *An Essay on Man*, Yale University Press 1963, pp. 21–22
Jacob Bronowski, *The Identity of Man*, Penguin 1967, pp. 8, 2–4
Ernst Cassirer, *An Essay on Man*, pp. 13–14

177
Dietrich Bonhoeffer, *Letters and Papers from Prison*, Fontana 1959, p. 189

179
H. Denzinger, *Enchiridion Symbolorum* (Documents of the First Vatican Council); in C. Brown, *Philosophy and the Christian Faith*, Tyndale Press 1969, p. 163
Cardinal J.C. Heenan, *Our Faith*, Nelson 1956, pp. 82–83
Francis Bacon, *Novum Organum*, 1:1.LXV; in Basil Willey, *The Seventeenth Century Background*, p. 32
Thomas Browne, *Religio medici*, 1:X; 1:XLVIII; in Willey, *The Seventeenth Century Background*, p. 59
Basil Willey, *The Seventeenth Century Background*, pp. 33–34

180
Lord Herbert of Cherbury, *De la Vérité*, pp. 51f.; in Willey, *The Seventeenth Century Background*, p. 114
Jacob Bronowski, *Science and Human Values*, p. 44
In Willey, *The Seventeenth Century Background*, pp. 118–20
Essay, 'What is Dogma?'; in A.R. Vidler, *Twentieth Century Defenders of the Faith*, SCM Press 1965, pp. 51–53

181
Dostoievsky, *The Brothers Karamazov*, Penguin, Vol 1, pp. 288–311
H.J. Blackham, *Objections to Humanism*, Penguin 1963, p. 28
George Harrison, interview in *Melody Maker*, 16 December 1967

182
Emil Brunner, *The Christian Doctrine of Creation and Redemption*, Lutterworth 1952, pp. 240–41
'Don't Crush the Little Faith I Have'; anonymous article in *Eternity*, 1965

183
Voltaire, Letter of 1741, in Colin Brown, *Philosophy and the Christian Faith*, IVF 1969, p. 85
Joseph Joubert, *Les Cahiers de Joseph Joubert*, in Paul Hazard, *European Thought in the Eighteenth Century*, p. 288
Basil Willey, *The Seventeenth Century Background*, Penguin 1967, pp. 106–7

184
R. Hookyaas, *Religion and the Rise of Modern Science*, Scottish Academic Press 1972, pp. 7–9, 12–13
Basil Willey, *The Seventeenth Century Background*, pp. 35, 37–39

185
Carl Becker, *The Heavenly City of the Eighteenth Century Philosophers*; in H.J. Blackham, *Objections to Humanism*, Penguin 1967, p. 10
Paul Hazard, *The European Mind 1680–1715*, pp. 295–96
John Locke, *On Civil Government*, Book II, chapter 11; in Paul Hazard, *The European Mind 1680–1715*, p. 325
Diderot; in Hampson, *The Enlightenment*, Penguin 1968, pp. 95–96

186
Ernst Cassirer, *The Renaissance Philosophy of Man*, University of Chicago Press 1949, pp. 10–11
Paul Hazard, *The European Mind 1680–1715*, pp. 159–60; 499–502

187
D.F. Strauss, *Life of Jesus*, tr. Marian Evans, 1846, Vol. 1, p. 71 (two quotations)
Paul Hazard, *The European Mind 1680–1715*, pp. 139; 274

188
A.J. Ayer, Essay in *What I Believe*, Allen and Unwin 1966, p. 14

Arthur Adamov, *L'Aveu*; in Martin
Esslin, *The Theatre of the Absurd*,
Penguin 1968, p. 90
Thomas Hardy; in Florence Emily
Hardy, *The Life of Thomas Hardy*,
Macmillan 1962, p. 224
Nietzsche; in Colin Wilson, *The
Outsider*, p. 133
Nietzsche, *The Joyful Wisdom*; in
Robert Adolphs, *The Grave of God*,
Burns and Oates 1967, pp. 13–14

189
Nietzsche, *The Will to Power 1041*; in
Blackham, *Six Existentialist Thinkers*,
Routledge and Kegan Paul 1965, pp.
33; 36
Nietzsche, *The Joyful Wisdom* No.
343; in Colin Brown, *Philosophy and
the Christian Faith*, Tyndale Press
1969, p. 139
Albert Camus, *The Rebel*, Penguin
1967, pp. 59–60
Nietzsche; in *Six Existentialist
Thinkers*, ed. H.J. Blackham, p. 40
H.J. Blackham, *Six Existentialist
Thinkers*, p. 41

190
Colin Wilson, *The Outsider*, p. 119
Michael Harrington, *The Accidental
Century*, Penguin 1965, p. 115
Jean-Paul Sartre, *Existentialism and
Humanism*, tr. Philip Mairet,
Methuen 1968, pp. 32–33
Jean-Paul Sartre, *Words*, Penguin
1967, pp. 62–65

192
T.H. Huxley, *Collected Essays
Volume V*; in *Encyclopedia of Religion
and Ethics*, ed. James Hastings, T.
and T. Clark, Edinburgh 1908, pp.
214–15
Charles Darwin, *Life and Letters of
Charles Darwin*, John Murray 1888,
Vol. 3, pp. 312–13
Charles Darwin, *Life and Letters*,
p. 313

193
Charles Darwin, Letter to D. Hooker
1870; *More Letters*, Vol 1, p. 85
Charles Darwin, *Autobiography*,
Dover Pubns., chapter 3
Charles Darwin, *The Descent of Man*
Charles Darwin, *Autobiography*,
chapters 2 and 3
Albert Einstein, in *What I Believe*,
Allen and Unwin 1966, p. 27
Aldous Huxley, *Do What You Will*
(Essays), Watts and Co. 1937, pp.
218–19
Barbara Wooton, in *What I Believe*,
p. 205
Somerset Maugham, *The Summing

Up*, Penguin 1963, p. 179
A.J. Ayer, in *What I Believe*, p. 14
H.J. Blackham, *Objections to
Humanism*, Penguin 1963, p. 13
Albert Camus, *Cahiers du Sud*, April
1943; in *Camus, A Collection of
Critical Essays*, ed. Germaine Brée,
Prentice Hall 1965, p. 70
Jean-Paul Sartre, *Nausea*, tr. Robert
Baldick, Penguin 1965, p. 26

194
Martin Esslin, *The Theatre of the
Absurd*, Penguin 1968, pp. 22–23
Martin Esslin, *The Theatre of the
Absurd*, p. 85
Eugene Ionesco; in M. Esslin, *The
Theatre of the Absurd*, p. 23
Time, 26 April 1968
Harold Pinter, Programme Note for
Royal Court Production of *The Room*
and *The Dumb Waiter*; in John
Russell Taylor, *Anger and After*,
Penguin 1963, pp. 300–301
G.J. Warnock, *English Philosophy
since 1900*; in Leslie Paul, *Alternatives
to Christian Belief*, Hodder and
Stoughton 1967, p. 139

195
Leslie Paul, *Alternatives to Christian
Belief*, pp. 150–51
Donald Kalish, 'What (If Anything)
to Expect from Today's
Philosophers', *Time*, 7 January 1966,
p. 20; in Leslie Paul, *Alternatives to
Christian Belief*, Hodder 1967, p. 159
Jacob Bronowski, *Science and Human
Values*, Penguin 1964, pp. 36–37
J. Wren-Lewis, *Fact, Faith and
Fantasy*, Collins 1964, p. 24
Douglas Spanner in *The Church of
England Newspaper*, 31 March 1967
C.S. Lewis, *Miracles*, Fontana 1960,
p. 110

196
Baron von Hugel, in Michael de la
Bedoyère, *Baron von Hugel*, Dent
1951, p. 291
F.C. Happold, *Religious Faith and
Twentieth Century Man*, Penguin
1966, p. 172
Christmas Humphreys, *Buddhism*,
Penguin, pp. 180, 185–86

197
David Knowles, *What is Mysticism?*,
Burns and Oates 1967
The Cloud of Unknowing, tr. Clifton
Wolters, Penguin 1971, pp. 55 and
57–58
Simone Weil, article in *Theology*
Lin Yutang, Essay in *I Believe*, Allen
and Unwin 1965, p. 83
Aldous Huxley, *Ends and Means*,
Chatto and Windus 1937, p. 286

198
Aldous Huxley, *Ends and Means*, pp.
289–90
Aldous Huxley, *Ends and Means*, pp.
290–91
Aldous Huxley, *Doors of Perception
and Heaven and Hell*, Penguin 1969,
pp. 23–25
Aldous Huxley; in Laura Archera
Huxley, *This Timeless Moment: A
Personal View of Aldous Huxley*,
Ballantine Books, New York 1971,
pp. 249–51

199
F.C. Happold, *Religious Faith and
Twentieth Century Man*, Penguin
1966, p. 106
H.R. Rookmaaker, *Modern Art and
the Death of a Culture*, IVP 1970,
p. 202
The Beatles Illustrated Lyrics,
Macdonald 1969
Brian Wilson; in *Rock and other Four
Letter Words*, Bantam 1968
Tom Wolfe, *The Electric Kool-Aid
Acid Test*, Bantam 1971

200
F.C. Happold, *Religious Faith and
Twentieth Century Man*, pp. 124, 68
Nicholas of Cusa, *The Vision of God*,
tr. E.G. Salter; in Happold, *Religious
Faith and Twentieth Century Man*,
p. 45
Dionysius the Areopagite, *The
Mystical Theology*, Shrine of Wisdom
Press, in Happold, *Religious Faith
and Twentieth Century Man*, p. 112
F.C. Happold, *Religious Faith and
Twentieth Century Man*, p. 51

201
F.C. Happold, *Religious Faith and
Twentieth Century Man*, pp. 51–52;
149; 152

202
K.M. Sen, *Hinduism*, Penguin 1969,
p. 53
The Bhagavad Gita, tr. Juan
Mascaro, Penguin 1965, pp. 85–88
H.D. Lewis, *The Study of Religions*,
Penguin 1966, p. 56
Paul Hazard, *The European Mind
1680–1715*, pp. 170–71

203
Paul Tillich, *Biblical Religion and the
Search for Ultimate Reality*, Univ. of
Chicago Press
Paul Tillich, *Systematic Theology*,
Vol. 1, SCM Press 1953, p. 227
Paul Tillich, *The Shaking of the
Foundations*, Penguin 1962, pp.
63–64
Teilhard de Chardin, *The

Phenomenon of Man, Collins Fontana 1966, pp. 322 and 338

204
John Robinson, *Honest to God*, SCM Press 1963, p. 7
John Robinson, *Exploration into God*, SCM Press 1967, pp. 36, 39 and 41
Julian Huxley, *Essays of a Humanist*, p. 223
John Robinson, *Exploration into God*, pp. 23, 83–84, 127, 15
John Robinson, *Exploration into God*, p. 58
John Robinson, *Honest to God*, p. 53
John Robinson, *Exploration into God*, pp. 134; 72

205
Peter Dumitriu, *Incognito*; in *Exploration into God*, p. 89
Julian Huxley, *Essays of a Humanist*, Penguin 1964, pp. 225–26
Barbara Wooton; in *What I Believe*, Allen and Unwin 1966, pp. 205–6
Alasdair MacIntyre, 'God and the Theologians'; in *The Honest to God Debate*, ed. David L. Edwards, SCM Press 1963, pp. 215–16

206
Alasdair MacIntyre, in *The Listener*, 15 February 1968
Alasdair MacIntyre, 'God and the Theologians'; in *The Honest to God Debate*, p. 220
Lenin, *Left-Wing Communism*, Central Books, 1975
Norman Hampson, *The Enlightenment*, Penguin 1968, pp. 124; 127
Dostoievsky; in Michael Harrington, *The Accidental Century*, p. 123

207
Leslie Paul, *Alternatives to Christian Belief*, Hodder 1967, pp. 60, 66

208
Richard Crossman, *The God That Failed, Six Studies in Communism*, Hamish Hamilton 1950, pp. 9–10
André Gide, *The God that Failed*, p. 198
George Orwell, *1984*, Penguin 1968, p. 220
Ignazio Silone, *The God that Failed*, p. 109
Nikita Struve, *Christians in Contemporary Russia*, Collins 1967, p. 288
Adam Schaff, *A Philosophy of Man*, Lawrence and Wishart, London 1963, p. 60

209
Arthur Koestler, *Darkness at Noon*,

Jonathan Cape 1940, pp. 253–54
E.L. Allen, *Existentialism from Within*; in Brown, *Philosophy and the Christian Faith*, pp. 181–82
Karl Heim, in Alec Vidler, *The Church in an Age of Revolution*, Penguin 1961, p. 211
Jean-Paul Sartre, *Existentialism and Humanism*, pp. 56, 27–28, 29

210
H.J. Blackham, *Six Existentialist Thinkers*, pp. 151–52
Jean-Paul Sartre, *Nausea*, tr. Robert Baldick, Penguin 1965, p. 241
Albert Camus, in *Camus, A Collection of Critical Essays*, ed. Germaine Bree, Prentice-Hall 1965, p. 116
Albert Camus, *The Rebel*, Penguin 1967, p. 14
Albert Camus, *The Outsider*, tr. Stuart Gilbert, Penguin 1971, p. 112

211
Jean-Paul Sartre, *Nausea*, pp. 123–24, 162
Jean-Paul Sartre, *Nausea*, pp. 176, 180–83
Jean-Paul Sartre, *Nausea*, pp. 113–14, 225, 115

212
Martin Esslin, *The Theatre of the Absurd*, p. 51
Albert Camus, *The Rebel*, p. 16
Albert Camus, in *L'Eté*, quoted in *Albert Camus and the Literature of Revolt*, John Cruickshank, Oxford University Press, 1960
Maurice Friedman, *The Problematic Rebel*, Univ. of Chicago Press 1970
André Malraux, 'The Walnut Trees of Altenberg'; in Maurice Friedman, *To Deny Our Nothingness*, Gollancz 1967
Arthur Adamov, *L'Aveu*; in Martin Esslin, *The Theatre of the Absurd*, pp. 89–90
Albert Camus, *The Rebel*, pp. 27–28
Albert Camus, *The Rebel*, pp. 258–60
Jean-Paul Sartre, *Existentialism and Humanism*, tr. Philip Mairet, Methuen 1968, p. 33

213
Jean-Paul Sartre; *Existentialism and Humanism*, pp. 32–33
Jean-Paul Sartre, *Existentialism and Humanism*, pp. 33–34
Jean-Paul Sartre; in Sartre, *A Collection of Critical Essays*, p. 167
Jean-Paul Sartre, *Existentialism and Humanism*, pp. 47–49

214
Colin Wilson, *The Outsider*, p. 39

John D. Wild; in *Sartre, A Collection of Critical Essays*, p. 145
Jean-Paul Sartre, *Existentialism and Humanism*, pp. 36, 31
Adam Schaff, *A Philosophy of Man*, pp. 24, 26
Albert Camus, 'Noces'; in *Camus, A Collection of Critical Essays*, p. 66
Albert Camus, *The Outsider*, tr. Stuart Gilbert, Penguin 1971, pp. 48–49

215
Jean-Paul Sartre, *Nausea*, pp. 160–61
Martin Esslin, *The Theatre of the Absurd*, p. 69
Albert Camus, 'Actuelles'; in *Camus, Collected Essays*, p. 56

216
Albert Camus, *The Rebel*, pp. 266–67
Albert Camus, *The Plague*, pp. 107–8, 214

217
Albert Camus, *The Plague*, pp. 170–71, 251–52
Jean-Paul Sartre, *Words*, Penguin 1967, p. 157
The Glossary of Humanism, under Humanism
H.J. Blackham, *Humanism*, Penguin 1968, pp. 13, 19
Edmund Leach; in *The Listener*, 16 November 1967
Lord Willis; in *An Inquiry into Humanism*, BBC 1966, p. 21
Geoffrey Scott, *The Architecture of Humanism*; in *Objections to Humanism*, p. 8
A.J. Ayer; in *An Inquiry into Humanism*, p. 2

218
H.J. Blackham, *Objections to Humanism*, p. 11
Julian Huxley, 'The Humanist Frame', in *Essays of a Humanist*, pp. 77, 107
Pearl Buck, in *I Believe*, Allen and Unwin 1965, pp. 24–25
E.M. Forster, in *I Believe*, p. 50
Fred Hoyle, *The Nature of the Universe*, Penguin 1960, pp. 120–21
Julian Huxley, *Essays of a Humanist*, p. 89

219
H.J. Blackham, *Humanism*, p. 116
Colin Wilson, *Beyond the Outsider*, Baker 1965, pp. 62, 165
John Wren-Lewis, *Fact, Faith and Fantasy*, Collins Fontana 1964, p. 44
Somerset Maugham, *The Summing Up*, Penguin 1963, pp. 181–82

Fred Hoyle, *The Nature of the Universe*, Penguin 1960, p. 122
Colin Wilson, *The Outsider*, Pan 1967, p. 38

220
Nikos Kazantzakis; in Helen Kazantzakis, *A Biography based on His Letters*, Simon and Shuster 1970
Francis Bacon; in John Russell, *Francis Bacon*, Methuen 1965; in H. Rookmaaker, *Modern Art and the Death of a Culture*, IVP 1970, p. 174
Allen Ginsberg; in Steve Turner, 'Some Notes from the Underground', *Voice* magazine, IVF 1972, p. 6
T.S. Eliot; from 'Fragment of an Agon', in *The Complete Poems and Plays of T.S. Eliot*, Faber and Faber, 1969
Somerset Maugham, *The Summing Up*, Penguin 1963, p. 203
C.E.M. Joad, *Is Christianity True?*, pp. ix-xx

221
Julian Huxley, *Essays of a Humanist*, pp. 91–92
H.J. Blackham, *Humanism*, pp. 58–59
J.S. Mill, *Autobiography*, 1873

222
H.J. Blackham, *Objections to Humanism*, pp. 15–18
Alvin Toffler, *Future Shock*, Bantam Books 1970
Jacob Bronowski, *Science and Human Values*, Penguin 1964, pp. 66, 77, 80, 68, 70, 75, 63

223
Jacob Bronowski, *Science and Human Values*, p. 8
Arthur Koestler, 'What the Modern World is Doing to the Soul of Man', Essay in *The Challenge of Our Time*, Percival, Marshall, London 1948, p. 15
Arthur Koestler, *The Ghost in the Machine*, Hutchinson 1967, pp. 153–54

224
Arthur Koestler, *The Sleepwalkers*, Penguin, pp. 552, 553
Fred Hoyle, *The Nature of the Universe*, Penguin 1960
The Humanist Manifesto II; in *The Humanist*, September/October 1973
John Updike, 'Pigeon Feathers'; in *Pigeon Feathers and Other Stories*, Fawcett, USA, 1959
Tom Stoppard, *Rosencrantz and Guildenstern are Dead*, 1967, p. 89
H.W. Van Loon; in *I Believe*, Allen and Unwin 1965, pp. 153–54

H.J. Blackham, *Humanist*, Penguin 1968, p. 116

225
Julian Huxley, *Essays of a Humanist*, pp. 130, 117, 252
Arthur Koestler, *The Ghost in the Machine*, Hutchinson 1967, pp. 267, 336, 335, 335–36
D.R. Davies, *On to Orthodoxy*, 1939, p. 61

226
Bertrand Russell, 'A Free Man's Worship'; in *Why I am Not a Christian*, Simon and Shuster 1966, p. 107
Bertrand Russell, 'A Free Man's Worship', in *Why I am Not a Christian*, pp. 115–16
Bertrand Russell, *Has Man a Father?*, Penguin 1961, pp. 126–27

SECTION 6

Page 231
E.L. Sukenik; in Berndt Gustafson, *New Testament Studies*, 1956, pp. 65–66
Ordinance of Claudius; in *The New Testament Background*, *Selected Documents*, C.K. Barrett, SPCK 1961, p. 15

232
Josephus; Professor Shlomo Pines, in Journal of Israeli Academy of Science and Humanities, 1973; quoted by Peter-Allen Frost, *Church of England Newspaper*, August 1973
Josephus, *Antiquities of the Jews*; in Robert Dunkerley, *Beyond the Gospels*, Penguin 1957, p. 34
Pliny; in *Documents of the Christian Church*, ed. Henry Bettinson, OUP 1946, pp. 3–5

233
Tacitus; in the same, p. 2
Suetonius; in the same, p. 3
Talmud; in Roderic Dunkerley, *Beyond the Gospels*, Penguin 1957, p. 50

234
Papias; in Eusebius, *Ecclesiastical History* 3.39
Acts 1:1–4

236
The Gospel of Thomas; in The

Apocryphal New Testament, tr. M.R. James, OUP 1924, pp. 62–63
Tale quoted in Dean Farrar, *Life of Christ*
Roderic Dunkerley, *Beyond the Gospels*, Penguin 1957, p. 97

237
Matthew 1:18–25
Luke 1:26–35

238
John 8:41
Galatians 4:4
Luke 2:18–19
Mark 6:2–3
Galatians 1:19

239
Mark 6:32–34
Mark 10:13–16
Mark 1:40–42
Luke 7:12–15

240
Luke 15:1–2
Mark 7:6,8,9
Matthew 23:13,16,17,25,28
Mark 11:15–17
John 5:30
John 6:38
Luke 22:24–27
John 13:3–5,12–15

241
Mark 7:37
John 8:46
1 Peter 2:22–23
1 John 1:8; 3:5
Mark 13:32
Matthew 11:27
Matthew 12:50
Matthew 16:27
John 10:30
John 5:22–23
John 14:6–7
Mark 1:15
Mark 10:45
Mark 14:24
Mark 14:61–62
Luke 4:17–21

242
Luke 24:44,46
John 5:39
John 5:46
Mark 2:5–10
John 5:21
John 11:25
Matthew 5:21–22
Mark 13:31
John 18:37
Matthew 25:31–32
John 5:22–23
Matthew 11:28–29
Luke 14:20
John 7:37

John 6:29
John 14:1
Mark 3:11–12

243
Mark 8:29–30
Mark 11:27–33

244
Mark 8:29–31
Mark 9:9–10
Matthew 26:63–65
Matthew 20:29–34
Mark 8:1–2

245
Matthew 15:31
Mark 2:8–12
Matthew 11:2–5
John 10:37–38
Mark 8:11–13
Matthew 12:14
John 6:15
John 5:18
John 11:53

246
Mark 1:22
Mark 2:12
Mark 3:21
Mark 4:41
Mark 5:15,17
Mark 6:2–3
Mark 7:37
Mark 8:29
John 20:28
John 6:69
John 16:30
Hebrews 2:14
Hebrews 4:15
James 2:1
1 Corinthians 15:47
Philippians 2:6–11

248
John 1:18
1 John 1:1–3
Romans 5:12–19
2 Corinthians 5:18–19
1 Timothy 2:5–6
Hebrews 2:17 18

249
Hebrews 4:15
John 17:20–26
The Truth Shall Make You Free,
Watchtower Society, pp. 248–50

250
John 14:28
John 10:30
John 14:9–10
Philippians 2:5–7
Luke 18:19
Luke 18:22
Colossians 1:15
Colossians 1:15–17

251
C.F.D. Moule, *Colossians and Philemon*, Cambridge New Testament Commentary, CUP 1957, p. 64
Hebrews 1:1–4
Herbert Danby, *The Jew and Christianity*, Sheldon Press 1927, pp. 8–9

252
The Jewish Encyclopedia, Vol. VII, pp. 161, 163

253
The Jewish Encyclopedia, Vol. VII, pp. 163–64, 162
Claude Montefiore; in Herbert Danby, *The Jew and Christianity*, p. 79
Sholem Asch, *My Personal Faith*, Routledge 1942, pp. 106–7

254
Herbert Danby, *The Jew and Christianity*, p. 23
The Koran, tr. N.J. Dawood, Penguin 1964, Sura 19:19–22; 3:42
Traditions; in M. Goldsack, *Christ in Islam*, Christian Literature Society of India 1905, p. 32
Sura 4:169

255
Traditions; in M. Goldsack, *Christ in Islam*, pp. 25, 41
Sura 5:112–15
Sura 19:26–31
Sura 5:112–15
Sura 5:110–11

256
Henri Michaud, *Jésu selon le Coran*, p. 10; in Geoffrey Parrinder, *Jesus in the Qur'an*, Faber 1965, p. 166
Sura 5:116
Sura 6:101
Sura 23:91
Hugh Schonfield, *The Passover Plot*, Hutchinson 1965, pp. 10–11

257
Paul van Buren, *The Secular Meaning of the Gospel*, Penguin, pp. 126–27

258
F.C. Happold, *Religious Faith and Twentieth Century Man*, Penguin 1966, p. 150
Hugh Schonfield, *The Passover Plot*, pp. 9–10

259
Paul van Buren, *The Secular Meaning of the Gospel*, pp. 16, 30
F.C. Happold, *Religious Faith and Twentieth Century Man*, pp. 145, 124, 52–53

260
Mark 10:32–34

261
Mark 14:6–10
Mark 14:22–25
Matthew 26:39,42
Psalm 75:8
Jeremiah 25:15–16
Isaiah 51:17
Deuteronomy 21:22

262
Mark 14:32–36
John 18:11
Mark 15:2–15

263
John 18:38
Luke 23:15
Luke 23:41
Luke 23:47
Luke 23:33–34
John 19:26–27
Luke 23:42–43
Mark 15:34
John 19:28–30

264
John 1:29
1 John 2:1–2
Luke 24:46–47
1 Peter 2:24
1 Peter 3:18
1 Corinthians 15:3
Hebrews 1:3
Colossians 2:13–14
Romans 5:8–9
1 John 4:10
Romans 6:10

265
Romans 6:23
Hebrews 10:12–14
Galatians 3:13
Romans 5:1,8
1 Peter 1:18
Colossians 2:13–15
Romans 5:8,10–11

266
Romans 5:9
1 Peter 2:21–22
1 Peter 4:13
Luke 9:23–26
Philippians 3:7–10
2 Corinthians 5:14–15
Philippians 2:5–8

267
1 Corinthians 8:11
2 Corinthians 1:3–7
2 Corinthians 5:19

268
Romans 5:12,15–17
Romans 5:18–19
Hebrews 9:26

Hebrews 10:12,14
Romans 5:1-2

269
J.W.C. Wand, *The Atonement*, SPCK
1963, p. 12
David Edwards, *God's Cross in Our
World*, SCM Press 1963, p. 41

270
John 3:16
1 John 4:8-10
Romans 5:8-9

271
1 Peter 2:20-24
Isaac Watts; last verse of 'When I
survey the wondrous cross'
Rudolph Bultmann, *Kerygma and
Myth*, ed. H.W. Bartsch, Vol. I,
SCM Press, pp. 36-39

272
Dietrich Bonhoeffer, *Letters and
Papers from Prison*, Collins Fontana
1959, p. 164
Paul van Buren, *The Secular Meaning
of the Gospel*, pp. 154-55

273
David Edwards, *God's Cross in Our
World*, SCM Press 1963, pp. 37ff
Nikos Kazantzakis, *Christ
Recrucified*, Faber 1968, pp. 466-67
Thomas Mann; quoted on the cover
of Kazantzakis, *Christ Recrucified*
F.C. Happold, *Religious Faith and
Twentieth Century Man*, p. 172

274
C.E.M. Joad, *Is Christianity True?*,
Eyre and Spottiswoode 1943, pp. 72-
73
J. Gresham Machen, *Christianity and
Liberalism*, Victory Press 1923, pp.
120-21
The Jewish Encyclopedia, Vol. VII,
p. 167
Hans Joachim Schoeps, *The Jewish
Christian Argument*, Faber 1965,
p. 23
Matthew 16:22

275
Matthew 16:23
John 12:27
Matthew 26:52-54
Luke 24:25-27,45-47
Sura 4:156-57, p. 370
Kenneth Cragg; in M. Kamel
Hussein, *City of Wrong*, tr. Kenneth
Cragg, Djambatan (Amsterdam)
1959, pp. x-xi

276
Hebrews 2:14-15

277
Hebrews 10:12-14
1 Peter 1:18-21

279
Acts 1:3

280
Acts 23:6
Acts 17:18-32

281
Acts 2:32,36
Luke 24:44-47
Ephesians 2:18
Hebrews 7:25
Romans 6:4-11
Philippians 3:8-11

282
Romans 14:7-9
2 Corinthians 1:8-10
The Jewish Encyclopedia, Vol. IV,
p. 51
Hugh Schonfield, *The Passover Plot*,
p. 7

284
Hugh Schonfield, *The Passover Plot*,
pp. 172, 180

288
David Hume, *An Enquiry Concerning
Human Understanding*, Section X, Of
Miracles, Collins Fontana, pp. 210-
13, 222-23

289
Rudolph Bultmann, *Kerygma and

Myth, Vol. I, pp. 42-43
Harvey Cox, 'A Dialogue on Christ's
Resurrection'; in *Christianity Today*
12 April 1968, p. 9
Paul van Buren, *The Secular Meaning
of the Gospel*, pp. 132-33
John Wren-Lewis, *I Believe*, Allen
and Unwin, p. 236
John Wren-Lewis, 'Does Science
Destroy Belief?' in *Fact, Faith and
Fantasy* Collins Fontana 1964, p. 43

290
Rudolph Bultmann, *Kerygma and
Myth*, Vol. I, pp. 42-43

SECTION 7

Page 296
Romans 1:21-22,25
Ephesians 4:17-18

297
Matthew 13:44-46
Augustine, *Confessions*, VIII.12

299
C.S. Lewis, *Surprised by Joy*, Collins
Fontana 1959, p. 189
John 9:25

Illustrations by John Thirsk

The photographs in this book have been supplied by Rex Features Ltd, London.

Additional photographs are reproduced by permission
of the following photographers and agencies:

Barnaby's Picture Library: page 115. The British
Museum: page 236. John Chapman: page 79. Crusade
Magazine: page 71. E.A.V. Ebsworth: page 120. Faber
and Faber/Angus McBean: page 220. Fritz Fankhauser:
pages 135, 141, 147, 148, 160, 270. Sonia Halliday
Photographs/Sonia Halliday: page 283. Lion Publishing/
David Alexander: pages 139, 247, 287; Jon Willcocks:
cover; pages 63, 83, 89, 161, 172, 199, 223, 262, 298.
Wulf Metz: page 150. John Rylands Library: page 235.
Stephen Travis: pages 109, 116.